365 days
of marketing

Year-round inspiration, ideas and marketing know-how to help you grow your business, develop customer loyalty and employee engagement, stimulate referrals, increase brand awareness and the Influence you have in your community using traditional, social media, community and event-based marketing.

Build a bigger role for your business in the lives of your clients.

Elizabeth Kraus

Be InPulse Branding Marketing & Design
www.12monthsofmarketing.com

For more on marketing or to read my blogs, visit my website at www.12monthsofmarketing.com.
Customized Distributor and Manufacturer publications available.

365 days of marketing

by Elizabeth Kraus
Owner/CEO, Be InPulse Branding Marketing & Design
www.12monthsofmarketing.com

Branded | Customized custom calendars, print and display materials, workshops and other resources available at www.12monthsofmarketing.com.

Author/Editor: Elizabeth Kraus
Cover and Interior Design/Lay out: Elizabeth Kraus (Be InPulse Branding, Marketing & Design)

Printing History: 2011 First Edition

ISBN:9781463660154

To my parents, who always made me believe
that everything is possible,
to my sister Carrie and my brother Craig,
who always have my back, and always cheer me on.

To my children, Amanda and Gavon, Eric and Laura,
Sarah, Sam, Noa and Rania
and to my grandchildren, Jaxon and Jaycee
whose possibilities are endless.

To my husband, Dan
who brought my heart back to life, makes me laugh
and makes sure I believe in myself.

Elizabeth

"It's not the dates on your tombstone that matter,
it's what you do with the dash in between."

Adapted, singer/songwriter Kevin Welch

With special thanks to my wonderful grammar freak, Sarah.

contents   365 days of marketing

105   march month-long observances

employee spirit month, music in our schools month, caffeine awareness, national on hold month, women's history month, girls in science and engineering month

109   march week 1

national beer day, old stuff day, read across America day, unique names day, national G.I. day, employee appreciation day, dentists day, girls write now day

112   march week 2

national money week, national crochet week, working women's day, get over it day, middle name pride day, worship of tools day, plant a flower day, jewel day, learn about butterflies day

117   march week 3

yo-yo and skill toys week, national wellderly (well elderly) week, chocolate week, consumer rights day, incredible kid day, lips appreciation day, st. patrick's day, happy hours, awkward moments day, companies that care day, spring equinox, proposal day, fragrance day

125   march week 4

national bubble week, doctor-patient trust week, national cleaning week, root canal awareness week, common courtesy day, chip and dip day, puppy day, organize your home office day, waffle day, make up your own holiday day, celebrate exchange day, decorating egg shells day, smoke and mirrors day, pencil day, i am in control day, she's funny that way day

132   april month-long observances

guitar month, national humor month, lawn and garden month, customer loyalty and appreciation month, stress awareness month

138   april week 1

laugh at work week, fun at work day, april fools day, children's book day, walk to work day, school librarian day (school library month), go for broke day, plan your epitaph day, caramel popcorn day

143   april week 2

networking week, international chicken wing week, draw a picture of a bird day, name yourself day, golfers day, siblings day, licorice day, scrabble day, teach your children to save day

146   april week 3

customer awareness week, administrative professionals week/day, income tax pay day, wear your pajamas day, cheese ball day, newspaper columnist day, hanging out day, look-alike day, volunteer recognition day

151   april week 4

national independent retailers week, whistlers week, safe kids week, jelly bean day, take your children to work day, administrative professionals day, red hat society day, pretzel day, tell a story day, poetry reading day, dance day, hairstylists appreciation day

158   may month-long observances

national photograph month, national blood pressure month, barbecue month, older Americans month, national salad month

161   may week 1

family week, executive coaching day, loyalty day, scrapbooking day, home brew day, melanoma awareness day, cinco de mayo, tourist appreciation day, military spouses day

168   may week 2

nurses week, child care provider day, lost sock memorial day, clean your room day, eat what you want day, receptionists day, night shift day, leprechaun and limerick day

173   may week 3

backyard games week, police week and emergency service providers week, work at home moms week, pizza party day, help clean up your street day, pack rat day, museum day, boys club day, employee health and fitness day, memo day

177   may week 4

waiters and waitresses day, taffy day, lucky penny day, towel day, tap dance day, senior health and fitness day, jazz day, musical instrument day, water a flower day, save your hearing day

contents   365 days of marketing

contents   365 days of marketing

introduction

365 days of marketing proves

there is no shortage of ideas for ways to build your business—no matter its size, monetary resources or location. You can engage in effective, low-cost marketing, communications and promotions, no matter what type of business you own. You can gain new clients, improve retention and increase the frequency at which customers return, the amount of money they spend with you and the number of referrals they send your way.

Regardless of the state of the economy, your business has the potential to engage, inspire and intrigue. And you have the ability to better understand and meet the needs of your clients while simultaneously developing employee loyalty, buy-in, morale and enthusiasm.

You are limited by nothing more than your own vision, a willingness to try and whether you are ready to do what it will take to truly identify and meet the needs and wants of your customers. It might take you out of your comfort zone, but as an entrepreneur and business owner, this is nothing you haven't done before, even if it's something you haven't done in a while.

The bottom line is, how much fun are you having in your business right now? How many customers have disappeared in the current economic slump? How many have cut back on the frequency of their visits or the amount of money they spend at your business? Or maybe you want to open your own business but you are hesitant to do so in this economy. "Business as usual" is not working well, that's true—but that same truth is why there is opportunity.

We all know there are opportunities in an expanding economy, but there are also opportunities in a contracting one. As consumers become more selective in how they spend their money and are forced to get by on less than before, competition is tighter for those dollars. What consumers look for, especially when it comes to spending disposable income, is the value they receive in exchange for their money. If they are spending money on themselves, they want to be sure their purchase has lasting value in addition to satisfying a momentary need, that entertainment is worth the expense, that an item will last, that money they spend will benefit the local economy and the community, that the practices of the businesses they patronize are environmentally responsible or that the dollars they spend will in some way benefit those less fortunate than themselves.

The good news for locally-owned, independent businesses is that in this economy, people *want* to spend their money with companies that provide local jobs, sell products made by local manufacturers and which provide the most benefit to the local economy. Consumers are increasingly savvy when it comes to where their dollars 'go;' when educated about how shopping with independently-owned, local businesses maximizes these types of benefits, they are even more likely to choose to patronize them, even if it means that they may pay more to do so.

That said, the consumer still needs you to educate them. Your customers need to be informed about "where" the dollars go once spent with your business versus the money spent at chain or remotely-headquartered competitors. Your clients are interested in the benefits that your business provides to the local economy: how it provides local jobs, about the money your business puts back into the community, schools or other local businesses, and even in knowing what your values are. They want to know which charitable and community causes you choose to support with monetary, product or service donations and through volunteer service.

The merchants in your area may already have a 'Buy Local' campaign or committee in place. One of the benefits of participating is gaining access to information and promotional collateral designed to educate consumers which contains persuasive statistics that clearly demonstrate how dollars spent with locally-owned independent businesses stay in and benefit the local community at a far higher percentage than do dollars spent at national chains. If there is no 'Buy Local' merchant association in your town, you have a moment of opportunity to become a leader in your community by starting one. You will have the advantage of being on the ground floor and be among the first to benefit as education efforts begin to penetrate the consciousness of local consumers. It might mean that you have to step out of your comfort zone, become more vocal in your local Chamber of Commerce, Rotary and other civic or social business networks or you may need to take the initiative to get things rolling, but you will be quickly joined by other like-minded business owners who will be more than willing to help shoulder the work. You will read more about 'Buy Local' campaigns and how you can build business through merchant group, city and civic leadership in the coming pages.

My hope is that 365 Days of Marketing will do two things. First, it will provide you with an almost endless number of ideas, resources and possibilities for developing your marketing plan for the coming year (and years to come). 365 Days of Marketing will give you ways to engage your audience like never before, so that you can create and maintain momentum in attracting new clients and building revenues.

Constructing effective marketing, promotions and events may come naturally to you; however, they may not, or your expertise may be more needed in other areas of your business. I hope this book provides you with practical ideas and tools to make the marketing and promotional side of your business easier to manage, less time consuming and a truly organic part of your overall operations.

As evidenced by a significant number of empty storefronts on main street and in the malls, "if you build it" does not necessarily translate into "they will come." You can have a great business, staffed by wonderful, caring, dedicated employees, provide a service that should sell itself, at a location people practically fall over every day; but you may still have empty chairs, shelves full of products, employees with nothing to do, blanks in your appointment books and dust collecting on the cash register. You can create the most meaningful, fun, valuable promotions and events, but if you don't tell your clients and prospective clients about them, even the best ideas can be totally ineffectual.

A lot of people get stuck here. They have a great idea, sell their staff on it, print up a few flyers for bag stuffers, order supplies and open the doors—then they are left scratching their heads and ultimately blame the idea, when they should be blaming their own execution. They mistakenly ascribe to the 'silver bullet' theory that it is the power of the idea that brings success. In fact, some of the most successful promotions and events are not those which are the most creative or elaborate of great ideas; instead, they are simple, but are executed well. The best promotions and events are held by those who consistently communicate with and truly engage their clients. The most effective campaigns become so because the community is already created—long before an event or promotion is held. To put it another way, the audience is already in the theater when the show starts.

365 Days of Marketing is a tool that can help you build short and long term marketing, strategy and business plans. It will provide you with the know-how to build buzz about your business, promotions, events and the benefits you provide your customers and your community. It will help you construct compelling events that attract new clients, increase sales, stimulate referrals and provide you with the legitimate means to garner media attention.

365 Days of Marketing will help you think about how the various components of your business and communications need to work simultaneously and cooperatively with one another in order to maximize opportunities, and will demonstrate how a strong, interconnected, low cost communications plan is essential to your business.

365 Days of Marketing will help you develop a truly engaged and loyal employee team. It will help you create a bigger role for your business in the lives of your clients and a more influential role for you and your business in your community.

Effective marketing is dependent upon your having a variety of communications channels including both traditional marketing channels and newer channels like social media, blogging, e-mail marketing, text messaging, etc. And the success of these channels is dependent upon building followings of subscribers, readers, 'friends' and fans. 365 Days of Marketing will tell you how to build and use these channels as well as how to build your contact lists.

Finally, I hope that 365 Days of Marketing brings you joy. I hope that it brings your business renewed life, energy, employee and customer engagement and enthusiasm; and as a consequence, that it also brings you a personal renewal of your own passion for your business and industry. I hope it deepens and strengthens your relationships with your employees and your customers. I hope that 365 Days of Marketing gives you the ability to build stronger relationships with other business owners as you work together to improve the economy within your community. And I hope 365 Days of Marketing inspires you and leads to personal as well as professional development.

Marketing 101

There are basic components, types of collateral and channels of communication no business should be without; the good news is that most are very low cost and easily accessible.

Business Cards

Don't go anywhere without business cards! They might just be the most efficient, cost-effective piece of collateral in your arsenal—a billboard, an invitation, a brand impression, a proposition, a tangible reminder of your business—all on a 2 x 3.5" piece of paper. They have the unique ability to pack the most critical information about your business and even some of the "feel" of your brand onto a small piece of paper that is generally kept long after other forms of collateral are filed or thrown away. Most importantly, business cards can give people both a reason and the means to seek you out, visit your website or come to your physical location. Make the most of this universally-recognized piece of collateral; keep them with you at all times, in a hard case so that they stay clean and crisp, and give them out like you would candy on Halloween!

Business cards (like all marketing collateral) should reflect the brand of your business in some way. Invest in a professional, custom design that relates to the feel and personality of your business. The business card is universally recognized and used; think of it as—and design it to be—the best 2 x 3.5 inch billboard you could ever have! It should look professionally designed, not feel dated, be memorable or striking and (this is so important!) contain accurate and up to date information—no crossed out phone numbers or hours, please!

Business cards can't do their job sitting in a drawer or even on the counter; make it your goal to give them away *as fast as possible* instead of hoarding them so you do not have to reorder.

While this will sound obvious, it's true; the more places to which your business cards travel, the more people will know about you. And the easier and more rewarding it is for someone to contact you, the more likely they are to do so.

What should always be on your business card:

- Your name and your business name
- Website address
- E-mail address
- Business address
- Phone number best to call to reach customer service, get directions, for days or hours of operation, to ask another question or make an appointment
- Alternate or special-purpose phone number or message line
- Facebook, Twitter, blog site and other social media page identifiers

Give them away 2 at a time—one to keep, one to give to a friend, co-worker, etc.

- Person to person
- In thank-you notes
- In gift baskets
- With gift cards or certificates
- At the point of purchase
- In merchandising displays
- As bag stuffers
- When paying the bill at your favorite restaurant, bar, wine shop, coffee shop, deli, salon, spa, dry cleaners, boutique, etc.
- Exchanged for display with businesses located near yours, those owned by friends or family, and in businesses with services that compliment yours or with whom you share target markets
- Given out with treats at Halloween, or with samples, gifts or goodies at events, during the Holidays, etc.
- Handed out at city events, street fairs and holiday parades
- Included in payments to local vendors (like your plumber, auto repair shop, housekeeping services, equipment rental, window cleaner, city services, etc.)
- On bulletin boards still found in many supermarkets
- Send them in bulk along with copies of your menu or catalog or with a specially-created offer tailored specifically for patrons and/or employees of local retirement living centers, local sports clubs or recreation centers, civic clubs, local churches, large employers, private or public schools, hotels/motels, hospitals, etc.

Ensure that your business cards will be kept by adding creative value to the card itself:

- Calendar year, half year or quarter year at a glance (to be replaced at the beginning of the next year, half year or quarter year, etc.)
- Weights and measures conversion chart, or a ruler
- Tips and tricks or step-by-step instructions on a specific topic
- Rewards / punch card
- A bounce-back offer or a special "code" redeemable for an add-on, discount, etc.
- Design cards to double as a bookmark
- Put a quote, "fortune" or inspirational saying on it
- Hand write a compliment or another personal sentiment on it, or write an alternative or personal phone number on it

Finding an affordable printer for marketing collateral is not always easy, but I have a great business card printing option to share with you. Visit the Resources page of my website at www.12monthsofmarketing. com for a quote, referral, design help or other assistance.

Note Cards

As a tool for expressing real appreciation, extending best wishes, sympathy, congratulations or other sentiments, a personal note remains unsurpassed in its ability to convey rich, genuine thoughts and feelings from the sender to the recipient. And like a business card, does so at a very low cost, in a very small space, requiring little time or effort to utilize. Like business cards, note cards can be customized to reflect your business and brand, and should always include your contact information. Like the business card, *personally-written* note cards are items individuals tend to keep.

Despite the number of articles written recommending their use in every area of business from interviews to customer relations, despite the very low monetary or time investment required, and even despite overwhelming evidence of its effectiveness, the personal note is still one of the least utilized forms of business communication. The personal note used to be a standard of society; now it's something that can set you apart from the competition. Just think about it, a few minutes of your time, some paper, an envelope and a stamp. A note to thank your most valuable customers, employees, local business owners or even your vendors for their patronage or assistance on a project, to remark on a personal incident in their lives, to extend congratulations for a new baby, sympathy for a lost loved one – you have no way of knowing how important the sentiment will be to the recipient.

Sometimes we behave as though we believe our customers should be thanking us for the products and services we provide (in exchange for money) to them. The reality is, we should be thanking them for their patronage, the first time and every time. Your customers have lots of choices; in fact, they may literally have hundreds of other merchants to choose from when it comes to the same services or products you sell.

Once you get the hang of writing a quick note to someone, it won't seem like a chore. Make it part of your daily routine. It will be uplifting for you to remember the high points of your day, express gratitude or extend encouragement to others.

Beyond just saying 'thank you,' here are some of the events that might trigger a note from you to a client, co-worker, vendor, consultant, friend, etc.:

- To say goodbye to a customer who is moving away, going off to college or leaving on a military deployment (or to encourage a military spouse or parent)
- In sympathy or to say you are thinking of someone due to the death of a loved one, job loss, divorce or separation, etc.
- To acknowledge milestones such as birthdays and anniversaries
- As a get well / feel better soon, or another card of encouragement, or to encourage someone who simply had a bad day
- As a personal invitation to an upcoming event or promotion

- Congratulations for major life events such as having a new baby, new job, promotion, new home, new marriage or engagement, graduation, awards, accomplishments, retirement, marathons, significant weight loss or other self-improvement

- 'Thinking of you' or 'miss you' notes to clients you have not seen in a while or to those who are visiting your business less frequently than usual

- To thank teachers, the principal and other leaders of local schools or district offices, or to congratulate local school sports teams, choirs, bands and scholastic groups for competitive achievements

- To thank your event and marketing partners following a campaign, for referrals or on-going cooperative efforts

- Included as a note of congratulations to contest or drawing winner/s and to extend a special offer to event attendees or contest participants

- Included as a note of congratulations to those who win or buy items you donate to local charity auctions or events

- To extend employee-appreciation, compliments or kudos

- As a note to city hall, a local politician or civic leader

- To communicate with the owners of local businesses

- To thank leaders or volunteers of local charity organizations, non-profits, community service, etc. for their work in your community

- To thank someone who made your day, or to thank a client for their loyalty or referral

- To thank and welcome new customers

- For holidays—Christmas, Thanksgiving, New Year, Valentine's Day, etc.

- At the point of sale, a bag stuffer expressing appreciation for the customer's patronage can be an inexpensive way to leave an impression with them. You can also tell customers about how the money they spend at your business benefits the local community, provides jobs and supports worthy causes, or you can give them a sneak peek at upcoming promotions or a save-the-date for a future event. You can direct them to visit your website or ask them to read your blog or subscribe to your newsletters.

Make it your goal to find ways to thank 100% of your customers, 100% of the time. Send thank-you notes to vendors as well as customers. Send thank-you notes to civic leaders who make a difference boosting neighborhood commerce or within the community in general. Give thank-you notes to employees who go beyond the call of duty. You will be remembered, you will change someone's day for the better, and you will set yourself apart in a world where people simply don't take time to say thank you anymore.

Website

Believe it or not, many small businesses still have not made the small investment needed to set up even a basic website. This, despite the fact that almost 80% of U.S. consumers use the internet to find businesses online, locate brick and mortar locations, comparison shop and research products prior to purchasing. More than half of all Americans spend more than an hour online every day, and that statistic is even higher when it comes to professional men and women, moms, Baby Boomers, and increases yet again with individuals aged Gen X and younger.

Your website can be as simple as a one page site that costs just a few hundred dollars a year (compare that with the cost of your yellow page listing!) with your contact information and one or two of the most compelling reasons people should book an appointment with you or visit your business. Or you can opt to develop a more complex site beginning with a landing page and expanded to include menu pages, product information, news, press releases, an online store, a blog, consumer education and reviews, specials, promotions—the possibilities are endless.

Your clients and prospective clients are looking for you online. You will be Googled, Bing'ed, Yahoo'ed, Yelped and otherwise searched for; your website is your 24 x 7 x 365 billboard to the world. Even so, many businesses still do not have an online presence, and so go overlooked—and therefore unfound. Additionally, in certain industries, many businesses that think they have nothing to 'sell' online have been slow to come to the internet, leaving the field to the competition. Even independent sellers (like individuals who sell wares at parties, independent agents, home-based businesses, etc.) can and should use basic piece of marketing collateral in order to be more successful, gain new customers and communicate with their clients. While e-commerce may not be in the cards for every business, having a website so that prospects and customers can find you is imperative.

You can have a website that does not break the bank but is still well-designed and (most importantly) is effective when it comes to getting your business found online; a website that does its real and most important job, which is getting prospect to take the next step, whether the next step is to book an appointment, visit your store or purchase something online. In fact, getting the reader to take the next step should be your top priority when developing or making changes to your website—a priority that overrules other goals where there is conflict of purpose or over-complexity caused by too many competing messages.

Many businesses make the mistake of designing a 'corporate brochure' type of website full of self-congratulatory, "ain't we great!?" statements, or one that contains so much information that the consumer doesn't know where to start (and so doesn't). Website content that is not designed to take the viewer on a logical journey, that does not compel the reader to take the next step, and that does not highlight only the top two or three things that prospects or customers would be most interested in knowing may be wasted space from a marketing and business-building point of view, and may even be so convoluted that it works against that number one goal.

Your website should be a reflection of the brand of your business. The client should get the same 'feeling' about your business whether they are visiting your business in person or online. Your website helps create expectations, is a promise of service and begins to set the mood for a new customer; after that, the in-store experience needs to deliver on these promises!

You may have to set aside your own personal preferences when it comes to the design of your website. Remember that color, font, and image preferences are just that, preferences. Subjective. It's more important for your website to 'feel' like the experience provided to customers by your business than it is for a designer to create something that you enjoy looking at.

If you are working with a skilled designer, be willing to trust some of their recommendations, or at least bring in one or two objective third parties to weigh in with second opinions on those areas you don't agree or don't feel sure about. (And conversely, it is also true that your designer may have recommendations based on their own preferences—again, this is where bringing in a couple of trusted, savvy associates can help to choose direction.)

Be concise. The more you dilute the number one purpose of your website—to move the reader to the next step in relationship with your business—the more you detract from its effectiveness. Just as you cannot be all things to all people, your website should not try to tell everyone everything that anyone could possibly want to know about your business.

You have just a few seconds to capture a reader's attention; do you really want them scrolling through a bunch of disclaimers and details trying to find your address and phone number? If you do plan to include areas of high text content, consider dedicating specific pages to them or include them as linked downloadable PDFs rather than as web pages.

Prioritize. Knowing that the primary responsibility of your website is to get the reader to take a desired action—book an appointment, visit your location, call your customer service center or purchase something online—design the journey through your website with that in mind. Your phone number and address should be prominent, incredibly easy to find and 'above the fold' on your landing page (if not every page).

Your website should:

- give site visitors intriguing, provocative reasons and the information needed so that it is as easy as possible for them to find your business, make an online purchase, book an appointment, contact your call center, etc.
- give site visitors a reason and an easy way to subscribe to your communications
- give customers reasons to more deeply engage with your business and to purchase additional services and products from you
- be a reflection of your brand
- be easy to navigate
- be concise
- be visually stimulating, intriguing, engaging and provocative

- lead the viewer on a logical journey beginning with what would (probably) be what is most important to them
- be kept up to date; your website should show enough 'signs of life' that it does not look like you built it years ago and haven't touched it since
- contain relevant, interesting content—content that is relevant and interesting *to your target audience and customer* base (which may not be the same as what is most interesting to you)

As the internet and applications used to create and maintain sites has evolved, it has never been less expensive or easier to build and update a website, all on your own if that is your only option. Work with a designer to create a site that will be easy to update and change frequently, so that you can use it strategically to support your most important goals.

Here are some of the ways that you can make your website work for you beyond its primary purpose:

- Increasing the perceived value of your business by showcasing the most important benefits you provide to customers
- Highlighting the unique credentials, talents, skills, education, celebrity or expertise possessed by you and your staff in order to show the benefit to the customer and to create a desire in prospects to want to be part of what you have to offer
- Giving people new or additional reasons to come to your business; such as, to purchase gifts for others, support charitable and community causes, or attend events
- Increasing client engagement and pulling customers deeper into your business through education, common interests and causes
- Featuring content that will help improve your site's standing in web search results (also known as SEO or search engine optimization)
- Creating a sense of "we" or a tribal mentality; helping your customers more closely identify with you and your employees, with the causes you support, with other local businesses and community resources
- Providing links to and from community and charity resources
- Promoting 'Buy Local' consumer education and initiatives
- Recognizing the accomplishments of staff, customers, local civic and community leaders, volunteers, public servants, etc.
- Conducting surveys and collecting information
- Promoting seasonal campaigns or time-limited offers
- Selling gift certificates, tickets or actual products online
- Promoting web-exclusive offers, coupons or code word savings programs
- Gauging customer interest in potential new products or services
- Sharing links to businesses with which you cross or cooperatively market in order to increase your value to them as marketing partners as well as to support your joint initiatives

Ding, Dong!

The doorbell rings while you are making dinner after a long, hard day of work; you (reluctantly) answer, opening the door to a total stranger who (you correctly assume) is there to make a sales pitch. Despite your repeated attempts to politely say, "no, thank you," the salesperson (trained to overcome your objections with at least 99 different scripts) continues to pressure, cajole, flatter and otherwise annoy you until you either give in and buy a little something or send them away with a firm rejection.

How do you feel afterward? Would you answer the door to this person again or pretend not to be home? Would you seek out the company that trained them in order to make additional purchases or thank them for teaching the salesperson 'not to take no for an answer?' My guess is that you would craft a less complimentary message for this company!

While for the most part traditional marketing and advertising is comprised of overt sales and brand messages and a 'call to action,' when it comes to social media marketing, one of the keys to a successful strategy lies in the first word: Social.

While over time you may include occasional undisguised marketing messages on social marketing channels, your primary focus in using this media should be to establish and further relationships with people by letting them know more about who you are (sharing values, principles, expertise, etc.) in order to create website and blog traffic, encourage word-of-mouth marketing and stimulate referrals, rather than blatantly promoting products or services you sell. Using social media marketing channels to frequently deliver 'hard sell' messages is a turn-off that will likely result in your sites receiving significantly less—not more—traffic.

Why?

In social media marketing you are inviting people to engage with you as a person, even in the case of a Facebook page or other social media site created for business purposes. You are asking them to trust you enough to give you access to their friends, family, co-workers and neighbors. How personal would you get with the salesperson at the front door? Would you introduce them to your family and friends?

When it comes to social media marketing, remember that this is not just another marketing channel. Before you set up a Facebook page for your business or professional services, set up a Facebook page for yourself. Add "Friends" and review their pages; chances are you will find that they are on Facebook primarily for social purposes and engaged primarily in interpersonal conversations.

Along the same lines, before you create a site for blogging, do some research and find two or three blogs that *you* really enjoy reading personally. Make a bullet list of the reasons that you like them, what drew you in, what brings you back.

Limit your messages to those that really deserve "interruption" status in people's lives, or to those clients who have expressly requested that you communicate with them via text message. Before you hit "send," decide whether the message would be more appropriately communicated in your monthly e-mail newsletter. Before you launch a text-messaging blitz, think about the types of messages you would welcome as an interruption on your own phone.

Use social media marketing channels in such a way that your messages will be welcome in the lives of your readers. Craft messages that are an interesting and organic part of the conversation found in their "feed" rather than sales pitches. Use these sites as if you'd been invited into their living room to visit. If asked, you would talk about your business, you would talk about things you are personally passionate about, and you would give advice based on your expertise; but my guess is that you would not try to sell them—well, anything!

One of the best aspects of social media marketing is that there is little monetary cost associated with its use; however, it can become a costly endeavor in terms of time, especially when maintaining it is just one more assignment added to a long list in the life of a busy professional (that's you). Some experts suggest that as much as 25% of your working time should be devoted to social media channels. While the time you will need to devote to this aspect of marketing may vary, the point remains; to be effective as a means of marketing, social media require that time be consistently invested in updating, blogging, posting, entertaining, educating and intriguing your readers.

Like any other initiative, social media marketing cannot thrive without being nurtured. If time is at a premium for you, if you have never ventured onto the internet or if the idea of setting up a Facebook page or Tweeting makes you break into a cold sweat, don't despair! Social Media sites have created interfaces that can—literally—be managed by even a relative novice to technology. You may find that once you begin to experiment with these social sites, it's easy to become addicted to the real conversations that are occurring every day in the virtual world!

Not your thing? You may have an employee or even a high school or college student in your family or among your clientele who would be thrilled to work for you for a couple hours each week either to set up and manage your social marketing channels on an on-going basis, or to train you to take over.

As you wade deeper in to viral marketing waters, use these channels to create 'customer love' by sharing the same kinds of stories about your business you would want to share in someone's living room—stories that they will remember and will feel inspired to pass on to others.

Due to the frequency at which Facebook, blogs and other social network applications change, it does not make sense to include step-by-step instructions on how to set up accounts here. The best way for you to become familiar with Facebook, a blog site or any other social marketing or networking site is to set up a personal account before you set up a page for your business. This will give you an opportunity to see how to set up your page, and to see how each application works as well as to see how other companies are using it to help build business.

Resist the temptation to use any of your social media tools primarily as a sales medium. Using social media as a forum for hard sales efforts is the quickest way to lose your following and alienate your "friends." It is not a contradiction to say that you can and should use your social sites to let your followers, friends and fans know about special promotions and events; in fact, you can even create Facebook-only, Twitter-only, blog-only or other social site-only offers, hold contests and conduct virtual events. But those types of offers are typically used more to attract new social media site followers or to direct people to visit your blog, website or store—rather than for direct sales.

Think of social media posts and status updates as if you are having one on one conversations with people in your living room (rather than your business). Speak to followers like you are speaking with friends and family, as if they are people you are being introduced to at a party, and people on whom you want to make a good first impression. Be relevant, be entertaining, be interesting, be provocative; stimulate thinking about what it is that you do in a way that relates to people personally, surpasses expectations and is better than the competition.

While social network sites need frequent attention and updates, the good news is that you don't have to be a prolific writer in order to create and maintain these sites, because your posts will usually be limited to a sentence or two in length. Even blog posts need not be more than a few paragraphs.

If you want people to pay attention, join, read, like, share and otherwise follow your sites, posts must be interesting and relevant *to your target audiences*. And you can talk about more than your business or area of expertise; unlike some of their more staid counterparts among marketing communication channels, people expect and want you to be personal when it comes to social media. This is a forum where you should communicate conversationally and with personality!

In addition to business topics, other things you might post:

- Quotes—inspirational, funny, poignant, profound—what speaks to you will probably speak to others
- Statistics; statistic-based facts relative to your business or industry, or that are humorous, profound, location-based—there are many possibilities, just be interesting!
- Personal anecdotes (nothing you wouldn't want your mother, most straight-laced client, the other people involved or an employer to read!)
- "Did you know...?" style questions about common customer challenges, conditions and product solutions
- Community information and links
- Links to relevant industry, product or service articles
- Events and follow up on events with photos and highlights
- Kudos, thank-yous and recognition of accomplishments
- Tips and tricks for the season, for special occasions, or on special topics
- Introduction and overview of new products and services

- Service and/or product of the month spotlight
- Upcoming events at your business or in the community
- Facebook, blog, or other social site-exclusive offers, coupons or contests
- Site-only immediate-response offers; such as, "the first 5 people to comment below will receive..."
- Reminders about expiring offers and teasers for new things coming soon

E-Mail

Make it your goal to collect 100% of your customer's e-mail addresses; ask for them at every point of contact! E-mail communication may be one of the most vital components of community-based marketing. Every event, promotion or contest you hold should include the means to collect contact information, including an e-mail address. Your website should have a form for subscription (as well as links to follow you on Facebook Twitter, etc.) Ask every customer for their e-mail address (and for permission to e-mail them) at the point of purchase, during the customer service phone call or at their appointment. Enter them into your contact database and ensure they start receiving communications as quickly as possible.

Nearly all of your customers and prospects use the internet to research businesses and to communicate with others on at least a somewhat regular basis. Even if you, yourself, have never used a computer, you can still utilize e-mail as a communications tool for your business. If you really don't want to learn to use it, again, recruit an interested employee or engage a local high school or college student. Even as little as a few hours a week will be enough help you start e-mail marketing.

If simplicity isn't compelling, price may be. Note cards and postcards are inexpensive and fairly quick to reach people, but e-mail is immediate, trackable and even less expensive (sometimes even free). Plus, e-mail sent in permission-based marketing has a *significantly higher response rate* than other forms of direct marketing.

Trying to run an effective e-mail campaign without e-mail addresses is like trying to invite people to a wedding without addresses. The invitations are printed and sealed, sitting there on the desk all beautiful and ready to go; but until you have an address to put on the envelopes, they won't go anywhere!

I know this sounds basic, but believe it or not, there are still many people who are afraid they will "annoy" their customers if they ask them for an e-mail address or send them an e-mail. Some assert that (unlike most U.S. consumers and contrary to all recent studies which say the opposite) their customers are "not on e-mail" or don't want to receive e-mails.

Maybe there are a few people who will request not to be contacted; but building your e-mail contact database is the only way for you to use e-mail communication to build business. Allowing negative feedback from one or two people to limit your ability to communicate with all of your customers is foolish.

In today's society, most people *expect* to be contacted by e-mail and many prospective as well as current customers will want to be on your e-mailing list. It is permission-based from end to end; people give you permission to e-mail them, so they want and expect you to do so. Once they receive the e-mail, there is still no coercion. They have the ability to open the e-mail, save it for later or delete it without even reading. They have the ability to print it or to forward it to a friend. They have the ability to unsubscribe from your list at any time. Your readers have all of the power in the e-mail relationship; all they want from you is interesting, relevant and compelling content! In order to keep your e-mails out of the junk e-mail folders and to keep your readers—well, reading, here are a few guidelines for using e-mail:

- Be as personal as possible. Even when you are sending a message out to all of your contacts, write as though you are speaking to just one person.

- Make sure all content is relevant *to the customer* and is written from a customer-centric point of view. It's not about what is good for you, it is about what benefits the customer. What's good for your customer *is* what's good for your business. If you write about your business as though you believe your customer's primary interest is in *your* bottom line, it won't take them long to delete your e-mails, stop opening them or unsubscribe altogether. And once you lose trust, it will be difficult to regain it.

- Keep messages brief and readable in a quick sitting.

- Keep e-mail addresses private; when sending a group e-mail from your personal account, put the e-mail addresses in the "BCC" (blind carbon copy) field, not the "TO" field where they can be seen by others.

  Better yet, use a resource like Constant Contact (www.constantcontact.com) to manage your lists and conduct your mailings. This will help prevent having your personal or business e-mail black-listed as spam, gives you the ability to manage your contact database and to quickly and easily send e-mail messages to all or targeted groups of subscribers. There is a link to Constant Contact on the Resources page of www.12monthsofmarketing.com, and as of the time of this writing, you can try their services out for free.

- Be authentic and personal, but remember that your e-mail communications should reflect the brand of your business in imagery and language.

- Include inspiration, insight and humor. If something you heard about touched or inspired you, chances are it will inspire and engage others.

- Be protective. If you would not want to read something about yourself, don't write it about someone else. Never share personal information of staff or clients without permission, even if you are sharing good news.

- Before you hit 'send,' re-read what you have written at least twice; read it out loud to see if it sounds like something that you would say.

- Ask a peer to proof-read any communications before sending out to clients for language, branding, tone and as your back up to prevent dissemination of any inappropriate information.

When crafting communications for any purpose, focus on the positive of what you do offer and provide (not on what you don't do or sell). Be honest and communicate what is necessary, but try not to focus on the disclaimers of your offers, the negative parts of your policies, or on exclusions or limitations. Speak in positive terms even when you are conveying policies.

And be concise. Your e-mail messages should be brief, with each item being no more than just a few sentences. People skim e-mails, looking for headlines or pictures which catch their eyes. If you do need to send something with large text content, place it at the bottom or on a separate web page or PDF with a link from the e-mail such as: [click here to read more].

Send new subscribers a welcome e-mail as quickly as possible and set up a regular schedule of communications to keep your business in the forefront of their minds. If you provide readers with interesting and relevant content, they will look forward to receiving your communications; and (for those still terrified of sending e-mails to their customers) remember that no matter how often you send e-mails, the power of opening them and the choice to read them or not resides with the recipient.

If you are just beginning to do e-mail marketing, try setting a goal for yourself to send one e-mail each month to your total e-mail database. Think of it as your business newsletter, a chance to let customers know what is new, what special offers, events, contests and promotions you have for them in the coming weeks, which offers are about to expire, and to share highlights about what happened during the previous few weeks. In harmony with your social networking communications, include a product or service of the month spotlight feature (you can use the same for both).

Once you publish your e-mail newsletter, put a link to the web version of your e-mail message on your website, blog, Facebook page and other social media sites so that even people who have not subscribed can still read what is, essentially, your monthly e-newsletter.

Are you beginning to see how all of these tools can work together to help support your brand and your marketing in order to help you break through the clutter? In an era when people are bombarded with thousands of marketing messages every single day, creating consistency across channels and giving your clients multiple ways to receive your messages greatly increases the chance that your information will get through to them. They might receive an e-mail newsletter, postcard, see your Facebook post and receive a bag stuffer—each highlighting the same special offer or spotlight product or service—and all without you having to deliver so much as a single sales pitch yourself!

By doing this, you will build brand awareness and gain mind share with clients and prospects so that by the time you actually sample, demonstrate or by the time they see the featured item at your business, they will already have been exposed to information about it and will already have an idea of how it benefits them. By the time you invite them personally to an event, they will already know what it is and who of their friends might also want to come.

Now that you have (hopefully) overcome any objections or fears you may have harbored about e-mail marketing and you are excited to get started, here are a few ways that you can put e-mail to work for you:

- Appointment reminders
- Sending directions and contact information
- Thank-you notes (personal)
- Electronic newsletters (also referred to as e-mail newsletters)
- Promotional service or retail offers
- Event announcements and reminders
- Collecting RSVPs, taking reservations
- Answering inquiries from your website
- Responding to complaints or suggestions, follow-up
- Cooperative marketing and advertising with your business partners
- Extending recognitions, kudos, and congratulations
- Invitations (mass or personal)
- New subscriber welcome
- New client welcome, thank-you, offer, reward, and/or menu of services
- Featured product and/or service of the month
- Seasonal special items or offers
- E-mail-exclusive offers (use a code word to help you track response)
- Highlight community resources or worthy causes
- Increase awareness of your business as a gift resource
- Extend birthday, anniversary, holiday or other special occasion greetings
- Extend special offers to large employers, seniors, schools, students or other groups
- Send referral rewards or reward status updates
- Announce contests or winners
- Conduct surveys or collect information about customer preferences, interests, etc.

There are many publications available in print and online when it comes to the appropriate and legal use of e-mail in business and marketing. One of the most important rules to follow is to e-mail with permission, 100% of the time. When asking for e-mail addresses, make it clear that they are being added to your contact database for business purposes.

If you make promises to clients regarding privacy or restricted use of e-mail addresses, honor your promises.

Catalog, Menu or Corporate Brochure

Take-away versions of your catalog, menus of products or services and/or a corporate brochures are great to have on hand at the point of sale, in your car or purse when you are out and about, and available for customers to read while waiting or walk off with. These types of publications can help ensure that your business remains in the minds of clients after they walk out the door or that they might take to give to friends, stimulating referrals. Include part of your business 'story, be sure it reflects your brand and include messages about the benefits you provide, client referrals, and other recommendations. Most importantly, make sure every piece of collateral includes your contact information including business name, address, phone number, website, etc.

Poorly designed collateral or collateral with errant or outdated information—or worse, text crossed through and written over—actually damages the brand you present to prospective clients, customers, vendors, etc. It sends a message to your own employees about your lack of concern over how your business is presented. It may even suggest that your business is struggling to the point that you cannot afford to replace paper collateral.

Create (or commission) a professionally-designed menu or brochure that is in harmony with your business cards, website and other collateral and that reflects your brand personality and style. Update it as frequently as needed. Ask your designer for a printable, downloadable PDF version to post on your website, blog, Facebook page and other social media each time it is updated.

Include information about what sets your business apart from competitors or alternatives. Describe the benefits of your services and products. Menus often go home with customers, so including product knowledge reinforces your marketing messages and serves a reminder when customers are considering future product and gift purchases.

Other take-home collateral you might create for customers include bookmarks, bounce-back offer cards, flyers and bag stuffers. Choose one retail product to feature each month and create a print piece to go home with clients, to be sent to contacts via direct mail and e-mail, to be displayed at the point of purchase or on shelves, and which will receive spotlight attention on your website and Facebook page.

When you create a new catalog, menu or brochure, ask your graphic designer to provide you not only with print-ready files for professional printing, but also with a PDF (portable document format) sized appropriately to be used as a link from your website, Facebook page, blog and e-mail newsletter. Depending on its size, your PDF will probably also be something you can (personally) e-mail to clients, prospects, vendors, new hires, etc. When you publish new collateral, be sure to update all of the electronic versions as well as replacing the print versions.

More menu ideas:

- Create a menu of "starter services" featuring a new customer reward as a catalog or brochure, or print a new customer offer on refrigerator magnets; send new customer collateral to people moving into new homes in your area, local businesses and prospect contacts collected at events.

- Add value so your menu is more likely to be retained; a year-at-a-glance calendar, school year calendar, list of holidays and observances, do it yourself tips and tricks, the schedule of the local professional sports team—anything appropriate to your audience that turns a piece of collateral into more of a keepsake.

- Once a year (or every time it is updated) mail or e-mail your catalog, brochure or menu to your entire contact database. This this as a reason and the means to reconnect with clients you may not have seen in a while or with prospects who may now be looking for something you offer, and can be a way to make people aware of services they may not have known you offered, or may not have tried before.

- Subscribe to new move-in mailing lists and send a copy of your catalog, brochure or menu to new residents or to residents living in neighborhoods representing your prime demographic market or ideal clients.

- Include as a bag stuffer.

- Distribute copies at local holiday fairs, job fairs, college and career fairs and to large employers in your area.

- Have your designer help you create a larger display version to frame and hang or have printed on a banner or professional sign.

- Create a display with your menu or other collateral to be displayed in businesses near yours or those with which you partner for marketing or events.

Space

If you have a physical business location and space to hold events, you're ahead; but if you don't, you still don't have to let a lack of space constrain you (another one of the benefits of the community-based marketing approach intrinsic to many of the ideas in 365 Days of Marketing). Finding space to hold events is as simple as finding businesses to partner with for cross and cooperative marketing, events and promotions. When you bring your clients and prospects to another business—a restaurant, wine shop, boutique, hotel or events facility, etc.—you are establishing yourself as a valuable referral partner. This gives you leverage to trade more equitably for event space, co-sponsorship, supplies, shared expenses and more. This type of cooperative marketing is a win for all of the businesses that work together, because each has the potential to reach new clients and prospects by bringing together and/or marketing to multiple customer groups and contact lists for combined events and promotions.

If space is an issue and you are not partnered with businesses that have adequate space, here are a few more ideas for capturing needed event space:

- In the current economy, travel is down, and travel-dependent businesses have experienced a significant slow down. Hotels and motels are scrambling to bring in business and may be willing to work creatively with you to utilize corporate meeting, restaurant, banquet and other facility space to accommodate your events.
- Local caterers, wine shops or restaurants may have lobby or meeting areas conducive to small group events and would also make great partners for cross-marketed offers, cooperative advertising, and co-sponsored events.
- Most businesses—even small, 1-2 person corporations—usually have conference rooms and may be willing to trade space to you in return for products, services or gift cards.
- Realty and insurance agents may have meeting rooms and could also be potential partners for cooperative marketing and events. They would likely be very interested in sharing prospect and client contacts for cooperative efforts.
- Community centers and retirement communities usually have multiple meeting areas for small or large groups and may also be a source of new client prospects.
- A strip mall or retail mall with vacant space may be willing to rent you space for a one-time event; after all, you are bringing potential 'shoppers' into their retail space—and you have the advantage of showing off your event to mall or street traffic. If your event is open to the public, be sure to have someone outside handing out flyers or business cards.
- Local wedding, party and event planners have lists of local venues in all size ranges and may also be great partners for cooperative marketing and events.

From a certain perspective, the lack of space can actually be a benefit to you since it means you will have to seek out partnerships for cross and cooperative marketing that have what you don't, and who want what you have. Use your events and services or products to create leverage in lowering your costs with space providers and other vendors.

Press Releases

As you read through 365 Days of Marketing and begin to plan events and promotions, set aside time and assign responsibility to document each event with a press release. If writing is not your strong point, recruit an employee, family member, friend or another individual to write press-style summaries of your events throughout the year. Send press releases to local media before events including an invitation for them to participate or observe. And provide them with summary releases, results and pictures afterward. Developing a relationship with local reporters will help you to begin to cultivate media coverage for your most news-worthy events.

Post a copy of your press releases online in the 'news' portion of your website, link to them on Facebook, your blog and e-mail newsletter, and place copies at the point of purchase or in the waiting area in your business for customers to read.

Your press release should be brief, no more than 1-2 pages. Include the information that would be most likely to qualify it as a press-worthy event, such as benefit to the community, an accomplishment of a community member, etc. Remember that reporters are often bombarded by requests for coverage; only the most compelling copy will cut through the clutter. Below you'll see a typical press release format, which you are free to utilize:

FOR IMMEDIATE RELEASE:
by [Business name]
[Contact name]
[Phone number and e-mail address]
[Fax number and website address]
[Mailing address]

Your corporate
logo here

YOUR HEADLINE HERE
Date
Introductory paragraph—what makes this press-worthy? What problem is solved, what benefit to the community or charity occurred, what major accomplishment or milestone was reached.

2-3 paragraphs of additional text - who, what, when, where, why - a brief history/overview.

If going onto page 2, repeat abbreviated headline, name of contact person, phone and e-mail address at top.

(After final paragraph)
For additional information, contact: (repeat all contact information)

Corporate bio and/or information in one paragraph about the business, its longevity, positioning and/or what makes it special or differentiates it from competitors.

#
(indicates end of release)

Cooperative and Cross Marketing

Partnering with other businesses for shared marketing and events makes sense. When you cross market with other businesses, you extend your marketing reach by hundreds (if not thousands) more prospective clients at a very low cost; perhaps as minimal an investment as the cost to purchase and place business cards, flyers, display sheets, tent cards or your catalog, menu or brochure in the waiting area, on the tables of, or at the point of purchase of other local businesses. And it's not just about exposure to their customers; by presenting your business to their customers, they are also giving you their unspoken (or even spoken) endorsement.

And there is more to be gained by working with other businesses in this way, there is also the shared sense of community and destiny—the realization that you are not in this by yourself and not limited to your own resources or creativity. So often as entrepreneurs, small business owners and independent professionals we feel that we need to be brilliant, creative and self-sufficient—and that we have to do it all on our own. Sharing resources, shelf space and contacts, brainstorming together to solve problems, enticing more people in the community to spend dollars locally, working together to create a greater sense of community   when we feel this shared sense of destiny with others, we work even harder to ensure the success of everyone.

Every promotion or event you hold has the potential to be attractive to some other business in your area for sharing contacts, responsibilities and costs. But how do you find them?

The most logical place to start building marketing and event partnerships may also be the most convenient; namely, those businesses located nearest yours. Other alliance possibilities exist among your friends and family, members of your Chamber of Commerce, Rotary, Kiwanis and other civic organizations, businesses in your community that share your target markets, and an avenue you may not have considered, among your customers themselves.

When building these working relationships, let businesses know up front about other businesses you are working with. This will help you avoid misunderstandings and will keep you out of situations where you might make commitments to businesses who compete directly with one another.

Cross marketing with other businesses can provide you with continuous exposure to new prospects. The businesses with which you choose to cross market should have a client base that overlaps with major segments of your own ideal types of clients or represents new target markets you want to attract. The same holds true for businesses you include in cooperative marketing or events.

Finally, when you endorse other businesses by allowing them marketing access to your customers, you are, in effect, recommending that your clients do business with those companies, so your endorsement should only be given to those businesses that you would truly recommend to others.

Cooperative Marketing

Cooperative marketing, as referenced in 365 Days of Marketing, is marketing done in cooperation with other professionals or businesses. It is implied that contacts will be shared to a central source for coordinated marketing, promotions, events and other campaigns. An example of a cooperative marketing promotion would be a salon joining forces with a dance studio to invite both sets of clients to an event which will feature services provided by both businesses, such as a hair and makeup fashion show along with an introductory dance class or demonstration. Exposure for each business is increased exponentially as offers are extended to multiple client contact lists. To honor promises made to customers about privacy of contact information, for cooperative marketing events, participating businesses can use a third party rather than trade contact lists outright.

Cross Marketing

Whereas cooperative marketing is working together, cross marketing is crossing over to market to clients of another business and marketing their services or products to yours. The main benefit to participants is increased exposure to prospective clients. Optimally, these prospects will share many of the traits you find in your 'ideal client' or desired target markets. You should still use a central source for marketing so that you do not violate customer trust by giving their contact information away to another business, or you can simply exchange marketing materials for distribution to one another's clients in displays, print or electronic communications.

Some of the items you might cooperatively share or trade for marketing space within other businesses include:

business cards or brochures	Facebook or blog posts
website links	e-mail newsletter inclusion
retail space	press release inclusion
lobby or client waiting areas	charity endeavors
break room or lunchroom space	real or virtual bulletin boards
point of purchase displays	event or program publications
flyers	direct mail postcards or letters

One additional benefit of both Cooperative and Cross Marketing is the implied endorsement of the businesses you partner with. Since you are—essentially—recommending that your clients do business with your marketing partners, expose your clients only to those businesses that will treat them as well as you do!

Marketing Partnerships

Your marketing partnerships will be most effective when you choose partners in context of specific promotions or events, and in relationship to your business, the nature of your clientele and your business goals. For the purposes of this book, when the words "partnership" or "marketing partners" are used, it refers to an informal partnership (rather than a legal or formal one). While there may be instances where you want to detail responsibilities in writing, most partnerships will be played out in cooperative work together as the result of verbal agreement, mutual trust and previous experiences.

Seek out and establish partnerships with businesses that have something you want (and want something you have) to create win-win scenarios. Here are some additional things to keep in mind when considering businesses you might partner with for marketing or events:

- Ideal client base—business partners whose ideal or main types of clients share some of the same characteristics or demographics as your ideal clients, such as geographic location, income or home ownership, gender, age, children, disposable income, leisure activities, charitable interests, etc.

- Social basis—partnerships or suggestions from among your current clientele, your family, friends, acquaintances, co-workers, former co-workers, etc.; partnerships whose businesses are represented by some of your current clients

- Proximity—partnerships with businesses located near yours

- Contact lists—partnerships with independent sellers, agents, realtors, etc. who have large client and prospect lists; they are typically familiar with your city and surrounding areas and may also have significant influence in your community

- Networking—participate in civic organizations and/or partner with businesses who are members of your city Chamber of Commerce, Rotary, Kiwanis, Optimists/Soroptimists, 'Buy Local' associations, business roundtables, etc.

Avoid sharing your contacts with other businesses outright. Whether you have a privacy policy or not, your customers believe that they are only giving you their contact information (and permission to communicate with them) and no one else. They will not mind if you endorse other businesses through shared marketing, but they will find it objectionable if you give their information away.

You can honor their trust by agreeing up-front that all businesses participating in cooperative marketing, promotions or events will provide their contacts to a central source or individual. This company or individual will utilize the contacts appropriately for a campaign or marketing activities occurring for an agreed-on period of time, but will not release the contacts to the other businesses involved. This applies both to cooperative and cross marketing campaigns.

Partnerships In Context

Building even one marketing partnership can bring new clients to your business and make both businesses more profitable. Building partnerships with several other businesses and using them in context with themed promotions, holidays, events and charity fundraisers can make a huge difference in growing your business, expanding your client base, engaging and retaining customers, increasing retail sales, helping others in your community and building for the future.

Marketing partnerships can maximize your exposure to the right types of prospects and give you the means to fill up events, sell through stock and promotions, and fill up appointment books and reservation slots. Partnerships give you the ability to hold bigger events and promotions than you could on your own, and reduces expenses since costs for events, campaigns and collateral are shared.

You don't have to partner with everyone. But partner with *someone*. Can't think of where to start?

Start with a list of 12. List of set of 12 different kinds of businesses in your community whose typical customers represent a segment of your target markets (for instance, businesses whose customers are women, men, moms, members of specific 'generations,' pet owners, parents of preschool, school or college aged children, empty nesters, home owners, boat owners, outdoor enthusiasts, hobby or craft aficionados, etc.) Or simply make a list of the 12 (non-competing) businesses closest to your location:

- For each of the 12 businesses on your list, make a list of 3 possible promotions or events you could imagine working on together;
- Write down the names of the next 12 months;
- Match up the business with which you want to partner with the month when one of the ideas for cooperative promotions or events you thought of would make the most sense; then,
- Approach the owner or manager of that business and suggest the cooperative marketing effort you want to run with them.

City, Civic and Leadership Organizations

While participating in city, civic and networking organizations requires that you commit precious time and resources, they also provide great contacts for your business—not only for networking and connecting with prospects, but also for your own personal development. Plus, being involved in these organizations gives you opportunities to influence local regulations and taxes that directly affect your business. Networking in city and civic groups also connects you with other independently-owned business professionals with whom you can work to develop community awareness of the benefits of buying from local, independently-owned businesses or even work together to establish a 'Buy Local' merchant group.

Chamber of Commerce and Civic Organizations

Chambers of Commerce exist to represent the interests of business and might also include economic development consultants and committees or local tourist and visitors bureaus. Membership is voluntary. Since they are generally populated by members of city government, local politicians and special interest leaders, they can also wield influence that may (or may not) coincide with what is best in general for local businesses. It is important for you to know how your local Chamber of Commerce works, how it is connected to local governing agencies, who belongs to it and who is influential in decision making. If you can, participate as a member or by providing input to help improve the overall business climate of your city, influence urban development, and have a say in the regulations and taxes which impact your business.

In addition to a Chamber of Commerce, you city may also have other committees on which you can participate or provide recommendations and input; some examples include arts commissions, tourism boards, transportation committees, human services, parks and recreation, planning committees, visitors information centers, street fairs, city celebrations, parades, historical foundations and others.

Chambers of Commerce often have multiple networking and member meetings, luncheons, business directories, provide services to local businesses, hold after hours mixers, breakfasts, grand openings, ribbon cuttings, golf outings, and even perform civic mission trips. They work closely with city government to promote the interests of business in your city, including investing in the infrastructure (roads, transit, parking, parks, etc.) needed to help attract more visitors (and more shoppers) to your city.

Close cousins of the Chamber of Commerce are local Optimist/Soroptimist, Rotary and Kiwanis clubs. These are service organizations made up of business and community leaders who voluntarily give of their time, abilities, money and other resources to help others in their communities and around the world. Clubs like these make significant contributions to meeting needs locally, but they have also provided meaningful support to the victims and rebuilding efforts following major catastrophes (such as Hurricane Katrina in 2005 and the earthquake in Haiti in 2010). Members have opportunities to work on local, national and even international projects.

These clubs (usually) meet once a week or once a month. They will probably also hold several social, networking-friendly events throughout the year and participate in city street fairs, parades and festivals. Their members are usually personally invested in promoting the economic health of the local business community. For more information about these organizations and how to find clubs near you, visit their websites:

Rotary — www.Rotary.org

"Rotary International is the world's first service club organization, with more than 1.2 million members in 33,000 clubs worldwide. Rotary club members are volunteers who work locally, regionally, and internationally to combat hunger, improve health and sanitation, provide education and job training, promote peace, and eradicate polio under the motto 'Service Above Self.'"

Kiwanis — www.kiwanis.org

"Kiwanis is a global organization of volunteers dedicated to changing the world one child and one community at a time. Our members develop youth as leaders, build playgrounds and raise funds for pediatric research. We help shelter the homeless, feed the hungry, mentor the disadvantaged and care for the sick. Working together, members achieve what one person cannot accomplish alone. And along the way, club members share friendship and laughter. Located in 80 countries, Members stage nearly 150,000 service projects and raise nearly $107 million (US dollars) every year for communities, families and projects."

Optimists — www.optimist.org

"Optimist International is an association of more than 2,900 Optimist Clubs around the world dedicated to 'Bringing Out the Best in Kids.' Adult volunteers join Optimist Clubs to conduct positive service projects in their communities aimed at providing a helping hand to youth. With their upbeat attitude, Optimist Club members help empower young people to be the best that they can be. Each Optimist Club determines the needs of the young people in its community and conducts programs to meet those needs. Every year, Optimists conduct 65,000 service projects and serve well over six million young people."

Soroptimists — www.soroptimist.org

"Soroptimist is an international organization for business and professional women who work to improve the lives of women and girls, in local communities and throughout the world. Almost 95,000 Soroptimists in about 120 countries and territories contribute time and financial support to community–based and international projects that benefit women and girls. The name, Soroptimist, means 'best for women,' and that's what the organization strives to achieve. Soroptimists are women at their best, working to help other women to be their best."

*The quotes, statistics and information above are directly from each respective organization's website in 2010

Opportunities abound for you to participate in professional organizations in order for you to both give and receive benefits, personally and professionally. In addition to business-building through networking, it is easy to see that your participation can also provide you with the ability to influence city government, planning, transportation and infrastructure issues as well as the rules, regulations, laws and taxes that directly impact your profitability and the way that you do business. Your participation will directly help these organizations and the local community members they serve, and you can also become the point of connection for your clients and the public to city and civic organizations, community events and local causes. You can even help lead efforts in your community by gearing your charity-benefit events to support club service activities and projects.

'Buy Local' Campaigns and Merchant Groups

One more option for you to consider when it comes to building valuable working partnerships: 'Buy Local' cooperatives. Revenue and profit for all businesses (and especially for small, independent professionals and stores) has been negatively impacted—in some cases drastically so—in communities throughout the U.S. during the last few years of economic recession and the so-called recovery. Many small businesses have few 'rainy day' funds or remaining resources to draw on; scores of businesses have closed down, and some are barely hanging on.

In response, 'Buy Local' organizations and initiatives have sprouted up nation-wide in efforts to draw more consumer spending to locally-owned independent businesses and away from national and international chain stores. Part of the consumer's willingness to buy locally in increasing numbers, even if it sometimes mean paying higher prices, stems from the educational efforts of 'Buy Local' merchant groups comprised of local, voluntarily-participating businesses and community leaders.

'Buy Local' campaigns facilitate dissemination of information to community residents about how much of each dollar they spend remains to benefit the local community when they shop at locally-owned independent businesses rather than national or regional chains headquartered elsewhere.

According to a 2002 study published online by AMIBA (the American Independent Business Alliance) while only $13 of every $100 spent at a national retail chain store "stays" in the local community, when spending that same $100 at an independently-owned local business, $45 out of $100 "stays" right in the community. Plus, local merchants spend a larger percentage of their total revenue on local labor, they keep more of their profits in the local economy and they provide strong support for local artists and authors, charities and other businesses, creating further positive local economic impact.

Organizations like AMIBA benefit participating members in several ways. They provide members with merchandising, signage and information to provide public education within the community about the specific social, economic and cultural benefits that are typically provided by locally-owned independent businesses. They provide members with cooperative purchasing, branding, marketing and resource-sharing opportunities so they can better compete with big, national chains. Members, together, have a stronger voice in local and state politics. And they empower citizens to help guide the economic future of their own neighborhoods and cities.

While most were initially founded to promote local shopping, many have gone on to leverage their group power to influence government policy in their communities. Many also choose to incorporate support for other principles into their campaigns, such as promoting "green" and sustainable business practices.

These organizations exist in many cities and often utilize resources provided by advisory non-profits like AMIBA (www.amiba.net). This is not intended to be an endorsement exclusive to AMIBA; there are several similar non-profit companies providing these types of services. I am simply familiar with it due to the existence of a local chapter.

Using Fundraising to Build Business

You can choose to support one or any number of charities in your community. When considering your options, why not choose to benefit an organization that has directly impacted your own life? You will express yourself the most honestly and persuasively when speaking to issues you understand personally. Plus, you will receive the most personal satisfaction when you help promote and donate to causes you genuinely believe in.

While in most cases I recommend that you put the desires of your customers first in decision making, in the case of supporting charitable causes and local social service organizations, choose those you most desire to benefit out of your own passions or personal experiences. You can also choose to provide support for customers or community members who have personally experienced tremendous loss or have personal need.

Here are some ways to benefit charities while building business (check with your tax professional to be sure that you construct your event most appropriately if you intend to write off any portion of your donations of money, products or services):

- Events or marketing promotions with all profits going to charity (usually this means net proceeds after costs are deducted)
- Events with all proceeds going to charity (costs are donated)
- Events with a cover charge going to charity

- Events or marketing promotions with a percentage of overall or specific product/service sales going to charity

- Product or service of the month with proceeds or percentage of sales to charity (or a certain dollar amount for each unit sold, etc.)

- Match all donations, a percentage of donations or total donations up to a certain amount, or acquire a corporate or individual sponsor willing to match donations

- Use your communications channels to feature information about a charity, its needs, and how it benefits others on an on-going basis in order to help build awareness, or build momentum for a specific event or marketing promotion

- Donate actual products or services to a charity, to patients or their family members, to care givers, to the employees of the charity, etc.

- Hold a walk-a-thon, cut-a-thon, massage-a-thon, read-a-thon etc., accepting donations for the charity in lieu of payment for services and encouraging contributions from all clients, corporate sponsors, advertisers, etc.

- Treat someone in need to 'queen for a day' or 'king for a day' type of treatment

- Create a 'make over a hero' program where customers and/or the public can nominate someone in the community who deserves special honor (create a bigger program/bigger prize packages by partnering with other businesses)

- 'Adopt' a family (or an individual) for a year (or another specified time period) for a specific product, service, shopping spree, gift cards, etc.

- Honor one employee from a different local charitable organization each month with a prize package, set of gift products, service coupons, etc.

One note of caution: A few years ago I attended an open house at a small business that had added support for a popular charity to their event in order to create an additional enticement for attendance and participation. At the end of the event, when the time came to write the check to the charity, it seemed apparent while watching the owner 'do the math' (i.e., deducting costs from proceeds, to determine what amount would go to the charity) that they did not genuinely intend to benefit the charity. I saw firsthand the damage that shorting the charity did to personal and professional relationships. As someone who had helped to facilitate the evening and donated a significant amount of my own time and money, I felt betrayed as well.

I share that only to say this: If you do not genuinely desire to support a charitable cause, don't add one to your event. You can benefit your business while also benefitting a charity, but this is another important reason why it may be desirable for you to approach this area with the goal of developing a long-term, on-going relationship with a specific charity or with a cause you truly want to benefit.

However you decide to do the math after an event, remember that the more you whittle down the portion designated for charity, the more it will appear that the event was not as much for the charity as it was for you. Hold yourself accountable by setting a minimum donation amount and by telling your clients, employees and marketing partners how much money was raised for the charity following your event or promotion.

In the weeks leading up to your event or promotion, send a series of press releases to local newspapers, magazines, radio stations, local and national offices of the charity you will be benefitting, city hall, and other media highlighting your chosen charity and the work that it does, the local community members it benefits and how your business hopes to help the charity.

- 6 weeks before event / promotion, send a general press release with "more details to follow"
- 3-4 weeks before the event / promotion, send a second press release with more details and a compelling reason for people to support the charity and your event
- 1 week before the event / promotion, send a full press release
- After the event / promotion, send a press release including one or two of the best photos and summary results

Planning Events

Plan at least three months ahead in order to anticipate and adequately construct events and promotions. That means that if today is your January planning session, you are finalizing any last details for February promotions and events, you are beginning to execute preparation work for March and you are laying out a general plan for April. Planning at least three months ahead will help ensure that you won't miss opportunities and will give you the time you need to garner employee enthusiasm and buy-in, identify potential marketing and event partners and delegate responsibilities, and it will provide you with the time you need to effectively market your event.

Working backward from your event date, add tasks and deadlines to your marketing calendar where it makes the most sense to marry these new tasks into your basic communications schedule and to lay out event preparation responsibilities.

Planning ahead three months at a time will help you keep your timeline and tasks manageable and practical in light of regular work, other responsibilities, staffing, etc. Defining tasks which need to be done ahead of time also makes it easier to enlist help, delegate tasks and share responsibilities with others. Having a written timeline, including assigned responsibilities, will give you the ability to stay on target, to quickly make up missed tasks, and to hold staff accountable.

Depending on the complexity and scope of a given event, you may need more time or less to execute an event from preparation through to post-event activities, but you can still use the general suggestions below to help set up your schedule:

7 Questions to Answer Before Setting a Date

1. What is the goal of your event? Most, if not all of the activities featured at your event should support your main goal in one way or another.

The event itself is not the goal—unless your (only) goal is to assemble people in one place. Setting specific goals will help you as you sift through all of the possible variables; who to invite, what will happen at the event, and who will be responsible for what.

You may actually have more than one goal for an event; if so, prioritize them in their order of importance so as to help as you make other decisions and plan the event itself. If you try to accomplish too many different things with one event, you may end up with an event that feels as fragmented as your competing goals. If you find yourself in this scenario, consider the need to hold more than one event or limiting your goals to the one or two which are most important. The activities you hold at the event should be largely dependent upon your main goal.

Some of the goals you may wish to incorporate:

- gain new customers
- launch new products or services
- sell through retail products
- pre-sell services, big ticket items, or bundled/packaged items
- increase customer engagement
- benefit a charity or an individual/family in the community

2. Who do you want to attend?

    a. Who in general will be invited? Think beyond answering "everyone," because 'who' should be invited to your event and the people on whom you expend the most effort and energy to attract should be specifically related to your goal.

    b. Who or what types of people will be specifically targeted with invitations?

3. What will happen at the event? What activities, demonstrations, consultations or education will you include to help you reach your goal that are customer-centric and persuasive enough to (a) entice people to attend and (b) to do what you want them to do?

Just as with all of your marketing, what will entice individuals to attend and to bring people with them, and what will persuade them to take the actions you want them to take at your event depends on what is in it for the client (not what is in it for you). The activities held during the event must entice, entertain and benefit the client, and the way that you craft messaging for invitations must be centered around the benefits, possible prizes, samples, demonstrations, education, social connections, etc. that would most interest the client.

4. When will the event be held?
   a. Date/s
   b. Beginning and End Times

You might instinctively try to schedule your event at a date and time that works best for your business, for you or your staff, or you might limit yourself to times when your business would normally be closed. But again, when deciding on the best date and time for your event, the goal and especially the client — those people you most want to attend — should be your primary consideration.

5. Where will the event be held? You may actually need to answer this question before #4 above as your location may dictate both your date and beginning and end times. Alternately, if the date of the event is more important than the location, the date you choose may limit or dictate possible event locations. In other words, you'll need to determine whether the place you want to hold your event is more important than the date you want to hold it, or vice versa.
   a. How many people do you expect to attend?
   b. How much space will you need to hold the activities you have planned?
   c. What will be the basic event timeline; how will guests flow through your space?

Noting (again) that your primary considerations must be your goal and desired attendees, here are some other things to take into account when choosing a location:
   - proximity to and convenience for your target audience / invitees
   - attractiveness and appeal of location to your invitees
   - ability to stage and accommodate all the activities you want to include
   - presentations or demonstrations you want to conduct
   - other businesses willing to co-sponsor event and their facility needs
   - total numbers of people invited, anticipated to attend, initial RSVPs, etc.
   - media, dignitaries or celebrities you want to invite
   - public address (P.A.) system, music or other sound system needs
   - tool and equipment needs
   - food and drink regulations
   - safety regulations
   - parking needs

6. Assign responsibilities: Who will do what? Adequately staffing and planning for set up, take down and clean up afterward is another key component of event planing. Too few people to help will mean exhaustion for you and your team and a poor impression for guests who may consequently be subject to an event flawed by long waits, hurried or inept demonstrations, uptight staff, or inadequate instructions about what to do after they arrive, after a presentation, etc.

Over-staffing could also result in a negative impression; if guests perceive you expected a larger turnout, they may feel that your event was not 'the place to be' after all, so plan for either eventuality. If too few people RSVP or attend, have a holding area for extra staff, have alternate responsibilities for them or simply send some home. If more people come than anticipated, (first, jump for joy! and then) be sure that you either have additional staff on call who can arrive quickly or that you have a plan to change the flow of the event, the number or duration of demonstrations, the ability to quickly set up more stations or additional chairs, etc. Since few events ever run completely as planned, plan for some of the most likely contingencies as a regular part of your process.

7.   What will happen after the event? In the post-event euphoria and exhaustion, it can be easy for activities like clean up, debriefing staff and co-sponsors and following up with contacts to slip through the cracks—the latter two of which are crucial activities if your goal is to build for the future. Approach it this way: Until post-event activities are completed, an event is not over.

Unless you are looking forward to doing it all yourself, plan for time and the personnel needed to take down chairs, tables, staging, equipment, etc. and for clean up, the return the facility to regular operational setup, the return any rented or catering equipment and for the return of unsold retail products, tools or equipment to regular locations or storage. If your event will be held at your business, be sure that you have a plan to return your facility to a business-ready state.

Meet with your staff (and/or your event partners) 2-3 days following an event in order to debrief and to ensure that follow-up activities are on track. Talk about what went right and what went wrong, but if any one aspect of the event went particularly poorly, don't allow any one individual to become the brunt of public criticism.

No event will ever go perfectly and people do make mistakes; regardless of any mistakes made, you want to be sure that your staff know their input and assistance was appreciated. Make it your goal as a team to honestly address problems with the goal of learning from them for future events—without throwing anyone under the bus. No one is going to want to help with the next event if they felt terrible after the last one, or watched a team member get torn apart. If something does go seriously wrong, or someone on your team behaves in a way that is truly out of line, address it privately rather than humiliating them publicly.

As soon as possible (or as soon as promised) after an event, add contacts collected to your database. Send out a "Thank You" e-mail or direct mail communication to all attendees. Send a confirmation to anyone who booked an appointment at the event, who purchased a pre-paid series or package, who ordered products from you for future delivery or who had questions or indicated interest in your products or services.

Plan a series of follow-up offers and scheduled communications to be sent during the 6 weeks following the event. First, because your best chance to cash in on the impression made by your staff and your business is when an experience is fresh and foremost in the minds of attendees, and second, to establish long-term prospect and client-awareness of your business through interactions. If your event included the opportunity to purchase a pre-sold series or package, extend the offer or another version of that offer to attendees for a limited time, and do the same for any product or service offerings made at the event.

Get feedback from attendees for future events and gauge potential interest in services and products through surveys taken either at the event itself or in follow-up communications. Ask for contact information so that you can match up an individual's interests or concerns to future promotional offers or provide other follow-up.

A sample post-event survey might ask for some of the following information:

Demographics and identifiers:

- attendee name
- e-mail address
- gender
- birthday date and month—this gives you an opportunity to send a 'happy birthday' greeting or offer on or at the beginning of the same month as their birthday
- age range (such as, 10-18, 19-24, 25-34, 35-44, etc.) to help you look for trends in different age groups and give you the ability to target specific offers to clients
- zip code (determine whether attendees are clustered geographically so you can target those neighborhoods in the future with direct mail, flyers, door hangers, etc.)

Event information

- how did you hear about the event?
- did you come by yourself or with a friend, if with a friend, who?
- what was your favorite part of the event?
- how would you rate the facility? (you can ask about specific areas as well, like cleanliness, décor, furnishings, rest rooms, food, music, seating, lighting, check-in, check-out, etc.)
- which products (or services) most excited or intrigued you? why?

Your Marketing Calendar

If you are just starting out in marketing (and especially if you will be, at least initially, the only one performing these tasks) it's unrealistic to try to create a website, set up a Facebook page, start an e-mail newsletter and launch a direct mail campaign all in the same month. Create a list of what you have and what you need to add to your communications tool box. Prioritize the list and focus only on the most important one or two items at a time, then move on to the next.

And along the same train of thought, don't create a schedule for yourself that would exhaust a marketing team of 10 people; it's unrealistic to commit to updating your website weekly and your Facebook page multiple times each day while you are simultaneously sending out reminders to all your clients, writing an e-mail newsletter, planning a customer event and—oh yes—also working within your business. Creating an impossible 'to do' list will leave you feeling exhausted and defeated; it's like starting an exercise routine after years of inactivity by running a 26 mile marathon; it just ain't gonna happen!

Be patient. Cut yourself enough slack so that a missed goal doesn't end in complete system failure, but simply a renewal of your next goal. Solicit help. If you already put in 8-10 hour days on top of your personal, family and social life, you can't add hours of additional communications work to your own plate each week.

Delegation and out-sourcing is the name of the game if you want to develop a highly effective, robust communications program. Since employee buy-in is critical to the success of your marketing program overall, as well as that of individual campaigns, employee participation and ownership of specific communications responsibilities would seem both to be a logical expectation as well as an effective means of creating more buy-in. When staff assist in the promotion of an event or a marketing campaign, they will naturally have a bigger emotional stake in the results. It also gives you the ability to tie performance expectations and salary reviews to measurable goals that directly impact the profitability of your business.

Some employees may choose to take on responsibilities in areas they enjoy and in which they are proficient; others may need encouragement or incentives to step out of their comfort zone and learn something new. Or you may have individuals within your client base who work in a related field, work from home or are students who would love either to pick up some part time work or would trade for services with you. Here's my suggestion for a manageable schedule with some basics to build on:

1st Week of the month (basic)

- Send an e-mail newsletter featuring the current month's promotions, new products, contests, events, results and highlights from any events occurring the prior month.
- Ensure that merchandising and signage is in place for the month's new promotions, contests and events.

1st Week of the month (supplemental)

- Change your window and/or store front displays.
- Write a weekly Blog post and/or daily Facebook posts on promotions, products, contests, events, etc.
- Seek out and firm up plans with marketing and events partners for upcoming promotions.
- Seek out one new business to partner with for marketing or events.

2nd Week of the month (basic)

- Begin marketing for the next specific major event or seasonal promotion/s.

2nd Week of the month (supplemental)

- Write weekly Blog post, daily Facebook posts.
- Write a press release for your next event and/or a follow up release for recently held events, contests, charitable endeavors, etc.
- Order branded promotional collateral, products or tchotchkes you need for your next event or seasonal promotion.

3rd Week of the month (basic)

- Send a 'last chance' e-mail or postcard noting any soon-to-expire promotions and previewing the next month's promotions, contests and events.

3rd Week of the month (supplemental)

- Check remaining stock of business cards, appointment cards, referral rewards and gift certificates, order any supplies that need to be restocked.
- Write a weekly Blog post and/or daily Facebook posts featuring favorite local date, group or special occasion destinations, local tourist or recreation attractions, favorite bars or restaurants, must-shop boutiques, etc. And hopefully some of these are your marketing partners!)

4th Week of the month (basic)

- Plan and finalize your marketing tasks, looking ahead 3 months at a time. Review information and/or meet with distributors and vendors in support of the launch of any new products. Identity businesses that would make desirable marketing partners for events and promotions.
- Take down expired signage and break down expired promotions.
- Ensure that contact lists have been updated with any new contacts from forms, events or contest entries

End of month

- Finalize contests and/or draw winners and award prizes.
- Write blog and/or Facebook posts summarizing the month's activities and highlights.

Holiday promotions, events, and displays/decorating:

- Early-to-Mid January: Valentine's Day promotions should be in full swing for the February 14th holiday.

- Mid-February: While love is in the air, highlight bridal/wedding services or products you provide and begin to book appointments for the upcoming wedding season. Better yet, work with other businesses to hold a bridal fair or create a bridal services directory.

- By the end of March: Mother's Day promotions should be underway.

- Mid-April: Prom and Graduation products/services and promotions need to be in place.

- By the 3rd week of May (just after Mother's day), Father's Day promotions need to be rolling.

- By mid-May: Wedding and Bridal services, packages and promotions should be highlighted from now through July.

- Early July: It might seem like school just got out, but it's time to launch back-to-school promotions.

- End of September: Begin working out how you plan to capture a share of consumer gift expenditures during the upcoming holiday season.

- October-December: Focus on holiday sales, contests, drawings, activities and events.

- End of December: January and New Year promotions.

365 Days of Marketing isn't intended to send the message that every day has to have a new activity. Some businesses may have the ability to run several small promotions, events, and contests during a year while some may choose to run only a few, but will spend more time and develop more robust programs around these few campaigns.

The number of possible promotions, events and themes that you and your staff can use to attract and engage customers and increase sales is virtually limitless. 365 Days of Marketing will feed the creative side of entrepreneurs and inspire new activities, cooperative marketing partnerships and breathe new life into traditional marketing plans. You'll notice recurring phrases meant to help you realize the importance of developing consistency in your communications channels and further develop branding and overall marketing programs.

The holidays and observances cited in 365 Days of Marketing have been gleaned from a variety of sources. Some are official holidays and observances and some are not. Where it seemed most important to do so, a holiday or observance is laid out on the actual official day that it occurs; where this is less important, an observance may be listed on another day in order to give it its due. Check a calendar to confirm the exact date of an occurrence in the current year (or check online). None of the organizations or causes mentioned in 365 Days of Marketing have endorsed this book or paid in any way for inclusion.

january
365 Days of Marketing

January Month-Long Observances

Be On Purpose Month, New Year Resolutions Month

Partner with executive coaches, counselors and personal organizers to hold a seminar to discuss the benefits of making New Year Resolutions and how to live with purpose in the coming year. Create a list of recommended reading. Add personal organizing tools, books about living with purpose or taking charge of one's life, inspirational or devotional books, t-shirts, calendars, mugs, etc. to your retail or to give away as a gift-with-purchase or contest prize.

Write your own "Top 10 New Year Resolutions," David Letterman style. Hold a contest for customers to submit their own Top 10 lists. Load the prize basket with items to help with New Year Resolutions (like consultations with weight loss, fitness or nutrition experts or counselors, gym gift cards, exercise equipment, etc.) Post winning entries on Facebook, your website, blog, e-mail newsletter and at the point of purchase. Use entry forms to help collect contacts for your e-mail and/or direct mail contact databases, and extend a special New Year offer to all entrants.

To take things a little more seriously, create a support group for customers to share their New Year Resolutions. Help to track progress and encourage accountability for members. Create rewards for those who meet their Resolutions. Constructed appropriately and kept separate from job expectations, this could also be a great team-building and personal development support for employees.

Blood Donor Month

Contact a local mobile blood bank and promote a blood drive among customers and employees, or hold a blood drive with a mobile blood bank at your business. Design inexpensive bag stuffers to promote the drive during the weeks leading up to it; tell customers how donated blood benefits others, how easy it is to donate blood, etc. Reward people who participate or bring you confirmation of a recent donation with a free add-on, gift card, branded tchotchke or some other reward.

Extend a special offer to the employees of your local blood bank, hospitals, nursing homes, etc. Create a special offer and design postcards which can be given out by the blood bank as a thank-you gift to all of their donors this month, or on an on-going basis.

Cervical Cancer Screening Month, Birth Defects Awareness Month

Charitable causes related to specific diseases or health issues can be especially meaningful because they touch so many lives. Raise awareness and provide support for causes which have impacted you personally; you will be most persuasive and satisfied by your participation when you work to benefit causes about which you are genuinely passionate. Provide support to a cause or charity through monetary donations, volunteering, raising funds or conducting other campaigns.

Designate that proceeds of a specific product or service or a portion of January sales will be donated to a cancer or birth defects-related charity. Tell customers how their participation makes a difference. Talk about community members who have been impacted by these conditions. Report results or post a chart to measure progress against your goal. Design signage for the point of purchase or a donation receptacle. Create bag stuffers featuring information about the charity or cause, where they can donate or volunteer, etc. Use your e-mail newsletter, blog and Facebook posts to raise awareness, encourage and incentivize participation and report results. Submit a press release prior to and following your campaign.

Support your charity on an on-going basis through the sale of specific promotional retail items (mugs, t-shirts, hats, tote bags, travel mugs, wristbands and other branded wares). Extend special offers to the charity's beneficiaries and to the employees and volunteers of the charity itself. Donate services or products from your business directly to local patients and/or family members affected by the causes you support. 'Adopt' a locally impacted family for a year; support them with products or services from your business, hold charity fundraisers or solicit donations from customers—what a sense of community you will convey to this family!

Family Fitness Month, Lose Weight-Feel Great Month

Partner with businesses such as local gyms, fitness and exercise centers, dance studios, martial arts studios and recreational facilities for cross or cooperative marketing. Partner with local fitness and exercise instructors, nutritional experts and/or medical professionals to hold a free workshop for customers and employees about the benefits of exercise, maintaining a healthy weight and eating right.

Partner with a local dinner preparation business, nutrition expert or organic food expert to hold a workshop on preparing healthy meals in general, for those with special needs, for those trying to lose weight, etc. Post healthy eating and weight loss tips on your Facebook page, blog and e-mail newsletter.

Extend a special offer to local fitness and dietary experts, to all employees of local fitness centers, to the employees of dinner preparation or health food stores, etc.

To seriously support customer (or employee) New Year Resolutions over the course of the coming year, create a system to record not only final goals but one that is broken down to pinpoint incremental milestones by setting short-term, achievable-sounding goals. For instance, the idea of losing a total of 50 pounds may sound impossible to someone, but losing a pound a week over the course of the year might sound more achievable.

Other items to consider putting on a New Year Resolution timeline are city or charity marathons, reunions, fitness competitions, performances or recitals, vacations and other points in time before which clients want to achieve their goals.

Set up a way for clients to track progress against goals online or at your business. Celebrate small wins as well as big ones at a monthly happy hour mixer. Encourage participants to bring friends to these events and invite them to register and track their goals as well (in other words, let new people start their 'New Year' resolutions any time during the year). Invite the employees and/or customers of businesses that partner with you for marketing or events to attend as well; make sampling, consultations, product demonstrations and bounce-back offers part of your happy hour events.

Create a dedicated web page, blog or Facebook page for this group:

- for participants to interact with and encourage one another
- to post encouraging quotes, relevant statistics and tips
- to share links to related articles about health, fitness, nutrition, etc.
- to post recognition as participants reach short and long-term goals
- to post 'after' pictures and results of those that achieve goals or pass milestones; invite a photographer to partner with you and help track intermediate progress
- to make readers aware of the benefits of products and services you offer that can help them reach their goals

Financial Wellness Month, Wealth Mentality Month

Partner with a local financial planner or investment professional to hold an educational event for customers. Hold a workshop, inviting both customers and prospects that fit within your target markets or 'ideal client' types, such as college students, seniors, individuals nearing retirement, young adults, new parents, etc. Create a relevant offer to cross market to the clients and/or employees of your event partners. Extend offers or send marketing collateral to the employees of local banks, tax preparation, accounting, investment and financial planning businesses.

Purchase items to add to impulse buy or regular retail such as notebooks, recommended reading, planners for financial planning or investment, piggy banks, etc. Or purchase related branded items for workshop give away, contest prizes, client gifts or to give away as a gift-with-purchase.

Create a 'financial wellness' package for your best customers with a discounted offer on a series of repeated services, bundled products or as a reward for referrals.

Oatmeal Month, Hot Tea Month, Soup Month

Food and beverage observances occur throughout the year, providing great opportunities for you to have fun, enjoy refreshments, conduct food drives for local food banks or shelters, hold contests and pay homage to the yummy, comforting, reminiscent edibles you and your customers love.

Take advantage of food and beverage observances to partner with local restaurants, bars, coffee shops, delis, bakeries, wine shops and grocery stores for cross or cooperative marketing. Extend special offers to their customers and employees.

Give away foods or drinks as samples, client gifts or to incentivize sales (or event attendance) as a gift-with-purchase. Ask marketing partners to provide you with free or reduced-cost foods or beverages to sample or gift-with-purchase to customers in exchange for a cross-marketing opportunity.

Hold contests to solicit favorite recipes, most creative uses of foods or ingredients, etc. Award prizes that include bounce-back offers and gift cards to ensure repeat visits to your business. Share recipes in your e-mail newsletter, in blog and Facebook posts, or even create your own (printed) recipe book to give away, gift-with-purchase or sell to celebrate edible bliss!

Contact a local food bank or shelter to ascertain their specific needs and hold a food drive or fundraiser event or campaign. Generate press releases prior to and following the event to report results and bring additional attention to the needs of those less fortunate in your community.

Get Organized Month, Clean Up Your Computer Month

Partner with personal organizers, stationers and office supply retailers to hold a workshop on personal or office organization or to hold an organizing-focused 'fashion show' featuring organizing accessories. Write a "Top 10 Ways to Cut Clutter" list that includes organizing or computer maintenance tips and tricks as well as product recommendations; sell related retail items. Compile a list of recommended reading and post links to books or resources on your Facebook page, blog and e-mail newsletter.

Add books on personal or office organization or computer maintenance to retail or purchase branded organizers, planners, calendars, and related supplies to add to retail, or to give away as contest prizes or a gift-with-purchase.

Hold a cubicle contest! Set up an office space and challenge customers to organize the layout efficiently in a limited time period (like 3 minutes). Or give contestants 60 seconds to view the space, then see how many items they can remember. Include gift cards in contest prizes to ensure repeat visits to your business. Partner with local businesses for a cooperative marketing offer or to create bigger prize packages. Afterward, extend an offer to all entrants.

Hobby Month, Book Blitz Month, Creativity Month

Partner with local book stores, stationers, hobby or craft shops or experts to hold craft or hobby workshops for clients. Create cooperative marketing offers for their clients and yours. Retail related supplies. Extend a special offer to the employees of local book, hobby or craft stores. Extend a special offer to local artists.

Feature the work of local crafters, hobbyists, or artists in your lobby or another public area. Host craft or hobby club meetings or work with marketing partners to host a craft, hobby or art sale or exhibit event.

Hold a most creative hobby contest for customers. Allow people to enter and submit a photograph in-store or online via e-mail, your website or Facebook page. Set up a real or online bulletin board for pictures of customer's hobbies or crafts. Add contacts from contests or photograph submissions to your database and extend a special offer to all each. Write press releases featuring contest winners or highlighting local hobby or craft artists. Post links to tell people how they can get involved in hobby clubs or attend workshops on your Facebook page, blog and e-mail newsletter.

Hold a 'Book Blitz' reading contest for elementary school-aged kids featuring prizes that might include things like a book store gift card, savings bond or gift card redeemable at your business.

Solicit customer suggestions on Facebook or in-store and create a 'Book Blitz' recommended reading list for customers (or their children). Add popular adult or children's books to retail. Purchase award-winning children's books to give away as a gift-with-purchase in January or to use as contest prizes.

Establish and host a book club or invite a local club to hold meetings at your business on a regular basis. Provide refreshments. Extend a special offer or an on-going special 'club member' rate to book club members. Purchase one book for a club member chosen by random drawing each month or help subsidize book purchases for the whole group on an on-going basis. Establish and host a business book club, inviting the leaders of other local businesses, fellow members of your Chamber of Commerce, Rotary or other civic service organizations, industry peers or other professional acquaintances to join.

Hold a 'Book Blitz' fundraiser, book donation event or month-long fundraising campaign for a local city, public or private school library, or the library of a community youth services organization. Extend special offers or rewards to customers who participate. Create marketing offers for library patrons and employees. Generate press releases prior to and following the campaign or event to report results and bring additional attention to the organization you are supporting.

Poverty in America Month

Make your business a designated point of donation for a local food bank, mission, or another poverty-relieving charity on a year-round basis. Publicize your efforts and draw attention to the charity through regular press releases to share needs and report results. Post statistics about poverty levels and related needs in your community on your Facebook page, blog and e-mail newsletter.

Contact a local shelter or social services agency about the possibility of 'adopting' a local family in your community. Support this family with free services or products, through fundraising or by partnering with other businesses for more free services or products or even to conduct a community-wide fundraising campaign. Keep the family's identity confidential to preserve dignity. Create a special offer or extend a reward to those who donate that is redeemable in a subsequent visit to your business. Raise awareness among clients regarding the needs of your 'adopted' family with signage at the point of purchase or designated donation area and posts on your Facebook page, blog, e-mail newsletter and/or bag stuffers.

Donate gift cards to local service organizations for distribution to needy families. Extend a special offer to their employees and volunteers. Contact local shelters regarding their specific needs or conduct a campaign to collect blankets, coats, boots, mittens and other cold weather gear. Hold an event where the cover charge waived when attendees donate money or a specified new item. Give branded tchotchkes, gift cards or extend special offers to those who donate. Don't forget the press release!

Self-Defense Month

Partner with a local self-defense expert or martial arts instructor for cooperative or cross marketing. Extend a special offer to their employees and/or customers.

Hold a self-defense workshop led by local self-defense experts, police officers, martial arts instructors or other appropriate professionals. Sell self-defense related retail products or post links to local or online resources, tips, recommended reading, etc.

Host meetings, provide refreshments or make some other donation to local victim's rights or victim support groups. Invite members to attend a self-defense workshop or hold a workshop for others who might be interested such as female college students, people who work or live in high-crime areas, etc.

Mentoring Month

Mentoring occurs in many different tutoring, religious, civic and other organizations within your community; a quick call to your local high school or public library can put you in touch with some of them, or you can canvas employees or customers for suggestions.

'Adopt' one of these organizations for the coming year. Hold volunteer, fund or supplies-raising campaigns, give rewards to participants and extend a reward or special offers to the patrons, employees, and/or customers who donate. Volunteer at a local mentoring organization. Create scholarships for local students. Publicize efforts before, during and after with press releases.

Connect customers with local resources by posting links on Facebook, your blog and e-mail newsletter. Create a community resources page on your website.

Create a special offer for teachers, tutors and youth leaders in your community. Send school or district offices postcards, business cards, menus, catalogs or flyers with a special offer for their employees for placement in break rooms, lunch rooms, lounges, etc.

January Week 1

January Week 1 – Some Day We'll Laugh about This Week

Partner with a local life coach or counselor to hold a workshop about dealing with stress, grief, difficult situations or difficult people. Provide customers with a list of recommended reading for self-help or post links to recommended reading and local resources on your Facebook page, blog and e-mail newsletter. Create a gift basket that includes self-help resources or books, wares with inspirational quotes, etc. for retail sale or to give away as contest prizes or a gift-with-purchase.

Hold a contest for clients, accepting entries online or at your business for the best funny story or joke. Reward the winner with tickets to a local comedy club or a prize basket featuring a funny book, stand up comedy video and/or a gift card redeemable at your business.

Design your own line of branded wares or add t-shirts, mugs, calendars, or other items with quotes or sayings that remind us to laugh at some of the more ridiculous aspects of life (including ourselves) to your retail or give them away as contest prizes or a gift-with-purchase.

January Week 1 – Home Office Safety and Security Week

Partner with local law enforcement, private security firms, alarm installation companies, technology experts and other home or office safety professionals for cross or cooperative marketing or to hold a home or office safety workshop. Post recommended reading, lists of recommended home or office safety products or services or links to local resources on Facebook, your blog and e-mail newsletter.

Invite the employees of businesses located near yours or those of your marketing partners to attend your safety or self-defense workshops, or work together to conduct safety training for all of your employees. Ensure that all of your employee stations are equipped with safety and emergency kits. Ensure that signage for customer or employee emergency instructions or evacuation routes are up to date and clearly identified. Tell customers and employees about improvements your make to safety or security within your business.

Add items like emergency and first aid kits, alarms systems, personal safety alarms, dog training, fire extinguishers, smoke and carbon monoxide alarms or battery replacements, etc. to your retail or to give away as contest prizes or a gift-with-purchase.

Partner with a computer safety expert to hold a seminar on computer security and online safety. Post computer safety tips on your Facebook page, blog, bag stuffers and e-mail newsletter. Partner with a mobile computer file backup business to hold a computer safety demonstration and education event. Create cooperative marketing offers to extend to the employees and customers of computer sales and service businesses.

First, the good news: The advent of a New Year presents many opportunities to reach out to help customers identify and reach goals, renew themselves and celebrate by bringing the New Year in together. And now, the bad news: Everyone else is trying to cash in on the same theme. To cut through the clutter, your New Year offers have to provide something of real value and benefit to the customer. What you bring to the table must be truly unique and engaging—not just another ad in a sea of sameness.

Stereotypically a day for football (for him) and shopping (for her), create an opportunity for one or the other, or if you are really ingenious, something to accommodate both. A big screen TV football party with a fashion show at halftime? Why not!

Even if your business will be closed on New Year's Day, you can still create special offers to help your customers start the New Year off with something to make the coming year better. Focus offers and messages on how products or services benefit or improve the lives of your customers. Communicate projected benefits in terms of real dollars and cents, pounds, dress sizes, health, well-being, luxury, pleasure, etc.

The New Year is also the perfect time to launch a customer rewards program or to sell pre-paid, extra-value bundled packages or products or series of services.

On New Year's Day, many Americans watch football, socialize and eat. If you own a catering business, restaurant, wine shop, bar or another food-related business, hold a New Year's social event or book your services out for home or office parties. If you can't cater to the sports crowd, host an anti-football gathering for 'football widows' featuring activities that would be more interesting to them.

Bring the New Year in with those closest to you and host a New Year open house for employees and their families, or for your most valuable, loyal or engaged customers.

Not in the hospitality industry? The New Year is the perfect time to seek out a marketing and events partner in the food industry for customer or employee events, to provide samples for your customers and for cross marketing throughout the coming year.

New Year, New You

If your business provides personal health, well-being, cosmetic or related services, create a New Year= New You promotion for the new year. Or partner with a salon, spa, cosmetic medical or dental practice, counselor or life coach, nutritionist, fitness centers, and dance, exercise or martial arts studios for cross or cooperative marketing, in order to extend special offers to their employees, to hold joint seminars or workshops, to sell related retail products, books, videos, etc.

Create suggested shopping lists and step-by-step instructional sheets that tell customers how they can utilize your products or services to recreate themselves in the New Year.

Resolution Helper

Help clients meet their New Year Resolutions by providing a network for support and accountability. Challenge customers to make their Resolutions public and participate in a 12-month support group on a special Facebook page or dedicated blog site. Track goals and results and celebrate incremental achievements. Create a business owner's resolution support group for yourself, peers, mentors, the owners of businesses located near yours and/or those of your marketing partners to help one another meet personal and professional goals in the coming year.

Invite employees to participate in New Year Resolution goal setting and tracking. Be brave enough to make your own goals public. We all improve our chances for success when we share our goals with others, track progress and hold ourselves and one another accountable. Ask your marketing partners to extend free or reduced-price options to your employees (and extend similar offers to theirs).

Imagine what would happen in the years to come if your business were able and publicly known to have helped 5, 10, 20 or even more people to meet Resolutions or goals set relative to weight loss, health, fitness, education, professional or personal development, etc. How much could you expand the role of your business in the lives of your clients? How would you change customer perception concerning the role your business plays in their lives? How would it impact your sales, or even impact the composition of your retail and service offerings? How would it impact your ability to attract new customers?

January 2 – Remember You Die Day

Not as morbid as it sounds! To remember that you are mortal is to realize that time is limited and that there is no time like the present. There are many areas you can focus on when it comes to living to the fullest and 'being present' in each and every aspect of our daily lives—with family, friends, co-workers or customers.

In partnership with a counselor, professional life coach or another qualified expert, hold a workshop for clients to discuss goals and obstacles, procrastination and overcoming things that might otherwise stop us from meeting our goals.

Include bag stuffers for customers with motivational quotes. Retail mugs, t-shirts, calendars, nail files or other promotional items with motivational quotes, from serious to light-hearted. Post motivational "seize the day" type of quotes on your blog, Facebook page and e-mail newsletters.

Share and/or solicit stories from customers and employees about moments when you took a chance that paid off or learned an important lesson from what seemed to be a failure. Sharing dreams, emotions, vulnerabilities and frailties with others helps us connect more deeply with them on an emotional level. It can encourage us when we take time to remember how far we have come or when we renew our commitment to goals or dreams that may have been set by the wayside.

Partner with a financial planner or investment professional to hold a workshop on investing, financial planning, retirement planning, estate planning, etc. Partner with a local law firm to hold a clinic on will preparation. Invite the owners and employees of your marketing partners or the businesses located near yours to attend.

Make sure your business is protected with the appropriate legal paperwork. Update or write your own will and succession plan. You may be able to barter with a local lawyer for your own document preparation or receive a discount on services for your customers or employees. Request group rates for your customers and employees or hold a group will-writing event in cooperation with a local law firm. Extend cross or cooperative marketing offers which include legal will preparation or professional review or personal wills.

January 3 – Chocolate-Covered Cherry Day

The chocolate-covered cherry is one of those great combinations of decadent, intense tastes and textures. Held on the heels of the holidays, Chocolate Covered Cherry Day might be just the thing to extend the feeling of indulgence that seems to pervade the holidays.

Partner with a local chocolatier or candy shop to provide samples or packaged treats for clients to enjoy during appointments, to give away as a client gift or gift-with-purchase or for retail sale. Send your most valuable clients a chocolate-covered cherry gift box to thank them for their continued patronage.

Hold a contest in-store and/or online (using your Facebook page, blog, e-mail newsletter and website) on chocolate-covered cherry trivia or by soliciting the most creative chocolate-covered cherry-related recipes. Hold a drawing (or hold drawings all week or all month) for a chocolate-covered cherry reward and/or a gift card to be redeemed during a visit to your business.

January 4 – World Braille Day

Sight—the literal ability to see—is some times taken for granted until lost or damaged. On World Braille Day, extend special offers to sight-impaired customers, raise awareness about eye health and connect people with local resources and vision professionals.

Partner with a qualified instructor to hold a seminar for businesses (such as local merchants, your marketing partners, members of your Chamber of Commerce, etc.) to demonstrate how people learn Braille, talk about the challenges faced in gaining employment or accessing public places by sight-impaired individuals, and make recommendations or brainstorm about how businesses can better accommodate sight-impaired customers or employees.

Partner with a local optometrist for cooperative or cross marketing. Partner with an optometrist to conduct free screenings for employees and/or customers or hold a seminar to discuss ways to promote and protect eyesight. Post information about eye health, protection and the recommended schedule for professional checkups on your Facebook page, blog and e-mail newsletter. Connect customers with local eye health professionals, resources for glasses or safety glasses, etc.

Create a point of purchase "Did you know...?" style eye health fact sheet to display with information provided by a local vision-care professional, foods or vitamins known to promote eyesight, safety glasses and other related topics.

Hold a happy hour, open house or community fair for the sight-impaired featuring local resources such as specially designed recreation centers and local professionals and programs. Post links to resources on your website and feature them in e-mail newsletter, blog and Facebook posts.

Conduct a campaign to raise funds or supplies in support of local service agencies for the sight-impaired. Provide support for organizations that train service animals or sponsor a service animal for a sight-impaired individual in your community. Partner with a local service animal trainer to hold a public event to raise awareness or funds toward training of service animals. Don't forget the press releases!

January 5 – Trivia Day

Partner with a local restaurant or bar to hold a social event for singles, couples, employees or customers in the form of a trivia contest or Trivial Pursuit-style game or tournament. Make it a themed party by going with a special set of trivia questions (the 80's, music, movies, etc.) and asking attendees to dress in costume. Give participants good reasons to come and visit your business afterward by way of gift cards, product demonstrations, samples, consultations and special offers. Offset event costs with a cover charge; in return, give recipients goodie bags, branded items or gift cards redeemable at your business.

Hold a trivia contest, either at the point of purchase with instant prizes, on the hour for those at your business, at an event held at the end of the day, week or month or even online. Write trivia questions relative to your business or industry; for instance, if you are in the car repair business, quiz customers on their knowledge of home car care and maintenance, the benefits of your multi-point service check, etc. Following the contest, provide contest entrants (and all of your customers) with the answers to these questions on your website, e-mail newsletter, blog and Facebook page. You will be providing them with added-value of expertise as well as giving them specific service and product recommendations.

If your business is dependent upon the technical expertise of your employees, hold a trivia contest for employees as a team building or training exercise. Solicit prizes from your cross and cooperative marketing partners. You provide even more value to your marketing partners when your employees (as well as your customers) patronize the businesses you are working with.

January 6 – Cuddle Up Day

Get closer to your customers, employees and community on Cuddle Up Day. Have hot chocolate and marshmallows, hot cider or other toasty treats on hand to warm people up. Purchase branded hot cups and cardboard sleeves to give away hot beverages at your business or even out on the sidewalk. Create your own design for branded, customized coffee or travel mugs for retail sale. Add branded throws, travel blankets, pillows or slippers to your retail or give them away as gifts (or a gift-with-purchase) to your most loyal or valuable clients.

In partnership with a local wine shop, restaurant or caterer, hold a "Cuddle Up" singles mixer or create date packages for singles or couples featuring a cocktail hour, wine tasting and/or dinner.

Cuddle up to staff! Set aside the negative today (as much as possible). Identify examples of great customer service or co-worker relations, deliver compliments and be a source of encouragement. Make yourself available for safe, informal staff feedback. Start having daily or weekly 'huddles' (informal meetings held to discuss challenges, talk about the 'plays' the team will make and give a short pep talk) to kick off the work day. Set up an employee suggestion box. Survey employees as to satisfaction, goals, ideas for improvements, etc. Create a program to reward employees who go beyond the call of duty, provide extraordinary customer service, submit ideas for improvements or cost-savings which are implemented, etc.

Cuddle up to your customers, especially if you don't normally interact with them on a daily basis. Initiate a customer feedback program, customer satisfaction survey or launch a new channel of communication. Interact 'live' with customers at a webinar or on your blog or Facebook page. Send personal thank-you notes to your most valuable customers.

Cuddle up to your community. Sponsor a city recreation program sports team. Attend games and meets of local high schools and colleges; bring treats for players and fans in branded goodie bags or with your business card. Promote the sale of gift cards designed specifically for coaches or extend a special offer to all coaches in your community. Extend congratulations to local coaches and point out the accomplishments of players and teams on your Facebook page, blog and e-mail newsletter.

Conduct a campaign in support of local arts, education, charities, service organizations (such as Rotary, Kiwanis or Optimists Clubs) or other community groups. Raise awareness, raise funds, solicit volunteers and tell customers about opportunities for participation. Post information about these organizations and the work they do in your community on your Facebook page, blog and e-mail newsletter. Write press releases.

January 7 – I'm Not Going to Take It Anymore Day

What tasks, circumstances or even people have become unpalatable to you? What is holding you back personally or professionally? Identifying things that should change and taking concrete steps to make needed changes can sometimes be easier said than done. We may be quick to advise others to throw off the unendurable, yet we continue to carry around own problems and continue to tolerate abusive people unnecessarily, to the detriment of our lives and our businesses.

I'm Not Going to Take It Anymore Day is not about stomping feet, throwing tantrums, taking our toys and going home; it's about identifying things within and outside of ourselves that we most want to change, and going about changing them in purposeful, meaningful ways. In partnership with a counselor, motivational speaker or life coach, hold a workshop for customers and/or employees about how they can 'not take it anymore' by identifying healthy, productive and constructive ways to throw off what is holding us back, improve assertive communication skills and set boundaries in interpersonal relationships.

Sometimes we all need to vent, or at least get some sympathy. Add clever, sarcastic, fun or motivational mugs, pens, posters, signs, notebooks, memo cubes or other wares that express "I'm not going to take it anymore" emotions, quotes and sentiments to your retail or give them away to employees or workshop participants, as contest prizes or as a gift-with-purchase.

'Don't take It anymore' when it comes to indifference in your local community. Get involved as a member of your Chamber of Commerce, Rotary, Kiwanis or Optimists or other civic groups so that you have a say in the rules and regulations, taxes and other decisions that affect your business and a role in bringing positive change to your community. If you are truly brave, run for office so you can effect even more change. It's not about what you don't do or won't take, it's about what you 'do' do!

January Week 2

January Week 2 – Women's Empowerment Week

"You've come a long way, baby!" This well-known phrase noting advances made by women in equality in the workplace also implies that there is still a ways to go. There are times we all need encouragement, empowerment and the courage to take risks, move forward and make changes. Take time this week to honor and celebrate notable women in your industry, in your business, in your community and in the world at large.

January is Self-Defense Month; pair that with women's empowerment and partner with a martial arts studio, shooting and gun safety instruction/range, security and self-defense experts or other professionals to hold a workshop on women's self-defense. In accordance with state or local regulations, retail personal safety products, recommended reading, etc. Partner with personal safety and self-defense professionals for cross or cooperative marketing.

Partner with a professional counselor, mentor, life or executive coach or another expert to hold a workshop on empowerment for women. Include a catering or wine shop marketing partner and enrich the event with appetizers during a cocktail hour or wine tasting.

Gauge the satisfaction of your female customers and/or find out about their personal interests through surveys and suggestion programs. Work with experts to hold workshops on topics in which your female customers are most interested, like gaining computer skills, developing leadership or professional communication skills, hobby, craft and art classes, activities that can be propelled into careers (cooking, arts, catering, party planning, computer skills, graphic design), etc.

January Week 2 – Elvis Presley Week

Whether your favorite is the young Elvis or old Elvis, celebrate Elvis Presley week with your customers by holding a contest or drawing to win an Elvis album or video. Work with marketing partners to hold an Elvis-appreciation happy hour featuring drawings or contests to win iPod or iTunes cards, albums, etc. Feature sampling, demonstrations and consultations at the event, give away branded tchotchkes and extend a bounce-back offer.

Hold online drawings for followers on Facebook or people that 'retweet' your posts on Twitter; reward winners with Elvis albums, products or gift cards. Post Elvis history and trivia on your Facebook page, blog and e-mail newsletter.

In cooperation with a restaurant, wine shop, bar, caterer or other facility, hold an Elvis Presley music event or a look or sound-alike contest. Photo-document the party with a photographer marketing partner. Hire an Elvis impersonator for entertainment and attendee photos. Provide attendees with goodie bags that include bounce-back offers, products or gift cards. Collect contact information to build your database, and extend a special offer to all attendees after the event.

January 8 – Bubble Bath Day

Are you old enough to remember the ad campaign featuring the slogan, "Calgon, take me away!" showing a woman relaxing in a bubble bath, imagining herself far away from the problems in her life? The ad perfectly conveyed all that a really good bubble bath can be—a luxurious, fragrant, comfortable, private escape. Whether or not you sell bubble bath or bath products, the idea of creating an emotional response within the customer experience is worth considering.

Look at the experience provided by your business from the client viewpoint. How do you welcome customers when they arrive? Is their time at your business anticipated or dreaded? Can they 'not wait to get there' or 'not wait to leave?' Can you treat clients to a moment of luxury, relaxation, aromatherapy, another sensory indulgence or a pampering extra to enhance their experiences, set your business apart, keep them coming back and motivate them to tell friends, family and co-workers about you?

Purchase branded or boutique bubble bath for retail sale or purchase sample sizes for client gifts or a gift-with-purchase. This could be a perfect item to stock for Valentine's Day or add to contest prizes in February.

Partner with a local salon or spa to create bath-themed gift, prize or retail baskets, and for cross or cooperative marketing. Salon and spa professionals are naturals when it comes to creating a moment of indulgence for clients; it's their job! Partner with a stylist, esthetician or another salon or spa professional to hold a workshop, provide makeup or skin care demonstrations, mini manicures, pedicures, etc. for your customers. Partner with a chocolatier for indulgent dark chocolate treats for sampling, gift or sale to clients. Purchase branded chocolates for clients to enjoy during appointments or while shopping, as a customer or employee thank-you gift or to add to retail.

Working with a local hot tub retailer or service provider, create a cooperative marketing offer to help everyone suds up! Design a branded rack card with pre or post-hot tub, pool or beach skin care, protection and repair instructions, recommended products and a special offer for the customers of local hot tub sellers, to be placed in locker rooms of local YMCA, community or hotel/motel pools, to be posted online and included on your Facebook page, blog and e-mail newsletters.

Conduct a campaign in support of a local shelter or community services group and donate bubble bath, shampoo and conditioner, towels, wash cloths and related items to local shelters or families in need. Write and submit press releases to help raise awareness within the community.

January 9 – Play 'God' Day, Recreate the World Day

If you had the power to do anything, what would it be? What kind of a world would you create? Many people interpret the phrase 'Playing God' in a negative way, referring to making decisions that essentially control others in ways they may not choose for themselves. Instead, take the idea in a positive direction; change the world around you in small and large ways and improve things for others.

How can you 'play God' for your customers? What changes can you make to improve the customer experience? How about for your employees? You may not be in a position to grant raises or hire more employees, but there are probably ways you can improve working conditions, employee break or lunch areas or make other changes to employee hours, responsibilities, incentives, thank-yous, recognition or rewards to enhance employee satisfaction.

Any good deity knows you should incentivize and 'reward behavior you want more of.' Now is a great time to launch a customer rewards program based on purchases, frequency of visits, dollars spent, big ticket items purchased, series or package deals, etc. You can even work with your marketing partners to create cooperative rewards programs design to incentivize purchases in multiple businesses. Tailor the rewards themselves so that they bring people back in for redemption.

Change the world around you. Hold an event or fundraiser to benefit local community services for the needy, the elderly, the young, the sick, etc. Set up a team made up of some of your employees (and/or also from among those of your marketing partners) in order to participate in a walk, run, car wash or another fundraising event. Raise awareness for your cause and solicit funds or donations with signage, e-mail and website updates, Facebook or blog posts, or set up displays with branded wristlets or ribbons, shelf talkers and more. Designate that the sales of a specific product or service will be donated in whole or in part to a local charity or needy family. Make positive change in your community!

January 10 – Cut Energy Costs Day

The start of a new year is a good time to pull things apart in order to put them back together more efficiently. And now, at the height of mid-winter, you're probably more than willing to think about ways to reduce energy costs. Not only will it benefit your bottom line, it benefits the planet. What's more, customers now expect that the businesses they frequent are aware of and will contribute to the sustainability and preservation of natural resources.

Many HVAC sales/service professionals can evaluate your equipment and facility to make recommendations of ways to cut energy consumption and reduce costs by improving efficiency, servicing or replacing equipment and implementing procedures that result in reductions in usage (such as completely powering down tools or equipment instead of leaving them on 'standby'). Pass on expert advice to your customers in posts on your Facebook page, blog and e-mail newsletter.

Partner with home appliance, windows, insulation/renovation or HVAC experts to hold workshops on cutting energy costs in the home or workplace. Create shelf talkers, point of sale displays or bag stuffers with tips telling consumers how they can conserve energy and reduce costs. Because newer appliances sometimes have greatly-improved energy efficiency, you should expect some recommendations to include replacing equipment so create cooperative marketing offers for clients who want to make energy-saving equipment upgrades, connect them with local resources, provide them with information about tax breaks related to "green" home renovations, etc.

Put a different spin on the subject by calling it "Reduce your Personal Energy Costs Day." What costs you in terms of personal energy? Poor diet, lack of exercise, stressful situations or difficult people? Partner with nutrition and fitness experts, counselors, motivational speakers or life coaches to hold a personal energy workshop. Create sheets for display or bag stuffers with tips on preserving personal energy. Compile a list of recommended reading and local resources to post on Facebook, your blog and e-mail newsletter. Add some of the best titles to your retail or as a gift-with-purchase.

Educate customers about the products or services you sell that can help cut their personal energy losses or which help to preserve and improve personal energy. Personal energy, properly managed, should be a totally renewable resource, with unlimited potential!

January 11 – Splash a Friend Day

Splashing is fun! Come on, admit it, you'd go out of your way to take on a big puddle with your car, and your kids absolutely love it. Remember splashing in the pool as kids? Remember lifeguards or parents taking all the fun out of it? Splashing is still fun; and when it's done right, it's fun for everyone.

On *Splash a Friend Day*, find a way to splash others with sunshine, kindness, joy, love and optimism. Treat clients to something that will make them smile by doing something fun, silly or unexpected at the cash register. Have you ever noticed that the individuals at the doors at big box warehouse stores often punctuate your visit by drawing a big smiley face on your receipt? How can you hit your customers with a splash of good feelings before they leave your business?

A splash isn't a soaking, it's more of a sampling. Enough to know how cold the water is without freezing (or how hot it is without getting burned). Sample products or services to your customers they have not tried before. Set up a station or point of sale display so that they can touch, smell, taste, hear or otherwise experience a new product or service. Create a mini, tasting or appetizer-sized version of an entrée or beverage to sample to customers as your version of a gift-with-purchase.

Provide samples of products from the businesses of your marketing partners (and provide samples of something of yours for their customers) to stimulate cross-referrals. Accompany samples with time-sensitive bounce-back or add-on offers to motivate immediate action and stimulate future sales.

To "make a splash" is to get the attention of others and leave a lasting, positive impression. Is your business leaving a positive, retention and sales-stimulating lasting impression on customers, or do they forget about you once they leave the building? Are there compelling reasons people should choose your business rather than one of your competitors—and do your customers know what they are? How are you communicating your points of competitive difference to your customers, community peers, vendors and employees?

Are you making a splash with clients that motivates them to refer others to your business? Create a referral rewards program to stimulate more word-of-mouth referrals. Working with your marketing partners, create a cross-business referral program to provide a bigger pool of potential referrals for all businesses.

Many people want to make a splash personally to improve their social or professional success. Partner with a Toastmasters group (www.toastmasters.org) or a public speaking or another consulting professional to hold a workshop for people who want to improve their public speaking or interpersonal skills and the impression that they leave on others in social or professional settings.

Get involved in your local Chamber of Commerce, Rotary, Kiwanis or another civic organization and make a splash that will benefit your business as well as your community.

Make a splash in the local economy by joining (or establishing) a 'Buy Local' cooperative of local businesses, providing education to the local community on the benefits of patronizing local businesses, holding neighborhood shopping events and providing incentives to stimulate sales.

Exchange website links with other local independent businesses or set up your own neighborhood business directory, blog or website. Create your own location-based marketing offers to attract new clients or launch new products or services.

While it's true that in many households women still make a majority of the actual purchases, this doesn't necessarily mean that men are not influential in the decision making process. That some are smart or lucky enough to have someone else to do the actual shopping for them should not be taken as a reason to dismiss them when it comes to marketing.

If your business normally markets to men, you likely already have marketing messages and strategies in place to bring them to your business. If not, then this is a market niche which may represent a new area of opportunity for you. Partner with businesses or clubs that cater to male patrons for cross or cooperative marketing events and offers.

Partner with a fitness expert, martial arts instructor or nutritionist to hold a workshop on men's fitness and health. Partner with a sporting goods store, recreational facility (such as a facility sporting batting cages, driving range, etc.) to host the event. Or simply cross market with one or more of these organizations.

Partner with a barber shop, salon or spa to hold a "shave off" or "best beard contest" at a local sports bar, brewery or wine bar (rather than in what could be an intimidatingly 'female' place like a salon).

To attract more male shoppers to your business and keep them coming back, make it easy for them to find what they want. When shopping, the male consumer often goes directly to the item they want, purchases it and leaves. In contrast, female shoppers may be more inclined to comparison shop, browse or see what else you have to offer during a shopping trip.

Make your business a male-friendly destination by featuring activities and attractions male customers would want to stay for. Be prepared to engage and interest the male shopper once he has entered your business. If he came for a specific product or service, connect him with it as quickly as possible. Use signage and scripting to let him know what else is available to him.

Create checklists that tell male shoppers "what else" they need to enhance product performance or for home care, what the next step is, suggest upgrades and add-ons, etc. Bundle other items with popular men's items to increase sales of peripheral, add-on, upgrade or complementary products. Hold a drawing for a product or gift card in order to collect contact information so that you can entice him to return, create opportunities for follow up, gauge his level of satisfaction, find out what he is interested in and ensure that he receives a bounce-back offer.

Every year, People Magazine features the "Sexiest Man Alive" in their magazine with a countdown of 50 gorgeous male celebrities. Hold your own "Fabulous, Wild Man" contest or take nominations and award a winner in your community. Honor some of the more notable nominees and the winner in a press release and in posts on your Facebook page, blog and e-mail newsletter.

January 13 – Make Your Dreams Come True Day

We all have dreams, or at least we did at one time—it's time for you to start dreaming again! During the last decade, "The Secret," a popular motivational video/book inspired many people to renew their dreams when it comes to becoming their best self and achieving things they might not have believed possible. When I viewed this video, I was going through a painful divorce and with four kids and my own business, I had a lot to worry about. What struck me the most was the suggestion in "The Secret" that dwelling on the negative—the things you can't do, things happening "to you" that are out of your control, fears, obstacles that are holding you back, the pain of past hurts, etc.—that dwelling on these things can keep you stuck there.

According to the author, what helps you move forward is spending time thinking about, envisioning and dreaming about the things you do want in your life. What really it resonated with me was the idea that the things we spend the most time wanting to do or have, we generally find a way to do or obtain. Those things we want to become, we can begin to become by being conscious of our desires, by naming them and beginning to take action. When we spend time thinking about how to get to a place in our lives we really want to reach, we naturally begin to problem-solve our way to that place, in our subconscious as well as our conscious minds. It makes sense.

So dream, first for yourself. About who you would be if you were all that you wanted to be—what you would do, where your business would go. And then begin to think about the pathways to those places: Education, counseling, coaching, financing, growth. Begin to layout a plan with the steps you know you need to take in order to move from the place you are now to where you want to be.

Dreams are intriguing! Work with a counselor or dream expert to create a fascinating seminar for customers on dreams and the subconscious. Partner with a caterer or hold your event at a local restaurant or wine shop. Create dream-related cross and cooperative marketing offers with your partners.

How does your business work to fulfill the dreams of your customers? Does it fulfill a practical need which can free them to pursue their dreams? Do you sell luxury or pampering products or services?

Passion is contagious. Don't be afraid to renew the idealism you once felt about your business and your industry, and to share it with your employees, vendors and customers.

Partner with a counselor or professional coach to hold a seminar for working professionals on achievement, obstacles and dreams. Partner with a local community, technical or business school to host a seminar on training for 'dream jobs.' With the downturn in the economy and high unemployment, this is the perfect time to introduce people to training and education that can propel them into jobs, into better jobs, dream jobs or a full-fledged career.

Work with businesses in your community (and/or your marketing and event partners) as well as technical or trade schools, high schools, colleges, etc. to hold a Dream Job Fair. Post links to local job boards and hiring resources on your website, blog, Facebook page and e-mail newsletter.

January 14 – Dress Up Your Pet Day

According to www.humanesociety.org, more than half of your customers and prospects have pets. Of these, dogs and cats comprise the vast majority. While you may be tempted to make fun of people who dress up their pets, don't; instead, celebrate this opportunity to attract new clients to your business!

Partner with local veterinary practices, animal hospitals, pet groomers or pet stores to hold a pet-oriented event at your business. Work with a pet boutique store to hold a full-blown pet fashion show. Partner with a mobile groomer to coordinate appointments or services you provide to customers (salon, spa, dining, workout, consultation, etc.) with mobile grooming outside for pets. Give pet owners a discount on both services when booked together, and make their lives easier!

Partner with veterinarians, pet boarding businesses and groomers for on-going cross marketing. This is a market that relies heavily on word-of-mouth and personal recommendations; pet owners in your clientele or people new to the area will be glad to know of good pet service providers in your area. Plus, pet owners periodically spend time waiting in the veterinarians office or waiting area of the pet's groomer where they could be reading or hearing about your business. Post links to pet-related businesses and pet-friendly destinations, hotels, parks, etc. on your Facebook page, blog and e-mail newsletter.

Conduct a campaign to benefit a local animal shelter, emergency animal hospital, rescue organization, etc. with funds, donated pet food, supplies, medicines or other needed items.

Add branded, bling-filled or fun pet supplies—leashes, collars, bowls, shampoos, brushes, etc.—or pet-themed mugs, t-shirts and other personal items to your retail or impulse buy wares, to give away with purchase or to be awarded in pet-owners drawings or contests. Solicit customer photos on Facebook and hold a cutest pet photo contest (dressed up or not!)

January Week 3
January Week 3 – Healthy Weight Week

Partner with a local physician, nutritionist or fitness expert to hold a seminar or create a list of Top 10 Tips for pursuing a healthy weight. Hold a workshop for kids or teens about healthy weight, body image and self-esteem. Post tips about healthy ways to lose weight on your Facebook page, blog and e-mail newsletter. Make customers aware of the services or products you offer that can contribute to healthy weight or weight loss. Partner with a local fitness facility, dance or martial arts studio to create a special offer for your customers.

Partner with a dinner preparation company, nutritionist and/or caterer to hold a hands-on food preparation and nutrition workshop for customers. Solicit customers' healthy recipes, weight loss success stories, etc. Share updates about individuals who made New Year weight loss resolutions or invite customers to join a healthy weight or weight loss support group.

January Week 3 – Hunt for Happiness Week

Partner with a local counselor, executive or life coach or motivational speaker to hold a workshop for clients on "The Hunt for Happiness." Compile a list of recommended reading and local resources to post on Facebook, your blog, or e-mail newsletter. Retail relevant books or videos to your customers.

Add branded wares like mugs, t-shirts, tank tops, pens, bags, etc. with "hunt for happiness" related quotes, designs or slogans to your retail or to give away as contest prizes or a gift-with-purchase.

Create a "Hunt for Happiness" scavenger hunt contest with clues spread among businesses with which you partner with for marketing or businesses located near your, or with clues related to products or services that you sell. Reward the winner with something good enough to make them truly happy!

January 15 – Get to Know Your Customers Day

Think you know your customers? Maybe, maybe not; but there are many ways to find out more about them. Establish channels for two-way communication and make it easy for customers to tell you what they want more of (or less of) when it comes to your business. Getting to know your customers will also help you plug into their lives more deeply and personally, so that they may become more connected emotionally with your business.

One obvious way you can get to know your customers is to create a formal way to solicit customer suggestions, complaints and other feedback. One-off complaints (or compliments, for that matter) may indicate cause for concern and further review, but should not be the basis for setting policy unless additional evidence surfaces. Relying solely on customer-initiated comments (which generally only occur when a customer is deeply dissatisfied with some aspect of your business) doesn't give you the whole picture and may actually give you a distorted, exaggerated perspective.

Instead, engage in regular customer surveys and short questionnaires:
- at the point of purchase
- at each table in your restaurant, wine shop or bar
- at your employee stations
- at kiosks
- near the exit and entrances of your business
- by way of follow up direct mail, e-mail or website form.

Make it easy for customers to provide you with a quick report about their visit to your establishment or website. Ask what went right (what they want more of or what they would not want you to change), what went wrong (what they want less of or what you should change), and what else they want (what did they not find or what else could you add to meet more of their needs).

Subscribe to publications and e-mail newsletters that provide news, trends and information about your largest customer demographic groups (men, women, Gen X, Boomers or other generations, kids, sports fanatics, celebrity buffs, hobbyists, home owners, parents, pet owners, financial status, neighborhood residence, etc.)

Educate yourself about commonalities and generalities within your client base and your community overall including the best ways to reach out to them, what interests them, what they most value, and what characteristics and qualities they most desire in business and personal interactions.

Create customer-centric bulletin boards (in store or online) to showcase customer achievements, hobbies, collections, performances, events, pets, children, favorite charitable causes, etc.

Hold daily, weekly or monthly polls to gauge customer opinion on your website, blog, Facebook page or e-mail newsletter. Collect responses and post poll results.

Conduct surveys in order to collect specific information and opinions about single departments, products or services. Include surveys as part of every customer (or employee) special event, collecting feedback either on comment cards at the event itself or by way of e-mail or web form response afterward. Unless you are conducting an anonymous survey, use surveys as a tool to help build your contact databases for direct mail and e-mail communications (and indicate that you are doing so or ask permission on the comment card or form). Anonymous surveys can still be used to collect demographics, interests, etc. in addition to opinions, ratings, complaints or suggestions.

Make it easy for customers to contact you online to express positive *or* negative views. Use reviews and opinion poll results to help promote specific menu items, products, or services. Use customer testimonials to tell prospects what to expect and why they should do business with you.

Follow up. When you receive customer requests, complaints or comments, be responsive. Ask for permission to contact them and for their preferred form of communication (direct mail, e-mail, phone, etc.) Ask for permission to add their e-mail address to your communications contact database.

When you receive a legitimate complaint, take immediate and meaningful action to correct the problem and to prevent its recurrence through employee training, facility repair, etc. Then tell the individual who lodged the complaint what action/s you took and thank them for bringing it to your attention. You will create more long-term, loyal customers if you are willing to be transparent, humble and address problems, rather than writing off the customer or ignoring the problem.

About 4 years ago when leaving a big box retail store I was asked if I had found what I needed. I mentioned one specific item I wish that they carried, and I was encouraged to fill out a comment card with my member number, name, e-mail address and request. The store still doesn't stock my item nor did they ever bother to respond to me—for all I know my card is still sitting in the bottom of their request box! It's better not to ask for suggestions at all, than to solicit them and not respond.

January 16 – Nothing Day

On Nothing Day, hold a drawing or contest and reward one lucky customer who will end up paying nothing for their purchase that day. You can award someone randomly on the spot (for instance, you could predetermine that the 10th or 100th customer of the day will win) or you can hold a drawing at the end of the day. Give the winning customer a gift card equal to the amount of their purchase that day (or more).

Create a "Something for Nothing" promotion where customers receive a free gift card or a gift-with-purchase for any purchase, for purchases over a designated amount or for purchases of specific products or services.

The term "Nothing Day" reminds me of a local low-budget, tacky-but-memorable TV ad which even found its way into national funniest commercials TV specials made by a business called Stereo Warehouse. In the ad, three "average joe" type of guys stand apparently unclad, except for socks, behind car stereo boxes, saying, "We stripped our prices naked!" While I am not advocating nudity, you might be inspired to create an advertisement or publicity stunt for your business where the central and memorable message conveyed is that there is "nothing" you wouldn't do for your customers.

Hold a "We're Making Nothing" charity benefit where all profits, a portion of profits or proceeds from the sales of specific products or services are donated directly to a local charity.

January 17 – Chili Day

When it's chilly outside, chili inside sounds great! Partner with a local caterer or restaurant and sample chili to customers throughout the day or have a customer or employee-appreciation luncheon. Have a homemade chili potluck lunch or dinner with employees.

Partner with a chef, nutritionist or caterer to hold a chili cooking class. Share recipes on Facebook, your blog, email newsletter and bag stuffers. Hold a chili making contest or tasting event. Solicit recipes on Facebook.

Treat people to a chili and beer happy hour. Hold a chili eating contest (based on quantity or heat).

Solicit donations of canned chili and soups to be given to a local food bank. Reward donors with a branded tchotchke or special offer. Accept donated canned chili or soup in lieu of a cover charge for a happy hour, chili tasting or contest. Afterward, donate the canned goods to a local shelter or another charitable meal provider.

January 18 – Winnie the Pooh Day

Set aside a special day to cater to kids. Partner with a makeup artist or esthetician and clothing and shoe retailers to hold a fashion and makeover show for pre-teen or teenage girls. Partner with a boutique to hold a baby or toddler fashion show. Partner with a local recreation or family fun center to host a family-friendly event or give gift cards to thank your most valued customers, employees, vendors, etc.

Donate Winnie the Pooh stuffed animals, play sets, children's clothing, bedding, books or other items to a local shelter, children's hospital or another children's charity. Invite customers to help underwrite donations or to provide support through the purchase of designated items.

Contact local youth services, mentoring or tutoring organizations and get involved by volunteering, raising awareness, raising funds, etc. Host an event or donate a percentage of sales to a local Children's Theater or music organization, such as the band program of your local elementary school. Raise awareness of local children's causes, campaigns, and opportunities with which customers can get involved on your blog, Facebook page and e-mail newsletter.

Hold a book drive or fundraiser to help support a local public or school library, day care or youth literacy program. Write press releases and put posts on your Facebook page, blog and e-mail newsletter to increase public awareness of needs. Contact your local public library to host or sponsor book clubs or to provide supplies or refreshments. Launch a reading rewards program for kids or hold a kid's, tweens or teen activity-filled read-in.

Start a book club at your business and/or partner with a caterer, wine shop or other local business to provide refreshments, meeting space, books or other items.

January 19 – Popcorn Day

Partner with a local party equipment rental business for cross or cooperative marketing. Rent a commercial popcorn cart so you can treat customers with a sample when they are on their way in or out of your store in branded bags as well as a promotional bag stuffer or bounce-back offer.

Place a popcorn machine at the back of your facility and use this fresh, hot, buttered enticement to draw customers directly past displays featuring seasonal or special offers. Set up a "point of popcorn" display with special offers, branded merchandise or seasonal products.

Purchase pre-packaged popcorn bags or popcorn balls and distribute them in branded bags along with a business card or brochure and a special offer from your business. Deliver popcorn treats to the employees of businesses near yours, to major employers in your community, to school offices or classrooms, nurses lounges, police or fire stations, union shops, etc.

Create an e-mail or web-exclusive offer for customers who say the word "popcorn" when they make purchases at your business or online.

January 20 – Disc Jockey Day

If you have a P.A. system, celebrate Disc Jockey Day by writing a series of fun, wacky and creative announcements to make or repeat throughout the day. To see if anyone is listening, add in special offers or freebies which expire in 15 minutes, at the end of the day, or which are good only for the first customer to mention a special code word.

Host a happy hour featuring karaoke. Hold a "Disc Jockey Contest" with serious or funny sample scripts to read. Give out a grand prize as well as small prizes or gift cards to anyone brave enough to participate; extend a special offer to all attendees.

Partner with a local radio station and/or college that offers broadcasting courses to hold a workshop for kids, teens or adults who are interested about what it takes to be a successful disc jockey, what types of careers it can lead to, or about careers in radio or broadcasting in general. Partner with a local radio station for advertising, endorsements, charity events, fundraisers and public appearances. Submit press releases to local stations on a regular basis.

January 21 – Squirrel Appreciation Day

It can be tough for squirrels and birds to find food during snowy winter months. On Squirrel Appreciation Day, show that you care about these little creatures. Send customers home with small bags of bird seed or a nutty mix recommended for squirrels and ask them to scatter the contents in their backyard or a local park or wilderness area.

Hold a squirrel-trivia contest. Conduct pop-squirrel-quizzes at the cash register. Ask questions on Facebook and reward the person who provides you with the first correct answer. Purchase stuffed animal squirrels as gifts to clients or their kids, or to donate to a local charity or preschool.

Write your own "famous squirrels in history" story. Ask customers to help name and describe the exploits of squirrels that might have been present at famous moments in history. Publish your story online or even in a print version, giving credit and prizes to customers who contributed in the form of gift cards redeemable during their next visit at your business.

January Week 4

January Week 4 – Take Back Your Time Week

Partner with a personal organizer to hold a workshop or provide tips to customers about taking back time by becoming more organized at work or at home. Partner with a professional coach or counselor to hold a workshop, compile a recommended reading and resources list or give tips to customers on ways to make the most of one's time personally and/or professionally.

Partner with a local wine shop or bar to hold a "Me Time" happy hour or wine tasting. Partner with a local fitness facility, yoga, dance or martial arts studio to create a "Me Time" dance, exercise or another fitness class offer for your customers.

Add wares to your retail or impulse buys such as mugs, clothing, hats, notebooks, memo cubes, etc. featuring 'time' or 'me-first' sentiments, designs or slogans.

Tell your customers about products or services you sell which can help them take care of themselves or which can help maximize the use of their time. Create a special offer for your best customers by creating a delivery or call-ahead service for products they repeatedly purchase. Implement text-ahead, call-ahead, e-mail-ahead ordering or personal shopping services.

January Week 4 – Private Schools Week

Cultivating relationships and creating special offers for school districts and schools in your community is well-worth the investment of time and resources—they may even be chock-full of your ideal prospective clients! School employees appreciate discounts and will patronize companies that understand the demands on their time and resources and are able to cater to their unique needs.

If you can market effectively to teachers and school employees, you have the potential to reach a large prospect pool very quickly, as opposed to trying to market to these same people individually in your community. School employees have the ability to share information with co-workers, parents and other school patrons—literally hundreds of people—by word-of-mouth nearly each and every day. School employees have the ability to spread reviews, information and endorsements quickly, virally and over a very wide net of the population in your community.

Private school employees (generally) have some of the same demographic characteristics as public school employees; however, when it comes to school patrons (parents and families of students), private schools may be even more relevant to your ideal target markets in terms of their demographic makeup and disposable income.

Create offers tailored to attract teachers, employees and patrons of private schools in your community. Private schools generally have more latitude in their policies than public schools and may be willing to work with you directly to tailor programs or offers for their staff or students, or even to allow you direct marketing access to school families. Another way to attract their patrons is to donate to school capital projects, fundraising auctions, take ads out in sports or performance programs, etc.

Ask local private schools about current capital projects, fundraisers or classroom needs and conduct a campaign to support their efforts. Establish a scholarship fund for students who would benefit from attending a private school but may not be able to for financial reasons, or to be granted as a reward for academic, athletic, artistic or other achievements. Create rewards redeemable in your place of business that schools can give to students for outstanding academic, artistic, athletic or other accomplishments.

January 22 – Blonde Brownie Day

I had to Google "Blonde Brownies" for this project, and once I did, I knew why I didn't know what they were. No offense to Blonde Brownie fans, but my personal conviction is that if the word "brownie" is used, chocolate had better be involved! To me, Blonde Brownies are *something* (maybe cookie bars?) but they are imposters in the world of brownies. Hold a contest for customers asking for examples of other infamous imposters when it comes to food (or other categories) in-store and online. Draw a winner who will receive a gift card or another prize. Extend a special offer to all entrants.

Satisfy customer's cravings with Blonde Brownie mini or full-size treats. Solicit blonde brownie recipes or share recipes on your Facebook page, blog, e-mail newsletter and bag stuffers. Partner with a local caterer to hold a blonde brownie cooking class or tasting event; make your event bigger by partnering with a local wine shop, bar or restaurant for a blonde brownie happy hour or hold a brownie eating or cooking contest.

Why wait for Halloween—people love to dress up! Partner with a local bar or restaurant and hold an "Imposter's Ball" costume or masquerade event. Solicit photos of your customers in their favorite disguises or costumes.

Partner with a local caterer or nutritionist to hold a workshop or provide tips about imposters that make a positive difference—foods and ingredients that can be substituted for less-healthy counterparts in order to help improve health benefits and nutrition, provide lower fat, calorie and cholesterol options, increase intake of anti-oxidants, etc.

January 23 – Pie Day

Partner with a caterer or chef to hold a pie-making class. Partner with a local restaurant, caterer or another business to take pie orders from your customers or in order to add pies to your retail.

Sell pies to raise funds for a shelter or food bank. Partner with a local restaurant or caterer to hold a cooperative fundraiser and donate pies to a local food bank, mission, shelter or to local needy families.

Hold a baking contest or partner with a local restaurant or bar to hold a pie eating contest. While there may only be one winner, everyone in attendance can receive a special offer from your business and those of your marketing partners. Hold door prize drawings to collect contact information for your direct mail and e-mail databases; afterward, extend a follow up offer.

(I love this one!) There is a unique organization that (literally) sells pies in order to raise funds which are then used to provide nutritious meals and food to some of the most needy people in the greater Philadelphia area called Manna. Create a campaign to support www.mannapa.org or promote them by way of links on your website and e-mail newsletter or on signage in your business.

January 24 – Beer Can Appreciation Day

Hold a beer trivia contest for customers with prizes including gift certificates from restaurants, bars or clubs with which you partner for marketing. Depending on local alcohol regulations, you may or may not be able to utilize beer as a prize; however there are plenty of other related items (like pretzels, peanuts or chips) that you can use to incentivize participation, shopping and enthusiasm.

Purchase branded items for gifts, rewards, incentives, prizes or retail like insulated beverage sleeves, beer mugs or glasses, etc. Purchase beer-themed wares to add to your retail offerings. Post trivia or beer-appreciative quotes on your Facebook page, blog and e-mail newsletter.

Partner with a local brewery to create a house beer named for your business for retail sale or to keep on tap seasonally, in support of a charity or customer event or to sell all year.

Partner with local breweries or wine shops to hold a beer tasting event, or hold a Beer Fair inviting participation from people in your community who create their own home brews and local micro-brew makers. Hold a blind beer tasting contest to see whether self-proclaimed experts can identify brands, local microbrews, or to determine the best local home brew beer.

January 25 – Measure Your Feet Day

Partner with a shoe retailer to hold a footwear fashion show or for cross or cooperative marketing. Partner with a local salon or spa that provides pedicure services, with a podiatrist or with another foot product or service specialist for cross or cooperative marketing. Demonstrate or provide mini-pedicures, how-to tips, a workshop on pedicures and foot care, etc.

Most of us (literally) played in our parent's shoes when we were young at one time or another, and many of us have parents, grandparents, older siblings and other role models to whom we still try to 'measure up.' Partner with a local counselor or motivational speaker to hold a seminar on measuring up in healthy ways, or how to identify and address unhealthy aspects of this tendency we may have carried into our adult lives. Compile a list of recommended reading to post on your Facebook page, blog and e-mail newsletter along with links to local resources. Volunteer, donate or hold a fundraiser to benefit local youth mentoring, tutoring and other services.

Hold a fundraiser or solicit the donation of footwear to be donated to a local shelter, school or community service organization. 'Adopt' a local needy family for a year and create a campaign to buy (or collect) needed footwear for each season for each member of the family.

Compile a list of the shoe sizes of employees, celebrities or famous historical figures and hold a shoe-size guessing contest with one grand prize, several smaller prizes and special offers for all entrants. Take entries in store and online. Create bigger prize packages by partnering with local shoe stores, pedicure salons or nail technicians, podiatrists offices or other related businesses.

January 26 – Spouses Day

Remind customers not to take their spouses for granted! Extend offers for customers to purchase something for themselves and receive a comparable product or service for their spouse for free or at a special price—from happy hour drinks to entrees to haircuts to massages to candy bars to wine tastings—be creative! Partner with other businesses in your immediate vicinity to hold a larger Spouses Day event or offer.

Partner with a counseling office to hold a healthy marriage workshop or host pre-marital workshops for engaged couples.

Partner with wedding and party planners, caterers, bakeries, bridal dress stores, formal rental stores, limousine rentals, salons and other relevant businesses to hold a bridal fair or to create bundled wedding product and service packages.

Partner with a local restaurant, wine shop or bar to hold a Spouse Appreciation dinner, happy hour or cocktail party. Make the event bigger by partnering with local area entertainment (movie theaters, playhouses, symphony or other arts, comedy club, sporting events, etc.) and include entertainment in the package. Partner with a local limousine or shuttle transportation business to make the outing a group event or reward a contest or drawing-winning couple with free transportation. Partner with a local salon to extend pre-event makeovers or award one couple with pre-event preparation services. Hold a cocktail hour or champagne reception at your business to kick off the evening's activities.

January 27 – Speak Up and Succeed Day

The ability to speak in public, make presentations or even to make short announcements or toasts doesn't come naturally to everyone. Some people are shy and some have deep-seated fears about speaking in public. Some people even have trouble speaking up for themselves if it will mean confronting or being in open disagreement with others. But the ability to 'speak up' appropriately and assertively is crucial to most avenues of professional success and for healthy, happy relationships!

Partner with a counselor or public speaking expert to hold a workshop for people who want to improve their skills in this area or join forces with a local Toastmasters group (www.toastmasters.org). Provide a list of recommended reading, public speaking tips or ideas people can use to practice at home on your Facebook page, blog and e-mail newsletter.

Partner with a counselor to hold a workshop on interpersonal communication skills. Host a workshop (or a series) in cooperation with other businesses near yours or those of your marketing partners about communicating with employees and customers, having difficult conversations, conducting effective employee communications and performance reviews, etc. Hold a workshop on professional and/or interpersonal communication for your own employees as a team-building and personal development exercise.

January 28 – Fun at Work Day

Work is serious business but it doesn't have to feel that way. *Have Fun at Work Day* can be fun for customers as well as employees. Take a page out of Southwest Airlines' playbook and design signage, announcements and offers that are fun to read or fun to hear over the P.A. Designate a theme and invite employees to get into costume for a day. Design bag stuffers with clever sayings and a fun offer to bring customers back to your business sooner, rather than later. Send an e-mail out to your contacts with fun business news, human interest anecdotes and a fun, redeemable offer.

Partner with area entertainment, sports, recreation or family fun centers for cooperative offers or gift cards to give your staff and their families. Have a game night, an after-hours cocktail party or some other get-together for staff (and/or their families) at the facility of one of your marketing partners.

Retail branded wares designed for use in an office setting that are fun to look at, have clever or facetious work quotes or have a unique or funny design. Purchase branded office supplies (pens, staplers, tape dispensers, post it notes, memo pads, etc.) to give away as contest prizes, client gifts or as a gift-with-purchase.

Partner with a counselor or another expert to hold a workshop for business professionals, your marketing partners, etc. about how to make the workplace a more fun and enjoyable place for employees and customers while still maintaining a healthy culture, a climate of continuous improvement and a commitment to the customer experience. It's not an excuse to ignore the rules; it's an opportunity to grow your employee culture to a place of deeper maturity, where most employees can be trusted to work effectively, productively and in accordance with policy without feeling as though they are in a micromanaged atmosphere.

Compile a list of recommended reading, team-building resources, workbooks, etc. to share with your peers, add to retail or post on your Facebook page, blog and e-mail newsletter.

January 29 – Corn Chip Day

Don't wait for Cinco de Mayo in May to break out the chips and salsa—Corn Chip Day is a perfect time to sample chips and salsa to customers or to give them away as contest prizes, a gift-with-purchase, an employee-appreciation gift or to enjoy during a customer or employee happy hour.

Hold a customer or employee-appreciation event at your favorite Mexican restaurant (hopefully this business is already one of your cross marketing partners!)

Partner with a local caterer to hold a class on making corn chips, or hold a workshop with a party planner using corn chips and Mexican foods as the central theme. Hold a contest for customers to create the ultimate corn chip dip, or have a corn chip and dip tasting party.

Retail corn chip serving bowls. Work with a local restaurant or manufacturer to create a branded line of corn chips for retail (or to serve) at your business.

January 30 – Inane Answering Machine Message Day

From corporations that rely on automated answering and directories to your friends and family who may in fact even be at home but screen calls for telemarketers—as Americans, most of us have some sort of interaction with an answering machine of some kind just about every day. While we may hear hundreds of automated recordings every year, we only really hear two or three variations of the same message. Inane Answering Machine Message Day is the perfect cure for repetitive answering machine message fatigue!

In signage, your e-mail newsletter and in your phone announcement recordings, state that in honor of the day you have committed yourself to this cause and go on to leave a witty, inspirational, clever or funny announcement. Encourage callers to leave spirited messages in return.

Hold a contest for the best customer message left on your voicemail system, entered via e-mail, posted on your Facebook page or blog, submitted on your website or even written on entry forms in your business. All entrants should receive a special offer from you in appreciation of their effort in addition to rewarding the winners.

Hold an employee contest for the best scripts for outgoing messages for your business or their extension or department.

January 31 – Inspire Your Heart with Art

This is another great opportunity to reach out and partner with local libraries and schools. Sponsor an art contest, feature the work of local artists, raise funds and solicit donations for local art programs. Support city, senior center, youth and other community art programs. Become a patron of your local symphony, orchestra, chorale or community theatre and place advertisements in their programs. Attend and support music, theater and the arts in local high schools and colleges.

Hold a young artist's contest and solicit entries from the children of your customers. Award the winner with a gift certificate to be used in a future visit to your business plus branded wares, toys, art supplies and/or with a scholarship to participate in a local art class or studio. Provide all entrants with a special prize to acknowledge their participation along with a special bounce-back offer or gift card redeemable in your business. Invite a local art studio or teacher to extend a special offer to all entrants. Write a press release to honor the work of the winner and some of the most impressive entries.

Partner with a local artist, art teacher or another expert to hold a workshop on the arts, on a specific art, or to hold art classes for customers (or for their kids). Compile a directory of local art supply stores, instructors and art studios to post on your Facebook page, blog and e-mail newsletter. Post links to the work or websites of local artists. Create a community resources page with local artist's resources on your website.

february
365 Days of Marketing

February Month-Long Observances
American Heart Month

Partner with local physicians or other medical professionals, fitness trainers, nutritionists, counselors and relationship experts for cross or cooperative marketing. With marketing partners or on your own, hold a workshop, seminar, class or series of classes on maximizing heart health, proper fitness and nutrition to improve heart health, or about emotional heart health and relationships.

Posts for Facebook/social media, Blog, E-mail, Bag Stuffers and/or Website:
- Tips, advice or local resources for improving heart health
- Awareness and early warning signs of heart disease
- Diet, exercise and fitness tips
- Highlight the products or services you provide that benefit heart-health, health or well-being in general or which provide stress-relieving benefits, aromatherapy, etc.
- Recommended reading (and add titles to retail or give away as client gifts, gifts-with-purchase or contest prizes)

Conduct a fundraising campaign to support a heart health-related charity. Support local cardiac services through fundraising or by donating gift cards, services or products to patients, their families or caregivers. 'Adopt' a local family impacted by heart disease for a free year of products or services.

Purchase branded heart-shaped wristbands, coin purses, stress balls or other items to add to retail or utilize in fundraising efforts. Ask all of your employees to wear red on a given day to help raise awareness or as part of a fundraising campaign.

Bake for Family Fun Month

Partner with a caterer, baker or another professional to hold a baking class or series of classes for kids and a parent. Expand the series by including a party planner and add education about party planning, tablescaping and other related dining, decorating and entertaining activities.

Black History Month

Hold a trivia contest to draw attention to important aspects of Black History, to important moments in history and notable individuals. Use your blog, Facebook page, website, e-mail newsletter and signage to post facts, trivia, history and "Did you know...?" style educational information. To help you get started, check out the resources available at www.infoplease.com/black-history-month/.

Boost Your Self-Esteem Month, Plant the Seeds of Greatness Month

Hold a self-esteem or personal development workshop or create peer and mentor support groups for kids, teens or young adults. Compile a list of recommended reading and local resources to post on your Facebook page, blog and e-mail newsletter. Add related books or videos to your retail.

Promote opportunities for kids and teens to become involved in projects or programs that benefit the community or sponsor a youth community-service project. Support youth services in your community by raising awareness, donating time, services or products, or helping with fundraising efforts. Solicit and feature success stories of local exceptional or accomplished youth on your Facebook page, blog and e-mail newsletter.

Care about Your Indoor Air Month

Partner with local HVAC service professionals to educate customers about seasonal and routine maintenance recommended to improve the quality of air in their homes. Share tips from HVAC experts on maximizing fresh air inside, especially during winter months.

Let customers and employees know that you care about the air they breathe by testing the air in your workplace and then sharing results and information about any corrective actions taken. Replace aging HVAC equipment with newer, more efficient, healthier systems.

Partner with HVAC sales or repair businesses for cross or cooperative marketing. Expand your reach by including home renovation and remodeling firms, builders, appliance stores, furniture stores, handyman services, etc. Work together to hold a home renovation, repair, services and equipment fair, or to compile a combined directory of services.

Canned Food, Cherry, Grapefruit and Sweet Potato Month

Food is always one of the most enticing ways to celebrate—because people love food! For Canned Food Month, hold a campaign to collect canned food for donation to a local food bank or another charity. In February, accept the donation of canned foods in lieu of event cover charges or let customers exchange donated canned goods for free add-on gifts, branded tchotchkes, a special offer or another incentive.

To celebrate Cherries, Grapefruit or Sweet Potatoes, hold events, trivia contests, cooking or recipe contests, tastings, happy hours and share recipes, nutritional tips and trivia. Partner with caterers, party planners and restaurants, etc. for cross or cooperative marketing. Share recipes, cooking tips and trivia on your Facebook page, blog and e-mail newsletter.

Purchase cherry or grapefruit flavored/scented items (lip gloss, lotion, candles, room sprays, etc.) to add to retail or give away as a gift-with-purchase or contest prize. Add a fruit flavored or scented product display to your point of purchase. Feature facts about aromatherapy on your Facebook page, blog, bag stuffers and e-mail newsletter.

National Weddings Month

Many 'June Brides' are in full wedding-planning mode beginning in the early months of the year. Hold a Bridal Fair to connect with a variety of wedding resources all under one roof (preferably yours!) Fair participants could include wedding planners, local wedding and hotel facilities, florists, caterers, bakeries, banquet and reception facilities, restaurants, bridal shops, formal rentals, equipment and supply rentals, officiants, musicians, jewelers, limousine services, horse and carriage rental, taxi and shuttle services, honeymoon or wedding guest travel planners and more.

Many proposals occur in February on Valentine's Day; help people who want to 'pop the question' create creative proposals to be made at your business or those of your marketing partners. Create proposal date packages with your marketing partners to include salon makeover, cocktail hour or champagne reception, a romantic dinner and special activity, chauffeured by a limo or shuttle service. Take videos and pictures, submit press releases to local news media and post videos, pictures and stories on your Facebook page, blog or website.

Hold a contest for the best proposal, wedding or honeymoon ideas or the best (or worst) stories. Use Facebook, your blog and e-mail newsletter to publicize your contests and share customer ideas and stories.

Pet Dental Health Month,
Bird Feeding Month

Create marketing partnerships with pet stores, groomers, mobile groomers, pet walkers, pet boarding facilities, trainers, equipment and feed suppliers, veterinarian offices, animal hospitals or area animal shelters, etc. Create cooperative and cross marketing offers, hold publicity stunts, hold events at pet-friendly parks or stores and connect customers with local professional pet services and resources.

Post information about pet dental health on your Facebook page, blog and e-mail newsletter. Make product or service provider recommendations. Compile a directory of resources for pet owners to add to your website or feature in an upcoming e-mail newsletter. Solicit customer recommendations or hold an online vote for favorite local veterinarian.

Raise awareness, hold a campaign to raise funds or solicit the donation of specific items for local animal shelters or animal hospitals. Partner with a local shelter to help promote pet adoptions. Donate gift cards to be given as a gift-with-pet-adoption. Tell customers about pets available for adoption in posts on Facebook or your e-mail newsletter. Give a free gift to individuals who show proof of a recent pet adoption or work with a shelter to hold an adoption event at your business.

During cold, snowy winter months, birds sometimes have trouble finding food. Help a bird out by giving branded bags of bird seed to your customers and to the customers of local businesses (or those of your marketing partners) to be distributed in backyards or parks. Partner with a local pet store to promote the sale of birds as pets or pet bird cages, food or supplies.

Presidents Day History Month

Entertain, engage and reward kids and teens while at your business with a youth President's Day History quiz or trivia contest. Or hold a trivia contest on Facebook.

Post "Did you know...?" style information about U.S. Presidents and government on your Facebook page, blog, bag stuffers and e-mail newsletter. To help you get started, check out the information available at the official White House website at www.whitehouse.gov/about/presidents.

Hold a President's Day essay contest for kids and reward the winner with a branded item, gift card redeemable at your business and/or a presidential history related video or book. Add presidential history books or videos to your point of purchase or regular retail, or purchase a presidential history coffee table book for retail or gift-with-purchase in February.

Relationship Wellness Month, Mend a Broken Heart Month

The pangs of loneliness or a broken heart hurt even more around Valentine's Day. Connect customers with local counseling or relationship resources. Partner with a counselor to hold a workshop or series on relationships, mending broken hearts, and becoming the 'who' they need to be to attract 'who' they want to have in their lives. Lighten the mood by adding anti-love or cynical sentiment wares such as tumblers, notebooks, totes, shirts, hats, etc. to your retail or give them away as contest prizes or a gift-with-purchase.

Retail love-related gifts and brandware, candies, chocolates, flowers, etc. Partner with a local florist to sell bouquets or take orders for Valentine's Day. Partner with a local chocolatier or candy maker to create branded goodies for retail sale, take orders for Valentine's Day, provide a display for cross marketing or to provide desserts at your relationship workshops.

Spunky Old Broads Month

Expanding on the senior theme, but not necessarily limited to seniors per se—because Spunky Old Broads come in all ages! One group that may resonate with this theme is the 'Red Hat Society;' similarly, there may be wine clubs, book clubs, card clubs and other groups of 'spunky old broads' that meet regularly in your area that would welcome your offer of meeting space or sponsorship in return for the opportunity to extend special offers or simple marketing information to their members.

Establish your own relevant support/social group in your community, either as an extension of a national organization or as a club unique to your community. Members may be interested in workshops, education, hobbies, crafts, art or games, or you can sponsor and coordinate group outings at shopping centers, wineries or breweries, sporting events, theater, symphony, the arts, etc.

Senior Independence Month

Create special offers for seniors. Establish relationships with senior social service organizations, community centers, activity groups, and senior living communities where your offers can be included in print or e-mail newsletters, on websites, in mailings, on bulletin boards, on dining room tent cards, etc.

Offer to host or sponsor senior book clubs, bowling or Wii bowling leagues, sightseeing or recreational outings, social clubs, craft or hobby clubs, shopping outings, etc.

Hold a Senior Independence Fair at your business or that of one of your marketing partners, bringing together resources for seniors such as senior living communities, health care services and providers, physical therapists and mobility experts, massage therapists, pedicure and senior skin care, hair and makeup experts, education, retail and other relevant professional services.

Create an off-site menu and take some of your products or services on the road for seniors who cannot get to your business; or help to arrange transportation to and from, and set aside specific hours at your business to cater to senior groups.

Time Management Month

Are you in charge of your time, or are the demands on your time controlling you? Time Management Month is the ideal time to add time management software, planners, books, and other time management tools to your regular retail or point of purchase, or to give away as customer gifts, contest prizes, a gift-with-purchase, etc.

Partner with a personal organizer or professional coach to hold a time management seminar for employees, marketing partners, businesses located near yours, city Chamber, Rotary or other civic organization members (or their customers). Include tips on time management on your Facebook page, blog, bag stuffers and e-mail newsletter.

Tell customers how your business saves them time, money or resources. Launch a new service to help customers save time and resources, such as online shopping, pre-ordering, call-text-or-e-mail ahead for pickup, personal shopping services, etc.

February Week 1

February Week 1 – Child Authors and Illustrators Week

Whether children, tweens, teens or young adults make up a significant part of your target market or not, their parents do! Hold a contest for their kids to enter in writing, illustrating or both. Set up a panel to review entries or hold a drawing to determine the winner. Enable voting in-store and/or online, and use the voting forms to help build your contact database. Award prizes redeemable in a future visit to your business, and be sure that all entrants receive a small reward and a special offer.

With parental permission, feature the work and names of winners in business communications and in a press release. Highlight some of the best young creative talent in posts on your website, Facebook page, blog, e-mail newsletter and media press releases.

Create a publication inclusive of all entries and have it printed by a commercial printer for retail sale. Give a copy to participants as a keepsake. Or use the best entries to create a book or calendar to give to clients, gift-with-purchase, use as contest prizes or for retail sale. Make sure entrants and/or their parents sign a release giving you permission to reproduce the artwork, or include a release on your contest entry form.

Conduct a campaign to raise funds or solicit donation of specific items for a local school art or literacy program. Host a children's art and/or writing class or series of classes. Hold story book reading hours for young children. Add art instruction books to your retail or give them away as contest prizes.

February Week 1 – Intimate Apparel Week

February is about kindling the romance! Partner with a local boutique or lingerie party seller to hold an intimate apparel fashion show or party for customers. Create a special offer to extend to the customers and employees of these businesses. Add intimate apparel to your retail or impulse buy offerings in the weeks leading up to Valentine's Day. Give away lingerie store gift cards as a gift-with-purchase or contest prize.

February Week 1 – Snow Sculpting Week

If your climate is conducive to snowy, frozen activities, hold a snow sculpting contest in front of your business or at a local park. Post pictures and highlights on your Facebook page, blog, e-mail newsletter and website. Generate interest ahead of time with press releases, bag stuffers, Facebook posts, e-mail newsletters and the promotional help of businesses near yours or your marketing partners. Partner with a caterer or restaurant to provide hot chocolate at the event. At the event, distribute hand warmers, business cards or your menu and a bounce-back offer. Or go big! Work with your marketing partners, members of your Chamber of Commerce, local merchants, etc. to hold a large, multi-sponsor true community snow sculpting contest or exhibit. Generate additional goodwill and media coverage by adopting a charitable cause and donating entry fees or a portion of proceeds.

February Week 1 – Solo Diners Eat Out Week

Create special offers for 'solo diners' this week, when so much of the focus is on Valentine's Day and couples. Partner with a local restaurant, bar or caterer to hold a Solo Diners Eat Out event or extend a cooperative offer. Hold a Solo Diners Eat Out charity fundraiser. Hold a series of solo dining-inspired happy hours, tasting parties, cooking classes, relationship workshops, etc. Design your own singles-themed slogans or sentiments to be printed on t-shirts, mugs and other wares with funny, sarcastic or cynical statements to your retail or to give away at events, as contest prizes or a gift-with-purchase.

February 1 – GI Joe Day, Freedom Day

If you live near a military base you have the ability to reach out to a large group of prospective customers while at the same time extending honor and appreciation to members of the military and their families. Create special offers for the military and/or their family members.

Conduct a campaign to provide care packages for soldiers deployed overseas. Donate services or products to families whose husband, wife, son or daughter is on deployment. If you normally provide services in your business that cost little more than your time, set aside February 1st for appointments solely for military or their family members at no charge or a very special price. Promote awareness and participation through press releases to the media, on the web, in your newsletters, etc.

February 2 – Groundhog Day

No offense to groundhog-lovers, but why leave the future of the next six weeks up to an overgrown rodent? Create Groundhog Day promotions for customers to enjoy whether Phil sees his shadow or not, redeemable during the next 6 weeks.

Hold a contest and ask customers to predict what the weather will be every day for the next 6 weeks. Reward winner/s with a gift card redeemable in your business as well as a stuffed groundhog or another gift item. Extend a special offer or give a branded tchotchke to runners up or all participants. Collect entries online and in-store and use entries to help build your contact databases.

No matter whether the groundhog sees his shadow or not, eventually, spring is coming anyway! Use February 2nd as the launching point for spring promotions to get customers geared up for warmer, sunnier days. Create "beat the winter blues" promotions designed to distract customers from the cold and gray and put them into a warmer, happier frame of mind.

In partnership with a counselor or physician, hold a workshop about the causes and symptoms of winter blues, and ways to combat them. Hold a Sunshine Party at your business, or partner with a restaurant or bar, and bring in spotlights and other faux-sunshine natural lighting to brighten spirits. Add sun lamps and other UV replicators to retail or give them away as contest prizes or a gift-with-purchase. Or go big! Partner with other businesses to hold a contest or drawing to win travel vouchers, receive resort or hotel gift cards, the chance to join their favorite Major League Baseball team for spring training in Arizona, or on another sunnier-climate trip.

You might at least look like you've been somewhere sunny—partner with a local salon or spa that provides safe, sunless tanning alternatives for cross or cooperative marketing. Retail (or give away with purchase) spray-on, lotions, wipes or other safe artificial tanners. Partner with a salon, spa or makeup esthetician to hold a spring or summer makeup and hair demonstration event and provide free mini-makeovers for customers. Add a local boutique clothing seller to this marketing partnership and hold a full-blown spring or summer style and fashion show.

Purchase branded flip-flops for gift-with-purchase or to add to retail to help customers get ready for warmer weather. Donate branded flip-flops to local pedicure salons or spas for use in services.

February 3 – Coaches Day

Most of us have had a coach at some point in our lives; whether for sports, music, academics, professional development or some other area. While we often think first of sports, there are hundreds of coaches in your community for whom you can tailor special offers, create gift baskets or extend student or team-related promotions. Like teachers, coaches have considerable word-of-mouth marketing reach; they interact with dozens or even hundreds of other people in your community who may be among your 'ideal clients' and target markets, so their referrals and goodwill are valuable to your business.

Be visible in your community when it comes to team fundraisers, sporting events, parks and recreation organizations, etc. Lazy summer afternoons in the park are great times to network with parents and other professionals in your community.

Create offers for coaches working at local schools, colleges or universities, volunteer/amateur coaches in your local parks and recreation organizations and for mentors, tutors, music teachers, etc. Gift branded tchotchkes like lanyards, water bottles, hats, duffel bags or t-shirts to sports coaches and/or their team members. Hold a party in a local restaurant to thank the coaches (and/or team members and their families) of parks and recreation or school sports teams at the end of a season, after a tournament or even after every game.

Use in-store signage, your e-mail newsletter, blog and Facebook page to suggest that customers purchase specific products, gift baskets or gift cards as gifts for coaches. Make your business known as a resource for gifts, greeting cards and thank-you cards designed specifically for coaches.

Sponsor a local school or city parks and recreation sports team (or a local school academic team or club). Provide offers for coaches, team members and their families. Hold fundraisers to help obtain needed equipment or supplies for local teams. Provide funding to help underwrite tutoring programs for needy or underprivileged children. Publicize efforts through press releases on your website, in your newsletters, at your point of purchase, and submitted to local schools and media.

February 4 – Girls and Women in Sports Day

Girls and Women in Sports Day is another way you can become more involved in your community by supporting women's athletic programs at local schools, parks and recreation city programs, etc.

Promote awareness of Girls and Women in Sports by holding a day, week, or month-long Girls and Women in Sports trivia contest. Prizes should include gift cards redeemable in future visits to your business, and all entrants should receive a special offer.

Design bag stuffers, shelf or point of sale displays, and use your website, Facebook page, blog and e-mail newsletter to post trivia or information about famous women in sports, the accomplishments of local women's and girls' teams and players, and opportunities for girls to get involved in local sports, gymnastics, swimming and other programs. Conduct a campaign to support local women's athletic programs and teams. Hold a fundraiser, donate items to auctions or create a point of donation for customers. Provide customers with education about local programs, their benefits and their needs.

Working with a local social services agency or school, sponsor a local deserving, underprivileged female athlete, or 'adopt' a local female athlete for a year to provide needed items such as uniforms, shoes, sporting equipment or funds to help with trips and tournaments.

February 5 – Bubblegum Day

There's nothing complicated about Bubblegum—it's a sweet treat and one that most of us associate with childhood. No matter how old we get, it's still fun to try and blow a giant bubble!   Hold a bubble-blowing contest. Hold a publicity stunt or try to set a new world record for the most people blowing bubbles at the same time.

Give away bubble gum or buy branded bubblegum for retail sale or to gift-with-purchase.   Donate branded bubblegum to local youth services organizations, parks and recreation teams, YMCAs, schools and other organizations. Give branded bubblegum to your employees, to the employees and/or customers of businesses located near yours and those of your marketing and event partners, fellow members of your Chamber of Commerce and civic organizations, etc.

February 6 – Wear Red Day

If you have chosen to focus on matters related to the heart in February, Wear Red Day is another chance to bring attention to heart health issues. Create your own custom design and purchase branded shirts for employees to wear.   Raise awareness and solicit donations for a heart-health related charity or a local patient. Purchase additional shirts to be sold via retail or given as a gift-with-purchase to help raise awareness and donate proceeds from t-shirt sales to your chosen heart-related charity.

Wear Red Day is the perfect day to hold a customer workshop on heart health in partnership with a local physician, cardiac specialist, nutritionist or fitness expert.

Partner with a local physician or another qualified health professional to hold a blood pressure education or screening. Or hold a blood pressure check event at a local wine shop, including education on the health benefits of red wine and chocolate. If you prefer not to tout the benefits of wine, choose a non-alcoholic juice or health drink that also provides anti-oxidants, stimulates release of endorphins, boosts energy or provides other benefits.

Retail custom-designed wares including t-shirts, mugs, ribbons, wristbands, water bottles or other items to raise awareness of heart-health or related charitable causes. Partner with local related service providers (counselors, nutrition experts, fitness experts, physicians, or other specialists) for cooperative or cross marketing.

Raise awareness within the community by sending press releases to local media, your website, newsletters, and at your point of sale highlighting your donations and efforts to support local or national heart health-related causes.

February 7 – Dump Your Significant Jerk Day

The fact is, sometimes it really is time to move on! With Valentine's Day just a week away, it might seem counter-intuitive to focus on break-ups, but sometimes break-ups are better than remaining in relationships that are unhealthy, dishonest or where both parties are not headed in the same direction.

It's not always just about people, sometimes there are other 'jerks' in our lives we need to dump. Partner with a local counselor, nutritionist or fitness expert and hold a workshop for customers who need to get healthy in any area of their life (not limited only to romance). For instance, customers may need encouragement and education to dump extra weight, poor self esteem, bad habits or other unhealthy aspects of their lives. From unhealthy relationships to nail biting, smoking, compulsions or disorders, you can't change what you don't acknowledge!

Have some fun with the theme and retail relevant wares sporting sentiments about break ups or ex'es. Design and market your own dump-themed products or a line of greeting cards to help break the news to a significant jerk. Hold a best break up story contest and treat the winner to a salon makeover and a night out destination. Create "Party of One" offers for customers or hold a singles, solo-dining or other non-date event. Promote products and services as "Valentine to myself" gift ideas.

Take things more seriously and partner with a local counselor to hold a workshop on healthy relationships, or even a how-to when it comes to breaking up. Compile a list of recommended reading and local resources to post on your website, Facebook page, blog and e-mail newsletter.

Or go big: "Dump Your Significant Jerk Week" is the perfect week to hold an "Insignificant Other" mixer. If this event proves popular, plan to repeat the event during June's wedding season as a "Best-Person–I-Never-Married" event. Whatever you choose to call it, this type of event will take some work, marketing partners, and some creativity to execute:

Partner with a local restaurant, wine shop or bar to host an "Insignificant Other" or "Best-Person-I-Never-Dated" mixer. Just what it sounds like, this is a chance for attendees to bring a non-date but great guy or girl out to a mixer at a local destination so they can both meet other great singles in the area. Collect contact information from all attendees with an at-the-door entry form which will also serve as an entry form in a drawing for a door prize package to be awarded at the end of the evening.

Before the mixer, collect entries from invitees who RSVP and hold a drawing for one or more lucky guy and gal to receive a free pre-mixer makeover, shopping spree for a cocktail dress or formal wear rental, manicure or pedicure, limousine service for the evening, food and drink vouchers and/or other relevant gifts from your business and those of your marketing partners. Since one of your primary goals for any event is to gather more contacts among both clients and prospects for permission-based marketing, make sure that you have a plan at each step to capture contact information and extend bounce-back offers after the event.

Working with your event marketing partners, create promotional offers for pre-event products or services (like pre-event makeovers, new clothing or shoes, transportation, etc.) Include appropriate product or service demonstrations and sampling and make branded items (like shot glasses, event t-shirts, tumblers or mugs, etc.) or professional products available for sale or part of attendees' goodie bags.

After the event, send a bounce-back offer via mail or e-mail to all participants and extend a save-the-date or an invitation to your next event.

February Week 2

February Week 2 – Flirting Week

Create a flirtatious offer for customers, encourage them to 'flirt 'with a new product or service or go one further and stock brandware with flirtatious sentiments and designs on t-shirts, mugs, notebooks, memo cubes, totes, chocolates, etc. for retail sale. Suggest specific items people could purchase to give as a gift in order to flirt with a special someone.

Some people find the prospect of flirting scary or awkward. Partner with a local counselor, relationship or dating expert to hold a workshop on safe, effective and appropriate flirting, how to attract and choose the right people for relationships, characteristics of healthy relationships, etc. Post flirting tips on your Facebook page, blog and e-mail newsletter. Solicit customer flirting stories and ideas on Facebook.

February Week 2 – Gelatin Week

As the Jello® Brand Gelatin ad slogan said, "There's always room for Jello!" People have created lots of tasty, sweet treats using gelatin. Hold a contest or allow customers to share their yummiest recipes. Hold a trivia contest or gelatin eating contest. If you're really brave and regulations allow, hold a gelatin wrestling match in partnership with a local bar or restaurant.

Gelatin is inexpensive! Gift-with-purchase or give away samples of gelatin or boxes to make at home that are tagged with a recipe, your business card and/or a special bounce-back offer. Solicit favorite recipes or hold a gelatin cooking contest.

Gelatin shots are yummy, and they don't necessarily have to be alcoholic. Kids love a good virgin berry blue gelatin shot as much as grownups love the spiked ones. Extend a free gift-with-purchase gelatin shot all week, reduced pricing on gelatin shots for groups or as an add-on, or partner with a local bar and give clients a voucher good for a gelatin shot at the bar.

February 8 – Man Day

Even though women still do most household purchasing, marketing to male customers should not be ignored. If your business has a significant male customer base, this is a day to celebrate and appreciate "the man." If women comprise the largest part of your client base, this is a day to reach out for more male clients or to focus efforts on promoting products or services which are primarily intended for men to the women most likely to purchase them on their behalf.

Create a "Man's Wish List" of suggested services and products for women to buy as gifts for them for birthdays, Valentine's Day, anniversaries or other special occasions. Create bundled gift sets of men's products or sell a series of services at a special price (such as 3, 6 or 12 men's haircuts) to be used within a given period of time (to ensure desired frequency of visits).

Partner with a local sports bar or a sports, recreation or entertainment facility to hold men's-only or men-get-in-free events. Since many bars regularly waive the cover for women on 'ladies night,' men will appreciate a role reversal for a change!

Partner with businesses who have primarily male customers like sports practice and activity facilities, martial arts studios, cigar shops, golf courses and clubs, gentlemen's clubs, barbershops, sportsmen's associations, sports bars, etc. for cross or cooperative marketing.

February 9 – Toothache Day

Celebrating Toothache Day can be a good thing if it unites you with local dental practices for cross or cooperative marketing. Provide tips and information about dental health and recommended services to your clients on bag stuffers, waiting room or point of purchase displays, e-mail newsletters and your Facebook page.

Ask your dental marketing partner to provide you with toothbrushes, toothpastes, floss samples or lip balms for gift or gift-with-purchase to your customers. Better yet, purchase these types of items branded to your business for gift or gift-with-purchase for their (and your) customers, for donation to local social service agencies, shelters, youth organizations, large employers, hotels, motels, restaurants, schools, day cares, etc.

February 10 – Umbrella Day

Here in the Pacific Northwest, an umbrella is as much a staple of the wardrobe as sunglasses are, and it's always a close contest to see which get the most use each year. And, for some odd reason, people just *like* umbrellas. Kids like to jump with them and pretend they are parachutes; kids (of all ages) spin them in a variety of "Singin' in the Rain" renditions.

Plus, this is an impulse-buy item that can attract buyers in sunshine as well as rain. Purchase branded umbrellas for retail sale, to gift to VIP clients, as an event attendance incentive, as a gift-with-purchase or a custom-designed premium add on—this is one piece of brandware that will be used while out and about, again and again.

The word 'umbrella' is sometimes used by businesses that offer several different products or services (usually with a discount for bundling) all under one 'umbrella.' Create your own 'umbrella package' of bundled services or products.

Or partner with insurance agents or financial planners to hold seminars for customers, provide them with tips, advice, or financial planning or insurance check lists (or for cross or cooperative marketing). Provide your clients with a free professional consultation as an add-on or gift-with-purchase.

If you hold a financial planning or insurance event, give away branded umbrellas as a memento or as part of a goodie bag. Your marketing partners may be willing to share the cost for a co-branded umbrella or to contribute their own branded items as gifts for your customers.

February 11 – Visit a Shut-In Day

On Visit a Shut-In Day, take time to reach out to those in your community are home-bound and who may be lonely. Identify people who need help in your community by contacting local social service, religious, senior, hospice or other agencies. In addition to taking time to visit someone who is not able to get out on their own, consider 'adopting' an individual for a month or a year, raising funds or soliciting donations from customers or your marketing partners. Use press releases to publicize local needs and your efforts keeping individual beneficiaries anonymous to preserve privacy and dignity.

Working with your marketing partners, create gift baskets which can be donated to local shut-ins or distributed via social service, religious, senior services, hospice or other organizations. Publicize efforts and raise awareness with press releases to media and linked to your Facebook page, blog and e-mail newsletter.

February 12 – Satisfied Single Day

With Valentine's Day only two days away, singles in your clientele might be needing some love. Hold a Satisfied Single event in cooperation with a restaurant, bar, catering or other marketing partners. Partner with a counselor to hold a workshop about what it means to be "satisfied single;" or how to change that fact if one is actually a *dis*-satisfied single.

If you serve food or beverages, create a "Satisfied Single" lunch or dinner offer—either in relation to dining alone or in relation to menu items that can satisfy hunger all on their own (e.g., a satisfying single item). Create a drink or menu item that can be added on for a single dollar with qualifying order.

Create promotions for "Singly Satisfying" items or services in your business, and communicate their benefits (i.e., how they satisfy the customer). Create $1 ("singles") promotions or add-on offers. For instance, a salon might offer clients a deep conditioning "satisfying" treatment at the shampoo bowl for a "Single" dollar—a treatment that satisfies the needs of the hair as well as the wallet. Designate items that can be purchased for a single dollar with qualifying purchase such as a branded item, a travel or miniature-sized version of a regular product or service, etc.

February 13 – Blame Someone Else Day

This is a chance to have some fun! Hold a contest soliciting the best 'shifting the blame' examples or stories, such as someone caught with their hand in the proverbial cookie jar who successfully diverts their consequences onto someone else (like, 'My mom shouldn't have made these cookies so darn good, it's her fault!') Hold a drawing or choose the cleverest entrants as winners. Use the contest to collect contact information and add names to your e-mail marketing database, and to build engagement with more followers on Facebook. Follow up by ensuring that all entrants receive a special offer redeemable at your business.

In partnership with a counselor or life coach, hold a workshop for customers (or local business owners and employees) on accountability in the workplace and how 'owning' our actions and decisions helps us become more successful and more in control of our destiny, regardless of the occasional mistake or failure.

If you have been shifting the blame in any area of your life, take ownership of your own actions and decisions. If you have been blaming slow business on the economy, your advertising, your staff or simply procrastinating on marketing tasks, make today the day that you stop shifting the blame and choose to get in motion.

February 14 – Valentines Day

If you didn't spend the last 6 weeks promoting for Valentine's Day—you're crazy! Treat Valentine's Day as though it were nearly as important as Christmas, because it can be a great time for you to attract new clients, sell a significant amount in gift sales and form deeper bonds with customers. There is no other holiday like it—a holiday of pure indulgence, love, fantasy and romance, a compelling reason to consume chocolate, drink wine and go out for dinner and entertainment.

No matter what your business, you can build Valentine's Day offers. Even a car parts store can run a creative Valentine's Day offer. As a woman, I personify the stereotype of someone who knows how to put the gas in the car but is otherwise completely ignorant about it's maintenance; if I had a flat tire, I could not use the jack properly, let alone change it. But I want to know these things.

I would welcome a Valentine from my significant other or my dad that included a workshop or classes in basic car maintenance. If my car were in need of service, I would welcome a Valentine's Gift that included the price of a needed repair or service; or even a series of pre-paid oil changes. Taking the anxiety and fear out of something as important as this would be a very loving gift! Heck—with gas prices high and on the rise, a gas card would make a great Valentine's Day gift from parent to child as well.

Partner with other businesses to create multi-stop Valentine's Day date packages beginning and ending with limo service, and preceded by a trip to the formal rental store, clothing boutique and/or the salon for preparation. Follow preparation with a cocktail hour, dinner, and a destination activity such as a movie, club, sporting event, or play. Your packages can be as creative as you and your marketing partners can make it; plus, it's probably that one person in nearly every couple involved will represent a new client for each participating business.

Create your own bundled Valentine's Day packages by purchasing discounted gift cards for local restaurants at sites like www.restaurant.com (where you can often purchase restaurant gift certificates at 50% or even 75% off). Create proposal/engagement date packages by partnering with local limo, formal rental, floral, jewelry and other similar partners. Suggest or solicit creative proposal ideas on your Facebook page, blog and e-mail newsletter.

Love yourself, first, whether you celebrate Valentine's Day as a single or a couple! Create special "Love Yourself" promotions around pampering services and retail products, or gift free branded chocolates or aromatherapy products with retail purchases to clients.

Expand impulse buy or regular retail in order to create a true gift center. Items that you can purchase in counter displays such as nail polish, lip glosses, jewelry, clutch bags, scented candles, etc. would make great additions to your retail for Valentine's Day and year-round for clients to purchase as gifts. Purchase boutique-quality, unique gift tags, greeting cards and gift bags. Make it easy for customers to envision your regular products and gift certificates as "gifts" by pre-packaging and displaying them as ready-to-go gift items.

Hold a contest in February and have a drawing to award one aromatherapy gift basket and/or gift card to a winner. Utilize entries to help build your e-mail marketing contact database, and extend a special offer in March to all participants.

February 14 – Organ Donor Day

Support organ donor registration efforts and remind customers to go online and register with the national organ donor registry. Visit www.organdonor.org, the US Department of Health and Human Services' organ donor registry and site for materials and resources to share with customers, campaign support materials you can use for your drive, education and links to transplant centers. Provide customers with stories of local recipients who have benefitted from this program. Post information about the need in your community for organ donation, blood drives, bone marrow donation, and a link to the national registry website on your Facebook page, blog, bag stuffers and e-mail newsletter. Raise awareness by writing press releases for your website, newsletters and local media.

February Week 3

February Week 3 – Friendship Week

This is the week you've been waiting for! Friendship week is the perfect week to bring in new customers and grow sales with "Bring a Friend" offers. Here are a few ideas:

- Bring a (new client) friend and receive a (free gift here)
- Buy an entrée (or a drink) and your friend eats (or drinks) for free
- Book services together and your friend (or both parties) receive 25%, 50% or a specific dollar amount off regular cost
- Receive two gift cards for the price of one (one for themselves and one to give to a friend); or buy a product, receive one free to give to a friend, etc.
- Purchase an event ticket, receive a ticket for a friend for free
- Purchase a location-based marketing offer with deep discounts for couples or new customer friend duos
- Hold an open house with a fashion show (or another draw) featuring free consultations, samples, door prizes and product demonstrations

February 15 – Call In Single Day

Hold an after hours or day-long Call In Single event for customers; not just to encourage truancy, but to help people recover from Valentine's Day. For the last month or more, all anyone has heard about is Valentine's Day, love and romance—give us a break! Establish a romance-free zone and celebrate the benefits of being single; offer up promotions to people who saved all that money by not buying Valentine's Day presents!

In a February 15th Call In Single promotion, give people who (literally) call in exclusive rewards like "love yourself first" pampering retail products or free branded gift chocolates (in partnership with a local chocolatier) redeemable at their next visit. Or modernize the observance and hold Text-In, Instant Message or Facebook Post offers.

Hold a February 15th Call In Single happy hour for the 'uncoupled' among your clientele, or hold a Call In Single party in partnership with a local bar or restaurant. Have a door prize drawing to collect contact information and reward the winners with free products, services or gift cards. Offer drinks or appetizers for "Singles" ($1 add-on, special, etc.) Extend a bounce-back offer to all attendees after the event.

Working with a professional counselor or life coach, hold a workshop for singles on how to successfully navigate the dating scene to achieve relationship goals, how to develop healthy, enduring relationships, or hold a workshop on flirting, body language and attraction.

February 16 – Do a Grouch a Favor Day

When I was in college, I worked as a cashier at a dry cleaning business. One regular customer (who was obviously a bachelor) drove through to drop off and pick up shirts every week. I'm outgoing, friendly and upbeat, and without exception, treated him to a free dose of my sunshine-ey personality every time he rolled through. He, on the other hand, without fail came and went without so much as making eye contact or saying more than two words to me. I always assumed he was a big grump, until one day at the end of the summer. On that day, he rolled in as silently as ever, traded dirty shirts for clean, paid his bill, and then just before he drove away, leaned out of his car door and gave me a bouquet of red roses. All he said was, "Thank you," and drove away. That moment has always stuck with me as a reminder that you don't always know what is behind someone's "grouch" and you don't always know when you change their world for the better. A word of encouragement, a good attitude, a consistent atmosphere of welcome—since you can't always know what your customer needs, you need to make these things happen, every time.

On *Do a Grouch a Favor Day*, take a step back to examine the customer experience at every touchpoint. Make sure each of your employees recognizes their ability to impact every customer who walks through the door, visits the website, subscribes to blog feeds, reads your Facebook posts, calls your customer service line or meets with a representative in the field. Ask a trusted friend to visit your business as a 'secret shopper' in order to obtain feedback about various aspects or departments of your business.

Implement a feedback system or conduct a customer survey to obtain specific feedback about what is great about your business, what they would never want to see changed and what could be better. Obtaining feedback before implementing change should always be part of your process; it can help you avoid implementing costly changes that are not necessary or that would change aspects of your business your clients want left alone, and it can help identify things that really do need to change, that you may not be aware of.

You can also approach this day more literally. If you catch an employee going the extra mile in spite of a grouchy customer, vendor or co-worker, give them a spot reward or recognition. Ask employees to share stories about "grouchy" customers and what they did to try to improve the situation.

February 17 – PTA Day

Contact local schools to reach out to PTA officials. (Parent-Teacher Association, sometimes also referred to as PTSA or Parent-Teacher-Student Association) Your local PTA is full of community influencers. They are practically politicians in that many even run for the offices they hold. They conduct community events and campaigns, they represent the interests of others, and they are responsible to make and influence decisions that impact the people in their constituency. PTA members have the ability to influence teachers, administration and district employees as well as the families of students. Extend special offers to leaders and parents of local PTAs. Create a special offer for the families of your children's schools, local private and public schools, trade schools, community colleges and other educational organizations.

Contact local PTAs and offer to host or sponsor meetings, provide refreshments or extend a free sample, gift or special offer to parents, teachers, school staff and PTA members. Donate money, gift cards or products to PTA fundraisers. Make yourself available to assist with school events; volunteer to work behind the scenes to help set up for or take down after events, auctions, concerts, graduation, etc.

February 18 – Battery Day

With the explosion of personal computing, video, gaming, music and similar devices over the last few decades, few U.S. homes exist without at least one drawer full of batteries in a variety of types that range in cost from inexpensive to pricey. When a piece of equipment is down and you need a battery, you want that battery right now. If you sell toys or equipment that require batteries, make them a free gift-with-purchase (or gift an extra set of batteries with purchase) on *Battery Day*.

The battery provides the energy necessary to power up, get in motion, start the engine, etc. As human beings, we all need to recharge our own inner batteries, and this can be done in a variety of ways. Partner with a salon, spa or massage therapist to offer clients or even employees a massage, makeover or another renewing service. Extend a food or drink offer designed to refuel the body. Give your most valuable customers a Starbucks or coffee card—the fuel that helps many of us start the day! Partner with a local coffee shop to extend special pricing or free add-ons to your customers. Create a special offer redeemable in your business for the coffee shop to extend to their patrons.

Partner with a counselor, nutritionist, physician, fitness trainer or other professional to hold a seminar for customers on how to stay recharged and maximize energy physically, mentally or emotionally. Provide tips about how to recharge one's inner 'batteries' from these professionals on bag stuffers, your website, Facebook page, blog, e-mail newsletters or point of sale displays. Tell customers about the products or services that you sell that help promote, preserve or maximize energy.

No group is as influential at word-of-mouth marketing than moms; research shows they share referrals and recommendations several times every day—more than 100 times each week! Reach out to MOPS (Mothers of Pre-Schoolers) and other mom-filled groups in churches, libraries, YMCAs, and other organizations with special offers, samples, branded tchotchkes, gift cards, etc. Sponsor or host meetings, support fundraisers or even contribute to child care needs while moms participate in activities that help them recharge their own batteries.

February 19 – Chocolate Mint Day

Thank customers for frequenting your business with complimentary chocolate mints (preferably in a gift box or wrapper branded to your business). Work with a local chocolatier to make chocolate mint items available for retail sale or give them away as a gift-with-purchase. Take or send branded chocolate mint items to local businesses, school or district offices, local large employers for placement in break and lunchrooms, city offices, police or fire stations, hospitals, health care or senior centers — to any organization in your community whose employees or patrons represent some portion of your target market. Treat employees to chocolate mint ice cream as a morale booster.

Solicit customer recipes or hold a chocolate mint cooking contest, tasting or happy hour. Challenge local bartenders to create chocolate mint cocktails or local chefs to a chocolate mint dessert contest. Share recipes on your Facebook page, blog and e-mail newsletter or add recipes to a collection you will have printed for retail sale or use as marketing collateral or a gift-with-purchase.

Post trivia or history about chocolate mints on your Facebook page, blog and email newsletter. Promote your chocolate mint products. Create a chocolate mint offer that pairs one of your products with one of your services or pairs two products or services together — after all, isn't it really just about a delicious pairing? Create an offer that pairs one of your products or services that of one of your marketing partners.

February 20 – Love Your Pet Day

Create cross and cooperative marketing partnerships with pet service and product providers — groomers, trainers, pet stores, pet food suppliers, pet boarding, veterinarians and emergency services, etc. Exchange business cards, catalogs, menus or brochures for placement in lobby, waiting room or break room areas. Create cooperative marketing offers for both sets of clients or hold a joint, pet-friendly event, training workshop, day in the park, etc.

Partner with a mobile groomer to provide services at your location. Let your clients know when they will be there (or take appointments) so that customers maximize their time and resources. For instance, a restaurant, salon or spa, or another appointment-oriented business can let their pet-owning customers know that a mobile groomer or trainer will be on hand and set up appointments for both. The mobile groomer would let their regular clients know that they will be at your business on a given date/time and encourage their clients to book appointments, make reservations or shop at your business at the same time.

Partner with a local veterinary office, pet store or boutique and create a "Love Your Pet" display combining your pet-oriented products with theirs. Create a directory of local pet-related businesses and connect customers with local resources on your Facebook page, blog, bag stuffers and e-mail newsletter. Purchase branded, fun, or blinged-out pet supplies for retail sale, gift-with-purchase or gifts for clients with pets.

February 21 – Single Tasking Day

I'm not that old—just over 40. Nevertheless, my husband and I already talk about 'the old days' when we were young—like about how weather permitting or not, we spent a lot of waking hours outdoors in contrast to kids today. We didn't have video games, cell phones, texting, Facebook, or IMing; in fact, we only had 4 TV channels, which we could only change by actually getting up, walking across the room and turning a dial—we *were* our dad's 'remote controls!' Heck, VCRs didn't even come on the scene until we were in our early teens. How *did* we ever pass the time?!

Today, people are bombarded 24x7 with stimuli. Hundreds of TV, movie, sports and music channels, DVDs, personal electronic devices, video games; we never escape our phones and since texting apparently isn't enough, the computer is also a medium for chatting, messaging, posting, blogging gaming and so on. It's almost hard for us to single task. Personally, it makes me feel nervous to sit still sometimes—I feel guilty, like I should be doing something with every moment of the day.

Today is *Single Tasking Day*, take a moment to just be, to breathe deeply, to focus completely on your significant other, your child, your pet—and of course your customers—and just listen. Take time to fully absorb and experience each moment, rather than quickly scanning a multitude of media or just listening for your name above the din.

On *Single Tasking Day*, think about ways to create moments for your customers where they get to just be, just breathe—where they can escape from constant stimulation and get away from their phones, personal electronics and computers. It might feel unfamiliar to them at first, but it's a moment customers will come back for!

February Week 4

February Week 4 – Crossword Puzzle Week

Design a crossword puzzle related to your business using the names of your products, services, divisions, locations—those things you most want your customers to remember—and use it to hold a customer contest. Enter all those who return puzzles (fully completed or not) into a special drawing for a prize at the end of the contest (or end of the day, week, month, etc.) and use the forms to help build your contact database. Award one winner with a grand prize and reward as many runners up as possible with branded gifts, gift cards, product or service samples, etc. Extend a bounce-back offer to all entrants.

Play a daily crossword puzzle clue game with followers using Facebook or Twitter posts to list clues. Reward customers who visit your business and provide you with that day's answer or who text you, retweet your posts on twitter or answer questions correctly online.

Create a Crossword Puzzle to use for employee training specific to product or service knowledge, customer service principles, human resource policies, store procedures, etc. Reward employees who return completed puzzles with a branded appreciation gift, lunch out, an extra paid hour off, a gift card, etc.

You don't have to be brilliant to build your own crossword puzzle! Type the phrase "free crossword puzzle generator" into your internet search engine for links to crossword puzzle applications (or other puzzle types such as word searches, jumbles, etc.). With the disclaimer that internet sites sometimes change or are deleted, try: http://www.thepuzzlemaker.net/crossword.php.

Print copies of crossword puzzles in order to entertain people in the waiting area. Print children's puzzles for kids to complete while their parents shop, dine, etc. Purchase crossword puzzle books to add to retail or to use as a gift-with-purchase, contest prize, employee gift, etc.

February Week 4 – Eating Disorders Awareness Week

Eating disorders have become an increasingly serious health problem in our society. Young, impressionable girls seem to be especially impacted by mass media in the form of ultra-skinny models and starlets. Add computer enhancements and PhotoShopped touch-ups to the mix, and the net results are distorted images no one can live up to—even the original subjects!

Help combat unhealthy eating habits and unrealistic body type idolization by raising awareness about this social phenomenon with "Did you know…?" style posts, listing eating disorder warning signs and local resources on your Facebook page, blog, bag stuffers and e-mail newsletter.

Tout the realistic body image or healthy diet and nutrition benefits your products or services provide on your website, e-mail newsletter, Facebook page and blog. Create a display with products that promote health and well-being featuring happy healthy people, or showing before and after pictures to demonstrate how many celebrities and models are not as perfect as they seem.

Partner with a counselor, nutritionist or eating disorder treatment facility to hold a workshop on eating disorders, healthy eating and local eating disorder treatment options. Hold a workshop for tweens and teens on healthy self Image and realistic body weights and types. Celebrate with visual imagery that features "real" women and men in your community as well as celebrities who are highly accomplished, have received extraordinary honors, have contributed to society, have launched their own businesses, etc. (without resorting to unhealthy body types or eating disorders).

Partner with a nutritionist, gym or physical trainer to hold a workout and healthy eating seminar or boot camp. Sponsor or host on-going classes for employees and/or customers. Create a special class geared for tween and teen girls to focus special attention on this subject during their most vulnerable years.

February Week 4 – National Pancake Week

In partnership with a local diner, restaurant or caterer, hold a pancake breakfast event and donate proceeds to your favorite charity. Work with a marketing partner to provide pancake samples to your customers or give away gift cards with purchase.

Hold a pancake-eating contest, a pancake tasting or cook-off. Hold a pancake or breakfast foods trivia contest for customers. Reward winner/s with a gourmet pancake mix, mixing bowl, spatula, measuring cups, measuring spoons, etc. and a gift card redeemable at your business.

Partner with a party planner and caterer to hold a class and teach customers all about making great pancakes, breakfasts and brunches for family and friends, bridal showers, etc. Hold a kids cooking class. Solicit and share customer and employee recipes or post links to celebrity pancake recipes on your Facebook page, blog and e-mail newsletter. Create a digital cookbook inclusive of recipes you collect throughout the year. And at the end of the year, design a printed copy for customer gift, gift-with-purchase or retail sale which also features your other kitchen must-haves such as timers, spatulas, serving ware, etc. and/or other products or services.

February 22 – Walking the Dog Day

Many businesses spend a great deal of money and time doing market research and surveying customers and prospects in order to determine which shared values, priorities and consumer behaviors are common to one or more of their target markets. If you could know, without even spending so much as a dime of your money or an hour of your time, that half of all of your customers and half of all of your prospective customers share one trait, wouldn't you want to know what it is?

It's statistically probable that over half of your customers—and your prospective customers—are pet owners. According to APPA (the American Pet Products Association), in 2008, 62% of all US households owned at least one pet (up from 56% in 1988). That equates to nearly 80 million homes. And according to the same study, more than 46% of US households own at least one dog, and at least half of these consider their dogs to be 'members of the family.' According to dogatar.com, pet owners spend about 5 billion dollars on holiday gifts for their pets. 5 Billion Dollars. On holiday gifts—presents—for pets! 36% of dog owners give their pet a present on its birthday and nearly 20% of pet owners reported making a decision about purchasing a house or car (at least partially) based on pet needs.

And check out some of the health benefits enjoyed by pet owners!

- People with hypertension who adopted a cat or dog had lower blood pressure readings in stressful situations than did those who did not own a pet. (Dr. Karen Allen, State University of New York at Buffalo study)

- Walking with a pet helps sooth nerves and offers instant relaxation. The impact of a stressful situation is lesser on pet owners, especially males, than on those who do not own a pet. (Josephine M. Wills, Waltham Centre for Pet Nutrition, United Kingdom)

- Because pets provide people with faithful companionship, they may also provide owners with greater psychological stability, thus a measure of protection from heart disease. (National Institute of Health Technology Assessment Workshop: Health Benefits of Pets)

- People with pets make fewer doctor visits, especially for non-serious medical conditions. (National Institute of Health Technology Assessment Workshop: Health Benefits of Pets)

- Pets help fight depression and loneliness, promoting an interest in life. When seniors face adversity or trauma, affection from pets takes on great meaning. Their bonding behavior can foster a sense of security. (Between Pets and People: The Importance of Animal Companionship)

What does all of this mean to you?

It means that more than 50% of your customer base, and of your prospective customer target market, likely owns at least one pet. It means that at least 25% of your customers and 25% of your prospects actually use a portion of their disposable income to buy presents for their pets during the holidays and for birthdays.

If you're not catering to the pet owners in your customer base in some way, you are missing out on a huge opportunity! Not only is money being spent elsewhere that might otherwise be spent at your business, but you are also missing out on the opportunity to forge a deeper emotional connection with your customers by providing them with resources for this important member of their 'family.' They love their pets; wouldn't they also love businesses who share their appreciation for these family members by bringing not only pet-love but other real, tangible benefits to their lives?

Celebrate Walking the Dog Day by sponsoring and rewarding pet adoptions through your local humane society or shelter. Sponsor a "Walking the Dog Day" dog walk for charity in your local city park or an city streets to raise funds and increase awareness of the needs of local animal shelters, rescue animal organizations, emergency animal services, etc.

Create cross marketing partnerships with businesses that cater to pet owning households in your community like veterinary offices, pet groomers, mobile groomers, breeders, boarding facilities, pet care product sellers, dog walkers, pet boutiques and pet stores. Work together to hold a "pet fair" for local pet owners in a pet-friendly location or facility.

Encourage pet owners to bring a bag or can of pet food to be donated to a local shelter in lieu of a cover charge for an event. At the event, retail pet-themed wares like t-shirts, tank tops, mugs, coffee cups, books, etc. and/or pet retail items such as boutique-quality collars, leashes, pet travel accessories, pet beds. Give branded pet items away as contest or drawing prizes. Consider adding these types of items as well as pet shampoos, gourmet foods or treats to your regular retail.

Donate a percentage of February sales or the proceeds of February sales of specific products or services to your local animal shelter or humane society.

February 23 – Personal Chefs Day

Partner with caterers, restaurants, dinner preparation businesses and gourmet food sellers for cooperative or cross marketing. Hold a contest for customers and partner with a local restaurant or caterer to reward winner/s with a 'personal chef' award package, gourmet lunches or dinners.

Partner with a chef, caterer or party planner to hold a cooking class for customers. Partner with an independent kitchenware store or seller for a joint event. Or go big! Partner with other businesses and hold your own local 'top chef' contest open to anyone or as a competition for local chefs.

Create a "personal chef tour" dining club where participants visit a different local participating restaurant once a month (or once a week) for tastings, special menu options or for a special price. Partner with a transportation company to provide group transportation so that your dining club can visit a prestigious restaurant further away or to hold a progressive dinner or wine tasting tour with participating restaurants.

Working with local restaurants, compile a recommended dining-out directory to be printed on a brochure, 'place mat,' fridge magnet or another publication to give away as bag stuffers and included on your website and in e-mail newsletter, blog and Facebook posts. Ask local chefs to contribute easy-to-make, delicious recipes to the publication (to increase its value and help ensure it will be kept) for appetizers, cocktails, side dishes, salads, soups, entrees and desserts. Republish the directory seasonally with new recipes. Marketing partners featured in the publication should help share in its cost and assist in distribution at their businesses and online.

Post chef's tips and tricks on Facebook, your blog, e-mail or print newsletters. Solicit recipes to share online. Ask customers what types of dishes they want recipes for, then ask local chefs and caterers to provide those recipes.

Add boutique-quality or specialty recipe books, aprons, cookware, utensils, tableware, table runners, tablecloths and napkins, napkin rings, salt and pepper shakers, etc. to impulse buys or regular retail. Purchase branded related items to give away as a gift-with-purchase or contest prize.

February 24 – Tortilla Chip Day

Sample tortilla chips to customers or set up a 'try me' station in your store or waiting room; cross market with a local gourmet food store or restaurant to provide samples for customers.

Hold a tortilla chip dip or salsa tasting event or recipe contest. Hold a contest and reward the winner with chips and dip or salsa as well as a serving dish and/or related tableware.

Ask customers to share dip and salsa recipes and post them on Facebook page, blog and e-mail newsletter. If you are soliciting recipes for various observances throughout the year, input them into the computer so that at the end of the year, you can create your own recipe book to have printed for sale, as a gift for your most valued customers, or as a gift-with-purchase or purchase incentive for an upcoming special event or holiday.

Purchase branded bags of tortilla chips to sell on an on-going basis along with chip and dip serving pieces and accessories. Purchase dried dip mixes to add to your retail or impulse buys or to be given away to customers as bag stuffers or a gift-with-purchase.

February 25 – Inconvenience Yourself Day

Go beyond the call of duty with employees or customers in some way; free add-ons, special gifts with purchase (preferably something branded to your business), man the entrance or exit doors of your business for the day – do something! Work as a team with employees (or even with customers who want to help) and volunteer to help complete projects for local seniors, a local shelter or food bank, help to clean up outside of your business park or a city park, etc.

Inconvenience yourself. Write thank-you notes to your most valuable customers. Write notes of appreciation to your employees. Do something unexpected for your employees. Stand in for them to extend their lunch break, to come in late or leave early. Wash their cars. Buy lunch. Do something!

Call or e-mail your most valuable customers personally to conduct one-on-one satisfaction surveys and to ask how you can better serve their needs. Feeling brave? Do the same for your employees! Follow up by posting survey results and telling people what actions you have or will take to address concerns. Post customer survey results online and tell customers about changes you make based on their feedback.

February 26 – Tell a Fairy Tale Day

Hold a children's Fairy Tale writing or Fairy Tale story telling contest (or one that is open to anyone).

Use your Facebook or Blog page to create a running Fairy Tale where each new post becomes the next line in the story. Or begin telling a Fairy Tale ("Once upon a time…") asking customers to suggest the next piece of the story or even to vote on options for the next piece in the story. Create your own fill-in-the-blank Fairy Tale in 'mad libs' style and ask customers to give you nouns, verbs and adjectives to insert in order to create a crazy version of a familiar fairy tale.

Tell your Tale—the story of your business—in your e-mail and direct mail marketing, in press releases and in posts on your Facebook page and blog. Add the story of your business to your website or update what is already posted. Take time to remember just how far you have come, to ask yourself what has changed, and to determine whether you are still being true to the vision you set out to achieve.

Hold a Fairy Tale workshop for employees and revisit the mission, vision, shared values and corporate messages of your business. Be sure your employees know the story of your business and that they know specifically how their role helps to fulfill the mission of your organization. Be sure that every employee understands how 'what they do' contributes to the vision of what your business should become.

February 27 – Polar Bear Day

Purchase branded polar bear toys or stuffed animals to give away as a gift to customers with kids, a gift-with-purchase or contest prize or to add to impulse buys or regular retail.

Send branded polar bears to a local day care as a gift for kids, or to a local dentist or doctor's office as a gift for young patients. Send polar bears to your local children's hospital or children's cancer treatment center to cheer up patients.

Hold a polar bear trivia contest or a polar bear drawing or art contest for kids and put together a prize basket with a toy polar bear, hat, gloves, scarf, hand warmers, hot beverage travel mug, hot chocolate fixings, etc.

Polar Bear Clubs are best known for having members who are willing to wade, dive or jump into freezing cold water during what may be the height of winter. Hold a Polar Bear publicity stunt for your employees or customers to participate in! If immersion into a freezing body of water isn't for you, think of your own variation on the theme.

February 28 – National Tooth Fairy Day

Partner with local dentists and orthodontists for cross or cooperative marketing. Ask dental practices to provide you with toothbrushes, toothpaste or floss/flossers for distribution to your customers as part of a cross or cooperative marketing effort. Provide oral health tips, advice such as when to seek treatment or when children should be seen, and other information in posts on your Facebook page, blog and e-mail newsletter. In partnership with a dental practice, hold a joint contest or drawing and reward the winner/s with electric tooth brushes.

Purchase branded toothbrushes, floss flossers to distribute as bag stuffers or a gift-with-purchase. Give away branded toothbrushes to local hotels, motels, day cares, senior living centers or other organizations whose employees or patrons represent some part of your target market.

Hire a Tooth Fairy to visit to your business to entertain children who are there with parents or for appointments and give them branded toothbrush or toy. Send a Tooth Fairy to local restaurants, ice cream shops, theaters, recreation centers, malls or other places where parents-with-children congregate to distribute branded prizes and gifts along with a bounce-back offer for your business.

Work with a local children's hospital or treatment center to sponsor an event and send a Tooth Fairy to visit their patients along with special prizes and gifts. Alternate destinations where you might send a Tooth Fairy might include local day cares, kindergarten classes, youth centers, etc.

Invite staff who are willing to do so to dress up as Fairies for the day and treat your customers to some fun, award random prizes, provide refreshments, feature kids activities, hold drawings and extend special offers.

march

365 Days of Marketing

March Month-Long Observances
Employee Spirit Month

Design a team-oriented image and/or slogan to add to branded jackets, shirts, t-shirts, tank tops, lanyards, name tags, aprons or other clothing suitable for employees to wear at your place of business. Request (or require) that brandwear be worn on Fridays, at special events or every day.

Make brandwear available for sale to customers. Give customers a reward or reward points if you find them wearing your brandwear out in public, to their appointments, while shopping in your store, etc. Reward customers who send you pictures of themselves wearing your brand gear in public. Create an online album or a bulletin board with pictures of people wearing items branded to your business.

Implement a formal channel for employees to suggest improvements, express concerns, request training, etc. Implement a rewards program for employees who suggest ideas (which are implemented) that improve efficiency or productivity or which result in cost savings or increased sales. Set aside time to meet with employees individually or as a group to review the vision and mission of the company as it relates to each employee's role in your business. Conduct an anonymous employee survey to gauge satisfaction or identify areas of concern.

Give recognition awards to employees who demonstrate the level of customer service, enthusiasm for initiatives and respect for co-workers that you want in your business. Write thank-you notes to employees who go beyond the call of duty or exceed expectations. Post customer compliments and raves in employee break or lunch areas and include them in your employee and customer newsletters, blog and Facebook posts. Highlight the outstanding work of employees, their personal achievements, special interests, etc. in Facebook posts, your blog and e-mail newsletter.

Partner with a masseuse to come and give mini-massages to employees, or give them vouchers for salon or spa services. Give gift cards from a local coffee shop, restaurant or bar to employees. Reward outstanding employees with a paid day, morning or afternoon off, or with an extended lunch break. Partner with a caterer or restaurant and bring lunch in for employees one day this month, or once each week.

Or go big! Hold an employee awards ceremony. Invite staff to a happy hour, dinner or cocktail party at a local wine shop, bar or restaurant and hold your awards ceremony there for staff, their significant others and/or families. An annual employee awards show could be a great alternative to holding an annual holiday party. More venues will be available and it will not add additional strain like it would during the busy holiday season.

Music in Our Schools Month

Donate a percentage of sales or proceeds from the sales of specific items to the music department of your local school. Hold a fundraiser and donate the proceeds to the music department of your local school. Raise awareness of the needs of local school's programs.

Work with marketing partners to sponsor a city-wide music talent show or contest. Connect aspiring musicians with local options for recording or performing music.

Let your community know that you support music in schools in posts on your Facebook page, blog and e-mail newsletter. Invite local school choirs, bands and ensembles to provide live music at your business. Contribute money or raise funds to help with competition trips or field trips. Post information about local school music programs needs, human interest stories about students or staff, promote local school music performances and highlight the accomplishments of local school musicians and groups on your Facebook page, blog, bag stuffers, e-mail newsletter and in signage at your business (tent cards, shelf talkers, point of sale displays, etc).

Donate gift cards, pampering products or vouchers redeemable for specific products or services to school music staff. Send private practice music teachers and school music staff information about products you sell or services you provide relative to recital or performance preparation or offer to host or help sponsor post-performance parties where musicians, directors, other cast or crew, etc. can celebrate. Promote your business as a pre or post-performance destination for music performance and arts patrons.

Extend a special offer to school music staff and/or to individuals who participate in community music groups such as city dinner theaters, chorales, orchestras or bands. Extend a special offer to all local music teachers and to the students/families in their studios.

Caffeine Awareness Month

Partner with a local coffee shop for cross or cooperative marketing. Ask a local coffee stand to extend a special offer to your customers on a one-time or an on-going basis. Give away coffee gift cards with purchase.

Post "Did you know…?" style trivia, history or benefits of caffeine. Talk about recommendations relative to the amounts and variety of ways it can be consumed on your Facebook page, blog and e-mail newsletter. Tell customers about products you sell that contain caffeine or which fulfill recommendations.

Establish a resolution support group (virtual or real) to help customers eliminate or reduce caffeine from their diets.

National On Hold Month

Review your incoming and outgoing telephone messages and automatic e-mail responses. Update your on-hold messages and customize automatic e-mail responses (messages confirming a subscription, an order, acknowledging an online form submission, etc.) in order to:

- Talk about new products or services, or provide information about current promotions
- Alert customers to changes in hours of operation, the opening of new locations, new ways they can shop with you (like the creation of an online store or automated ordering system)
- Tell customers about services you provide they may not be aware of (delivery services, online ordering, take out or off site services, etc.) or which they have not previously tried
- Highlight a product, service, customer or employee of the month; introduce new staff members
- Highlight community involvement, charitable endeavors, improvements made to the customer experience, describe your business's "green" practices, etc.
- Promote participation in contests and drawings, solicit subscriptions to your e-mail newsletter, blog, Facebook, Twitter, Linked-In and other social media
- Connect with customers more personally by creating messages that are humorous, sentimental, interesting or which express appreciation, done in a way that is unexpected, causing the listener to really listen—make them *want* to be left on hold!

Hold an employee or customer contest to solicit scrips for entertaining on-hold messages. Take entries in-store or on your Facebook page, blog and website. Reward winners with gift cards redeemable at your business or with products or services. Incorporate some of the best ideas into your on-hold and automated e-mail messaging or create an online collection.

What projects are you currently keeping "on hold" due to lack of employee enthusiasm or support, lack of funding or resources, lack of strategic marketing partners or for some other reason?

If the hold up is you, get out of the way! Do what you need to do to get projects back on track, or to delegate tasks to co-workers who have more ability, motivation or interest than you in said tasks or in a given project as a whole. Hold yourself accountable by inviting other employees, vendors, or marketing partners to work on projects with you in order to avoid procrastinating and to have access to more resources (in order to overcome any other obstacles that come in the way of implementation or success).

Make a list of what would it take to get projects off hold and on track and lay tasks out on a timeline. Delegate assignments and hold everyone (including yourself) accountable. Incorporate milestone incentives or periodic rewards into long-term initiatives. Remind people when tasks are coming due, especially if it has been a while since you discussed the project with them.

If an employee is the cause of a project being "on hold," be sure they know and fully understand how important the project is. Ask them to make the choice to support the goal or to re-evaluate their level of commitment to the business. Tie performance evaluations and salary determinations into objective, measurable factors including support of, enthusiasm for and on-time task performance relative to individual projects and on-going initiatives.

Women's History Month

Extend a special offer, add-on or a gift-with-purchase to women during March, on a given day of the month or to incentivize attendance or purchases at an event.

Use a fishbowl to collect the business cards of working women for a drawing to be held each week (or at the end of the month). Keep a stack of blank entry forms near the bowl to capture the contact information of those who might not have a business card with them, or so that anyone can enter the drawing. As soon as possible, add contact information to your database and send a message to announce contest winner/s and to extend a special offer to all entrants.

Post "Did you know...?" style information on your Facebook page, blog and e-mail newsletter about the accomplishments of female employees, customers, local leaders, influential community members, local women business owners, famous women in history, etc. Hold a women's history trivia contest in-store or online.

Hold a Women's History Month happy hour targeted toward business women, moms, singles or other groups that have demographic commonalities with your target markets or 'ideal client' type. Participate in women's or girls mentoring programs. Create a women's internship or job shadowing program for local high school or college students.

Hold an event to celebrate women of distinction within your company or industry. Or go big! Partner with other businesses in your community to hold a large-scale celebration of local women or a women's history exhibit or workshop, establish a women's college scholarship fund or launch a community-wide women's mentoring and internship program.

Girls in Science and Engineering Month

Target your celebration of Women's History Month toward the future instead of the past. Establish a scholarship (from as little as a $500 scholarship toward college tuition, books or supplies) to be awarded to a female member of your community who is entering college with the intent of pursuing a degree in science, math or engineering, or to an upper level college or graduate student who is actively pursuing a related degree. Create criteria for entry and set up a committee to review applications and select an annual recipient.

Promote the scholarship program on social media profiles, your blog, e-mail newsletter and website, in displays at your business and in those of your marketing partners, in press releases to local newspapers, city magazines, and radio stations, in community news releases sent to city hall, Chamber of Commerce, Rotary, Kiwanis, Optimists/Soroptimists, local business women's associations, etc.

After a scholarship is awarded, take a photograph with the recipient and send a press release to local media, city hall, local civic or women's groups, etc. Or go big! Work with marketing partners to establish a larger scholarship (or to award multiple scholarships) and hold a media event to present awards and celebrate with recipients.

March Week 1

March 1 – National Beer Day

Hold a beer-centric promotion or happy hour and gift a beer or bar gift card when you pre-sell men's product or services or as a gift with the sale of bundled products or series of services.

On March 1st (or all month) offer clients a beer (or root beer) at their appointment or as a gift-with-purchase. Before launching any alcohol-related promotion, check state and local regulations regarding sale or distribution of alcohol.

Use National Beer Day to target current and/or prospective male customers with a special offer. Reach more prospects by partnering with businesses whose primary client base is men or that have a significant male customer base (like sports and recreation facilities, fitness centers, barbershops, cigar stores, sportsmen's associations, golf or men's clubs, etc.) for cross or cooperative marketing.

Design and purchase a branded coaster featuring an offer from your business to be placed on the counters, tables or used at the bar of local bars, restaurants, coffee shops, etc. Use branded coasters at your own hospitality stations, as bag stuffers or even in lieu of traditional business cards.

Extend a beer happy hour offer to employees and/or customers of local businesses or those of your marketing partners. During happy hours, feature demonstrations, sampling, consultations or mini-services in a social setting.

March 2 – Old Stuff Day

One person's "old stuff" can become someone else's new stuff! Hold a swap event where clients can exchange books, jewelry, shoes, jeans or another type of item and enjoy mini-services, demonstrations, consultations and sampling. Charge a cover fee to be donated to a local shelter or another charitable organization. Or go big! Work with businesses located near yours to hold a large scale swap event or overstock sale.

Give customers a branded tchotchke, small gift card, free add-on or discount when they provide a receipt indicating recent donation to a local thrift store, a shelter, your favorite charity or another non-profit organization.

Solicit customer photos and stores about their collections and memorabilia. Post nostalgia related to your city, industry or business on your Facebook page, blog and e-mail newsletter, contrasting what 'was' then with how things work now, products that have evolved or become obsolete, etc.

March 2 – Read Across America Day

Hold a reading contest for children with prizes awarded based on the number of books or pages read during the month. Create an on-going children's reading rewards program. Incentivize participation by awarding points that can be redeemed for new books, toys, electronics or other items. Hold periodic celebrations for participants and their parents with food, games, door prizes and drawings, product or service demonstrations, samples, etc.

Hold a book drive and collect books to be donated to a local library, day care, or youth organization. Donate a percentage of sales, proceeds from the sales of specific items, make a donation or ask customers to make donations to raise funds for a local public library, school or literacy program.

Work with marketing partners to hold a children's book swap event or children's book fair. Set up a reading area or a book exchange library in your business. Incentivize the purchase of new books by allowing customers to trade in old ones in exchange for a discount or free add-on.

Compile a recommended reading list including short reviews or average rating of books for children (or adults) and populate it with suggestions from customers and employees. Post suggestions on Facebook, your blog and e-mail newsletters. Make some of the best titles available for sale or to be used as a gift-with-purchase or contest prize. Launch or host book club meetings.

March 3 – Unique Names Day

Hold a contest to determine which of your customers has the most unique name provable by driver's license or birth certificate. Put some of the most unique entries up for a public vote. Reward winner/s with a gift card and some of your most unique or uniquely-named products. Extend a special offer to all entrants and add contacts to your database.

Ask customers to help rename one or more of your products or services with unique names or with names that rhyme, are slang, are made-up words, etc. Reward winner/s by treating them to the product or service for which they created a unique name. Hold a contest just for fun or actually rename products or services for a period of time or on an on-going basis. Use entries to rename a different product or service each month as part of your product/service of the month spotlight.

March 4 – National GI Day

Express appreciation for military members who live in your community in posts on Facebook, your blog and e-mail newsletter. Hold a military open house. Extend offers to local military personnel and their families. Give away a branded tchotchke as a gift, gift-with-purchase or free add-on to members of the military. Give away small flags as a gift-with-purchase. Post military trivia on your Facebook page, blog and e-mail newsletter or hold a military trivia contest.

'Adopt' a member of the military, a spouse, or a whole family for a year's worth of specific products or services. Take entries in-store and online to honor a military member of the month or for a drawing at the end of the month for a shopping spree or gift card. Ask your marketing partners to contribute gift cards as additional prizes.

Ask the public to nominate military personnel and reward the winner with a shopping spree, free services or products, etc. Or go big, and work with other businesses to create multiple or large 'hero' gift packages or date nights, family nights or group outings to extend at a special rate to local military personnel and their families.

March 5 – Employee Appreciation Day

Identity and recognize employees who exemplify the spirit you want in your business. Partner with a retailer, restaurant or night-out destination to reward employees with gift cards. Surprise employees with a branded item, a service or product gift and/or a personal thank-you note. Post client compliments and kudos for staff efforts and customer service on your Facebook page, company bulletin boards, blog and newsletters. Hold an annual employee-appreciation or all-employee meeting or family event.

March 5 is also *Nametag Day*. Take this opportunity to refresh the design of your nametag or uniforms. Celebrate the day by creating special funny, artistic or otherwise creative name tags for the day or to be worn all month. Create a branded nametag or button that can be given to customers as a gift-with-purchase or handed out at the door.

March 6 – Dentists Day

Partner with local dentists, oral surgeons and orthodontists for cross or cooperative marketing. Display one another's business cards, promotional offers, gift certificates and service menus.

Cross market a youth offer with a local dental practice. Purchase branded toothbrushes to be given away at the door or point of sale as a gift, gift-with-purchase or as a gift to local day cares, youth services or other organizations.

Working with your dentist and orthodontist marketing partners, post advice on your Facebook page, blog and e-mail newsletter about dental hygiene, the recommended schedule of services for children and adults, the benefits of orthodontics, the relationship between overall health and oral health, etc.

Compile a list of suggestions for natural ways to combat bad breath, improve the appearance and condition of teeth and gums, etc. Create a promotional product kit for the "perfect smile" including (branded) toothbrush, toothpaste, floss/flosser, lipstick, lip gloss or branded lip balm, wrinkle reducing serum or cream for the area around the lips, mint breath strips, teeth whitening products, etc.

Set up a display featuring whitening and dental hygiene tips as well as lip balms, lip glosses, lip plumpers or lipsticks needed to help customers achieve a great smile. Create a step-by-step instructional sheet for proper application of liner, plumper, lipstick, gloss and wrinkle-reducers (products that reduce fine lines around the mouth). Post tips, instructions and tricks on your Facebook page, blog and e-mail newsletter.

Hold a contest and solicit pictures of people's best smiles. Or go big! Partner with a dentist, orthodontist, salon, skin care and/or makeup esthetician with before-and-after makeover photographs to demonstrate the power of a great smile.

Hold a Best Smile Contest at a local bar or restaurant and reward winner/s with a gift card or products. Gift branded lip balms to those in attendance and a bounce-back offer redeemable at your business. Collect contact information at the event and extend a special offer to all who attend.

March 7 – Girls Write Now Day

Hold a story, poetry, song, journalism or multi-category writing contest for girls. At the end of the contest, reward winners with gift cards or writing-oriented prize baskets. Partner with a caterer or restaurant to hold an awards ceremony and celebration. If possible, give a small gift card or branded item to every entrant. Post highlights from entries on your Facebook page, blog and e-mail newsletter. Send a press release to local media, city hall, women's business and civic organizations, local schools, etc. Or go big! Partner with other businesses or women's groups to extend publicity for the contest, create more and larger prize packages, etc.

Feature writing tips, quotes from female authors, trivia about female authors, the accomplishments of local women authors, etc. in posts on your Facebook page, blog and e-mail newsletter. Publish a list of recommended reading with books written by female authors. Set up a display featuring your favorite female author's books for impulse buy near the point of purchase.

March Week 2

March Week 2 – National Money Week

Partner with a financial planner, tax expert or retirement planner to hold a money management, banking, retirement or another financial workshop for clients. Make recommended reading, software, workbooks and other resources available for sale. Post recommended reading, local resources and links to online resources (such as government and financial sites for small business, women and minority business owners, educational sites for children, etc.) on your Facebook page, blog and e-mail newsletter.

Working with your accountant, a financial planner or a representative from your local bank, hold a workshop for youth about money management, saving, credit, planning for college or even about how to start their own business. Help children or teens set up their first bank and savings accounts. Add $5 of your own money to each account started at the event or reward those who set up accounts at your event with a gift card or branded tchotchke. Hold a workshop for parents on preparing for college (saving for college, applying for scholarships and financial aid, etc.), planning for retirement, opening a business, buying a home, repairing credit scores, etc.

Your bank may offer rewards for referring new clients to them who start their own accounts, purchase CD's, establish savings plans, etc. Ask your banker for information about accounts they offer which offer cash back, high interest accrual or other rewards and work to move your personal and business accounts to those which will most benefit your business. Begin a dialogue with your banker about retirement and succession planning.

March Week 2 – National Crochet Week

In recent years, the art of crochet has evolved and reinvented itself in order to become relevant to younger generations. Way beyond what you learned from your grandmother about crocheting simple blankets, old fashioned pot holders or doilies, crochet is currently employed to embellish fashion and accessories that are featured on high fashion runways throughout the world. You can become part of this resurgence and help connect customers with this tradition both in order to stir feelings of nostalgia as well as to help shape the future of this craft.

Partner with a hobby, craft or fabric supply store for cross or cooperative marketing. Partner with a local boutique that features clothing with crochet or a local designer to hold a crochet-for-today fashion show.

Work with a local crochet expert to hold a workshop on use of crochet in the modern era and host an introductory crochet class or on-going classes. Start and host a crochet club. Add crochet supplies, patterns and craft books to retail.

Hold a contest or a crochet show featuring the work of local experts and artists. Ask customers to submit photographs of their work or of their most beloved crocheted heirlooms along with a story about their origin. Create a site or invite crochet-lovers to exchange patterns or photographs or connect on your Facebook page, blog at an event or as part of a club that meets at your business.

March 8 – Working Women's Day

Set up a fishbowl near your entrance, exit or the point of sale for women to drop in a business card for a daily, weekly or month-end drawing. Place blank entry forms near the bowl to collect the information of those who might not have their business card with them.

Hold a working women's happy hour, cocktail hour, wine tasting, luncheon, dinner or another social and networking event. Demonstrate or sample products or services at the event. Conduct professional consultations. Give away gift cards or products as door prizes. Create goodie bags for attendees that include branded tchotchkes and a bounce-back offer redeemable at your place of business. Set a cover charge to help offset costs or to be donated to a local women's service organization or charity. Partner with other businesses to create a larger event, extend your marketing reach to more prospects and create larger door prizes.

Post interesting facts about working women or famous working women on your Facebook page, blog and e-mail newsletter. Hold a working women's trivia contest.

Partner with businesses like salons or spas, restaurants, dry cleaners, housekeeping services, gourmet foods, caterers, etc. for cross or cooperative marketing. Work together to create a women's scholarship fund or establish apprenticeships and internships for young women.

March 9 – Get Over It Day

Partner with a counselor or motivational speaker to hold a seminar for people who want to learn how to "get over" past hurts, defeats or setbacks in healthy, productive ways. Compile a list of recommended reading to address specific issues (such as books to assist in recovery after the end of a relationship, the death of a loved one, the loss of a job, addiction, intrusive or hurtful relationships, etc.) Add related books to your retail or impulse buy offerings. Post links to local or online resources and recommendations on Facebook, your blog and e-mail newsletter.

Do you want your customers to "get over it" when it comes to visiting your competitors? What are you doing to create unique, irresistible, surprisingly delightful experiences for your customers so that they wouldn't dream of going anywhere else? Examine each customer touchpoint, from the parking lot through to the end of sale, from the first visit to your Facebook page, blog or website through to the follow-up that occurs after the sale. There are probably dozens of improvements you can make in the course of the customer life cycle. Solicit employee ideas, conduct surveys and create focus groups to help pinpoint ways to create a truly exceptional customer experience.

March 10 – Middle Name Pride Day

Hold a contest and solicit entries for the best, most creative, most awful or for multiple categories of middle names. Use Facebook, your blog, website and/or in-store forms to collect entries. Award a prize basket or gift card to the winner/s and extend a special offer to all entrants.

Hold a middle name trivia contest in-store or online. Post interesting middle names of historical figures or local celebrities on your Facebook page, website, blog and e-mail newsletter.

Add baby name books or books about the origin of names to your impulse buys or regular retail. Purchase copies to be given as prizes in your Middle Name Pride Day contests. Post links to sites with information about the origin or meaning of names, genealogy, etc. on your Facebook page, blog and e-mail newsletter.

March 11 – Worship of Tools Day

Partner with hardware stores, lumber suppliers, tools, equipment, home building or renovation businesses for cross or cooperative marketing. Partner with an expert to hold a do-it-yourself class for women in the general use of common tools for common household maintenance, decorating, repair tasks, car repair and maintenance, etc.

Compile a list of the Top 10 most needed, most popular, or most unusual tools customers should buy from you for spring household, lawn or garden tasks. Create an in-store display, post signage at the point of purchase and post this list on your Facebook page, blog and e-mail newsletter.

Educate customers about worship-worthy multi-purpose tools, such as tools that can be used in unusual ways, have unusual origins, etc. Hold a history of tools trivia contest or post facts in "Did you know...?" style status updates.

Compile a list of the Top 10 tools customers need to make over their appearance, improve scalp, skin or hair, for seasonal cooking or entertaining or for any other seasonal "to do " list you can think of relative to your products or services. Design displays, tent cards or other collateral to be placed on the tables of at local restaurants or displayed by other marketing partners. Feature your Top 10 lists in posts on your Facebook page, blog and e-mail newsletter. Create a Top 10 lists page for your website that is devoted to seasonal merchandise.

Any time you feature a product or service on your Facebook page, blog and e-mail newsletter, link it directly to corresponding item for sale online, to an appointment or quote request or another inquiry form. Make it easy for your customers to purchase the item or obvious as to the next step you want them to take. Post downloadable PDFs of your Top 10 lists online so that customers can print sheets at home to bring with them when they shop. Offer special pricing or free add-ons when customers return with your Top 10 list or reference a code word to help track marketing channel and promotion effectiveness. Always (always, always!) include your business name, web or physical address and other contact information on each and every piece of marketing collateral.

March 12 – Plant a Flower Day

Partner with landscapers, nurseries, florists, etc. for cross or cooperative marketing. Work together to hold a workshop on outdoor space planning, regional growing recommendations, garden care, landscaping or indoor plant care.

Educate customers about native regional flora and fauna in "Did you know...?" style Facebook, blog and e-mail newsletter posts. Post advice for indoor or outdoor plant, flower, lawn and garden care. Hold a trivia contest. Solicit customer questions, stories or recommendations and photos of their lawns, flowers and gardens.

Purchase branded or boutique-quality spring garden tools and//or items like gloves, gardening shovels, watering cans, seed packets, flower pots, etc. to give away as gifts or prizes, for retail sale, as a gift-with-purchase or to help incentivize workshop attendance. Purchase packets of seeds or small plant starts to give as a gift or gift-with-purchase to customers on a given day, during a week, or all month long.

Put together a spring planting basket to be awarded as a contest prize and hold a drawing at the end of the month, collecting entries at your point of sale, on your Facebook page, etc.

Organize a group clean-up event outside your business or business park or at a local community park to weed flower beds and plant flowers. Volunteer to help with yard work at a local charity, senior center or for local seniors or shut-ins.

March 13 – Jewel Day

Partner with jewelry stores, boutiques, local independent jewelry artists and independent jewelry sellers for cross or cooperative marketing. Working with marketing partners, hold a seasonal or bridal jewelry fashion show or sale event. Or go big, and hold a full-scale spring fashion, accessory and beauty show or bridal/wedding fair. Hold a jewelry swap event where customers can exchange quality used fashion jewelry or other items.

Add a seasonal, boutique or targeted (children/tween/teen or adult) jewelry display to impulse buys or regular retail. Partner with local jewelry crafters for locally-made jewelry, hair accessories or related items to sell on their behalf for commission or on a resale basis.

March 14 – Learn about Butterflies Day

Butterflies aren't born butterflies, they are transformed from one state to another. They represent beauty, grace, delicacy and transformation. They start out only able to crawl, then undergo a transformation that gives them the ability to fly. Can you see how many analogies you could make relative to your business? Tell customers about the services and products you sell that can help to transform their appearance, health, well-being, attitude, home, garden or other aspects of their lives for the better.

Hold a butterfly trivia contest or post "Did you know...?" style facts about butterflies, beauty and transformation on your Facebook page, blog and e-mail newsletter.

Add butterfly-themed products to your impulse buy displays or regular retail, such as custom-designed T-shirts or tank tops for girls or women, mugs, notebooks, note cards, jewelry, bags, table coverings, dishes, napkins or napkin rings, etc. Add butterfly temporary tattoos or nail art to your retail or to give away as contest prizes or a gift-with-purchase. Use famous quotes or create your own slogan and design your own line of brandwear with a butterfly or transformation theme.

Partner with businesses and practices that are in a transformation business for cross or cooperative marketing (hairstylists, makeup estheticians, fitness and weight loss experts, cosmetic medical and dental professionals, physical therapists, counselors, life and professional coaches etc.)

Hold a transformation workshop with a local beauty industry professional, cosmetic surgeon, fitness and training expert, physical therapist, nutritionist or weight loss specialist, dentist, orthodontist, counselor, motivational speaker, executive or life coach, etc. Provide customers with personalized, individual transformation plans and offers. Demonstrate products or services that help people make inner or outward transformations.

Partner with a counselor or motivational speaker to hold a workshop on how customers can be transformed on the inside. Working with these professionals, compile a list of recommended reading relative to internal transformation, self-esteem, interpersonal relationships, dating, etc.

March Week 3

March Week 3 – Yo-Yo and Skill Toys Week

You might think yo-yos are just little toys, but these little toys are big business. There are yo-yo and skill toys conventions, contests, instructional DVDs—you can even hire yo-yo 'athletes' to conduct physical education courses in school. Maybe most compelling of all, yo-yos and other skill toys can be used to teach kids (of all ages) about the principles of science without it feeling like work at all.

Partner with a local hobby or toy store for cross or cooperative marketing. Hold a yo-yo demonstration or introductory lesson. Expand this into a continuing series of skill toys classes (puzzles, mazes, frisbees, footballs, boomerangs, gyroscopes, spinning tops, etc.)

Hold a yo-yo or skill toys contest or tournament in your place of business. Hold a tournament or workshop for older 'kids' at a local bar or restaurant as a social event.

Hold an online contest and ask entrants to submit videos of their yo-yo or other skill toys talents. Hold a drawing for a skill toys gift basket; reward all entrants with branded tchotchkes and/or gift cards. Post information on Facebook, your blog, e-mail newsletter and bag stuffers featuring step-by-step tricks and tips, history and science-related facts.

Purchase branded, customized or specialty yo-yos and other skill toys to give away as contest prizes, a gift-with-purchase or for retail sale. Donate branded yo-yos to local day cares, schools, church youth groups and other youth-oriented businesses and organizations. Add related instructional books or videos to your retail, contest prizes or gift packages.

March Week 3 – National Wellderly (Well Elderly) Week

Educate clients on the benefits your products or services provide specifically for seniors, how they address conditions common to seniors or which they should use for healthy, beautiful aging and to minimize negative effects of aging.

Partner with beauty, fitness, nutrition, financial planning and other experts to hold workshops on healthy aging, common diet and exercise needs, preparing for or transitioning to retirement, etc.

Extend a special offer to seniors for relevant products or services. Set aside special shopping hours just for seniors. Have staff on hand to demonstrate and sample products or services just for seniors. Offer seniors special pricing on these products or services or for bundled sets of products or a series of services.

Extend off-site services or deliver products to seniors with mobility or transportation challenges in their homes or at a senior center. Many retirement living communities provide individual and group transportation for residents; coordinate with a local senior living community and set aside blocks of time each month for their appointments or for senior group visits to your business. Extend a senior shopping incentive or provide them with refreshments during transport or once they arrive.

Send manufacturer's samples or "Try Me" stickered product testers to local senior centers along with your business cards, service menu and a special offer for seniors.

March Week 3 – Chocolate Week

My favorite celebration of the year! Partner with a local chocolatier for cross or cooperative marketing. Purchase branded chocolates to give away as client, vendor or employee thank-you gifts, a gift-with-purchase, contest prizes or for retail sale.

Purchase branded or specialty gourmet chocolates or chocolate products (like hot chocolate mix, flavoring for coffee drinks, cookies, recipe books etc.) to add to retail or to enable you to create the ultimate chocolate gift basket for contest prizes, retail sale or a gift-with-purchase. Add chocolate dessert and drink recipe books to your retail.

Hold a chocolate recipe contest, tasting or cooking class; beyond basic categories you might include best chocolate-covered, most unusual use of chocolate, hot or cold chocolate beverages, most original combination, etc. Post recipes featuring chocolate on your Facebook page, blog, e-mail newsletter and bag stuffers. Solicit recipes to share online and/or to add to a collection of recipes to be printed at the end of the year, featured in a marketing calendar, etc.

Design and purchase custom, branded or boutique wares featuring a chocolate theme (t-shirts, tank tops, coffee mugs or travel cups, cold beverage cups, wall or desk decor, etc.) for retail sale.

March 15 – Consumer Rights Day

Remind customers about the guarantees and promises you make about products, services and the quality of the customer experience they should expect every time they do business with you. Review your mission statement; are you confident your business is fulfilling the promises it makes? Tell customers what benefits the receive in return for doing business with you. Describe the good that you bring to their lives and to the community. Include your mission and vision statements in your e-mail newsletter, blog and Facebook posts and on bag stuffers.

Conduct a customer-satisfaction survey relative to the overall customer experience or in order to hone in on a particular department or a specific aspect of your business. Print copies of the survey for in-store submission and make an electronic form available online. Link to the survey from your e-mail newsletter, blog and Facebook page. Afterward, report results and publicize the changes you implemented as a result of feedback to improve the customer experience or address specific concerns.

Hold a focus group, inviting key stakeholders among your client base to participate. Review your corporate mission and vision and ask the group to keep them in mind while evaluating the overall customer experience or specific areas of concern. Other times you might want to utilize a focus group might be In order to gain preliminary buy in or discover objections prior to making major changes in the way that you do business; prior to making significant changes to the products or services that you sell; or, to review the results of customer surveys and to develop solutions to remedy problems.

Create a 'Customer Bill of Rights' and educate, train and periodically retrain employees in how they will be honored. Share your Customer Bill of Rights on your website, in letters, proposals, on flyers or bag stuffers, in posts on your Facebook or blog page, on displays or posters at your business, etc.

Review your mission and vision statements with all employees at least once a year. Be sure new hires receive training during orientation clearly explaining these statements and the values they represent. Review your mission, vision, corporate values and customer bill of rights during orientation, at your annual all-employee meeting, during annual performance and salary reviews and in formal training. Talk about how the role of each individual impacts the customer experience, and how the mission of the company is fulfilled by them (or not) based on how they fulfill their role.

Tie every performance and salary review to the customer experience in some way. Ask employees to choose to support the values, mission and vision of your business. Ask them to be honest about any reservations or objections they have, even if it means that it might be time for them to move on to another organization. Retaining employees who cannot support the values and mission of the organization is damaging to the customer experience and unfair to co-workers.

March 15 – Incredible Kid Day

Allow clients (and/or the public) to nominate local "Incredible Kids" via entry form in-store and/or online. Award one or more nominees with a product and/or service prize; extend a special offer to all entrants. Write a press release about the entrants and the winner (with permission). Post links to stories featuring local incredible kids on Facebook, your blog and e-mail newsletter. Work with fellow members of your Chamber of Commerce or civic organization, businesses located near yours or your marketing partners to hold a larger-scale, community-wide event.

March 16 – Lips Appreciation Day

Partner with a makeup esthetician, salons, boutiques, and independent makeup sellers for cross or cooperative marketing. Hold a makeup application class, demonstration or beauty show for customers.

Incentivize event attendance or sales by giving away a free lipstick or lip gloss with purchase in general or with purchase of specific items. Purchase branded lip balms to give away as a gift or gift-with-purchase to customers. Purchase a lipstick, lip gloss or similar display to add to your point of purchase that is tailored to adults, teens, tweens or children (or multiple displays).

Partner with a cosmetic medical, dental or orthodontic professional to hold a seminar on creating a perfect smile for children or adults, having a healthy mouth and the best ways to ensure they have healthy lips, teeth and gums for a lifetime.

Partner with a bar or restaurant to hold a Lips Appreciation happy hour with a "best lips" contest. Ask attendees to vote for their favorite smile or pucker. Create a prize package for winners with gift cards, bounce-back offers, branded tchotchkes and lip enhancers like lip balms, plumpers, lipsticks or lip glosses.

March 17 – St. Patrick's Day (Happy Hour Extravaganza!)

Smile, it's happy hour! When it comes to designing your own happy hours, there are many ways to construct events that will make people feel good about coming in, coming back, and bringing co-workers and friends with them. What's more, your happy hours should not only make clients happier, they should also make you happier; design them to help fill up the books during slow hours, promote new services and products, promote retail sales and add-on services, promote sales of big ticket items, bundled products or series of services, etc.

Usually, Happy hours are "happy" specific hours when patrons receive special pricing or mini versions of some of your most popular products or services. With a little creativity, any type of business can do this, no matter what type of products or services they sell.

While most restaurant and bar happy hours feature alcohol, it doesn't mean that yours has to be intoxicating, so don't dismiss the idea out of hand. If you can serve alcohol but worry about clients driving afterward, work with a local bartender or chef to develop a low-alcohol Sangria recipe or a non-alcoholic cocktail unique to your business—you can cut the alcohol without losing a drop of taste or the spirit of the event. If you would prefer to (or must, due to state or local regulations) go non-alcoholic, keep the spirit alive with "mocktails" for client consumption. Partner with a nearby natural foods store, deli, restaurant or juice bar to help create unique beverage offerings; or hold a co-sponsored happy hour and invite all customers.

No matter how or where you celebrate, incorporate a way to collect contact information and extend a bounce-back offer. Hold drawings or contests to facilitate contact collection and to incentivize attendance and participation.

Make your happy hours special; do something in contrast to what occurs during regular hours in some way. It could be a chance to turn up the music and let clients sing or dance, hold contests or drawings, feature demonstrations or provide free consultations. Include referral or bring-a-friend rewards, drawings, contests and games or feature live entertainment.

Here are a few more variations:

Weekday-Relaxer or Weekend-Readier

Position your business as the first stop for couples going out on a date, or create a 'date prep' or 'de-stress' happy hour where clients can get ready for their night out while they relax for an hour or so. Or help people let go of the stress of the week and get in the right frame of mind to relax on the weekend by providing a setting where customers can unwind after a long stressful week.

Gift-Wrap your Clients

Partner with a boutique clothier and/or with a hairstylist and makeup esthetician to hold happy hours featuring services designed to "gift-wrap" clients for the evening with a fresh hairstyle, professional makeup application, and clothes or accessories for that special night out on the town, etc. If you sell cosmetics, clothing, bags or other accessories, don't miss out on the opportunity to send products home with happy hour attendees; offer special Happy Hour pricing on retail products as well!

Building Happy Books

If you provide services or products to customers by appointment, reservation or on a walk-in basis, hold happy hours or extend special pricing on appointments booked during what are normally slower times on your books to plump up bookings. Hours in between lunch and dinner rushes may also be slower hours for restaurants as well; partner with a local restaurant or bar to provide snacks or gift cards in return for the opportunity to gain cross marketing referrals from among your clients.

Happy Hour How-To, Must-Haves and Menus

Include social appeal. Feed them. Entertain them. Treat them to something truly unique. Make the feel like they are part of an exclusive, insiders club. Give people a reason to come to your business beyond their regular appointment, reservation or shopping trip and to bring friends with them.

Ask yourself: Who do you want to attend? If the answer is "everyone," you aren't likely to construct a uniquely-attractive happy hour. Identify types of 'ideal' attendees from larger subgroups within your clientele or from your target market (the type of clients you most want to attract); such as:

- Single or married working professionals for an end of day or end of week decompress or prep for night on the town
- Stay-at-home or soccer moms and dads who want and deserve a few minutes to themselves
- Special interest groups (sports, fashion, beauty, craft, art, music, environmental, political, or otherwise-oriented groups)
- Senior citizens, Baby-Boomers, Gen X, Gen Y, college students, young professionals, working parents, teens, tweens, etc.
- Men or women
- Couples or best friend duos, groups of girlfriends, etc.

Setting up a target group is important; what appeals to one generation or group vs. another will vary widely, from what entertains or interests them, to what they want to eat or drink, to the music they want to hear.

Partner with a restaurant or bar so that during happy hours at their businesses, their patrons receive a business card or coaster with an offer from your business; and during your happy hours, clients receive an incentive to visit your partnering bar or restaurant.

If other businesses near you are interested, create bigger, combined happy hours for clients, sharing costs and contacts in a cooperative marketing effort. Feature demonstrations, product samples, consultations and professional recommendations for services or products.

Happy Hour Brand Extensions

Order branded coasters and gift them to local bars or restaurants that have happy hours. Their alcohol distributors sometimes provide them with free coasters; why not substitute those with coasters that draw attention to your business or your services as a professional? A typical coaster is about twice the size of a business card, so it should be no problem for your design to incorporate a referral reward or new client offer, promote an upcoming event, or include a compelling offer people can redeem when they visit your business. Include entertaining or intriguing information, facts or trivia. Make an emotional connection. Ask questions or promote solutions to common problems or conditions. Include step-by-step instructions, tips or advice. Give people a reason to want to come in and find out more about you and your business.

Extensions of your Brand, with a Twist!

Order branded coasters with your contact information, happy hour details and/or a special offer and use them as bag stuffers or when providing water, coffee and other beverages to customers, for prospects or vendors use in meetings, or even when you take a client out for a meal to touch base or make a proposal. How impressive would it be to a potential vendor, lender, marketing partner or even a job candidate if you went to a restaurant that featured your advertising right at the table! Distribute coasters as business cards within your community. Ask your marketing partners to use them or distribute them at the point of purchase to advertise your happy hour and services.

On the Flip Side

Your coaster, which can also be used as a business card, bag stuffer, or other advertising medium, has two sides. One of the first rules of marketing design is this: Do not waste the flip side of any marketing piece! The flip side can do double duty and include an area for people to give you contact information or you can use the flip side to extend offers, provide an overview of business and its mission, vision or customer guarantees, feature a testimonial or list special features you provide (such as special equipment, trendy services, TV/video, Wi-Fi connectivity, etc.)

If you will be serving alcohol, have safeguards in place. Make sure you know what the regulations are in your city / county / state for serving alcohol or whether you need to have a food handler's permit. There may be different regulations for serving alcohol at no cost than there is if you have a cover charge or charge per beverage. Remember that attendees will probably be driving from your location to their next destination or home; so, do not over-serve and be sure to incorporate food as well. If a client arrives intoxicated, appears impaired, or you believe that you have a guest who is experiencing a problem, have a plan in place and procedures for arranging transportation and safely delivering clients home or summoning medical or other attention if necessary. Finally, these are working hours for you and your staff; save your own drinking for when you are off the clock.

Luck of the Irish

Irish or not, give customers an opportunity to win something this month. Create a gift basket with a pint or two of a favorite regional micro brew (or root beer) and 'a pint' (mini or full-sized) of retail products to support your National Beer Day or St. Patrick's Day promotions or partner with a local bar or restaurant to provide gift cards or vouchers for free cocktail, appetizers or entrees as contest or drawing prizes. As with any event, contest or drawing you hold, use entries to help build your contact databases and make sure all entrants receive a special offer from you.

March 18 – Awkward Moments Day

Hold a contest for the best awkward moment story, collecting entries in-store, on your Facebook page, blog, by way of an electronic form linked to your website or e-mail. Invite people to vote for their favorite story online or in-store. Include a gift card redeemable at a future visit to your business in the winner's prize package.

Partner with a counselor, life coach, communications or etiquette expert to hold a workshop on how to avoid awkward moments, how to behave in common awkward situations, how to overcome shyness or on improving social skills overall.

Hold an etiquette trivia contest. Provide etiquette and social situation tips in Facebook posts, your blog and e-mail newsletter. Use your Facebook page, blog and e-mail newsletter to discuss common awkward moments, soliciting advice from readers about how to behave in certain social situations.

March 19 – Companies That Care Day

This could become one of the most important and rewarding days of the year for you and your team! Commit to giving back to your community annually in support of organizations in whose mission you value and believe. As an employee team or on your own, provide volunteer work for a charity, shut-ins, patients of a local cancer or other treatment facility, for seniors, etc. Participate in an event like a walk, run or other "a-thon." Encourage customers to participate with your employees on community service projects, events and fundraisers.

'Adopt' a local needy family or patient (such as an individual affected by a serious disease or long-term medical condition) and donate free products or services to that patient or family for a year.

Keep track of the big and small things your business and its employees does throughout the year. Design an annual community service and charity report to send to customers, media, city hall and to other businesses in order to raise awareness of local needs, increase corporate participation in community service projects, appeal to marketing and event partners, and to entice those who share your values and ideals to become patrons of your business. Display a poster or in-store signage highlighting projects completed the previous year and those you are supporting at the present time. Add a page to your website featuring your annual report and links to local charities or your current campaign. Use your Facebook page, blog and e-mail newsletter to provide periodic updates on projects, solicit volunteers, donations and raise funds.

Volunteer to help beautify a section of a local road or neighborhood. Host a work day to clean up outside of your business, or at a local city or neighborhood park. Wear branded t-shirts, hats, or other items to help identify your business as a corporate sponsor of community service. Reward volunteers or hold a social event afterward for participants.

Sponsor or hold an event of your own (or with marketing partners) like a car wash, cut-a-thon, massage-a-thon, walk, run, floss-a-thon—any type of event you can think of where funds are pledged or donated. The more creative and off the wall, the better, when it comes to getting the attention of customers and media. Offer to match employee and/or customer donations, or to match donations up to a certain dollar amount. Seek out other corporate sponsors to help match donations.

March 20 – Spring Equinox

Celebrate the advent of spring by gifting seed packets, a plant or tree start or another spring-symbolic or branded item as a gift-with-purchase to clients or a gift for children shopping with parents. Work with an expert on regional flora and fauna to hold a workshop on spring plant care and yard preparation.

Celebrate Spring Equinox in a punny way by giving away branded slinkies (which are after all, just giant springs) as a gift, gift-with-purchase or addition to your impulse buys or regular retail.

March 20 – Proposal Day

Brainstorm with your staff or your marketing partners to come up with creative ways to help to facilitate marriage proposals either in your place of business, at the business of a marketing partner, at a local park, recreation, wilderness, public venue, tourist or date night destination, etc.

Promote the sale of bundled products or a series of services to be held over the next 3, 6 or even 12 months in order to "propose" that your customers form a long term engagement with your business.

Hold a contest for the best proposal story, taking entries in-store and online and allowing the public to vote on their favorite stories and/or pictures. Post crazy or creative proposal ideas and stories on your Facebook page, blog, website and e-mail newsletter.

Partner with a relationship expert to hold a pre-marriage workshop. Create a list of the Top 10 things you should know before you become engaged or before you get married, the Top 10 things you should look for in a prospective mate, the Top 10 things you need to know after you get married, the Top 10 marriage pitfalls to avoid, etc. Compile a list of recommended reading, websites and local resources to post on your Facebook page, blog and e-mail newsletter. Add some of the best titles to your retail or as gifts for newly engaged couples, gifts-with-purchase or for contest prizes.

March 21 – Fragrance Day

Work with a manufacturer (like a fragrance or professional salon products manufacturer) to develop a custom fragrance for a candle, room spray or body spritz or other products unique and branded to your business. Add them to retail or give them away as gifts to your most valuable customers, a gift-with-purchase or contest prizes.

Add aromatherapy products to retail. Educate customers about aromatherapy benefits featured in the products you sell on Facebook, your blog, bag stuffers, website and e-mail newsletter.

Partner with independent fragrance sellers, or those who create 'personal' fragrances using essential oils to create personal fragrances and hold a fragrance workshop to help customers create their own custom fragrances for perfumes or room sprays.

Post trivia about fragrances or aromatherapy on your Facebook page, blog and e-mail newsletter. Hold an aromatherapy trivia contest featuring prizes that provide aromatherapy benefits.

March Week 4

March Week 4 – National Bubble Week

Purchase branded bubblegum, bubbles or bubble-filled toys as customer gifts, gifts-with-purchase or to add to retail. Partner with a local candy maker to develop your own custom line of bubblegum to add to retail, utilize in cross marketing with other businesses or to give away to clients.

Hold a best or biggest bubble-blowing contest. Distribute branded bubbles or bubblegum at local parks or as gifts to kids at local day cares, schools, youth groups, etc.

Post bubble recipes on your Facebook page, blog, bag stuffers and e-mail newsletter (like this one from www.bubbleblowers.com/homemade.html, April 2011):

> Combine:
>
> 1/2 cup dish washing liquid soap
> 2 cups water and
> 2 teaspoons sugar
> - Add a dab of food coloring for colorful bubbles
> - Use pipe cleaners bent into shapes, cookie cutters and similar items to create interesting shapes

Do you sell or work with cleansers? Educate customers about ingredients commonly found in cleansers and provide advice on how to choose healthy cleansers, about the eco-friendly practices of your business or your manufacturers, vendors, etc. Tell customers why the products you choose to use in services and sell via retail are better for them than those they could purchase elsewhere.

March Week 4 – Doctor-Patient Trust Week

If you provide services, reassure clients, reminding them about your privacy policies and the ways in which you safeguard information entrusted to you. You may find that you need to create or revise policies relative to customer records, prospective customer data, employee gossip, use of contact information for marketing or communications, or for other areas.

Use this as an excuse to reach out to customers you have not seen in a while or who have been extending the time in between their normal visits to your business with a special offer, to ask why they have not returned or to determine how you might better serve their needs.

March Week 4 – National Cleaning Week

Partner with industrial and residential cleaning businesses or independent housecleaning professionals for cooperative or cross marketing. Purchase a gift certificate from a local housecleaning or dry cleaning business as the prize for a drawing or contest, or use them as gifts-with-purchase to incentivize sales. Reward one or more of your employees with a housecleaning or dry cleaning gift certificate.

Take nominations online and/or in store in order to reward a mom, teacher, military spouse, local hero or another deserving individual who deserves free cleaning for a week, a month or even a year. Hold a contest to find the most neurotic cleaner. Solicit stories or photographs online and in-store.

Hold a car wash to benefit charity. Volunteer to help clean at a local senior center, for a local charity, for a local cancer patient or for a local hero, overworked mom or another individual. Solicit employee and/or customer volunteers to help clean up outside your business or at a local city park. Or work together and 'adopt' a local stretch of road or highway.

Partner with other 'cleaners' for cross or cooperative marketing; hold a pet's teeth or coat cleaning event or partner with local groomers for cross or cooperative marketing. Invite a local dentist to provide your customers with product recommendations for better teeth cleaning or for cooperative or cross marketing. Partner with a local auto detailer or auto parts store to provide cleaning products, tips or a special offer for your customers.

March Week 4 – Root Canal Awareness Week

Partner with a local dentist for cross or cooperative marketing. Ask a local dentist for recommendations and information to pass on to customers about dental health and oral hygiene, recommended schedule of services, preventive care, services for infants or children, whitening, orthodontic referrals, symptoms and causes of common tooth, jaw or gum complaints, foods or drinks that contribute to (or detract from) good oral health, etc.

If you are a dentist or orthodontist, take time (please, forgive me for this!) to "get to the root" of things with your patients. Conduct a survey or hold a focus group to determine how well you and your staff are meeting their needs or to develop new services for the future. Contact patients who have expressed dissatisfaction or have recently left your practice (or stopped making their routine appointments) to determine what you could do differently or better or to tell them how you are addressing their specific concerns. Contact patients who did not return for their last scheduled visit (or the last several) to book their next appointment or to find out why they have not returned.

March 22 – Common Courtesy Day

Partner with an etiquette expert to hold a workshop on common courtesy or classes on social etiquette for children or teens. Include etiquette and courtesy trivia and advice on your Facebook page, blog, bag stuffers and e-mail newsletter. Include posts on the origin of common courtesy rules or traditions or hold a contest relative to the origin of common courtesy rules or what constitutes common courtesy in other cultures. Hold a contest asking customers to make up outrageous new rules for common courtesy. Ask people what courtesy rules they would make if they could relative to modern society.

Write personal thank-you notes to your most valued customers, vendors, marketing partners and employees. Make it a habit to write at least one thank-you note every day.

Solicit "things my mother taught me" courtesy stories; reward or recognize those who provide the most interesting, funniest, oddest, most meaningful or important common courtesy stories with a gift card or branded tchotchke. Invite the public to vote for their favorites in-store and online. Use entries and voting forms to add contacts to your database. Extend a 'common courtesy' offer to all entrants and voters after the event.

March 23 – Chip and Dip Day
And see February 24 – Tortilla Chip Day

Sample chips and dips to customers or set up a chips and dip hospitality station in your store or waiting room. Cross market with a local gourmet food store or restaurant and invite them to provide samples for your customers.

Hold a chips and dip recipe contest, tasting or happy hour. Reward contest or drawing winner/s with chip and dip serving pieces, chips, dips, salsa or mixes and/or a gift card redeemable at your business. Extend a special offer to all participants. Solicit and/or share chip and dip recipes on Facebook, your e-mail newsletter, or even in a printed-book for client gift or retail sale.

Purchase branded bags of chips to serve or to add to retail on an on-going basis, along with chip and dip serving pieces and accessories. Add a variety of dried dip mixes to your retail or impulse buys or give them away as bag stuffers or a gift-with-purchase.

March 23 – Puppy Day

Host or sponsor a pet-adoption event. Reward shelter pet adoptions. Give gift cards or branded prizes to your local shelter to be distributed to pet adopters. Invite breeders or local animal shelters to showcase pets available for adoption at a live event or by photograph/display at your business.

Partner with dog obedience trainers, pet groomers, veterinary practices, boarding or breeding facilities, etc. for cross or cooperative marketing (remember, more than half of the people living in your community are pet owners!) Or go big! Partner with other businesses and hold a pet fair or your own amateur dog show for pure breeds or mutts.

Add branded or boutique puppy accessories (leashes, collars, carriers, sweaters, etc.) or care products (shampoos, brushes, custom-designed food and water bowls, pet beds, etc.) to an impulse buy display or regular retail. Design your own line of pet-themed wares such as mugs, shirts, notebooks, memo cubes, wall art, etc. to add to retail.

March 24 – Organize Your Home Office Day

Partner with a professional organizer to hold a workshop on home or office organization. Add branded office and organizing supplies to your retail or impulse buy offering or give them away as contest prizes, client gifts or as gifts-with-purchase to incentivize sales.

Compile a list of recommended reading, local resources and websites to share on your Facebook page, blog and e-mail newsletter. Post tips and recommendations of items that provide multi-purpose solutions for common home or office organization problems.

Display a Top 10 list of office or home organizing supplies at your point of sale, on shelves in your store, on your website, Facebook page, blog and e-mail newsletter. Tweet a link on Twitter and hold a drawing for a prize for all those who 'retweet' your post (to help you grow your following on Twitter).

If you sell products online, be sure that your electronic posts link directly to the corresponding item in your web store, a coupon or certificate that a customer can print and bring to your store. Offer special pricing or a free add-on when customers return with a list or reference a code word you inserted into your coupon, online post or other electronic communication to help track effectiveness.

March 25 – Waffle Day

Partner with your favorite breakfast spots for cross or cooperative marketing. Hold a customer-appreciation breakfast at your business or your favorite breakfast restaurant.

Solicit waffle recipes and cooking tips to share on Facebook. your blog and e-mail newsletter. Hold a customer waffle tasting or a waffle cooking contest. Invite local breakfast restaurants and chefs to participate in a professional waffle-making contest or work together to hold a charity waffle feed. Assemble a waffle gift basket with waffle maker, mix, syrup, spatula, apron, etc. as a contest or drawing prize basket or to add to your retail gift-giving options.

Create "no waffling" offers combining options your customers normally have to (waffle) choose between, so that they can enjoy samples or miniature sizes of both, buy-one-get-one free or purchase both at a special price.

March 26 – Make Up Your Own Holiday Day

Working with your employees, create your own special company holiday and plan to celebrate it annually as an all-employee or employee-and-family event. Establish a costume or purchase branded shirts, hats, aprons or other brand gear to wear on your holiday. Post your corporate mission, vision and tagline on bag stuffers and store signage and tell the story of your business in posts on your Facebook page, blog and e-mail newsletter.

Hold a contest for customers to make up a new holiday for March 26. Entries could include ideas for what it should be named, what the brief fictional history of the holiday is, who celebrates it and how.

March 27 – Celebrate Exchange Day

Establish a support network among peers and hold monthly meetings to share challenges and ideas, pool resources for group buying, conduct joint charitable or community service projects, impact local politics and business regulations and to create cross and cooperative marketing initiatives.

Hold a swap event to benefit charity where clients can swap items like jeans, jewelry, books, home accessories or some other type of item. Donate the cover charge or a portion of proceeds to charity. Provide product demonstrations, consultations, samples, branded tchotchkes and bounce-back offers to attendees. Collect contact information at the point of entry or hold door prize drawings. Use registration or entry forms to add contacts to your database. Afterward, extend a special offer to all attendees.

Hold a promotion allowing customers to trade old or expired products or those sold by your competitors for something new from your business, or in order to upgrade to new models or products from old ones. Allow customers to bring a new item (such as children's toys or books) to be donated to charity to exchange for a gift card, special add-on offer, brandwear or branded tchotchke, discount on purchases, etc.

Why should Starbucks have all the fun? Set up a reading area and book exchange library at your business for clients or employees. Partner with a local vendor to bring in coffee or other beverages or make a selection of sandwiches or cookies available for purchase. Extend an invitation to their customers to visit and enjoy your book exchange library. Set up a seasonal, impulse buy or "ask me about" signage display within the book exchange/reading area.

Take a look around your business; are you wasting space that could be "talking" to customers for you? Set up a seasonal promotion or "try me" sample display near your entry or in your lobby, waiting room, etc. Change your display so that it changes with the same approximate frequency as customer visits so that they are likely to learn, sample or see something new every time they visit.

Add a "Swap Ideas" question and answer section to your website, blog or Facebook page where clients can ask one another questions, get information or provide recommendations about local resources such as tourist points of interest, shopping centers, repair or renovation resources, etc.

March 28 – Decorating Egg Shells Day

Hold an egg decorating event or contest. Set aside a supervised area for kids to decorate eggs with supplies and instructors. Post links to beautifully decorated eggs on your Facebook page, blog and e-mail newsletter. Solicit pictures of eggs decorated at home.

Give customers a free egg decorating kit, dye packet, Easter Egg sticker sheet or related item with purchase. Add egg decorating kits, supplies or how-to books to your seasonal impulse buys or point of purchase retail display.

March 29 – Smoke and Mirrors Day

Magicians use "smoke and mirrors" to distort the view of the audience and distract them in order to support the illusion they are trying to convince the audience to accept. Think of it as helping people who *want* to believe in the possibility of magic to do so. What can you do to establish, reinforce or restore customer, investor, employee and vendor belief in the ideals of your company—things they already want to believe? What can you do for your customers to symbolically illustrate or reinforce the brand image you want to create in their minds?

Hire a magician to entertain customers in-store or to do a show for kids while their parents shop. Partner with a magician to hold a workshop to teach beginning magic and card tricks. Hold a kid's magic contest. Add magic kits to your retail or impulse buy offerings, as a gift-with-purchase or gift to children of customers. Or go big! Invite local magicians to come and showcase their skills, promote their party services or even to compete with one another for the title of best local magician.

Post magic tips and tricks in Facebook posts and your e-mail newsletter. Write a special e-mail newsletter just for kids that teaches simple magic or card tricks and provides links to online magic resources, games and instructional sites. Post links to YouTube videos or ask customers to submit their own magic videos to share online. Post facts or trivia about the history of magicians and magic on your Facebook page, blog and e-mail newsletter.

March 30 – Pencil Day

Purchase branded pencils to be given as a gift-with-purchase or gift for customers, employees, vendors, etc. Gift branded golf pencils and score pads to local golf courses or miniature golf courses. Create a special design for branded pencils to be given to local schools for student use.

Design boutique-quality pencil and/or pen gift sets for customer purchase or as gifts for your most valued customers, employees or vendors.

Hold a pencil art drawing contest or partner with a local artist to hold a class or series of classes. Solicit photos of customer's pencil drawings or pencil-related art on your Facebook page, blog and e-mail newsletter. Partner with local art supply stores for cross and cooperative marketing.

March 30 – I Am In Control Day

Partner with a counselor or life coach to hold a seminar on how to take control of various areas of life (temper, feelings, relationships, etc.) in order to promote personal and professional success. Create and sponsor an on-going personal development support group.

Post interesting and motivational tips or quotes on your Facebook page, blog, bag stuffers and e-mail newsletter about what we should or shouldn't try to control, the futility of striving to control others, taking control of relationships, taking control of one's own professional success, etc.

Post suggestions for recommended reading, videos, and links to websites and local resources for personal development on your Facebook page, blog and e-mail newsletter. Add some of the best reading to your regular retail or create an impulse buy display. Purchase books in quantity to donate to support groups, employees, give away as employee or client gifts, etc.

March 31 – She's Funny That Way Day

Hold a quirkiest habit contest, soliciting entries and votes in-store and online. Ask customers to tell you about their pet peeves or things they are especially picky about when choosing products or services.

Find out what your customers are 'funny about.' Survey customers relative to their preference for communications from your business. Find out they look for or what would characterize an "ideal" shopping (dining, appointment, etc.) experience. Ask people to tell you about an experience they had in another business where someone went beyond the call of duty, or one in which they felt particularly under-satisfied. Ask customers to tell you about the last time they felt more than satisfied by an experience with your business, and what they felt made the difference. Ask questions about other topics that could provide you with clues for ways to enhance the customer experience.

Partner with a counselor, life or career coach to hold a seminar about quirks or habits people have that may be destructive or which may be holding them back from success and about habits people need to develop in order to be more successful personally or professionally.

april
365 Days of Marketing

April Month-Long Observances
Guitar Month

Partner with music stores and music teachers for cooperative or cross marketing. Add albums featuring great guitar performances as contest prizes or to retail, gift or gift-with-purchase. Add guitar sheet music or music books to your retail. Connect your customers with resources for local guitar and musical instrument stores or lessons. Hold a trivia contest or post interesting guitar or guitarist-related facts on Facebook, Twitter, your blog and e-mail newsletter.

Invite local music teachers to perform or to provide a free introductory lesson for people interested in lessons for themselves or their children. At the event, provide samples and demonstrations of any products or services you sell which can help people for performances or recitals (or other products which might interest your audience). Create a recital or performance makeover service or a list of fashion, beauty and styling products with a list of step-by-step instructions. Host post-performance happy hours or other celebratory events. Place ads in performance programs.

Extend a special offer to local music teachers, their students/families or to all employees of music stores. Take nominations and reward one or more local deserving music teachers with a gift basket or gift card redeemable in your business.

Partner with a local bar or restaurant and hold a guitar music-themed event or happy hour. Hold a talent show or contest for local guitar players. Invite or hire musicians to provide live music, showcase wedding or party music services, or perform at special customer or employee events. Compile a directory of local musicians for hire for weddings, corporate events, bar mitzvahs, anniversaries, etc.

National Humor Month

Hold a best joke or best prank contest and collect entries online as well as in store. Reward the winner with a humor-themed gift basket or a night-out package that could include transportation, dinner, a pre-event makeover, boutique clothing or accessories and/or tickets to comedy club. Extend a special offer to all entrants. Or go big! Partner with a local bar, club or restaurant and hold your own amateur standup comedy contest or charity benefit.

Partner with a local comedy club to extend a joint offer or purchase tickets from them for client gifts, awards or resale. Ask the club for a group rate and hold a customer or employee-appreciation event.

Add joke books, gag gifts, or humorous brandware to retail or impulse buy offerings. Solicit customer jokes or post jokes, funny marketing messages, made-up stories about your business, industry or community on your Facebook page, blog, bag stuffers and e-mail newsletter. Write humorous marketing messages to announce over your P.A. system. Create a humorous podcast to post online.

Lawn and Garden Month

Partner with local garden stores, lawn and garden equipment sale or repair businesses, landscapers and nurseries for cross or cooperative marketing. Ask for a special offer or free gift to extend to your customers as a gift-with-purchase, contest or drawing prize. When partnering with other businesses for cross marketing, think about where characteristics of your 'ideal clients' or target markets intersect with those of your marketing partners. Where your customer or target markets overlap lie the group of individuals you should reach out to with offers and invitations. For instance, when working with lawn and garden-related businesses, you'll know that many customers will be male, will be home owners and share an interest in outdoor work and activities; this provides you with an opportunity to boost your own customer base if this type of individual falls within a segment of your target markets or represents your 'ideal client.'

Put seasonal and regional lawn and garden recommendations on Facebook, your blog and e-mail newsletter. Add gardening supplies or tools to your retail or impulse buy offerings. Create a lawn and garden-themed gift basket for retail sale, gift-with-purchase or for a contest prize. Purchase branded seed packets or seedlings to give as a gift-with-purchase or event give-away.

Customer Loyalty and Appreciation Month

Nothing is healthier for your business or will do more to alleviate your personal stress (April is Stress Awareness Month!) than cultivating a happy, loyal client base. Retention and loyalty initiatives may require the investment of time, supplies or money on your part; but it can cost up to 5 times or more to gain new clients than it does to retain current clients.

The steps you take to ensure customers will return, and do so at the frequency you desire, as well your efforts to increase the number of solutions your business provides for customers (so that they will spend more money with you, more often, and little-to-none with direct competitors) are worth the effort. One of the keys to customer retention is good old "customer satisfaction," and this requires that you actively solicit, obtain and honestly analyze customer feedback—good or bad.

Analyze the customer experience from their first visit to your website, receipt of an advertisement, or the placing of that first phone call to your business through to the points that would comprise "the end" of their experience or visit. Evaluate each and every aspect of a customer's journey at each possible touchpoint, because you never know where you might be losing customer interest or fail to live up to their expectations in some way. You could be losing prospective and current customers at *any* of the following touchpoints:

- Advertisements designed to draw in a new customer
- Offers or new client reward designed to draw in a new customer
- Website landing page, targeted offer pages, site navigation, "contact" or "directions"
- Facebook page, blog and other social media sites
- Responses to "new customer" inquiries via telephone, e-mail, website or social media sites

- Incoming call answering, automated messages or on-hold messages
- After hours outgoing telephone messages
- Performance of referral rewards system
- Ease of finding your location and parking
- Outside of store (or outside of business park) or web store landing page
- Window displays and signage on doors, windows or anything on the outside meant to draw the customer in (or lack of anything to help draw a customer in)
- If and how the customer is greeted upon entry
- If and how/where the customer is directed to begin shopping or get directions
- Where and how the customer checks in for an appointment or scheduled visit
- Waiting area or length of wait
- Furnishings or decor
- Refreshments or hospitality stations (free or for pay)
- Rest rooms
- Ease of shopping, ease of finding desired items in store or online
- Friendliness of support staff such as receptionist, bookkeeper, assistants or aides
- Professionalism of any professional care or service providers and support staff, perception of knowledge, education and expertise
- Prescriptive advice for professional or home-use products, or the "you might also like" suggested selling of additional items on web store
- Knowledge of staff about products or services, online descriptions of products or services (even if purchases will be made in-store)
- Staff ability to up-sell, knowledge of products, ability to suggest upgrades and add-ons
- Any point where the customer or prospect is asked for contact information or asked to subscribe to communications
- Ease of point of purchase or check out experience
- Length or complexity of check out, staff ability and attitude, self check out options, etc.
- Helpfulness and availability of staff at the point of check out
- If and how the customer is thanked before leaving
- How the customer is dismissed or told 'goodbye'
- What happens after the visit; follow-up, bounce-back offer, re-booking process, surveys, etc.
- Experience at home with products purchased or results of services

That's more than 30 basic customer touchpoints at which you have the opportunity to damage or enhance a customer's experience in any one given encounter!

It is precisely the attention you devote to making the customer experience truly special—the 'extra' things you do—that tells the client you are personally interested in their well-being, louder than any words you speak. And it is the extent to which you intelligently and intentionally create an ideal client experience at every customer touchpoint that will set you apart from the competition, ensuring that clients feel you truly value their business (rather than take it for granted).

It's often difficult to view your business objectively, from the standpoint of a new customer, for the simple reason that we are too close to it. There are many things a new customer may notice as either a glaring problem or a shining plus; but since we see the same things day in and day out, they may not stand out in the same way to our eyes or ears.

One effective way to see your business through the eyes of a new customer is to enlist the help of a secret shopper, either by hiring a professional service or by asking a trusted friend or business peer (not known within your company) to try out your business as a new customer and report back on various aspects of their experience.

You can also set up a focus group comprised of key stakeholders (they might all be customers, but you can also include key vendors, investors or employees). Create simple feedback systems and surveys and ask (or even reward) key stakeholders and customers for their participation. Afterward, provide participants with a summary of the group's findings, what you did to implement changes based on their work and how the changes impacted your business.

If you plan to build your own surveys, you can either ask several general questions to identify areas of concern or you can focus questions on specific areas in order to assess one area at a time. You may have preconceived ideas or strong personal opinions about certain employees, services, products or other specific aspects of your business, but you should try to keep these ideas from influencing how you ask questions.

In other words, don't try to guide your secret shopper, focus group or survey participants to support pre-drawn conclusions by creating questions that reveal your bias. Be open to being wrong, be open to the idea that you don't know everything there is to know about your business. Be willing to try things you have not considered before, based on findings. You will receive the most accurate information and find the best solutions only if you approach both the process and the analysis of results with an open mind. Ready to create a loyalty rewards program? Here are a few ideas to get you started:

A Simple Personal Act (that cultivates Loyalty)

People will notice if you take the time to do something personal for them. A personal thank-you note written to each service client or to your most important or influential customers (these might be those who do a significant amount of business with you or those likely to refer and influence others) would take only minutes a day. You can even pre-address and begin each note prior to your encounter with each client. It costs very little (e-mail costs even less), but it will go a long way toward strengthening your relationships with clients and keeping your business in the forefront of your customers minds.

A hand-written note is a personal touch in an impersonal world. It conveys your gratitude for their patronage—for them choosing your business—when there are so many others they could choose.

Giving a personal thank-you note or sending an e-mail gives you the opportunity to connect with your customer by remarking on a topic of conversation or an area of concern they shared with you (showing that you really listened and truly care about what is important to them). It's an opportunity to ask them to book another appointment, to return soon or to consider you for their next major purchase, renovation, repair, etc. It's an opportunity to mention new products or services, or mention those you spoke about during their last visit. It's an opportunity to ask for referrals. It's an opportunity to ask questions meant to solicit specific feedback such as:

- Whether they were satisfied with a specific service or product or their overall experience
- Whether they have any questions about the products or services they purchased
- If there any way in which their experience could have been improved
- Whether they were able to find all that they wanted, does your business carry what they were looking for or was it in stock

Writing a personal note is a very simple act that can be completed in a few minutes; but ironically, while many business owners will spend a fortune on more complex forms of marketing and advertising, very few people are taking advantage of this very basic, proven method for strengthening customer relationships and touching base with prospects. Therefore, if _you_ make this part of your routine, it will get noticed, it will set you apart, it will bring clients back (and back more often) and it will stimulate more referrals. It will provide you with more opportunities to communicate and to truly connect with your clients.

Order branded note cards, create your own custom design or purchase boutique-quality, amusing, attention-getting or otherwise memorably-designed note cards. Every time you send or give a personal note, include your business card (preferably two, one to give away). If space allows, place a menu, client referral reward or a special offer on the inside flap or back of the thank-you note. If you have a reward points system, you can customize the note by including any points the client has accumulated as well as how many additional referrals, purchases, service visits, etc. they need to move to the next rewards level. You can even design and keep a number of variations of on hand so that every time you send one to a client, you are also including other information that may interest or intrigue them.

Simple Rewards

Due to the recession of the last decade, more people than ever have returned to using coupons both out of economic necessity and a desire to get the most value for the money they spend. Reward your most loyal and engaged clients with a periodic discount or free add-on service when they rebook, after they complete a certain number of appointments, purchase a certain level of retail products or when they refer people to your business. Give service and retail coupons to clients and prospects in personal thank-you notes, newsletters and e-mails and make them available on your website.

Simple Steps

You may be able to increase service and/or retail sales through a simple rewards program where incentives are awarded in direct proportion to client expenditures, either in gross dollars or dollars spent on specific services or retail products, or both. The more a client spends in a given time period, the greater their reward. Or keep it simple and offer a frequency-based punch-card style reward or a package discount for items bundled together or series of services purchased in advance.

Simple Recognition

Recognition is free! Put the spotlight on a "customer of the week" (or month). Recognize clients for work in the community or other achievements. Draw attention to worthy causes they support. Herald (with permission and respect to privacy) new babies, marriages, anniversaries, promotions, retirements, etc. Select a deserving 'client of the month' to receive a gift card, free product or service, gift-with-purchase, branded tchotchke, etc. Ask clients to nominate a deserving member of the community who deserves a reward. Recognize honorees in displays, press releases and posts on your Facebook page, blog and e-mail newsletter.

Simple Appreciation

Implement a (formal) thank-you note program for all clients with the goal of thanking 100% of your clients. Try it for a month and see how easy and effective it is! Order personalized or branded thank-you notes and envelopes or postcards. Or use e-mail. Include special coupons and incentives for new client referrals. At a minimum, send an electronic thank-you or place a note of thanks on their Facebook page.

Stress Awareness Month

In April, highlight stress-relieving benefits provided by your services or products. From intended or primary benefits provided by products or services themselves to aromatherapy fragrances and other enhancements to health, well-being or attitude, you may have more to talk about than you first realized when it comes to how your products or services contribute to stress relief.

Aromatherapy benefits can be found in many products (or in products used in the course of services) or it might be something that you incorporate into the environment of your store itself. Educate customers about specific benefits your products provide with signage at point of sale and in retail displays, in Facebook, blog or website posts and your e-mail newsletter.

In moderation, dark chocolate and red wine can have beneficial effects including endorphin release, anti-oxidants and improved attitude through indulgence. In the spirit of health, create a one-time or on-going Wine and Chocolate Wednesday happy hour as a client (or employee) thank you event. Reward a drawing-winning client with wine and chocolates to take home.

Enhance retail sales by drawing attention to stress-relieving or aromatherapy gifts for moms, teachers, coaches, friends and others, or use them as client thank-you gifts or contest prizes.

Incentivize retail sales of gift cards or other products and services with aromatherapy gifts-with-purchase (such as a small sachet, branded personal fragrance, room fragrance or candle).

Partner with a local massage therapist to add mini hand or neck massages to your menu or as a free add-on with certain purchases. This extra 5-10 minutes of personal pampering could help create a client experience that could never be replicated in another business.

Hold a contest or drawing to win a stress-relieving, pampering prize like a salon or spa gift card, voucher for free massage, fragrance infuser, candles, gift certificate for free housecleaning, etc. Hold this contest and market these types of products as perfect gifts for Mother's Day. Reward the winner with a gift for themselves and their mom (or daughter). Follow up! All entrants should be added to your database and receive a special related offer from your business.

Market de-stressing products to caregivers, public servants, health care professionals, working women, day care providers, stay-at-home moms, teachers—anyone who really deserves, and really needs some extra pampering and stress relief.

Hold a stress-awareness and stress-relieving workshop or happy hour featuring wine and dark chocolate. Sample and demonstrate stress-relieving products and services. Partner with a massage therapist, yoga or fitness instructor, etc. to hold a workshop teaching massage, relaxation and other techniques customers can perform at home. Hold an introductory yoga lesson or host on-going classes. Subsidize yoga classes for employees or hold classes at your business for employees.

April Week 1

April Week 1 – Laugh at Work Week

It's time to have some fun! Post random quotes, weird facts, dumb jokes, links to short comedy videos and off-the-wall observations on your Facebook page, blog, e-mail newsletter and employee newsletter or bulletin board. Write a humorous version of your regular customer or employee newsletters. Write humorous marketing or other messages to announce over your P.A. system. Create your own humorous podcasts for employee training. Create funny commercials to post about your business on YouTube and as video links from your e-mail newsletter and website.

Hold a best funny story, prank or joke contest. Hold a dumb joke contest or have a stand-up comedy talent show or contest. Hold a contest to find out which of your customers or employees has the best laugh. Hold a Facebook or Twitter new fan acquisition contest and reward a winner with a comedy video, humorous book, or a funny branded hat, t-shirt, mug or other tchotchke.

Reward contest winners with items like tickets to a local comedy club, a comedy video or humorous book as well as incentives to visit your business such as vouchers redeemable for a fun product or gift cards. Add contacts to your database and extend special offers to all entrants.

Partner with a local bar or restaurant and have your own open mic comedy talent show or contest as a customer-appreciation, new client attraction or employee-appreciation event. Hold a movie night at a local bar or restaurant for employees and/or customers—view a comedy, of course!

Partner with a local comedy club for a joint event or purchase tickets from a local club at a reduced price and gift, award or resell them to customers. Play comedy videos in your business for clients to enjoy via TV/Video, on computers, or even on smartphones or iPod devices.

Purchase items with humorous sayings to add to retail such as mugs, t-shirts, tank tops, books, nail files; you can even create your own branded line of humorous wares.

April 1 – Fun at Work Day, April Fools Day

A healthy, happy business begins from the inside out. Ask your marketing partners or businesses located near yours to contribute to goodie bags for your employees including samples, coupons, and special offers designed specifically for, and offered only to, your employees and their families. Partner with a local business to provide lunch for your employees or with a local restaurant to extend happy hour offers exclusively for your employees after work.

Surprise employees on *Fun at Work Day* with thank-you notes, recognition or rewards. Include client kudos and raves in your employee and client communications.

April 2 – Children's Book Day

Children's causes in particular are easy to build momentum around. Solicit new book or cash donations to help support libraries of local schools, day cares, children's services organizations or similar charities. Give customers a branded or boutique-quality bookmark to thank them for participating. Beautiful, one-of-a-kind boutique-quality bookmarks could also be a unique impulse-gift item to add to regular retail year-round.

Solicit input from local teachers and from customers and employees and compile a reading list of great children's books. Publish a list of recommended reading for children. Add some of the best titles to your retail or impulse buy offerings, or create a gift basket or prize package that includes children's books.

Hold a read-a-thon event or create a reading program and reward children in your community for participation. Hold periodic events for reading club members and their families; or partner with local sports and recreation facilities or destination points to create fun outings for families.

Hold a children's story writing contest or work as an employee team to write a children's story about your industry, business, community or some other theme. Solicit stories from children in order to create a collection of short stories for publication either online or in print, which you can use as a client gift or even sell via retail. Contact me at elizabeth@12monthsofmarketing.com or visit the Resources page of my website at www.12monthsofmarketing.com for editing, book design and/or publishing resources.

April 3 – Walk to Work Day

Promote the health benefits of walking in print and electronic communications and signage. Encourage employees to walk during breaks and lunch. Organize a walking club to walk together near your business, at a local park or at a fitness facility. Partner with a local fitness expert or trainer to hold a free workshop, boot camp, introductory class or demonstration for customers and/or employees. Host classes at your business.

Since improved health and well-being directly impacts business expenses related to health insurance and worker's compensation, offer to subsidize employees' gym memberships or reimburse membership fees based on frequency or use or results. Incentivize employee participation in fitness programs with rewards based on fitness, meeting weight loss or fitness training goals, etc.

Organize a walk-a-thon in support of a charity or a local deserving beneficiary; such as your local library, a local patient or persons/ impacted by a personal setback, a social services or youth services organization, etc.

Purchase branded water bottles, workout towels, pedometers and other fitness or workout related items to give away as a contest prize, gift-with-purchase, to include in gift baskets or for retail sale. Wear or take branded items with you on employee or walking club walks. Distribute free branded pedometers or water bottles to mall walkers (and customers), park patrons, fitness center clients, etc.

April 4 – School Librarian Day
(and April is School Library Month)

Most Americans will enjoy the use of a free school or public library more than once during their lives. These icons of American history are much more than book repositories; they are havens for underprivileged youth (and adults, for that matter) who want to learn and develop new skills, they provide resources for job hunters, educators and professionals, and they hold copies of a wealth of national and world history, art and literature, without which our society and civilization wouldn't be what it is today. City and state budgets have been hit hard during the last several years of recession due to losses in projected taxes collected from individuals and corporations. Like other public organizations, libraries have felt the budget crunch at all levels, from cuts in staffing to cuts in funding for supplies, new books, technology and other resources.

Working with your local school or public library, hold a benefit event, read-a-thon (or other "a-thon"), donate a portion of April sales or donate proceeds from the sales of specific items to a local library. Ask your local library for a list of specific supplies they need and solicit donations from vendors, employees and customers to purchase books or supplies for a local library. Or go big! Partner with other businesses in your community to hold a large-scale campaign or event in order to provide your local library with a more sizeable donation or funding for a capital project.

Extend a special offer to the library staff (or all employees) of your local schools and/or public library.

April 5 – Go for Broke Day

The term "go for broke" means to give it everything you have, to risk all in pursuit of a specific goal in spite of any obstacle, challenge or possible consequence. It carries with it the idea that you are pursuing a prize with fierce, single-minded determination, choosing to remain focused on it with tunnel vision, ignoring that which might otherwise scare or distract you. When was the last time that you pursued a goal for your business or for yourself personally with that kind of ferocity?

We often accept excuses from ourselves or allow obstacles or challenges to hold more weight than they deserve. The fear of the unknown, fatigue, the cynicism or pessimism of others, past failures—if you are looking for a reason not to try you can almost always find one.

Partner with a counselor, life coach or motivational speaker to hold a seminar or workshop for customers (employees, vendors, etc.) on how to identify what is holding them back personally or professionally, to distinguish between real or imagined threats, to teach strategies for overcoming obstacles and to develop a mindset that allows them to "go for broke."

Establish a peer-support group and host on-going monthly meetings for individuals who want a forum to verbalize their dreams and problem-solve their way toward them together. Identify those things you say are holding you back and determine within yourself that they are not going to stop you. Set your mind on the prize and go for broke in pursuit!

April 6 – Plan Your Epitaph Day

An epitaph isn't just a headstone or what's written on it. An epitaph is a literary work (sometimes even a poem) written in honor of the deceased. Running the gamut from caution to glory, and from humorous to immortalizing, a well-written epitaph gives the reader a look into the real person about whom it was composed in order to leave them with inspiration, a warning or other food for thought. In other words, you must be extra-ordinary in order to generate an extraordinary post-mortem remembrance. You must live memorably in order to touch people's lives in some important and meaningful way.

What do you want to accomplish in your lifetime—personally as well as professionally? Articulate specific personal and professional goals for the next 6 months, 12 months, 5 years, 10, 20, etc. Write out at least one goal for each of those time periods. For each of those goals, write down at least 5 things that would need to happen to enable you to meet them. What would have to change? How would you have to change?

Writing out goals and creating a timeline of incremental action steps can help you get started; sharing this list with other people who will encourage you and help to hold you accountable will take you even further. This would be a great exercise or topic of discussion to include in a peer support, mentoring or problem solving group (which could be a natural outgrowth of some of the marketing partnerships you have formed).

At a minimum, identify a mentor, trusted friend or entrust your significant other with your 'dreams' worksheet and planned action timeline. They may have resources or advice to help, and should be individuals who will commit themselves to providing you with moral support, encouragement, and the occasional kick in the pants we all need to combat negativity or pessimistic self-talk.

Looking outward, what would happen to your business if it were known to be a resource that helped customers, vendors, or employees achieve their personal and professional goals? Can you see how this could impact your ability to grow deeper relationships with customers and to attract new ones? How about your ability to hire and retain the best employees?

Partner with a life coach, counselor or motivational speaker to hold a "Plan Your Epitaph" workshop. Compile a list of relevant recommended reading. Create your own branded collateral for group or individual use such as a goal planner, timeline or tracker. Post inspirational or motivational quotes on your Facebook page, blog, bag stuffers and e-mail newsletter. Purchase your own custom line of fortune cookies with inspirational and motivational quotes and words of encouragement.

Create a personal or professional development program for your staff. Subsidize or reward continuing education. Recognize employees' personal and professional achievements. Tie performance evaluations and salary reviews directly to corporate goals. Provide incremental incentives to mark milestones toward individual, department or company-wide long-term goals.

April 7 – Caramel Popcorn Day

Treat customers (and/or employees) to caramel popcorn treats. Add related fragranced candles, air or car fresheners or room sprays to your retail or to give away as a gift-with-purchase.

Fill a large glass container with caramel popcorn pieces (count first!) Let customers enter to win by guessing how many pieces are inside. Take entries in-store and/or post a picture online and accept entries on Facebook, via e-mail or by way of a web-based contact form. Create a caramel popcorn-themed gift basket for the winner, to gift-with-purchase or for retail sale to customers. Add all contacts to your database and extend a special offer to all entrants following the contest.

April Week 2

April Week 2 – Networking Week

A lot of people confuse 'networking' with 'socializing.' While socializing can create networking opportunities, simply meeting up with other business owners or prospective customers is not networking. Let's break down the meaning of this word so that we truly understand it and appreciate its real intent. According to www.merriam-webster.com:

net-work-ing, *noun*
meaning: the exchange of information or services among individuals, groups, or institutions
specifically: the cultivation of productive relationships for employment or business

Just think about the word itself: net-work.

A good analogy might be to think about how a fisherman uses a net in his line of work:

- The net is used to surround and then scoop up fish (marketing)

- A smart fisherman uses his nets strategically—he puts them out in places where he believes specific kinds of fish will be, at specific times (targeted marketing, strategically timed and targeted based on knowledge and experience)

- The last thing that he wants is to pull in his nets only to find them empty (marketing that produces no results and is therefore a waste of valuable resources)

- Nor does he want to find them filled with creatures other than those he specifically wants to catch (marketing to those outside of ideal client target market, with the effect that the people responding to your marketing lack either the means or desire for your product or services)

Now we're getting somewhere!

According to www.wikipedia.org, business networking is a "socioeconomic activity by which groups of like-minded businesspeople recognize, create or act upon business opportunities. A business network is a type of social network whose *reason for existing* is business *activity*." The purpose of networking in business is—or at least should be—to facilitate the building of new business relationships and to generate business opportunities (at the same time).

Networking is more than attending meetings with other business owners or showing up at events where prospects might be in attendance. Effective networking is purposeful. It either involves working together with peers to help improve the business climate in your community or it involves being present, visible and alluring in the same places as are your target market/s prospects or ideal types of clients.

Maybe that's why so many business professionals give up on networking or put it on the bottom of their priority list; they've been doing it wrong! Now that you have a better understanding of what networking is (and isn't), how are you going to put this tactic to work to help build business?

April Week 2 – International Chicken Wing Week

So many people love chicken wings! Partner with a local bar or restaurant and invite them to provide samples for your customers, or hold a joint chicken wing happy hour. Partner with a local caterer or BBQ restaurant to hold an employee event after hours featuring great wings.

Hold a chicken wing eating contest. Invite local chefs to participate in a chicken wing cooking contest. Hold a chicken wing and wine tasting or a customer cooking contest. Solicit customers' best wing or sauce recipes to post on Facebook, your blog and e-mail newsletter or to add to your recipe collection to be printed at the end of the year.

Purchase gourmet sauces or dips to retail, add to contest prizes, for gifts or gifts-with-purchase. Create your own custom wing recipe and share it with the public on your Facebook page, blog, bag stuffers and e-mail newsletter.

April 8 – Draw a Picture of a Bird Day

Hold a children's bird drawing or coloring contest and allow entries in-store as well as on Facebook, your blog and e-mail newsletter. Reward winner/s with an appropriately themed gift basket, gift card, toy store gift certificate, etc. Use the opportunity to extend special offers to children whose parents may be loyal customers, but who may take their children to a competitor for some of the same products or services you provide. Extend family rates or multi-appointment rates and set aside blocks of time for family or group bookings. Offer to provide a child's version or child-size product or service at half price when parents purchase the full-size version for themselves. Bundle sets of products for use by the whole family at a special price.

Partner with an ornithologist or another expert on regional birds for a workshop or a group bird watching outing. Post facts about local birds or those which come and go seasonally on your Facebook page, blog and e-mail newsletter.

Partner with a local wildlife artist to hold a class on drawing birds and wildlife. Display the work of local wildlife artists at your business. Post photos or links to their websites on your Facebook page, blog and e-mail newsletter. Work with marketing partners to hold an art exhibit featuring the work of local artists.

April 9 – Name Yourself Day

Most of us had little say in the matter of what our own names would be. Start a conversation or hold a contest on Facebook, Twitter and in-store asking, "If you could rename yourself anything you wanted, what would you rename yourself and why?" You can ask for real names or you can ask participants to submit philosophically symbolic words, phrases or even made-up words.

Create a new service or product offering and hold a contest, asking customers to name it by submitting ideas online and in-store. Use entries to build your database. Reward the winner with a free version of the product or service they named, and extend a special offer to all entrants.

Solicit customer testimonials asking customers to tell you what they would name your business if they were going to name it based on their experience doing business with you, based on the values they feel exist in your organization, relative to your products or services, etc.

April 10 – Golfers Day

Spring is here (or just around the corner) and golf course business should be heating up. Partner with local golf courses, driving ranges, men's and women's golf clubs, sporting goods stores, practice facilities, etc. for cross or cooperative marketing. Hold a drawing for their patrons and reward a winner from each of these organizations. Use entry forms to help build your contact database and extend special offers. Create targeted offers for the members of local golf courses, clubs and recreational and sports facilities.

Add branded or boutique items or create your own custom design for golf items to add to your retail or give away as a gift-with-purchase or contest prize, such as golf balls, tees, shirts, towels, tools, bags, coolers, desk or wall plaques, picture frames, etc.

April 11 – Siblings Day

Extend offers for customers to purchase services to be enjoyed with siblings or specially-priced pairs of "sibling" products (wine and cheese, gum and mints, scarf and gloves, etc.) Partner with businesses that would be "siblings" to yours for cross and cooperative marketing, such as an auto repair business with an auto parts store, a salon with a spa, a shoe or accessories store with a clothing boutique, etc.

Host a happy hour, luncheon or tea for siblings. Hold a contest to find the siblings who most look, act, or sound alike. Other categories you might include are most alike in education or profession, funniest, closest in age (with or without being twins) or furthest apart in age.

Solicit heartwarming (or hilarious) sibling stories online and in-store. Turn your blog, Facebook page and in-store bulletin board into a forum for people to post loving and appreciative sentiments to their siblings.

April 12 – Licorice Day

Treat customers (and/or employees) to licorice. Partner with a local candy or gourmet food store for cooperative or cross marketing. Purchase gourmet, branded or specialty licorice for resale to customers, client gifts or gifts-with-purchase.

Hold a happy hour featuring licorice-flavored drinks, appetizers or desserts. Hold a licorice recipe or licorice cocktail concoction contest, tasting or customer-appreciation event.

Hold a trivia contest or post facts about licorice such as the history or making of licorice, who loves it, crazy flavor variations, etc. on your Facebook page, blog and e-mail newsletter.

Donate branded or gourmet licorice to local church or city youth organizations, parks and recreation teams, dance or music studios, social clubs, charitable organizations, schools, etc. Include a bounce-back offer for your business, include a special code word for offer redemption, invite them to an open house or event or direct recipients to your website to participate in a contest or drawing.

April 13 – Scrabble Day

Hold a Scrabble tournament or happy hour at your business or in cooperation with a marketing partner such as a bar, restaurant or another business. Sell Scrabble games or Scrabble travel games or give Scrabble games away as contest prizes or a gift-with-purchase.

Print blank Scrabble board-style grid sheets and give clients letters (or simply list available letters on the bottom, clients can "x" them out as they are used in each word). Ask customers to use the letters provided to build out their own Scrabble-style contest entry with the names of your products, services and/or words that they would use to describe your business. At the end of the day (or week or month) total up each entry using the points system you assigned for letters, and reward the winner/s with a special service and product prize basket. Create a Scrabble-style rewards program where customers earn letters through purchases, contests, referrals, etc. while working to win a grand prize or to collect letters to spell out prizes.

Make it possible for people to play not only when in your business but also make your game sheet available online via linked PDF on your website, Facebook page, blog and e-mail newsletter. Ask customers to return entries personally in return for a free branded tchotchke or product sample. As with any event or contest, use entry forms to collect contact information and extend a special offer to all entrants following the event.

April 14 – Teach Your Children to Save Day

Partner with a financial planner or bank representative to hold a workshop on money management and saving for children (or adults). Help attendees get started with a new account by incentivizing with branded gifts, special offers, gift cards or even by placing an additional $5 in the account of each child who starts their account at your workshop.

Post tips about saving and money management on your Facebook page, blog and e-mail newsletter. Purchase branded or custom-designed savings banks (piggy banks) to add to your retail or to give away as contest prizes or a gift-with-purchase.

April Week 3

April Week 3 – Customer Awareness Week

I'm going to go out on a limb here and say that one of two things is likely true about your business: Either your business is so amazing and wonderful and so perfectly meets the needs and desires of all of your prospective customers, or, while your business is truly pretty amazing and wonderful, and you rightly believe is has a lot to offer the individuals who you believe represent your ideal clients, for some reason, you are not attracting enough clients, you are not attracting enough of the right kind of customers, or your customers are not purchasing (enough of) the products or services that you offer.

If the latter is true for you, it's possible that you have a 'customer awareness' gap to address. You might not have a full understanding of what type of individuals most want or need what you have to offer, and so you might be marketing to the wrong people. Or you may not have a full understanding of the true needs and wants of your customers, and so might be offering them the wrong products or services. In either case, here are some simple steps you can take to increase your level of customer awareness:

- Identify some of the main features and benefits of your business overall; and/or of specific products or services you sell.

- Based on the main features and benefits, list the reasons why a customer would want or need to do business with you (or purchase a specific product or service). In other words, what human needs and wants are you fulfilling?

- Based on the two points above, list the traits, attributes, lifestyles, interests or qualifications (income level, home ownership, education requirements or other preliminary requirements, etc.) that are likely to characterize people who would want or need what you have to offer.

Once you begin to identify the commonalities that would be found in the types of people who would be most likely to want or need what your business provides, you can begin to create a profile of "who" should really make up your primary target markets. And then you can lay out a strategic plan to target those types of individuals with marketing tactics.

April Week 3 – Administrative Professionals Week
(see April 24 – Administrative Professionals Day)

April 15 – Income Tax Pay Day

Hold an income tax relief happy hour, your customers need it! Give clients a 'rebate' with the purchase of specific items or after reaching a specified dollar amount in expenditures in the form of a gift card redeemable in your business or one of your marketing partners. Pay the sales tax for customers for a day or for purchases of specific items.

Connect tax filing procrastinators with accountants and tax preparation professionals who can help them get back on track—fast! Partner with accounting, tax preparation, financial management and related businesses for cross or cooperative marketing. Post tax information, IRS links, contact information for local resources, tips and tax deadlines on your Facebook page, blog and e-mail newsletter.

Go to your local post office on the evening of April 15th to give out bounce-back offers along with samples, refreshments and/or branded tchotchkes to those waiting in line to mail their tax returns at the last minute. (Repeat this exercise for other events such as city parades, individuals lined up to vote, standing in line in front of clubs or stores, etc.)

April 16 – Wear Your Pajamas Day

Wear your pajamas today—why not? As a public relations stunt, you and/or your employees can work in pajamas to raise awareness and solicit donations for a local charity or needy family. Hold a "wear your pajamas" happy hour or open house, collecting a cover charge to be donated to a local charity. Invite customers to shop in their pajamas all day long or for a specific event.

Hold a pajama or lingerie fashion show. Open up after hours and invite your most loyal, influential and/or valuable customers in to enjoy a midnight movie, dining, shopping event or fashion show. Incentivize attendance by offering blowout offers or by planning a unique and exclusive experience. Partner with other businesses to hold a larger event. Invite attendees to wear pajamas to the event, or to bring a pair of new pajamas in lieu of a cover charge which will be donated to a local shelter.

Create your own funny, beautiful or otherwise one-of-a-kind pajamas to add to your retail or give away as a gift-with-purchase or contest prize. Hold a contest for the best pajama design and have the winning entry printed as a gift for the winner and sold with a portion of proceeds going to a local charity.

April 17 – Cheese Ball Day

Solicit customer cheese ball recipes for sharing or hold a cheese ball contest, tasting, or happy hour. Hold a cheese ball trivia contest. Post interesting cheese and cheese ball related facts on your Facebook page, blog, bag stuffers and e-mail newsletter.

Partner with a local gourmet food store, caterer, restaurant or chef and sample cheeses, cheese balls or cheese-based dips to customers or purchase a selection for retail sale, gift-with-purchase or contest prizes.

Ask customers to give you the "cheesiest" reason why they think they desert to win a Cheese Ball Day prize and gift card. Add all contacts to your database. Invite them to attend your cheese ball happy hour, give them a voucher redeemable for a free cheese ball with their next purchase or extend another offer.

April 18 – Newspaper Columnist Day

How is your public relations program? Have you established contacts with local media and do you regularly submit press releases for your business highlighting community involvement, charitable endeavors, human interest stories and business announcements? Depending on the size of your community and its local media, you may need to do some research in order to determine which reporters would be your most appropriate contacts.

Just getting started? Use the press release template located in the Marketing 101 chapter of this book as a template for writing your own releases. With some practice, you'll find that it's not as difficult as you might think and it shouldn't take a lot of time once you learn how to edit a story down to its two or three main and most powerful points.

Visit local newspaper offices. Ask for the name of the individual who would be the most appropriate reporter to whom you should submit press releases on behalf of your business. Introduce yourself to that individual and give (or send) them a copy of your corporate press kit, brochure or menu and a few business cards. Ask them how they prefer to receive submissions (e-mail, direct mail, phone, etc.) Ask what types of stories they feel most interest their readers. Ask what they, themselves, look for in a story. Incorporate these angles into your press releases as often as possible. Make writing a press release part of your monthly marketing routine and a scheduled, assigned task as part of any event, contest or charitable benefit you hold.

Become your own columnist! Commit to putting new content on your blog, Facebook page and other social media and the "news" page of your website on a regular basis. For Facebook, Twitter and other social media, this might mean writing a new post every day or even multiple times each day. Commit to putting a new post on your blog *at least* once each week. Once you put a post on your blog, immediately share it on Facebook, Twitter and your other social media sites. Any time you write a press release, place a link to it on the "news" page of your website and post a link to it on your Facebook page, blog and other social media sites as well.

Write your own newsletters at least once each month to be sent by e-mail and/or direct mail to your customer database and printed for distribution at reception, in your waiting area or as bag stuffers. Ask your cross marketing partners to display or distribute your newsletters to their customers. Send copies to local businesses, large employers, fellow members of your Chamber or Commerce, etc. Each time you publish a new newsletter, post a link to it on your website, blog, Facebook page and other social media sites.

Make it easy for people to subscribe to your communications by providing as many points as possible for them to sign up. Make it your goal to ask for 100% of your customer's e-mail addresses. Collect contact information including e-mail addresses at every event and for every contest or drawing you hold. Provide a sign up sheet at every point of purchase. Place links to subscribe on your blog, Facebook page and other social media sites. Ask your vendors and marketing partners to subscribe. Invite influential members of your community (business leaders, civic organization leaders, local politicians, members of the media, etc.) to subscribe. Send these influencers a print copy of your newsletter from time to time to stay in touch.

Pay attention to the statistics which are available to you in most e-mail and blog programs to learn which items most interest your readers, what types of subject lines prompt them to open your e-mails, who among them regularly opens your e-mails, which readers post comments or interact with you online, etc. Survey and poll readers from time to time to find out what interests them, what they want to see more of, what types of promotions or events they would respond to, etc.

April 19 – Hanging Out Day

Give customers reasons to come and hang out at your business. Have an open house or happy hour, feature live music, a magician or some other entertainer, serve food or samples, have a wine tasting, invite experts to perform demonstrations or hold workshops, have a poetry reading, form a book club, hold an art show, hold hourly drawings for door prizes—give people reasons to visit your business beyond purchasing the products or services you sell—reasons to stay and "hang out" for a while!

Give your employees (volunteers, vendors, investors, etc.) reasons to hang out so that you can build a more cohesive, goal-oriented and interdependent team. Schedule regular team-building and training workshops. Hold an appreciation event, awards or recognition event, pot luck, game night, cocktail hour, family-friendly outing, picnic at the park, wine tasting, vendor-sponsored fair, an all-employee annual meeting or retreat. Gather your team together in order draw focus to the goals, mission and vision of the organization, and the ways in which each individual contributes to their fulfillment.

April 20 – Look-Alike Day

We'd all like to look like movie stars! Partner with a salon or hairstylist and makeup esthetician and hold a contest for the best celebrity look-alike makeover. Partner with a photographer to take before-and-after pictures and let clients vote in the winning stylist/client pair.

Hold a celebrity look-alike contest, soliciting entries in-store and online. Use entry forms to help build your contact database. Reward the winner and extend a special offer to all entrants.

Partner with a local bar or restaurant for a happy hour or night out event with "look-alike" contests that might include categories such as people who look most like each other, pets that look most like their owners or celebrity look-alikes.

April 21 – Volunteer Recognition Day

Write personal thank-you notes or letters of appreciation to your volunteers. Just as you would for employees, set aside time to hold volunteer events for appreciation, recognition/awards, to attract new volunteers, to engage more deeply with your current volunteers, to communicate organizational goals, and to let volunteers know how they contribute to the fulfillment of your mission and vision. Write a press release highlighting the contributions of some of your most outstanding volunteers or awards given at events. Include pictures and tell other people in your community how they can become involved.

Contact a local charity that relies on regular volunteer labor and offer to provide them with funding for a volunteer appreciation event or to provide gift cards or products to be given to their volunteers as a gesture of thanks. Or go big! Working with marketing partners or on your own, host a volunteer appreciation happy hour, dinner or another event on behalf of your favorite local charity, church or public service organization. Invite a photographer to attend to help document the event. Write a press release highlighting the organization, honoring its volunteers and noting the gift or donation made by your business.

You might feel strange writing about good deeds done by your business; however, it's more than just blowing your own horn. When you step forward to raise funds, make donations, volunteer or support the efforts of those who do, you are fulfilling your responsibility to the community. You are setting an example for other businesses and individuals within your community to follow and you are drawing attention to the needs and community contributions of the charitable organizations you support.

Solicit nominations of deserving volunteers within your community. Partner with other businesses to create a reward package fit for a hero in order to reward a deserving community member each year (or each quarter, month, etc). Your prize package might include a makeover or day of spa pampering, new clothes, dinner, a family or date package, transportation, house cleaning, etc. By partnering with other businesses you can create larger or multiple prize packages.

You can also use these same marketing partnerships to create family night out and date night packages of events, products and/or services that are bundled together at a special price for retail, or as a gift for an outstanding employee or your most valuable customers.

April Week 4

April Week 4 – National Independent Retailers Week

That's you! If you are using this book as an idea resource, chances are that you own or work in an independently-owned business. Invite leaders from other local, independently-owned businesses to participate in a community summit to improve the health of the local business economy.

Join or form a 'Buy Local' merchant association. Tell people how the local economy benefits when they patronize local, independently-owned businesses versus national chains. Write press releases to highlight the ways local, independently-owned businesses support charities and public works, create local jobs, support local schools, music, arts, children's organizations, etc.

Work together in cross and cooperative marketing and joint events; reach out for additional partnerships with medical, dental and other service-oriented practices. Participate in street fairs, parades, festivals and farmer's markets. Get involved in your Chamber of Commerce. Expand your channels of communication. Build your contact databases. Create marketing collateral to be displayed in rack card holders at local tourist spots, restaurants, hotels, motels, etc. Reach out; opportunity abounds for you to build a bigger role for your business in the lives of your customers and the community!

April Week 4 – Whistlers Week

Hold a whistling contest or a whistling happy hour; for instance, you could play music that has whistling in it or even (if you can take it!) is whistling. Hold a Karaoke event or contest with whistling instead of singing. Remember the old game show, Name that Tune? Hold your own "Name that Tune" contest, whistling style.

Purchase branded whistles for customer gift or gift-with-purchase or to be sent to local schools, day cares, etc. Purchase safety or specialty whistles for retail, gift or gift-with-purchase. Post history and facts or hold a whistle trivia contest on your Facebook page.

April Week 4 – Safe Kids Week

Partner with local experts such as members of the police or fire department or other personal safety experts to hold a workshop on safety for kids in general, baby-proofing the home or on another topic. Partner with a local photographer to hold a child's identity card event in conjunction with your safety workshop or on its own. Use your camera and computer or photo-badging equipment to provide children's I.D. cards (or sponsor a child I.D. card event).

Use event entry forms for registration or hold drawings at your safety-related events to add contacts to your database; following the events, extend a special offer to all attendees. Purchase branded lanyards with I.D. card holders, whistles or other items to give away.

Put together a gift or contest prize basket filled with related safety items. Hold a drawing or sell these bundled sets at a special price at events or on an on-going basis. Write a Top 10 list on the topic of kids safety, home safety, etc. including product recommendations to post on your Facebook page, blog and e-mail newsletter and for an in-store product display.

Partner with a babysitting expert, nurse or another professional to hold babysitting classes. Hold a CPR class for people in your community, your employees, the employees of your marketing partners or businesses located near yours, etc.

Hold a fundraiser to help provide bike helmets or other common youth safety equipment for local children. Or go big! Partner with other businesses to hold a community-wide campaign or event in order to raise funds to improve public safety or purchase safe outdoor climbing gyms, toys, etc. for a local park, school or youth services organization.

April 22 – Jelly Bean Day

Fill a large glass container with jelly beans and hold a quantity-guessing contest (be sure and count before or while filling the container). Take entries in-store as well as online by posting a picture on your website, blog, e-mail newsletter and Facebook page.

Post interesting jelly bean history and facts or hold a jelly bean trivia contest. Beyond the history and making of jelly beans, post things like celebrities who love them, which flavors they love, what flavors they make the most of, how many countries they are sold in, etc.

Partner with a candy or gourmet foods store to provide samples for customers or for products to add to retail. Treat customers to jelly beans while at your business. Purchase branded bags of jelly beans to send home with customers as a gift, gift-with-purchase, contest prize or to add to point of purchase or regular retail. Purchase branded jelly beans to distribute to local businesses, schools, day cares, libraries or other organizations whose employee or client base overlaps with some part of your 'ideal customers' or target markets.

April 23 – Take Your Children to Work Day is in April

Check the current year's calendar for the official Take your Children to Work Day. Work with your staff to construct an event that includes an interesting tour of your business, demonstrations of some of the products or services you provide and activities that kids would enjoy. Set up a mock version of your business and let kids practice their own business skills. Create worksheets and give kids play money to spend, invest or launch their own pretend business.

Provide a great lunch. Hire a magician or another entertainer to make the day more special for them. Invite a photographer to attend, photo-document the day in pictures and to create custom honorary employee I.D. cards. Purchase branded lanyards and I.D. badge holders as well as branded yo-yos, coloring books, stuffed animals, notebooks, pens, etc. for goodie bags kids can take home as mementos of the day.

Partner with other businesses located near yours for a multi-business Take Your Children to Work Day event, tours and activities. If your business is not conducive to this type of activity, create goodie bags to send home with employees for their children and include an kid-friendly brochure about your business that describes some of the activities their parents do each day at work.

April 24 – Administrative Professionals Day is in April

Check the current year's calendar for the official Administrative Professional's Day. Beginning in March, promote sales of gift cards and specific products or services best suited as gifts for Administrative Professionals. Set up a display in-store. Send e-mail and postcard reminders to the executives of local businesses, your marketing partners, businesses located near yours, schools and other organizations noting the upcoming date for Administrative Professionals Day and making specific gift recommendations Offer to deliver gifts on their behalf for an additional charge or incorporate the cost of delivery into the price of the gift.

Solicit nominations of outstanding administrative pros and reward winner/s with a gift card or gift basket. Make additional gift baskets available for retail sale. Purchase branded folios, notebooks, lanyards, laptop or tote bags, lunch bags, pens or other items suitable as business gifts or to create a business-oriented gift basket.

Send a personal item (scented lotions, aromatherapy candles, room sprays, branded wares, gift cards, etc.) along with a bounce-back offer to local administrative professionals such as the secretarial staff of your local school district and school offices, hospitals, city hall, police and emergency services departments, businesses located near yours, your marketing partners, etc.

Add branded, custom-designed or boutique-quality office supplies and tools to your retail. Purchase branded pens to give away as a gift-with-purchase to all customers in April.

April 25 – Red Hat Society Day

According to their mission statement on www.redhatsociety.org, the Red Hat Society is "a global society of women that supports and encourages women in their pursuit of fun, friendship, freedom, fulfillment, and fitness." Members are generally over the age of 50, but younger members are not turned away. As of April, 2011, annual membership fees are under $50 and entitle members to participate in a local chapter; according to their website, there are currently 23 chapters operating within 10 miles of my home zip code, in a rural area south of Seattle.

Members enjoy internet resources and participation in a global online community. They also have access to the Red Hat Society's online calendar of events where "Hatters" post information about events, outings and gatherings for local chapter members.

Reach out to members of local chapters with a special offer, gift or event. Offer to sponsor an outing, host chapter meetings or partner with other businesses to sponsor a large-scale event. Extend offers to members and hold door prize drawings so that you can ask for contact information. Provide food, supplies, manufacturer samples or branded tchotchkes as gifts for chapter members. Promote organization memberships or offer to sponsor one or more of your customer's membership fees.

In the same spirit of fellowship among women, hold a women's happy hour, a movie and a makeover event, a group event at a local club, a fashion and makeup show, a spa day of pampering or organize a tour to a major shopping or tourist destination.

April 26 – Pretzel Day

Partner with a local gourmet food or grocery store to provide pretzel samples to customers. Purchase gourmet or branded pretzels for client gift, gift-with-purchase or retail sale.

Solicit pretzel or pretzel-related recipes. Hold a pretzel eating contest, a pretzel making contest or a pretzel dip and decorating contest. Post trivia or history about pretzels on your Facebook page, blog and e-mail newsletter or hold a pretzel trivia contest.

Make or purchase gourmet dipped, decorated pretzel bouquets suitable for gift giving (Mother's Day is just around the corner!) Send a pretzel bouquet to the office of your local school or district, the nurse's lounge of your local hospital, to your local police or fire station, or the offices of a local charity.

Here are ways to translate Tell a Story Day into business building and engaging, fun activities:

- Hold a story writing or story telling contest
- Partner with a local author, editor or another writing expert to hold a workshop to help budding authors in your community know better how to get started writing, how to work with an editor, how to self-publish or appeal to book publishers, etc.
- Create a running story on Facebook with each new post being the next entry in the story; allow followers to determine alternate endings or vote on options for the next element of the story
- Hold a contest for customers (and/or employees) to create fictional stories around the origin of some of your products or services
- Add some of your favorite books to prize baskets, give them as gifts to your most important customers, use them to incentivize purchase of specific products, menu items or services or give them away as gifts-with-purchase
- Hold a book swap event or create an In-store reading area and a book swap library
- Post a list of recommended reading including customer and employee favorites on your website, blog, Facebook page and e-mail newsletter
- Host or sponsor a monthly book club

When was the last time you told the story of your business to your customers, or even your employees? It's more than the date you opened your doors, the story of your business also includes things like:

- The chronological, major event and turning points in the history of your company
- What ideals or inspiration led you into the industry or to start your business
- Why you choose to operate your business in certain ways
- The values that underlie employee performance expectations and the values you expect employees to understand and share
- What customers can expect as a result of doing business with you
- How you hope to change the lives of your customers for the better
- What you hope to provide to employees of your business beyond a paycheck
- The good that your company does and/or ultimately wants to accomplish
- What your business will ultimately become when it's all 'grown up'

Here are some ways to tell your story in the coming weeks in order to engage and strengthen relationships with your customers, investors, employees, vendors, the media and local leaders:

- Tell the story of your business in Facebook posts and in your e-mail newsletter

- Post interesting facts at the point of purchase or on bag stuffers

- Create an 'annual report' to be sent to your customers, employees, vendors, investors, community leaders and other stakeholders telling the story of your business, describing how the business is fulfilling its mission and pursuing the vision and the good that it is doing

- Review employee hiring, orientation, and annual training to ensure it includes telling and re-telling the story of your company, especially as relates to employee expectations, standards, values, promises to the customer, etc.

- Include vendors who directly impact the customer experience or who interact directly with customers in mandatory orientation and training

- Tell the story of your business in correspondence and during the proposal process with prospective customers, investors, vendors, etc.

- Create or update the "about us" sections of your website

- Create or update your corporate brochure or press kit

- Send a copy of your corporate brochure or press kit to local media and to offices of large local employers, school districts, city government or other influential organizations

- Plan a corporate anniversary celebration or annual meeting and include the re-telling of your corporate story in some way

April 28 – Poetry Reading Day

Share poetry on in-store displays, Facebook, your blog and e-mail newsletter. Ask clients to post the names or quote great lines from their favorite poems. Post quotes from poems and hold a contest to see whether customers can guess or match up the name and author with the poem. Compile a list of recommended poetry or poetry-writing resources to post on your Facebook page, blog and e-mail newsletter.

Hold a poetry writing contest in one or multiple categories (kids, humorous, romantic, etc.) Partner with a local author or literary expert to hold a poetry writing workshop or series of classes. This could be a great opportunity to extend to members of local senior living communities, educators, students, Red Hat Society members or other women's organizations, etc.

Partner with a local library, book store, author or editor to hold a poetry reading event or happy hour. Launch a poetry club or sponsor meetings for a local club. Hold a fundraiser to benefit a local library. Sponsor reading clubs, school literary clubs, after-school library activities or other youth services. Create a special offer for the employees of local libraries, book stores, newspapers and other literary organizations and clubs.

April 29 – Dance Day

Partner with a local restaurant or bar to hold a customer and/or employee-appreciation dance event. Working with a local senior living community, host or sponsor a senior dance event; partner with a photographer to document the event and submit a press release to local media after the event.

Invite local dance teams, teachers or professionals to demonstrate styles of dance to customers. Hire a D.J. to "spin records" live at your business. Organize a flash mob dance event in your business to entertain customers. Solicit dance videos on Facebook or post links to dance or dance instruction videos on your Facebook page, blog and e-mail newsletter.

Partner with local dance instructors or dance studios for cross or cooperative marketing. Work together to provide a demonstration, workshop or introductory dance lesson for customers who are interested in classes for themselves or their children. Add dance instruction videos to your retail or for drawing or contest prizes.

Hold a fundraiser in support of a local children's dance studio or upcoming event. Help promote ticket sales to the performances of local youth dance studios (and be sure you attend yourself!) Take out advertising in performance programs to show your support for the arts. Extend a special offer to the employees and patrons of local dance instructors and dance studios.

April 30 – Hairstylists Appreciation Day

Partner with local salons or stylists for cross and cooperative marketing. Offer to post photographs or display a "look book" featuring the work of local stylists. Connect customers with local stylists by holding a salon or spa expo or creating a directory. Invite local stylists to come and demonstrate their artistic and technical ability, feature seasonal looks, provide mini makeovers or consultations and talk about their salon or spa and products to customers.

Host a happy hour or extend a special offer to local stylists (or all salon and spa employees). Send gift cards to the employees of your favorite salon and spa or send gift cards to the employees of a different local salon or spa every month.

Partner with a local salon to hold a cut-a-thon to benefit charity. Ask participating stylists to donate their time, set a suggested donation for participants and ask other customers to donate as well. Invite a photographer to document the event. Afterward, submit a press release to local media, industry and trade publications. Post links to your press release and photos on your Facebook page, blog and e-mail newsletter.

Purchase salon gift cards as gifts for your employees, as gifts for some of your most important customers or to give away as a gift-with-purchase. Include salon gift cards in pampering gift baskets created as contest prizes or for retail sale.

Partner with a local stylist to provide services prior to major corporate events such as conferences, photo opportunities, company meetings, all-employee photographs, videos or photos that will be included in advertising, etc.

may

365 Days of Marketing

May Month-Long Observances

National Photograph Month

There are a lot of ways you can partner with local photographers, and a lot of great reasons for you to do so! They can work with you on photo shoots for use in advertising, attend and photo-document customer and corporate events, photograph your work for use in marketing and press releases, provide you with photographs to help you create your own catalog, recipe books, coffee table books or marketing calendars, help you make employee I.D. badges or child I.D. cards and more. You can be a source of cross-referrals for them, giving them marketing access to your customers and referring people to them for weddings, graduation, family and holiday pictures and other photo-worthy events.

Here are some ways you can market cooperatively or create joint offers with a photographer marketing partner:

- Major life events, family photos, Christmas and Holiday card photos, anniversaries, family reunions, engagements, weddings and receptions

- Events: holiday parties, corporate events, conventions, graduation, prom, etc.

- School photos, senior photos, school events, competitions, fine arts performances, prom, homecoming, graduation

- Head shots, photo shoots, social media profile photos, corporate blog and website photos, professional corporate publication photos

- Before-and-After photos for makeovers or to document major life external transformation projects (such as restorative or cosmetic surgeries, weight loss programs, etc.) or before-and-after shots for events or contests (like for celebrity look alike makeovers)

- Holiday events, sales and offers

- Catalog, brochure or other marketing collateral featuring your staff, products, services, building, customers, etc.

- Public relations stunts, charity benefit events and fundraisers, corporate meetings, employee-appreciation events, etc.

National Blood Pressure Month

Partner with a local medical practitioner to hold a seminar or screening. Set up a self blood pressure check station and invite customers to check their blood pressure before and after receiving stress-relieving services or interacting with products that provide stress-relief benefits such as aromatherapy or endorphin release. Post expert information about blood pressure, links to websites and local resources on your Facebook page, blog and e-mail newsletter.

BBQ (Barbecue) Month

Create barbecue-themed gift sets with branded or gourmet barbecue supplies, sauce mixes, rubs, utensils, cookbooks and other items for gifts-with-purchase, contest prizes or retail sale. Hold a drawing and collect entries for a gift basket or gift card from a local barbecue restaurant. Add all contacts to your database and extend a special offer to all entrants.

Partner with a caterer or restaurant to hold a customer or employee-appreciation barbecue parking lot event. Hold a barbecue contest, tasting or happy hour. Solicit recipes and cooking tips for sharing on Facebook. Add recipes to the collection you plan to have printed for retail sale or to give away as a gift-with-purchase or contest prize.

Older Americans Month

According to the 2010 US Census, Older Americans (those 65 and older) now comprise almost 15% of the total U.S. population. That's almost 39 million people (a.k.a. "consumers"). By 2050, this number is projected to grow to 88.5 million and represent 20% of the total population! This is a target market worth cultivating; their needs and wants will dictate a considerable portion of total spending over the next several decades. They will continue to live longer, healthier and better than previous generations. They will be increasingly technologically savvy and so will be well-able to access information, communicate and shop online. And what's more, they have so much to offer younger Americans when it comes to experience and wisdom!

Hold an older American's event showcasing local older American artists, photographers, musicians, dancers, etc. Solicit stories or nominations from customers about accomplished, notable or famous local older Americans. Create a special prize for a drawing or to be awarded by public vote in one or more categories. Be sure to draft a press release and submit information about these amazing people to local media for additional honor.

Hold a contest and/or solicit stories from customers about their grandparents or other older Americans who have meant something very special in their lives and why.

Get involved personally by yourself or with your employees to provide volunteer services or visit older Americans living at local retirement facilities, assisted living and nursing homes. Help with indoor cleaning or repairs, mow lawns, weed garden and flower areas, wash windows or cars, etc.

Sponsor a social event at your local senior center or living community. Work with your marketing partners to host a fair for older Americans to introduce them to more community resources. Sponsor or help coordinate transportation to your business for local seniors. Create delivery or in-home services that can be provided at a senior community center or in seniors' homes.

Sponsor a senior picnic or night in the park featuring refreshments, live music, a movie projected onto a screen, etc. Organize a senior game and activity social to be held at your business, at a local restaurant or bar, etc.

Partner with a local salon or stylist, dentist, physician, fitness expert, nutrition and dietary expert and related professionals to hold a graceful aging workshop, screening, demonstration or consultation event. National Senior Health and Fitness Day is observed at the end of May—this would be a perfect time to hold this event! Partner with a fitness expert to hold on-going exercise and fitness classes for local seniors at your business.

Give away branded tchotchkes as a gift-with-purchase to older Americans in May. Post facts about the generations represented by older Americans including The Greatest Generation, Baby Boomers, etc. Take entries, hold drawings and give away free products or services to older Americans this month.

For more ideas, see March Week 3 "Well-Elderly Week."

National Salad Month

Partner with a local restaurant, caterer or grocer to provide delicious salad samples to your customers or with take-out salads to gift-with-purchase or sell to customers or to treat your employees to lunch. Work together with a local clothing retailer and hold a working women's or mom's lunch hour fashion show with salad fare.

Partner with a local caterer or party planner to hold a workshop teaching participants how to prepare great salads as the main course for bridal showers, anniversaries, luncheons and other occasions as well as how to beautifully tablescape and serve their salad-based party menu.

Hold a contest or have a salad tasting or happy hour. Solicit the favorite salad recipes of customers, employees, local chefs, caterer, etc. to share on Facebook, your blog and e-mail newsletter. Create a salad recipe brochure or add recipes to the collection that you will have printed at the end of the year for retail sale, gift-with-purchase or contest prize inclusion next year. Whether you will print a brochure or full-blown cookbook, use space in your publication for marketing your business, services and products, providing customer testimonials, talking about the good that your business does in the community, etc.

Put together ingredient kits that can be sold as a set to make it easy to recreate the salads that are featured at your events or to sell as the perfect summer hostess gift. Purchase serving and silverware pieces to complete gift sets for resale (or to give to your most valuable customers, to give to employees at your annual corporate meeting, etc.)

May Week 1

May Week 1 – Family Week

Partner with a local restaurant and bowling alley, movie theater, recreation or sports center to create a family night out package or hold a customer or employee family appreciation event. Bundle your gift card together with those of marketing partners to be sold at a special price or awarded to a contest winner. Partner with family-oriented restaurants and destinations for cross and cooperative marketing. Extend a special offer to the owners, managers and employees of family-friendly businesses.

If you provide services in the course of your business, coordinate times when family members can receive services simultaneously and/or at a special family rate. Let customers know that you are happy to provide services for their children. Create a graduated schedule of pricing for families that purchase products or services together (such as, 1st at full price, 2nd at a percentage or dollars off, 3rd or 3 or more at a percentage or dollars off, etc.) Extend a discount for children's or child-sized services or products when purchased at the same time as those of their parents.

Provide incentives for people to patronize your business as a family like free treats or toys for children, free children's products, meals, etc. Set aside an area for children's activities. Purchase branded crayons and coloring pages, silly putty or clay and assign staff to supervise children. Hire a magician, clown or mascot. Purchase branded toys or treats to gift or gift-with-purchase to customers who frequent your business with their children. Send branded toys to local kindergarten classes, day cares or youth services organizations.

Create a gift basket filled with family-oriented items like "mad libs" books, craft kits and board games and hold a drawing; make additional baskets, family-friendly games and activities available for retail sale or a gift-with-purchase.

Post links to family games and activities on your Facebook page, blog and e-mail newsletter. Solicit customer suggestions or photographs of family activities or outings. Create a directory of family activity centers, theme parks, outdoor parks, sports and recreation facilities.

May 1 – Executive Coaching Day

Partner with a local executive coach or motivational speaker to hold a workshop on executive development or a related topic. Partner with local coaches, speakers, employment agencies and similar professionals for cross or cooperative marketing.

Work with marketing partners to set up a leadership training course for employees who are interested in professional advancement. Invite business educators, executive coaches or leaders from within your partnerships or from other businesses to speak to members on leadership topics, common management problems and best management practices.

Launch a formal networking support group made up of peers in leadership at other businesses within your community. Meet once a month or once every two months to discuss a specific topic, have a guest speaker and brainstorm on problems and solutions.

Create a list of recommended reading for executives, managers and leaders or for job seekers. Add some of the best titles to your retail or to a special impulse buy display. Include your favorites in gift packages tailored for professionals.

Partner with other local businesses to hold a job fair. Participate in job fairs at local high schools and community colleges. Host a community job posting bulletin board in your business or online. Invite other businesses to help populate this listing and keep it updated.

Create a facts sheet about your business to share with students or individuals interested in learning more about your business or your industry, noting the most important skills, education or knowledge required for success in your line of work. Send a copy of your facts sheet and press kit to the career counseling services offices of local high schools, trade schools, colleges and universities.

May 2 – Loyalty Day

Do you know what makes customers (and employees, for that matter) develop loyalty to you? Your devotion to them. You earn loyalty by meeting and exceeding the needs of people in ways they perceive to be valuable and unique to your business, over and over again, over time. There is no shortcut to loyalty and there are no guarantees that it will last; loyalty can be eroded through poor customer experiences more quickly than it can be built.

If it's so much work, is it worth it? Absolutely. Loyal customers will buy your stuff. Loyal customers will return again and again to buy even more of your stuff. Loyal customers won't be interested in your competitor's stuff. Loyal customers will refer friends, family, co-workers and acquaintances to you. Loyal customers will even talk to strangers about you—they'll sing your praises to anyone they think you can help.

Loyal, engaged clients will begin to view themselves as insiders; part of your 'club,' so to speak. They will attend your events and bring people with them. They will participate in two-way dialogue with you, provide you with constructive feedback and even help you generate new ideas. They will participate in your conversations on Facebook, leave reviews for you and vote for you in "best of" contests. They will be an active source of referrals and will work to earn rewards and participate in your programs.

Engaged clients believe that they are part of something. They believe they are important to you and to your business. The *only way* a client will become engaged will be because you deliberately engineer a series of consistent experiences and touchpoints which clearly demonstrate to them, over the passage of time, that *they* are a unique, valued and vitally important person in your life and in your business.

This is a fact that many people in business don't seem to understand: A client is never going to put more into your relationship than you do. Imagine a still pool of water that provides a reflection. The reflection on the water may be a fair image of the original, but the original is still by far the strongest, clearest side. Like it or not, the engagement (or lack of engagement) demonstrated toward your business by your customers (and employees, for that matter) is a direct reflection of your engagement with, and demonstrated interest in, them. Your level of engagement and interest in the them is the original, their response is the reflection. Just as with the clear pool of water, the reflection is never going to be stronger than the original!

Realizing that should motivate you to thoroughly examine the experience you provide for each and every customer. Challenge your own preconceived ideas and those of your staff about the quality of your products and services, the employee culture, your physical environment, your marketing and communications, your promotions—everything. Move beyond your own fear relative to confronting or even removing staff who are in the wrong positions, who need more education, who need to update their skills, who need to change the way they present themselves or who simply need to move on.

While discounting has been the name of the game for the last couple of years, especially once the effects of the recession really started to hurt the US consumer, discounting does not breed loyalty. Once you lower your price, a competitor is sure to follow, and you find yourself undermining the vitality of your own organization with little to show for it. As those who jumped in to location-based "daily deal" marketing have learned, many bargain shoppers are loyal to just one thing: the discount.

Many small business owners who tried using deep discounts to get customers through the door or lowered their prices and then marketed the heck out of their price point advantage have been left scratching their heads, because what they believed to be true was not true. They believed their products or services were totally relevant, that their facility was acceptable, that their staff were qualified and competent. They believed that if they could get a new customer in the door once, they would come back again—but it didn't happen.

Why not? Because one (or more) of their assumptions was incorrect. In part, they didn't understand that the customer was responding to a discount, not buying as the result of a strong need or desire. But ultimately, the answer is that the customer experience they created was not compelling enough to stimulate intrigue. Intrigue, you ask? I thought we were talking about loyalty. We are!

Creating intrigue is the natural first step to establishing long-term, loyal relationships with customers.

*intrigue (*v.*) *meaning:* to fascinate, arouse the curiosity of, or amuse
*Kernerman English Multilingual Dictionary

It might help to think of it this way: While you invest thousands and thousands of dollars in your facility, personnel, inventory and training—and you invest even more than that in time and energy— the customer only sees a microscopic portion of that investment. Some part of their 30, 60 or even few-hour-long experience must stimulate intrigue in them to make them *want* to come back and to cause them to want to try other products or services you offer.

The editors of television reality shows condense what they feel are the most compelling, provocative and important conversations, activities and events that occur over the course of a week or even longer into a one or two hour-long show. That might mean distilling upwards of 168 hours (more than ten thousand minutes) into just 35 or 40 minutes of actual show time when you account for commercials and "coming up next" teasers. They try to produce the most intriguing, engaging and provocative 40 minutes possible in order to entice viewers to watch the show again, to follow contestants, to visit their websites and, in some cases, even to decide the outcome of the series via public vote.

Think of each customer visit as if it were a personal, condensed reality show for each and every individual. In other words, each customer will see, hear, smell and experience the elements *that you decide* —either intentionally or unintentionally—to edit down into the block of time they will be present within your business. As the producer and real time editor of the customer experience, how can you orchestrate each one to be intriguing, engaging and provocative to the client?

May 2 – Scrapbooking Day

Scrapbookers have a tight-knit, interactive community. Most have families and many are moms— and these women talk to each other, constantly. In fact, "Moms" are unrivaled champions when it comes to reviews, recommendations, referrals and word-of-mouth marketing. Far outpacing any other demographic in this area, on average, moms have more than 100 product or service-related discussions every single week! They are connected online and off, they have common interests and they share referrals on any number of topics—it's a community worth courting.

Partner with a local boutique paper, hobby or craft store for cross or cooperative marketing. Invite a scrapbooking expert from one of these businesses or from within your community to hold a workshop for customers in beginning or advanced scrapbooking.

Make chic, kitsch-y, unique and/or elegant scrapbooking supplies or kits available for sale. Create a prize basket and hold a contest or drawing, soliciting entries from local scrapbookers. Ask customers to share pictures of their favorite layouts and exchange resources online. Create a gallery page on your website, blog or Facebook page. Set up a display at your business featuring the work of local artists.

May 3 – Home Brew Day

There aren't many statistics online relative to home brewers; however, while not scientific, I did find some stats worth sharing at usabeertrends.com from a 2009 survey. The age of survey respondents were between 21-50, with about a third each represented in the 21-30, 31-40 and 41-50 brackets. I'm going to go out on a limb and suggest that a majority of all responders were probably male (so marketing around this theme is another opportunity to target male clients).

While it's officially Home Brew Day, you can expand promotions and events to include microbrews, which have become exponentially more popular over the last decade in the US (and the world). Events in observation of American Craft Beer Week (held the 3rd week of May) were held in all 50 states for the first time in 2011. Beer tasting is now a common alternative or add-on to traditional wine tasting events. Close cousins, it's a great marriage for the purpose of attracting more people with similar lifestyles and interests to shared tasting events.

Extend offers to home brew cooperatives, vendors and suppliers or partner with them for cross and cooperative marketing and events. Connect people with home brew suppliers, websites and local resources. Launch a local club for home brewers; plan to hold monthly or quarterly tastings or meet at the facilities of local micro-breweries for networking and education.

Partner with a local home brewing expert to hold a workshop for interested customers. Add homebrew books or starter kits to your retail, or create a homebrew starter kit prize basket. Post facts or have an online trivia contest on home brewing, microbrews or beer in general.

Hold a contest for local beer crafters (check state and local regulations first), or a tasting or a combined wine and beer tasting event; just fyi, there are people who make wine at home as well. Partner with a local brewery to hold a beer tasting or microbrew happy hour. Compile a list of local micro-breweries to share on your Facebook page, blog and e-mail newsletter. Soliciting customer input as well as suggestions from local brewers, bartenders, distributors and other experts, post a recommended tasting list of microbrews on your Facebook page, blog and e-mail newsletter.

May 4 – Melanoma Awareness Day

Supporting a charitable cause and helping real people in your community is an important part of being a responsible business owner. Your business is not the end, it's the means to many other ends. It's what you do to support your real 'habits'—things like providing for yourself and your family, saving for college, travel and retirement, pursuing hobbies and activities, and, in this case, giving back to the community by supporting causes that impact you personally or stir your passions.

The reason I espouse so many cancer charities as potential fundraising beneficiaries (any time you need a cause to rally people around, please feel free to steal mine) is that when I was just 22, my husband (also 22) died of melanoma cancer, leaving me a widow with two very young kids. Not fair, right? Melanomas most commonly occur on the outside of the skin and can be removed; however, melanoma that occurs internally, especially if it has spread to more than one location, is incurable. It's an incredibly fast-moving, insatiable, painful and grotesque cancer—no Hollywood-movie romantic sugarcoating for this one!

Get behind efforts to fight a cancer that has impacted your life or that of a loved one. Donate and raise funds to support research. Provide support and encouragement to patients and their families, some of whom will face medical bills in the millions of dollars in the space of a year, or even less.

There are simple ways to help protect the skin and increase awareness to help prevent melanoma and other skin conditions caused by the sun's damage. Educate employees and clients on the harmful and premature aging effects of the sun and how to protect hair and skin. Partner with local medical specialists and skin care experts to hold a seminar or screening and to provide information to your customers about what to look for, when to have a skin abnormality checked, etc.

Purchase branded sunscreens for retail or sample sizes for gifts-with-purchase, client gifts and employee use. Add safe, sunless tanning lotions to retail or to give away as a gift-with-purchase to customers. Put together a safe tanning-themed basket for contest prize or retail sale, including items like sunless tanners, sunscreen, lip balm and/or makeup with sunscreen, cover ups, hats or visors, messaged brandwear, after-sun skin repair products, etc.

Purchase branded items or create your own slogan or design for cover-ups, t-shirts or tank tops with messages about protecting the skin, having checkups or screenings, fighting cancer or in support of your campaign. Use branded, custom-designed items to help raise awareness. Gift them to employees to wear at benefit events and community gatherings, in public forums (such as when manning the booth at street fairs) or on special awareness days at your business. Sell or gift additional wares to extend both your brand and the message out into the community. Hold a benefit event to raise money or donate a percentage of overall sales or proceeds from sales of specific items (like custom-designed wares) to a local cancer treatment facility or patient.

Recommend products that help protect the skin during sun exposure or repair skin afterward and give advice about what to do before going out in the sun, when the suns harmful rays are likely to be the strongest, what to do in event of sunburn, etc. Post recommendations, tips and trivia on your Facebook page, blog. e-mail newsletter and bag stuffers. Post information about melanoma, the harmful effects to skin because of overexposure to the sun, chemicals to avoid, potentially dangerous tanning practices, links to local skin care or skin cancer specialists, etc.

May 5 – Cinco de Mayo

According to wikihow.com, on May 5, 1862, against overwhelming odds, the Mexican Army defeated French forces in the Battle of Puebla. While Cinco de Mayo (Spanish for the 5th of May) is celebrated in the Puebla region because of this, the observance has taken on more meaning outside of Mexico than within, similar to how St. Patrick's Day is actually more popular in the U.S. than in Ireland. Originally a celebration of freedom and independence, in the US, Cinco de Mayo has taken on the meaning of celebrating Spanish history and traditions.

In honor of the 'Cinco' extend a $5 promotion to clients such as $5 off every $50 spent in May on retail and/or services or $5 off a specific service or product.

Cinco de Mayo is also a great opportunity to partner with a local restaurant or bar for joint happy hours or another event complete with a piñata, door prizes, limbo contests, etc. Take pictures of guests wearing sombreros. Hold a hot chili pepper eating contest. Hold a drawing for a gift card or prize basket and utilize entries to add contacts to your database. Afterward, extend a follow-up offer or an invitation to your next special event to all those who attended.

Put together a gift basket with Mexican foods, mixes or sauces, table ware, decorations, etc. for retail sale or for a contest prize. Add piñatas to your retail or give them away as a contest prize or gift-with-purchase. Partner with a local hobby or craft store to hold a piñata-making workshop. Post links to instructional sites for making pinatas at home on your Facebook page, blog and e-mail newsletter. Hold a contest for attendees and reward winner/s with a piñata, the craft supplies needed to make one or candy to fill it.

Post interesting facts or have a trivia contest about Cinco de Mayo and related traditions on your Facebook page or in-store. Host Spanish language classes. Donate proceeds from Cinco de Mayo events or product sales to local ESL (English as a Second Language) learning or literacy programs.

May 6 – Tourist Appreciation Day

Extend offers to local tourists by partnering with hotels, motels, restaurants, car rental agencies, gas stations, etc. for cross or cooperative marketing. Place rack cards at tourist points of interests. Advertise in tourist directories. Extend special offers to the employees of businesses that cater to the tourism industry (like hotels, motels, car rental agencies, bus tours, historical sites, national parks, theme parks, etc.) Get involved with your city's tourism and commerce committees. Contact your local Chamber of Commerce or city hall to find out about additional opportunities to reach out to tourists or tourist industry businesses.

Hold an open house event where you treat guests like 'tourists.' Give tours of your facility. Collect contact information. Create a punch card designed to look like a ticket, map or in another tourism-themed format and have guests "check in" at each "tourist stop" in order to learn more about your business, receive free samples, professional consultations and see demonstrations.

Reward participants when they have visited all of the stops on your "tour" with a goodie bag containing samples and bounce back offers. Hold one or more door prize drawings at the event and collect contact information to add to your database. Afterward, thank attendees for coming, ask if they have additional questions, provide them with information about the products or services featured at the event and extend a bounce-back offer. Or go big! Partner with other businesses in your community to create a larger scale, multi-business customer tour route and rewards program.

May 7 – Military Spouses Day

Extend a special offer or host an event for military spouses or families. Send business cards, postcards or flyers advertising military-only special offers, promotions or events to military family support organizations. Place ads in military base directories. Extend on-going free add-ons, discounts or other promotions to those with military I.D.

Express appreciation for the military and highlight the accomplishments or sacrifices made by servicemen and women around the world, as well as their spouses, in Facebook and blog posts, your e-mail newsletter and bag stuffers. Highlight local resources available to military families. Post information about military charities and community events.

Support military charities through fundraising, holding benefit events or by donating a percentage of sales or proceeds from sales of specific products or services. 'Adopt' a local military family for a year of free services or products, a one-time shopping spree, gifts for their children or to help fund a reunion or vacation.

Partner with other businesses (salon or spa, restaurant, club, theater, limo company, tux or formal rental, etc.) to hold a contest, taking nominations of local military spouses to win a pre-date makeover and date night package. Create bundled date night out packages to sell on an on-going basis at a special rate, to be used as contest prizes, to be donated to charity auctions, etc.

May Week 2

May Week 2 – Nurses Week

Extend a special offer to the nurses (or all employees) of local hospitals, nursing homes, assisted living facilities, medical treatment centers, independent medical and dental practices, etc.

Hold a drawing and reward a local nurse with a gift card for a free massage, spa services or another pampering experience. Purchase aromatherapy products like massage oils, candles and lotions to award as prizes or to gift or gift-with-purchase to local nurses. Purchase branded hand or body lotions, oil, incense, candles or other aromatherapy minis to place in break rooms of local hospitals in appreciation of the work of local nurses along with a bounce-back offer from your business. Coordinate with a local hospital or care center and provide a meal or dessert as a thank-you gift for nursing staff.

Purchase custom-designed or boutique-quality nurses scrubs for resale or for drawing or contest prizes. Create your own design or add humorous or inspirational nursing-themed messages to your own line of scrubs, lanyards, travel or coffee mugs, candy pill bottles, totes, nail kits, wall plaques, bumper stickers, license plate surrounds, notebooks, pens and other promotional items to add to your retail or to give to local nurses as gifts of appreciation or contest prizes.

Hold a reception or happy hour for nurses and other caregivers at your place of business or in partnership with a local bar or restaurant. Provide attendees with free samples, branded tchotchkes, demonstrations and consultations. Take entries (to build your contact database) and award door prizes or a grand prize at the event. Afterward, extend a bounce-back offer.

Purchase a giant thank-you card and ask customers to sign it when at your business or use a large roll of paper to create a thank-you banner to be sent to the nursing staff of your local hospital at the end of the month or to be presented at a special event.

Hold a walk-a-thon or another fundraiser in support of your local hospital, hospice, nursing home or specialty care center.

Use Facebook, your blog and e-mail newsletter to solicit customer stories honoring local nurses for the care they provide or special accomplishments. Post trivia, facts, statistics or history, famous nurses in history, etc. on your Facebook page, blog and e-mail newsletter. Ask people to nominate their favorite local nurse to win a prize package or gift card. Partner with a salon or spa to reward a local nurse with a free makeover.

Or go big! Work with marketing partners to hold a larger scale open house or reception for nurses. Award one or more larger prize packages that might include gift cards for salon or spa, dining, entertainment, massage, flowers, wine, chocolates, housecleaning services, etc.

May 8 – Child Care Provider Day

Also referred to as 'Provider Appreciation Day,' Child Care Provider Day is usually observed on the Friday before Mother's Day; check the internet to determine the exact day it will be held in the current year. In the weeks before Child Care Provider Day, make specific gift suggestions to parents on your Facebook page, blog, e-mail newsletter and bag stuffers. Purchase greeting and gift cards with sentiments that express appreciation and gratitude appropriate for giving to providers.

Extend special offers, send branded products or gift cards to local child care providers, day cares, etc. Sponsor an event for local day care or home child care providers at a family recreation or activity center. Hold an open house, park or parking lot event featuring kids' activities, games, prizes and refreshments. Extend invitations to day cares and child care providers in your community. Send branded tchotchkes and bounce-back offers home in goodie bags for providers (and/or parents). Invite stay-at-home moms and dads, MOPS (Mothers Of Pre-Schoolers) and other parent organizations in your community to enjoy this activity day as well.

Take nominations and reward a local child care provider with a salon or spa gift card for a makeover, a free massage and/or a night out on the town package. Partner with other businesses to create larger or multiple prize packages (salons or spas, boutique or formal rentals, limousine, restaurant, club, theater, bar, etc.) Don't forget the press release!

Supply lunch or treats for the employees of local day cares. Hold a fundraiser or make a donation to purchase new toys or equipment for a local day care. Establish a scholarship fund for continuing education for child care providers. Hold a contest, taking nominations of favorite local child care providers. Feature some of the most outstanding stories in a press release honoring local providers and highlighting the community contributions and/or needs of local child care centers.

Compile an online directory of child care providers and day cares. Connect parents with local child care options, recommended providers and other resources (guidelines, babysitting classes, children's activity sites, etc.) using Facebook, your blog, website, e-mail newsletter, bulletin board, etc. Solicit stories about outstanding local providers and the difference they make for parents and children.

May 9 – Lost Sock Memorial Day

Create a Lost Sock Memorial! See how many socks whose mates have been lost that you can get your customers to contribute. Hold a publicity stunt to build the largest 'Lost Sock Memorial' possible. I tried to find out whether there were any world records on file for a lost sock collection. While I found records for the most socks worn on one foot and the most people simultaneously knitting socks, I did not find one for the biggest collection of un-mated socks—this one could be all yours!

Hold a trivia contest or post facts about the history of socks. Believe it or not, I found a rather lengthy set of historical sock facts at www.lonelysock.com.

Use the excitement you are undoubtedly now building about socks to kick off a sock BOGO event or the retail sale of zany, beautiful, boutique, branded or otherwise one-of-a-kind socks. Purchase unique socks to sell, gift-with-purchase or use as contest prizes. Create your own sock design.

Hold a contest and solicit customer stories on the most unique use of socks. Post reasons why people should save single socks and what they can use them for besides footwear. Ask for pictures of their most unique, colorful, worn, etc. socks.

Donate new socks to a local charity or to children of local day care centers, kindergartens, children's hospitals, etc. Offer clients a free add-on or reward when they bring packages of new socks with them to your business. Purchase branded socks and invite customers to bring their socks-with-lost-mates in for a free exchange. Purchase branded baby socks to send to clients who are expecting or have recently had a baby.

May 10 – Clean Your Room Day

Hold a contest and ask customers to send you pictures of the cleanest or messiest rooms (teenager's bedrooms, children's bedrooms or play rooms, garages, offices, etc.) Reward winner/s with home organizational supplies or cleaning tools.

Partner with a professional organizer and a local house cleaner to hold a workshop for customers on home organization and cleaning. Post cleaning and organizational tips on Facebook, your blog, e-mail newsletter and bag stuffers.

Solicit home organization and cleaning tips, homemade or organic cleaning solution recipes and recommendations and post them on Facebook, your blog and e-mail newsletter. Turn this effort into a contest and reward those who submit the most unusual, wacky, effective or innovative ideas.

Partner with a local housecleaning service and add a gift certificate for two or more hours of housecleaning to your prize package/s. Purchase a gift certificate from a local cleaning service to give away as a contest prize, gift-with-purchase, or an employee-appreciation or incentive reward.

May 11 – Eat What You Want Day

Do it! And while you're indulging, think through the customer experience at your business. Come up with ideas on how to create client-indulgent experiences to make them feel as though they are being treated to *extra*-special care, service or pampering.

Hold an "eat what you want" promotion and allow customers to choose from a variety of items that are not normally priced the same, at a single, special price. Redesign your catalog or menu to read like an à la carte menu. Make suggestions for common add-on items or give the customer the ability to bundle several products and/or services at a special price.

Provide treats for customers while shopping or during appointments. Invite a local caterer, restaurant, candy shop, etc. to sample treats to your customers. Provide samples or create a special offer for their customers. Purchase branded or gourmet foods to add to your retail or impulse buys or to gift or gift-with-purchase to clients.

Partner with a nutritionist and/or healthy eating expert to hold a workshop for customers on ways they can 'eat what they want' while still maintaining a healthy diet. Provide customers with healthy, delicious recipe alteratives and substitutions for less-healthy ingredients.

Partner with a local bar or restaurant and hold an 'eat what you want' happy hour with all appetizers, entrees or desserts offered at a special price, bundled into a sampler or featured buffet-style.

May 12 – The 2nd Wednesday in May is Receptionists Day

The 2nd Wednesday in May is Receptionist's Day; check a calendar for the actual date of observance in the current year. Extend an offer or send a gift to receptionists at businesses located near yours or those of your marketing partners. Give your own receptionist a special pat on the back, gift, thank you or acknowledgement (hopefully you are doing this more than once a year!)

In the weeks leading up to Receptionist's Day, send flyers, e-mails and postcards to the managers and executives at local businesses to let them know the observance is approaching, to make specific gift suggestions and extend special offers.

Partner with a local caterer or restaurant to provide lunch for the receptionists of local businesses, your marketing partners, your local school district or school offices, etc.

Invite local receptionists to a reception, open house or happy hour. Feature delicious after-work refreshments. Hold a fashion show and/or partner with a stylist or esthetician to provide free mini-makeovers, manicures, pedicures or massages. Invite a local photographer to take pictures that attendees can use as corporate head shots, social media profile pictures or purchase for themselves. Purchase branded picture frames to give to all attendees or as a gift-with-purchase. Give away branded items, have door prizes, collect contact information and extend bounce-back offers.

Purchase branded or create your own line of humorous or inspirational office/work-themed t-shirts, tank tops, pens, notebooks, folios, totes, lunch bags, travel and coffee mugs, memo cubes, phone message pads, stress balls, office supplies, etc. to use as contest or drawing prizes, to give away at your event, to give away as a gift-with-purchase or to add to your retail.

Sponsor a monthly or quarterly lunch hour for local receptionists. Invite guest speakers to speak on topics of personal or professional interest, provide information on continuing education or give motivational speeches. Set aside time for attendees to share common problems, brainstorm solutions and share resources. Sample products and provide professional consultations and demonstrations at all of your Receptionist's meetings and events.

May 13 – Night Shift Day

Send samples, branded tchotchkes and/or refreshments to the night crews and third shift employees of local businesses; don't forget your own night security and cleaning staff. Send dessert, snacks or provide a 2 AM "lunch" to thank the night shift of your local police force, emergency services, hospitals, etc. With each, send bounce-back offers, copies of your menu or catalog and business cards. Other businesses with third shift employees to whom you might extend special offers: hotels and motels, grocery stores, gas stations, convenience stores, 24-hour restaurants, call centers, manufacturers, etc.

Hold a Night Shift charity benefit all-nighter, after hours social event or sale, extending your regular hours to a full 24 hours for one day or into the wee hours of the morning. Have games, contests, tournaments, door prizes, consultations, sampling and/or demonstrations. Give away branded tchotchkes. Hire an entertainer or provide live music. Partner with a local bar or restaurant to host or provide food for your event. Invite those within your community who do work the night shift to stop in during their lunch hour.

May 14 – Leprechaun Day (and May 12 – Limerick Day)

Hold a trivia contest or post interesting facts, history and other lore about Leprechauns on your Facebook page, blog, e-mail newsletter and in-store on flyers, bag stuffers or a point of service display.

Design "lucky" bag stuffers or mailers that include codes that can be redeemed for free add-ons, special pricing, branded tchotchkes or other rewards. Number each individually and hold a drawing to reward one or more of your customers with a free gift, shopping spree or gift card redeemable at your business. Hold a "must be present to win" drawing to bring customers in to your location.

Place a 'pot o'gold' at the point of purchase filled with gold-wrapped chocolate or branded coins for customers to take. Or fill a large container with gold coins (count first!) and allow customers to enter a contest by guessing how many coins are in the container. Use entries to build your contact database. Extend a bounce-back offer when you send an e-mail announcing the winning entry.

Hold a limerick-writing contest or hold a happy hour at a local bar or restaurant featuring a standup limerick recitation contest. Post limericks on your Facebook page or have an employee or customer contest to write limericks that describe your business or its products or services.

Purchase books with limericks, jokes or general poetry to include in prizes, sell via retail or to gift or gift-with-purchase to customers.

May Week 3

May Week 3 – Backyard Games Week

Add a selection of backyard games (croquet, badminton, volleyball, bocce, hula-hoop, horseshoes, toss games, etc.) to your retail for the summer months. To remind customers that you have them, give one away free in a drawing or in drawings held each week, every day this week or every day this month.

Put together a Backyard Games gift basket to give away as a contest prize or to be donated to local school or charity auctions. Donate backyard games to local day cares, senior centers, youth services organizations, churches, etc.

Purchase branded tchotchkes like water bottles, sun screen, lip balms, stadium seats, visors, sunglasses or other outdoor gear for retail, gift or gift-with-purchase.

Hold a Backyard Games tournament as a customer or employee-appreciation event at a local park. Create a larger scale event by working with your marketing partners. Extending invitations to both/all sets of customers and to special interest groups like day cares, private or public schools, senior centers, churches, large employers, media, civic organizations, etc.

May Week 3 – Police Week and
May Week 4 – Emergency Services Providers Week

Extend a special offer to civil servants such as police, fire and other emergency service professionals and their families. Partner with other businesses to create a reward package including dinner, a destination point, and other gift cards or prizes, and launch a new "Hero" rewards program. Take nominations and once a month (or more or less often), reward one deserving community servant in order to say "thanks" on behalf of the community.

Send gift cards, products or branded tchotchkes to be placed in the break and lunch rooms of your local police and fire stations. Coordinate with your local police department or fire station and provide lunch for local civil servants. Or go big! Work with other businesses in your community to sponsor an open house, happy hour, dinner or reception for local civil servants complete with recognition, awards and door prizes.

Purchase giant greeting cards or create a large banner and ask customers to sign it as a giant thank-you note to be sent to your local police or fire station.

May Week 3 – Work at Home Moms Week

Extend a special offer to work-at-home moms and/or self-employed women. Hold happy hours, a reception or an open house for these busy people. Host a monthly lunch, breakfast or round table to help connect them with a network of peers with whom they can pool resources, share problems and brainstorm solutions.

Take nominations for exceptional work-at-home moms, or hold a drawing to reward one or more local work-at-home moms with a pampering or work-oriented service, product or prize package.

Do you have slower daytime hours during the week? Attract work-at-home moms by offering free add-ons or offering special rates on products or services sold during slower hours, or by holding a work-at-home moms networking or social event.

As a work-at-home mom myself, there are many days when I feel isolated; sending e-mails, writing blog posts and doing graphic design does little to fulfill my social needs. Partner with motivational speakers, executive coaches and/or professional organizers, or simply tap the deep pool of work-at-home moms in your community for guest speakers and hold regularly-scheduled work-at-home mom workshops, wine tastings or happy hours.

May 15 – Pizza Party Day

Host a pizza party for your employees. Partner with a local restaurant or caterer and give pizza samples to customers. Partner with local restaurants for cross and cooperative marketing.

Solicit nominations of local favorite teachers and sponsor a pizza party for the class of the winner. Send pizzas to local schools for teachers, coaches, administrative staff and other school employees along with copies of your menu, special offers you extend to educators and a bounce-back offer.

Turn the tables and send gift cards to your favorite local independently-owned pizza place which their customers, employees and/or family members can redeem at your business.

Have a pizza history or trivia contest in order to add contacts to your database. Put together a collection of gourmet pizza-making supplies for a contest prize, to gift-with-purchase or add to retail. Add pizza pans, pizza cutters, pizza-themed dinner or party wares to your retail.

Ask customers to share their favorite pizza recipes or pizza-making secrets. Have a pizza making contest, pizza tasting or happy hour. Create a catalog with pizza recipes and related products or add recipes to those you are collecting in order to create your own printed recipe book. Partner with a local restaurant, caterer or nutritionist to hold a pizza-making class or demonstration. Post gourmet recipes or links to celebrity recipes and cooking tips on your Facebook page, blog, bag stuffers and e-mail newsletter.

May 16 – Help Clean Up Your Street Day

Work as an employee group (or with other businesses) to clean up public areas outside your building, in your parking lot, neighborhood sidewalks or a local public parks. Contact your local public works or transportation department and 'adopt' a section of a local highway.

Partner with other businesses in your community to hold a true community service event, taking to the streets to pick up trash, sweep sidewalks, weed and plant flowers, trees, shrubs, etc.

Purchase branded windbreakers, t-shirts, tank tops or hats for employees to wear during clean-up events. Create custom-designed shirts, hats, travel mugs, pens, etc. to sell or for employees to wear at clean-up events with a message related to community service in general or which features the name of your city.

May 17 – Pack Rat Day

Partner with a professional home or office organizer to hold a workshop for customers, or for cross or cooperative marketing. Partner with local storage unit businesses, movers and large vehicle rental agencies for cross or cooperative marketing.

Post home and office organization tips on your Facebook page, blog, e-mail newsletter and bag stuffers. Connect customers with local home and office organization professionals, storage units, movers, mobile data backup, mobile document-shredding services, etc.

Create a messy home or office space and hold a contest challenging customers to clean and organize it during a 60 second period of time.

Solicit pictures of personal collections (things people can't bring themselves to get rid of for sentimental reasons or because they are valuable). Hold an exhibit at your business and invite customers to show off their prize possessions, or create an online photo gallery and solicit submissions. Create your own line of collectibles to release periodically (such as a series of glasses, toys, pins, hats, shirts, or some other item).

Compile a list of recommended home and office organization supplies. Add home and office organization products to your retail. Purchase branded organizers to add to retail or give away as contest prizes or a gift-with-purchase.

Volunteer to help local seniors with spring cleaning and re-organizing their homes, garages or yards. Help coordinate the transportation of seniors' or shut-ins' unwanted items to the dump or for donation to a local thrift store or charity.

May 18 – Museum Day

Partner with local museums, tourist destinations, historical attractions, etc. for cross and cooperative marketing. Purchase passes to museums and historical exhibits to give away as a gift-with-purchase, use as contest prizes, donate to local schools or seniors or even to resell. Exchange free branded tchotchkes or products with people who turn in ticket stubs indicating they recently visited a local museum or attended an arts or cultural event. Place ads in the programs, magazines or directories of local museums, theatrical, orchestral or choral performances.

Feature information, posters, photos or a display in your business for local museums and historical points of interest. Provide trivia about the history of your community with posts on Facebook, your blog, e-mail newsletter and bag stuffers. Hold a local history trivia contest. Post links to local attractions, historical sites and cultural organizations.

May 19 – Boys Club Day

Hold a Boys Club sale, recreation or entertainment event. Create boys club among your customers for activities, events, rewards, etc. Instead of a 'ladies night,' hold an event where men get in free.

Draw customer attention to your male-oriented products or services. Design collateral featuring suggested products, services and add-ons that address common needs or wants of male customers (such as a male grooming kit, golf or other sports-themed kit, etc.) Survey male customers to gauge the customer experience or to discover additional services or products they might enjoy.

Extend special offers to patrons (and/or employees) of local golf clubs, sports and recreation facilities, hunting, fishing and wildlife associations, barbershops, sports bars and other male market-oriented businesses.

May 20 – Employee Health and Fitness Day

Work with your employees to set a group fitness or weight loss goal. Partner with a local trainer and/or nutritionist for expert help or subsidize gym costs to incentivize participation. Provide gift cards or free workout clothes. Have periodic weight and fitness checks; celebrate milestones along the way. Expand your effort by inviting customers to participate.

Partner with a local fitness and nutrition expert to hold a workshop, boot camp or series of classes for customers and/or employees. Hold your own weight loss contest modeled on the popular TV series. Start a walking group or form a team to train for an upcoming marathon, walkathon or another event (like the Susan G. Komen 3-Day Walk for breast cancer treatment, research and awareness).

Compile a directory of local trainers, fitness facilities, resources and reading to feature on your Facebook page, blog and e-mail newsletter. Add related books to your retail or impulse buys; help people get ready to wear skimpier summer clothes!

Partner with a local physician to hold a workshop or share information on your Facebook page, blog and e-mail newsletter. Provide information about recommended checkups, screening, healthy weight and fitness, early warning signs for heart attack or stroke, local resources, etc. Post links to websites with health and fitness information, advice for healthy weight loss, dietary recommendations, recipes, etc.

Partner with local restaurants and help promote healthy eating options. Provide information to employees and customers about how to eat out and still eat healthy, what kind of substitutions they can ask for, how food should be prepared, what questions they should ask, etc.

Focus attention on health or fitness-related products or services you provide. Extend special offers to nutritionists, trainers, dance and martial arts instructors and the employees of local gyms. Design your own branded workout wear. Purchase like water bottles, pedometers, towels, etc. to retail or give away as contest prizes or a gift-with-purchase.

May 21 – Memo Day

Purchase branded office supplies or create your own slogan or design to be printed on memo cubes, pads, notebooks, pens, pencils, etc. to add to retail, gift-with-purchase or for contest prizes. Hold a contest for the most clever, funny, beautiful or otherwise-original design for notebook covers, memos or message pads.

Give away branded memo pads to customers, employees, vendors or your marketing partners as a token of appreciation, kudos or thanks. Distribute branded sticky notes to customers as bag stuffers. Send branded memo pads as gifts for the office staff of local businesses, large employers, local schools, city hall, charities, etc. Write memos of appreciation to employees, customers, local leaders, community service organizations, public servants, etc.

May Week 4

May 22 – Waiters and Waitresses Day

Extend a special offer to employees of local restaurants, bars, and clubs. Invite wait staff to happy hours at your business. After any great dining experience, send a note of thanks to the manager of the restaurant or bar noting the name of your server and how they exceeded your expectations. Include copies of your business card.

Post kudos about great wait staff or great dining experiences on your Facebook page. Post dining etiquette facts and tipping guidelines on your Facebook page, blog and e-mail newsletter. Solicit stories about great and not-so-great dining experiences. Hold a contest for the best or worst waiter or waitress related story. (Avoid problems, litigation or negative results—don't "name names" or otherwise identify specific restaurants or people when sharing negative stories or experiences!)

Partner with local restaurants and bars for cross or cooperative marketing.

When you eat out, tip well and include a copy of your business card, your menu of services, a gift card, or a copy of a current promotion or special offer. Keep branded note cards with you (or in your car) in order to write out notes of thanks to wait staff and other service professionals like stylists, massage therapists, auto service technicians, baristas—there are many individuals you interact with every day who would appreciate a (branded) note of thanks!

May 23 – Taffy Day

Fill a large container with taffy pieces (count first!) and hold a quantity-guessing contest. Take entries in-store and online allowing people to enter via print or web form, Facebook post, e-mail reply, etc. Use entries as a means of collecting contact information to grow your database or get more e-mail subscribers, Facebook and other social media followers. After the contest, extend a special offer to all entrants. Extend special offers to the employees of local candy or gourmet food stores.

Purchase branded taffy or partner with a local candy or gourmet foods store to provide samples of taffy to gift-with-purchase, sell or use as contest prizes. Give gourmet taffy to your most valuable customers, vendors or employees.

Post facts about taffy or taffy making on your Facebook page, blog and e-mail newsletter. Hold a taffy trivia contest. Solicit taffy recipes or have a taffy making contest, tasting or happy hour.

When I think about taffy from the standpoint of analogy, two principles come to mind; the first is flexibility. When taffy is fresh, it's malleable, flexible; you can work with it, you can stretch and reshape it without breaking it. What a great principle for you as a leader as well as for your business.

When it comes to dealing with other people, are you flexible? Are you able to stretch yourself to new lengths? The next time you field a customer complaint, a challenging employee or an unusual situation in your business, "be the taffy." Be willing to be stretched and folded over and over again, blended with new experiences and reshaped into the best piece of taffy you can be!

The second principle that struck me had to do with stickiness. How sticky are your marketing messages? If you practice one-and-done marketing, your messages aren't likely to be very sticky in the minds of customers. Creating a strong brand across all marketing channels (and across all customer and employee touchpoints) will require the delivery of a multitude of messages, delivered consistently and clearly, over time and across all of your customer touchpoints in order to penetrate the minds of consumers. There aren't shortcuts; this is the only way to build a brand that sticks in the minds of customers and is reflected in the behaviors, attitudes and actions of your employees.

The same holds true for single marketing campaigns. You can't just tell customers about a product or service one time and expect that they will jump for joy and elation and rush to your business. It might take months and a dozen messages before customers suddenly "remember" that new product or service you have that they all-of-a-sudden can't live without. Consistency and constancy are the keys to sticky marketing!

May 24 – Lucky Penny Day

Hold a Lucky Penny promotion to provide add-ons, minis, samples, gifts or special pricing on multi-quantity purchases for a penny (e.g., buy 2, get the 3rd for a penny). Create Lucky Penny signage to display by specified items.

Mark one (or more) of the pennies in your cash register with a special marking or color. Tell customers they if they receive these as change, they can exchange these 'Lucky Pennies' for special rewards. Reward customers who pay in exact change (requiring pennies) with a gift card or branded tchotchke as a surprise.

Place a fountain or tub of water near your entrance as a designated wishing well. Set up your own penny toss game, awarding prizes for pennies that land in cups or land in specially-marked cups. Donate all of the change collected to a local charity, youth team, school fundraiser, etc.

Partner for cross or cooperative marketing with a local bar or restaurant and hold a happy hour featuring Lucky Penny cover charges, appetizers or drinks.

Post penny trivia online or have a trivia contest. Allow customers to redeem "Lucky Pennies" (like pennies made in 1966 or another specified year) for branded tchotchkes, products or services.

May 25 – Towel Day

Summer is coming and people will soon be making trips to the beach and the pool. Purchase branded towels for retail sale, client gifts or to give away as contest prizes or a gift-with-purchase— sending your brand beyond your walls and into the community. Expand your retail by purchasing specialty hair-drying, extra-absorbent, uniquely designed, etc. spa or boutique-quality towels for resale. Purchase branded hand towels, place mats and napkins for use on hospitality stations, tables, counters, etc.

Branded towels can do double duty when used within your business to help reinforce your brand at the counter, at the back bar or in the course of services you provide. Purchase enough so they can be also be included in client gift or contest prize baskets throughout the year.

May 26 – Tap Dance Day

Extend a special offer to dance teachers and the employees of local dance studios, performing groups, stores that sell dance wear, shoes, etc. Partner with local dance studios, performing arts organizations, clothing, shoes and supplies stores, etc. for cross or cooperative marketing. Partner with local dance instructors to hold a free demonstration or introductory lesson for your customers.

Hold a talent show or contest. Hold a drawing and reward one or more winner/s with gift certificates they can use for dance lessons or to purchase dance wear or shoes.

Hold a tap dance trivia contest or post facts and connect people with local related resources. Solicit videos of people tap dancing. Post links to local dance studios or instructors, website and local resources on your Facebook page, blog and e-mail newsletter.

May 27 – Senior Health and Fitness Day

Partner with health and fitness professionals to hold or help sponsor a senior health and fitness event including demonstrations, introductory classes, consultations, screenings, senior fitness clothing and shoes fashion show, etc. Hold your event at your business, in your parking lot, at a local fitness facility, in the park or at a local senior center.

Organize a senior walk, exercise, dance, swim or another fitness group. Provide or subsidize transportation, workout gear, equipment and/or other wares and refreshments. Post senior health and fitness advice, tips and resources on your Facebook page, blog and e-mail newsletter.

Create special promotions and focus marketing message on products or services you provide that contribute to the health and fitness of seniors (and/or others).

May 28 – Jazz Day

Choose some of your favorite (or customer-recommended) jazz albums to give away as a gift-with-purchase or contest prize, to add to your retail or in order to create a special impulse buy display.

Purchase tickets for local jazz or other live music performances to be resold or given away as a gift-with-purchase, contest prize or an employee-appreciation gift or group event.

Invite local jazz artists to provide live music at your business, or partner with a local bar, club or restaurant to hold happy hours or an event featuring jazz.

Partner with local instrumental and vocal music teachers to hold a jazz demonstration or an introductory lesson for customers. Hold a drawing and give away a free vocal or instrument lesson, a music scholarship, music store gift card or an instrument. Partner with a local music instrument store to provide special offers for your customers. Extend a special offer for their customers or create a display to be featured in their store. Extend special offers to local music teachers and their students. Extend special offers to all local music instructors, school music staff, music store employees, performing arts organizations, etc.

Hold a jazz trivia contest or post interesting facts on your Facebook page, blog, bag stuffers and e-mail newsletter.

May 29 – Musical Instrument Day

Hey, we're on a roll! In addition to some of the ideas above, you could also hold a musical instrument and/or sheet music swap or garage sale event. Hold a music happy hour and donate the cover charge or a portion of proceeds to the music program of a local public or private school.

Purchase toy musical instruments to be given as a gift or gift-with-purchase to the children of your customers, to be added to your retail or donated to local day cares, schools, children's organizations, youth groups, etc.

May 30 – Water a Flower Day

Partner with local florists, garden centers, nurseries, landscaping professionals etc. for cross or cooperative marketing. Extend special offers to the patrons and/or employees of local florist shops, nurseries and garden centers.

Donate flowers, shrubbery, trees and/or your time (to plant, weed, etc.) to a local retirement community, church, school, senior center or other civic organization. As an employee team, wear branded shirts and hats while you work together to weed and plant in order to improve the outside of your business or business park. Create your own customized community service or city-related design and purchase shirts, hats, mugs, totes, license plate surrounds, bumper stickers, etc. for retail sale, client gifts or to give away as a gift-with-purchase or contest prize. Designate that a portion of proceeds from the sales of these items will be donated to community service projects or a civic service organization.

Purchase branded flower pots and partner with a nursery for flower or plant starts for retail sale, client gift or gift-with-purchase. Add branded or custom-designed watering cans, misters, shovels or gloves to your retail or to give away as a gift-with-purchase.

Partner with an expert on regional native flora and fauna to hold a workshop for your customers or to provide you with advice and tips for indoor or outdoor plant, flower and garden care to post on your Facebook page, blog and e-mail newsletter.

May 31 – Save Your Hearing Day

Partner with a local professional to hold hearing screenings at your business or provide screening services for your employees and/or their family members. Hold a seminar on the causes and warning signs of hearing loss and connect customers with local resources. Invite a hearing aid specialist to participate or demonstrate the latest and greatest in hearing aids.

Bring members of your business community together for a summit on the needs and challenges of the hearing impaired in your community as employees or patrons. Invite an expert to provide recommendations for accommodations that can be made to help the hearing impaired.

Hold a sign language class or series of classes. Hire an interpreter and hold an event for the hearing impaired featuring professional demonstrations, consultations and product sampling. Hold a benefit event to raise money and raise awareness of the needs of agencies in your community which serve the hearing impaired.

Post links to sign language educational sites, local resources and related websites on your Facebook page, blog and e-mail newsletter.

june

365 Days of Marketing

June Month-Long Observances

Childhood Cancer Month,
Cancer of the Skin Month

Hold a benefit event to raise funds or donate a portion of June sales (or proceeds from the sale of specific items) to fund cancer research or benefit a local treatment center. Create your own slogan or design to be printed on t-shirts, tank tops, hats, travel mugs, etc. to raise awareness. Donate proceeds from sales of these items to a local related charity, treatment center, patient or to housing and support centers that provide services for patients and their family members.

Partner with skin care professionals to hold a screening or workshop on cancers of the skin and preventative measure. Give away branded sunscreen and add branded sunscreen, lip balm or makeup with SPF protection, sun umbrellas and cover-ups to your retail.

'Adopt' a local patient to whom you will donate free products or services for a year or a shopping spree. Work with other businesses to acquire additional products or services for this individual and/or their family members. Write a press release to put the spotlight on local treatment centers, talk about what typical patients go through, list some of the common needs of patients and their families, and feature the ways in which your business is making a difference in the lives of local cancer patients.

Form an employee team to participate in a marathon or walkathon (like the Susan G. Komen 3-Day Walk). Train together (this could also be a great cause around which to launch an employee health and fitness program.) Increase the impact by inviting customers, your marketing partners, businesses located near yours and other community members to be part of your team or to make a donation.

Use your Facebook page, blog, e-mail newsletter, bag stuffers and signage to help raise awareness, post facts and preventive measures, list early warning signs and tell people how your business is making a difference. Write press releases before and after benefit events and to periodically document your team's progress.

Entrepreneurs Month

Become a visible, active member of your business community in order to build influence, gain referrals and attract marketing and event partners. Host a club for local entrepreneurs. Get involved in 'Buy Local' associations, your Chamber of Commerce and other groups where entrepreneurs tend to congregate. Take the lead to initiate projects that help improve the local economy and business climate. Add links to community and entrepreneurial resources to your website and feature them in posts on your Facebook page, blog and e-mail newsletter.

Effective Communication Month

Whether you need to tweak existing communications or make them over completely, it should be comforting (and exciting!) to know that it has never been easier, faster or less expensive to communicate with clients and prospects—anywhere in the world they might be! Technology has gone a long way toward leveling the playing field for small businesses (vs. corporations which have the resources to reach out worldwide on their own).

Does all of the new technology available for use in communications mean that decades and even centuries-old tools like the telephone, brochures, catalogs, flyers, business cards and mailers are out of vogue? No, they are more important than ever, in part because you have to utilize more channels of communication, more often, in order to leave an impression in the minds of clients and prospects in today's world. People are bombarded with thousands of individual marketing messages in any given day. You cannot focus solely on internet marketing, social marketing, word-of-mouth, viral or buzz marketing or print marketing—you have to do it all.

Establishing multiple channels for communications and creating habits of engaging frequently and consistently with clients and prospects is crucial. Plus, once established, you will be able to use all of these channels to support special initiatives, educate and engage people, stimulate sales, build more brand awareness and capture more client and prospect mindshare.

So how do you prioritize your marketing investments when it comes to limited resources like time and money? How do you construct communications that work to reinforce not only a one-time message, but also your brand and long-range marketing plan?

First, become aware of all of the tools available to you. Then, decide which communications tools you will use, when, and to what extent you will use each based on the specific campaign, marketing goals or business problem you want to address.

It may sound like a lot of work, but it is through the use of planned, robust, relevant and engaging communications that business is built, new clients are gained, and buzz, viral marketing and referrals are stimulated. The fact that it can seem like there are a lot of moving pieces is precisely why it is crucial for you to know which tools are at your disposal, how they work best and when to use them. It will help you establish a regular schedule of on-going communications and to develop a plan for supplemental communications you can deploy to support special campaigns and events.

Some of the basic tools that are (or should be) at your disposal:

- Business Cards (general)
- Business Cards (with client referral or rewards form)
- Business Cards (with seasonal or new customer offer)
- "Ask me about…" product or services signage, postcards, buttons, etc. celebrity-endorsement testimonial "As Seen In" display sheets and shelf talkers

- Reminders via phone, text, e-mail or direct mail per client's preference (appointment reminders have been shown to significantly reduce no-shows and rescheduling)

- Doctors and other professionals use intake forms at every appointment to verify contact information and get other information about their clients (allergies, symptoms, problems, etc.). Create your own customer intake form or at least re-verify client contact information verbally when appointments are booked, reservations are made, at each appointment, with each purchase, etc. .

- Note Cards (blank, thank-you, sympathy, congratulations, birthday, etc.)

- Postcards (direct mail or to use as bag stuffers, handbills, shelf talkers)

- Signage, indoors and out

- Merchandising, price tags, price lists and displays

- Flyers (direct mail, post as PDF online, bag stuffers, business-to-business offers, event handouts)

- Coupons / vouchers (print and/or electronic)

- Press Releases

- Invitations and RSVP forms (print and/or electronic)

- RSVP or reservation forms (print and/or electronic)

- Brochures (corporate, annual reports, new product or service introductions, guarantees, customer policies, etc.)

- Menus—general, special menus for events, special occasions, or specific groups, such as for bridal or corporate events, etc.

- Menus or brochures for pre-sold series or packages of products/services

- Menus—combination menus featuring your offers as well as those of your business cross and cooperative marketing partners

- Catalog, seasonal catalogs, new product or service announcement brochures (print and/or electronic)

- Website/s

- E-Mail (personal)

- E-Mail for marketing use such as Constant Contact—you don't want to send bulk marketing messages from your personal e-mail account for many reasons

- Facebook and/or other social sites, (most are free to use)

- Blog (many are free to use on sites like blogger.com, wordpress.com, etc.)

- Rewards, Loyalty and Referral Programs collateral

Once you have identified all of the tools at your disposal, decide how and when you will employ each and how you will use them in concert with one another. Set up a basic, manageable schedule of communications tasks to perform each month; to help you get started, use the suggested schedule in the Marketing 101 chapter of this book.

It's unrealistic to try to create a website, a Facebook page, start an e-mail newsletter and launch a direct mail campaign all in the same month (especially if you are the only one who will be doing these tasks). Create a list of the channels and collateral you already have and a list of things you want to add to your communications tool box. Prioritize the list of what you want, and focus on the top one or two items at a time until they've been incorporated, then move on to the next. And find other people within your organization who are willing, would enjoy, and are capable of helping with communications responsibilities—you can't do it all yourself!

For Effective Communication Month:

Review your existing channels of communications. Determine which are the most effective, which need to be discontinued, redesigned or reinvigorated. Decide which channels you don't currently use that need to be added. Set up a list daily/weekly/monthly scheduled tasks. Make/renew your commitment to completing scheduled tasks on a regular basis. Solicit help and instruction where you need it.

Do you know all you need to know about e-mail and social media marketing? There are many free resources on the internet that can bring you back up to speed in terms of new (or updated) communication channels and computer applications or teach you what you need to know to get started. A local community college may have marketing classes you can take or audit, or you can outsource some or all of these tasks to an interested employee or to a marketing professional.

Evaluate internal communications like signage, price tags, displays, etc. Are they legible, clean and still new looking? Do you use your logo, fonts and formatting consistently? Do your communications speak effectively to the needs and wants *of your customers*—are they actually stimulating sales, customer conversations or otherwise producing desired results?

Evaluate employee communications. When was the last time you had an all-employee meeting? When did you last meet individually with each of your staff? Do you have a system for employees to ask questions, make suggestions or share information with you or one another? Do you have an employee newsletter or another means of disseminating corporate news, sales scripts, encouragement, inspiration, education, policies, values and instructions?

When was the last time you solicited feedback from customers or employees? Do you conduct surveys? Do you act on suggestions? Do you communicate results? Are you consistently collecting customer contact information so that you can communicate directly with them on a regular basis?

Fresh Fruit and Veggies Month

Partner with a nutritionist to hold a seminar for customers about the nutrition, health and well-being benefits of fresh fruits and vegetables. Talk about fruits and veggies that contribute to improved mood, and energy or help combat the effects of aging or the environment. Post education, recipes and trivia on in-store signage, tent cards, menus and/or your bag stuffers, Facebook page, blog and e-mail newsletter.

Hold a fresh fruit and veggies tasting or a cooking contest based on the use of specific ingredients. Hold a trivia contest. Hold a fruit and/or veggie smoothie or cocktail contest or tasting. Solicit home remedies based on fresh fruits and vegetables.

Chances are your community has a summer Farmer's Market or street fair. Increase your visibility in the community by taking a booth and providing samples, consultations, demonstrations and featuring your best-selling products or services. Hold a drawing for one or more prizes so that you can collect contact information. Award prizes including gift cards, popular products and some of the branded items you have been purchasing during the year. Be sure that contacts are added to your communications database and extend a bounce-back offer to each.

June Week 1

June 1 – Flip a Coin Day

Provide some excitement for customers and let them take their chances by flipping a coin when they arrive or at the point of purchase for a chance to receive free or specially priced add-ons, samples, branded items, extra rewards or points. If you're feeling really brave, hold a drawing for one customer to win a chance to flip a coin to determine whether you or they will pay their bill.

Post trivia about the history of the coin flip on your Facebook page, blog and e-mail newsletter. Design and purchase your own branded coins to use as part of a rewards program or to be distributed outside of your business to be returned in exchange for a product, service or special offer.

June 2 – Go Barefoot Day

Purchase branded flip-flops for customers to use in the spa, at the pool, on the beach or at the park, sending your brand outside the walls of your business. Branded flip-flops make great gifts for pedicure or spa customers, for members of fitness clubs to wear in the showers and for hotel guests to wear in their rooms or to the pool.

Partner with a salon or spa that provides pedicures for cross or cooperative marketing. Create a contest prize basket that includes items like a branded robe, cover up, flip-flops, pedicure gift card, nail polishes, lotions, etc.

Add a nail polish display to your impulse buy or regular retail. or add displays with nail art, toe rings, temporary tattoos, ankle bracelets, foot creams, pedicure files and similar items designed to help people put their best feet forward all summer long.

June 3 – Leave the Office Early Day

Hold happy hours designed to lure working professionals out of the office early. Conspire with local business owners to release employees to attend or allow them to come over in shifts to enjoy samples, refreshments, consultations, demonstrations and door prize drawings.

As a gesture of employee-appreciation, reward one of your own employees with a paid afternoon or even a whole day off in recognition of a job well done, exceeding customer expectations, making a significant improvement or cost savings for the company, etc.

Leave your own office early today. Get out into your community and meet with peers, visit some of the businesses which routinely refer new customers your way to say thank you, patronize a restaurant, bar or another business with which you partner for marketing or events, spend time with your spouse, family or spend some time all by yourself in order to relax, get a massage—even nap! Getting out of your normal work environment for a quick walk, fresh air and new surroundings can help you renew your own creative juices, provide you with new inspiration and help you feel recharged.

June 4 – Rocky Road Day

Invite a local grocer to provide samples of Rocky Road ice cream to your customers. Partner with a local candy or gourmet foods store to sample Rocky Road-flavored refreshments for your customers or to provide you with Rocky Road-flavored items to add to retail. Partner with a local ice cream parlor, yogurt shop, restaurant or coffee shop for cross or cooperative marketing.

Hold a Rocky Road-themed cooking contest, tasting or solicit related recipes. Have a happy hour featuring Rocky Road ice cream or another flavored drink, appetizer or dessert.

Figuratively speaking, we all have to travel a 'rocky road' from time to time. Partner with a local counselor or motivational speaker to hold a seminar on how to cope in troubled times. Create a list of recommended reading; add some of the best titles to retail or to give away as contest prizes or a gift-with-purchase. Connect people with local counseling resources or compile an online directory of community counseling and/or support group resources.

Create your own slogan or design an image to add to shirts, hats, mugs, notebooks, totes or other items with inspirational, motivational, sarcastic or funny quotes or slogans related to tough times.

Partner with bark, gravel and sand supply companies for cross and cooperative marketing. Reach out to their customers with male customer-oriented offers. Give these businesses gift cards redeemable at your business or branded products to use to incentivize their sales and stimulate cross referrals.

June 5 – Doughnut Day

Partner with a local doughnut shop or bakery for cross or cooperative marketing. Invite a local bakery or doughnut shop to provide samples for your customers. Create a "sweet" offer to extend to their customers. Hold a doughnut making and/or decorating contest. Partner with a professional baker to hold a class for customers. Have a doughnut tasting or happy hour.

Add doughnuts to your menu or purchase them from a local bakery in order to treat your clients at appointments, as a gift-with-purchase or for retail sale. Treat your employees to doughnuts or send boxed doughnuts home for their families. Send doughnuts to be enjoyed by local nurses, caregivers, teachers, civil servants, to businesses near yours or to those of your marketing partners.

Contact a local Krispy Crème (unless you make doughnuts yourself) or another local doughnut shop and take advantage of their charity sales program. Sell doughnuts in your business, your parking lot or some other public place to raise money to support a local charity or service organization.

June 6 – June is Recycling Month

Unless you've been operating your business under a rock for the last decade, you are probably already engaged in many 'green' practices, including recycling. But is there more that you could be doing? Are there improvements you could make to equipment, tools or lighting that would result in lower costs and decreased energy consumption? Check with your local power company for tips on conserving energy and recommendations for appliances and fixtures that improve efficiency. Invite companies that service or repair appliances tools or equipment to provide you with an assessment and recommendations. Seek out vendors and manufacturers that are committed to sustainable environmental practices, preservation and use of renewable resources.

American City magazine defines a business' environmental 'footprint' as, "The environmental impact any company or entity makes as it performs any activity. A footprint is determined by how well raw materials or by-products are (or aren't) absorbed by the surrounding environment." (www. americancity.org) Tell customers and employees about improvements and changes you make to improve efficiencies, decrease energy consumption, lower expenses (resulting in improved profitability and lower costs to customers) and reduce the size of the 'footprint' left by your business.

Extend and offer allowing customers to bring in products sold by competitors or items that are obsolete or expired to 'recycle' in exchange for free replacements or special pricing on equivalent products that you sell.

June 7 – Cheer Coach Day

Extend special offers to cheer coaches—or all coaches—of local schools, city youth and adult sports leagues, etc. Purchase branded water bottles, towels or other sports-related items to donate to local teams, to sell or to give away as contest prizes or a gift-with-purchase.

Sponsor a local sports team. Become a booster of athletics at local schools. Purchase advertising space in programs. Extend special offers to team members and their families.

Partner with local gymnastics, martial arts, golf and other sports instructors to give your customers a free demonstration or introductory lesson; create an offer to extend to their customers.

Work with local cheer coaches or high school cheerleaders to hold a one day youth cheer camp a series of classes. Purchase branded pom poms, hair ribbons and water bottles for participants. Top off cheer camp instruction with a reception and performance for parents.

Purchase candy-filled pom poms to donate to local cheer teams who can then sell them in order to raise funds for a trip, tournament, uniforms or other supplies. Purchase branded or candy pom poms in the team colors of local schools to distribute in the stands at local high school, college, or city league games, sell or give away as a gift-with-purchase.

June Week 2

June Week 2 – Headache Awareness Week

Working with a medical expert, provide customers with information about common causes and natural remedies for headaches. Hold a seminar or conduct a screening event. Let customers know about products or services you provide which help alleviate the symptoms or causes of headaches.

Partner with a local massage therapist to provide mini head, neck and hand massages for customers or employees. Or hold or a massage workshop.

Since stress can cause headaches, highlight the benefits and/or create promotions around stress-relieving products and services. Purchase branded products with aromatherapy benefits (lotion, candles, air fresheners, bath salts, room sprays, etc.) or which provide stress relief (stress balls, massagers, cool gel eye masks, etc.) for retail, gift-with-purchase or for contest prizes.

June Week 2 – Business Etiquette Week

Send a note of thanks, a token of appreciation or extend an offer to the owners and/or employees of businesses located near yours or to your vendors, landlord, marketing partners, etc.

Partner with an etiquette expert to hold a workshop on business etiquette. Invite your marketing partners, local business owners, members of your Chamber of Commerce, Rotary, or other civic organizations, customers, employees, college business students, etc. to attend. Partner with other businesses and professional experts to hold a larger scale business etiquette summit or conference.

Review your own collateral and business cards. Is it time for an update? Is any information obsolete or incorrect? Does your logo look like something from another decade? Update and/or redesign your collateral in such a way that it communicates something authentic about you and your business, and captures the attention and interest of the reader.

Hold a contest and/or solicit etiquette blunder stories (hopefully they are not about your business!) in-store and online. Share business etiquette tips, facts, trivia and origin of common rules on your Facebook page, blog and e-mail newsletter.

Solicit complaints (yes, I said complaints) and suggestions from customers in order to identify aspects of your business which need to change; these may range from minor improvements to complete overhauls. You might be losing customers and thwarting your own success inadvertently, in areas of which you are unaware. Address employee-related complaints honestly, but without 'throwing people under the bus.' Invest in redesign of your systems, processes and in retraining for employees. Tell customers about changes or improvements made as a result of their feedback, and keep the lines of communication open. Remember, you often lose a customer not because of a problem, but because you failed to address a complaint or make amends when a problem occurred.

June Week 2 - The 2nd Wednesday in June is Receptionists Day

Send a gift card or branded gift as well as a bounce-back offer to receptionists and hostesses at local businesses. Ask the receptionists of local businesses and offer to provide them with a display, catalogs, brochures or flyers with information about your business and a special offer for their employees for placement in break or lunch rooms.

Hold a prize drawing, soliciting entries from local receptionists, hostesses, greeters, etc. or asking for nominations from local businesses. Send e-mails, postcards or flyers to local executives and managers noting that Receptionist's Day is coming up, making specific gift suggestions for their receptionists. Make it easy for people to buy a gift for their receptionist by adding delivery service or taking advance orders by phone, e-mail or website.

What kind of reception do your customers receive? Are you leveraging this important point of contact within your business, whether by telephone, website or in person, to its fullest potential? Don't assume all staff are well-versed in professional interpersonal relations. Implement a formal training program and annual refresher training for individuals staffing your first points of contact. Hire a secret shopper to assess your first points of customer contact. Invite a courtesy expert to speak to your staff. Write scripts and include role-play for greeting people, dealing with customers or co-workers who are upset or dissatisfied, or for other common situations that can occur in your employee training. Script and design your first points of contact to surpass customer expectations—something that makes them more interested in your business and more willing to make a purchase, book an appointment or take the next step of engagement.

June 8 – Best Friends Day

Partner with other businesses (caterer, bar, restaurant, makeup artist, boutique, independent seller, etc.) to hold events that naturally inspire people to bring friends with them such as happy hours, jeans or lingerie parties, teas, wine tastings, skin bars or fashion shows. Give a gift card or a special reward to customers who refer or bring a guest new to your business (as well as to the new guest). Take advantage of Best Friend's Day to launch a referral rewards program.

Celebrate Best Friend's Day by reconnecting with customers you have not seen in a while. Send them a personal note, letter, phone call, e-mail, postcard and/or a special offer. Call your most valuable customers or send them a personal note to thank them for their continued patronage and tell them they are important to you and to your business.

Invite your most valuable customers, vendors and/or employees to a reception so that you can celebrate Best Friend's Day with your best friends. Hold a special party or event to which you and your employees will all invite personal friends to attend. Include sampling, provide product knowledge, talk about the future of your business and hold drawings for door prizes, demonstrations and consultations.

Or go big! Partner with other businesses and find an outdoor venue (use your parking lot if appropriate) and invite local musicians to participate in an open air community concert. Feature sampling, demonstrations, and consultations; give away door prizes and branded tchotchkes.

June 9 – Name Your Poison Day

Partner with a local bar or restaurant to provide samples or drink vouchers for your customers. This would be a great time for you to purchase branded coasters for placement in their establishment that features a special offer or your 'happy hour' offers.

If you serve beverages, set a single price for beverages and hold a Name Your Poison happy hour. If you don't, think of products or services you provide for which you could set a flat, special rate during slower hours. The ultimate goal for any 'happy hour' is to make both the customer _and_ your bottom line happy. As an alternative, offer add-ons or accessories at special one-price rates, allowing customers to "name their poison" (in other words, to choose which add-on or accessory to receive for free or a flat-rate, discounted price).

Solicit drink recipes from customers or local bartenders to share on your Facebook page, blog and e-mail newsletter. Hold a cocktail or "mocktail" mix-off, tasting or happy hour. Share recipes for cocktails, punch, sangria and other favorite drinks on your Facebook page, blog, bag stuffers and e-mail newsletter.

Attach a hang tag with one or two of your favorite drink recipes to branded glassware for retail, gift, or gift-with-purchase. Put together a gift basket with glassware, a cocktail recipe book, shaker, wine opener, charms, etc. to give away as a contest prize or for retail sale as the perfect wedding, anniversary or summer hostess gift. Purchase branded shot, high ball, wine or cocktail glasses or design your own collectible line of glasses to release over the summer to collectors as a gift-with-purchase or to retail to clients.

June 10 – Ballpoint Pen Day

You probably take the ballpoint pen for granted, but did you know that it hasn't even been in use for a century? While early versions began 'making their marks' before 1900, a practical, working model was not perfected until the mid-1900's. New York City's Gimbels Department Store was the first to release ballpoint pens on a large-scale basis; in 1945, they sold all 10,000 of their stock in just one day at $12.50 each – that's equivalent to nearly $150.00 each now when adjusted for inflation! There's a lot more ballpoint pen history available online; hold a trivia contest or post facts on your Facebook page, blog and e-mail newsletter.

No sticker-shock today, now you can purchase branded ballpoint pens for less than a dollar each. Think of them as blue collar, working business cards. Your contact information, website, brand elements—every time a customer takes your pen out of their purse, backpack, pocket or briefcase at the store, the bank, the office or a business meeting—the ballpoint pen is increasing mindshare as a constant reminder of you and your business in addition to doing its practical job.

I have been in businesses that not only did _not_ have their own branded pens available in public areas, they actually had pens _branded to other businesses_ there for customers use. The message? They _took_ someone else's pen, for free, for their customers to use. The impression they want to leave on the customer is not only _not worth_ the cost of a branded pen, it's not even worth the price of a generic one!

Purchase branded pens for use in all public-accessible areas, but especially at your point of sale, on the desks of your salespeople or agents, to complete contest or drawing entry forms—anywhere a customer is likely to need to use a pen while in your place of business. And don't freak out when customers steal them; remember, it's a blue collar business card and you want it to go to work!

Create a custom design for pens to turn them into boutique-quality products that can be sold or given as a gift-with-purchase, client thank-you gift or contest prize. Beautiful, zany, inspirational, sarcastic, romantic, mod, quirky—there are no limits to the type of design you can create. People still buy quality, unique pens for gift-giving year round for both personal and professional acquaintances.

June 11 – Iced Tea Day

Offer iced tea to customers as a delicious sample or full size refreshment. Partner with a local tea shop or gourmet food store and invite them to sample iced teas to your customers; create a special offer to extend to their customers on a business card, flyer, postcard, coaster, table tent card, etc.

Create your own custom recipe for a flavored or herbal iced tea to serve as an exclusive beverage, or serve a different flavored iced tea every day. Purchase boutique, tea shop-quality teas to add to retail or give away as a gift-with-purchase. Create a tea-themed gift basket for retail sale or contest prize.

Set up a beverage station in your waiting area. If you already have one, make sure it's clean, sanitary and inviting. Its purpose is to provide comfort, hospitality and the sense that you feel your customer is worth the expense and work necessary to provide it—is this the message that your hospitality station is sending? Be sure that it is someone is assigned responsibility to check customer hospitality areas throughout the day to ensure they are welcoming, to wipe down any spills and refresh supplies.

Partner with a local tea or coffee shop to hold a joint event or for cross or cooperative marketing. Partner with a tea expert and/or party planner to hold a workshop teaching how to create exceptional tea parties for bridal or baby showers or other ladies group events. Solicit recipes to share on Facebook, your blog and e-mail newsletter. Post iced tea-related trivia or hold a trivia contest. Hold an iced tea recipe contest, tasting or happy hour.

June 12 – Tired of Being Tired Day

June 12 is Fatigue Syndrome Day. Use posts on your Facebook page, blog and e-mail newsletter to provide clients with information about Chronic Fatigue Syndrome symptoms, treatment options and local resources (for more information, visit http://www.cdc.gov/cfs/). If this is a condition which has impacted your life or that of a loved one, raise awareness about Fatigue Syndrome and/or the needs of local individuals impacted by Fatigue Syndrome. Hold a benefit event or donate a portion of sales or proceeds from sales of specific products or services to raise awareness, research a cure or benefit a local patient.

Highlight products or services you offer that help relieve fatigue or contribute to improved energy levels. Partner with a local dietician to educate customers about energy-boosting foods or supplements.

Partner with a dietician, organic food store, supplement store, sleep expert and/or fitness expert for cross or cooperative marketing. Work together to hold a workshop for customers on how to take a multi-faceted approach to help alleviate fatigue and improve energy.

Post tips and information on your Facebook page, blog, e-mail newsletter and bag stuffers about recommended levels of sleep, nutrition, etc. as relates to renewing and maintaining energy levels in general or for specific conditions, for specific ages, during stressful times, etc.

Partner with a local hotel, resort or spa to create a fatigue-relieving getaway package customers might enjoy as couples, girlfriend groups, by new moms, etc. Hold a drawing and reward a customer with a fatigue-relieving prize. Sponsor a free fatigue-relieving getaway or spa day as an incentive for employee performance or acknowledgement of a special accomplishment.

June 13 – The Wicked World of Croquet Day

Hold a croquet game or tournament at a local park (or in a grassy area outside of your business) as a customer or employee event.

Hold a trivia contest or post facts about croquet on your Facebook page, blog and e-mail newsletter. Purchase croquet sets for retail sale or to give away as a contest prize or gift-with-purchase.

Design your own croquet-themed game board to use as a customer rewards card or sweepstakes contest. Place 'wickets' on the game board (or even the back of a business card) and let customers earn 'strokes' when they visit, bring a friend, make a purchase, etc. Reward customers for completing the course or construct a winner-take-all game using scratch off game cards, dice rolls or game cards they draw to find out what their next 'hit' is.

June 14 – Dance Like a Chicken Day

Hold a chicken dance contest at your business, via online video submission or during a chicken dance happy hour. Partner with a local bar for happy hours or to hold a customer or employee-appreciation event with music and dancing. Give branded prizes, extra rewards or the opportunity to win a drawing to customers who will dance like a chicken upon entering your store or at the point of purchase.

Partner with local dance teachers, dance studios and performing artists for cross or cooperative marketing. Work together to hold a workshop or introductory dance lesson or to introduce local dance performance companies to your customers. Host dance classes. Enroll in group classes for employee team building, for fun or as part of a fitness program.

June Week 3

June Week 3 – Meet a Mate Week

Did you hold an "insignificant other" mixer in February? With bridal season in full swing, this would be the perfect time to repeat this idea in the form of a "Best Guy (or Girl) I Never Married" event. Partner with local singles organizations and activity clubs or church singles programs for cross or cooperative marketing. Sponsor or host an outing for local singles.

Partner with a relationship expert or counselor to hold a workshop on how to prepare oneself in order to be ready to meet a mate, how to know whether you found "the one," strategies for building a strong relationship or a healthy marriage, what to look for in a potential mate, etc. Partner with an individual who understands the world of online dating, its potential pitfalls and dangers, and how to navigate the options available to hold a single-but-looking workshop.

Compile a list of recommended reading and add some of the best titles to an impulse buy display or regular retail or to give away as contest prizes or a gift-with-purchase. Post recommendations, local resources, websites or relationship advice on your Facebook page, blog and e-mail newsletter. Connect singles in your community with local singles clubs, organizations and activities.

Hold a contest and/or solicit dating, courtship and proposal stories. Post interesting, philosophical, inspirational, heartwarming or hilarious quotes about marriage, dating or relationships on your Facebook page, blog, e-mail newsletter and bag stuffers. Create your own line of custom love or relationship-themed brand wares for retail sale, contest prizes or a gift-with-purchase.

June 15 – Smile Power Day

Build cross and cooperative marketing partnerships with local dental and orthodontic practices. Work together to promote Smile Power Day. Provide customer consultations or hold a workshop together. Purchase branded toothbrushes, floss, lip balms or lip gloss for distribution by local dentists and orthodontists in support of beautiful smile for their customers, along with a bounce-back offer from your business.

Give clients tips about dental hygiene or the benefits of orthodontics, including recommended products, services and scheduling (how often they should be receiving preventive care, when a child should first visit a dentist, etc.) in posts on your Facebook page, blog, e-mail newsletter, bag stuffers and displays.

Purchase branded toothbrushes for retail sale or a gift-with-purchase or to give away to local day cares, youth services or other organizations.

Set up a "create the perfect smile" display including teeth whitening and dental hygiene tips as well as lip balms, lip glosses, lip plumpers or lipsticks. Create a branded tip sheet with product recommendations and instructions for the application of lip liner, plumpers, lipsticks, wrinkle-reducers (for fine lines around the mouth), etc. Post tips, tricks and recommendations in your e-mail newsletter and on your Facebook or blog sites.

Partner with a local cosmetics seller, esthetician or local makeup artist to hold a makeup class for customers. Hold drawings for free products and provide samples, demonstrations and consultations and sell the cosmetics or bundled cosmetic sets (in order for workshop attendees to recreate looks at home). Incentivize attendance with gift cards. Reward customers who bring a friend to the event (who is new to your business). Collect contact information at the point of registration. Use registration forms even for free events in order to obtain database contacts. Add contacts to your database and send a message after the event to ask attendees if they have follow up questions, to refresh their memories relative to the products or services you demonstrated at the event, to invite them to another event and/or extend a special offer.

Add "smiley" items to retail or purchase branded smiley products to gift-with-purchase, retail or for donation to the clients of local dentists, orthodontists, salons, independent cosmetics sellers and other professionals who work to make people smile, or to make smiles look better.

Survey customers to find out what makes them smile when it comes to your business, or what you could change to put a smile on their face in the future.

June 10 – Blooms Day

Partner with local florists, nurseries, landscapers and garden suppliers for cross or cooperative marketing. Partner with a local florist to provide you with a bouquet and cross marketing display for your reception area or point of purchase, a floral "look book" or another display and with flowers for events, contest prizes, etc.

Partner with a local florist to provide a bouquet or plant and hold a drawing (or let employees vote) to see which client of the day should go home with a bouquet (a dental practice once did this for my mom after a particularly long appointment—she has never forgotten it!)

Personally, I love that my local oil change technician leaves a single bloom in my car after my oil change; provide customers with a single bloom as they leave your business today or partner with a local plant supplier and send them home with a small plant or flower start.

Add floral jewelry, hair accessories, bags, totes, travel mugs, water bottles, pens and other items to your retail. Add a floral-themed product display to your point of purchase to stimulate impulse buys. Create colorful "bouquets" of bundled products to offer at a special price (such as lip sticks, nail polishes, barrettes or headbands, brushes, bracelets, pretzel rods, martini glasses, etc.)

Partner with a local counselor or motivational speaker to hold a "bloom where you're planted" seminar for customers or employees. Create a "bloom where you're planted" employee rewards or personal development program. Subsidize continuing education. Establish a scholarship to award annually to a local high school senior who will be entering college in the fall.

Post highlights about staff accomplishments, extraordinary efforts, community involvement and good deeds on your Facebook page, blog and e-mail newsletter in order to honor your staff and to increase the personal connection customers feel toward them and toward your business as a result.

June 17 – Reorganize Your Life Day

Update, organize and appropriately archive your own customer and/or employee files. Reach out to clients you have not seen in a while to let them know that you still think about them, that you would love to see them again, to ask whether there was a specific reason they left or to extend an incentive for them to return.

Take a tour through all of the public areas of your business. Remove or replace old signage. Ensure that floors, counters and tables are clean and free of clutter. Assign responsibility for display creation and changes, restocking of impulse buy areas, daily cleaning, beautification and upkeep.

Set policies indicating how quickly boxes will be unpacked, shelves restocked, etc. Don't leave boxes sitting in aisles or any other public area. Be sure your merchandising displays are current, that expired promotions have been broken down and that anything that detracts from your business goals—anything that is not there in order to help promote sales or stimulate customer engagement—is out of sight.

June 18 – Recess at Work Day

Remember Bring Your Children to Work Day back in April? Expand on the concept and turn your business into a field trip destination for local schools, day cares or other youth groups. Hold recess activities and games. Create your own coloring pages and buy branded boxes of crayons to give as a gift to children of customers, donation to local schools or day cares, etc. Have refreshments. Provide samples, branded tchotchkes, prescriptive consultations and product or service demonstrations.

Hold a hopscotch, jacks, kickball, tetherball and/or another recess game tournament. Set up a hopscotch game for kids (or grownups) to play in your business. Create a rewards card or game board styled like a hopscotch. Set up a hopscotch-style game on the floor or on a poster on the wall and have customers roll or toss something (such as a bean bag, or roll rocks, old school style!) into the squares. Assign a unique offer, gift, sample, branded tchotchke, etc. to each of the numbered squares, award the customer the same number of rewards points as are in the square, etc.

Donate or raise funds to purchase recess games, toys or equipment for your child's school or another local public or private school.

Gift one or more of your employees (or even an entire department) with an extra paid hour off during lunchtime for 'recess' in token of appreciation for a job well done, tenure of service, going beyond the call of duty, meeting corporate goals or just to say thank you for their service.

June 19 – Museum Day

Increase customer awareness of local museums and tourist destinations (monuments, exhibits, galleries, historical homes, etc.) by creating an online directory, in posts on your Facebook page, blog and e-mail newsletter or in a printed brochure, catalog, postcard, flyer or menu. Partner with local museums, tourist and related destinations for cross or cooperative marketing.

Purchase tickets from local attractions (or partner with them to provide you with free tickets or tickets at a reduced price) to include in contest prizes or to gift, gift-with-purchase or resell to customers, to give as gifts to employees, vendors, etc.

Hold a fundraiser or benefit event in support of a local museum or historical site. Sponsor school or day care field trips to local attractions.

Create a museum within your business! Ask customers to bring in an item of historical significance or solicit customer photos and accompanying lore online to share on Facebook, your blog and e-mail newsletter. Turn this into a contest by creating categories for competition such as most interesting local artifact, oldest artifact, wackiest artifact, ugliest artifact, etc.

Turn your business into an art gallery! Invite local artists to feature their work in your lobby, waiting area or as part of a special display. Post links to the websites of local artists on your Facebook page, blog and e-mail newsletter or add artists websites to your online museum directory.

June 20 – The 3rd Friday in June is Bike to Work Day

Reward employees who bike, walk or carpool to work on a one time or on-going basis. Educate employees and customers about the benefits of biking to work; not only the environmental benefits, but the personal benefits as well, like improved health and fitness.

Distribute a map showing local designated riding trails and bike routes; post information on your Facebook page about local routes and trails.

Partner with a local bicycle shop or sporting goods store and create an in-store display featuring a bike or photos as well as a special offer for your customers. Create a special offer to extend to their customers and provide them with a countertop display, postcards, scripting for their website or newsletter, etc. Post historical facts or interesting trivia about bicycling or famous cyclists on your Facebook page, blog and e-mail newsletter. Or hold a trivia contest.

Partner with a local bike shop for special pricing on bicycles and/or accessories (helmets, attachable water bottles or bags, etc.) for your employees. Hold a customer or employee contest or drawing and reward the winner with a bicycle shop gift card, a bicycle or a bicycle-related accessory.

Add bike accessories, equipment, repair kits, etc. to your retail or purchase branded items like bike-attachable water bottles, storage bags, helmets, bicycle-themed hats, t-shirts or tank tops to add to your retail or to give away as contest prizes or a gift-with-purchase. Purchase miniature toy bicycles to gift to children or add to retail.

June 21 – The 3rd Sunday in June is Fathers Day

Purchase items to add to retail intended specifically for men during the month prior to Father's Day (and plan to sell those that do well again during the holidays). Create marketing collateral for cross marketing with typically male organizations like men's golf clubs, recreation and sports facilities, church groups, sports bars, etc. Working with these same types of organizations, collect entries and hold a prize drawing; use the entries to build your database. After the contest, send a communication to announce the winner/s, promote male-oriented products or services, invite them to an event or extend a bounce-back offer.

While sales of men's grooming and other personal care products have increased exponentially over the last decade, the vast majority of male grooming products are still being purchased on their behalf by women.

If your regular and/or 'ideal' client base is primarily female, create Father's Day promotions designed to market to women the products they should purchase for their special men. If your business already caters to a significant male base, or males are your primary target market, utilize gifts-with-purchase and buy one, get one type of promotions, or create incentives that encourage clients to refer even more men to your business. Create special Father's Day gift baskets with men's favorite products, gift cards, sweet treats, etc.

Hold a contest and take nominations from the public or solicit "great dad" stories. Reward one or more of these deserving fathers with a prize. Use contacts to build your database. After the contest, send a communication to announce the winner/s, promote male-targeted products or services, invite dads to an event or extend a bounce-back offer.

Partner with a local sports bar or sports activities facility and create gift certificate duos that include a service or product from your business and a game of bowling, round of golf, bucket of balls at the driving range or batting cage, etc. Partner with a local sportsmen's club or retailer and create a package with hunting or sporting goods (or gift certificate) as well as men's products and/or gift certificates from your business.

June 21 – Summer Solstice

Celebrate Summer Solstice (the day of the year with the longest period of daylight) by hosting a customer or employee party. Add sun-themed branded or custom designed products to your retail or give them away as contest prizes or a gift-with-purchase (such as sun glasses, tank tops, flip flops, sunscreen, beach towels or totes, visors, beach umbrellas, etc.) Give sun-themed items away every hour of the day in "must be present to win" door prize drawings.

Hold a drawing or contest to collect contact information and reward the winner with a sun-themed gift or set of prizes. After the contest, send a communication to announce the winner/s, invite them to an event, promote seasonal products, services or current promotions and extend a bounce-back offer.

June Week 4

June Week 4 – Freedom from Fear of Speaking Week

Partner with a local counselor, motivational speaker, teacher or another expert to hold a workshop on fear-free public speaking or a series of classes to improve public speaking skills. Contact your local 'Toastmasters' and offer to sponsor or host a meeting. Host your own public speaking practice and support group meetings to facilitate public speaking practice opportunities.

Take a public speaking class, or enable one or more of your employees to take a class. Invite an etiquette and/or speaking expert to provide training for your customer service and other 'front line' employees, volunteers and vendors. Work together to write scripts for up-selling or cold calling and engage in role-play practice with sales staff during training.

Compile a list of recommended reading and add some of the best titles to your retail or to give away as contest prizes, client gifts or a gift-with-purchase. Post public speaking tips and tricks on your Facebook page, blog and e-mail newsletter.

June 22 – Buy a Musical Instrument Day

Partner with local music instrument stores and music teachers for cross or cooperative marketing. Purchase a branded item (such as guitar picks, music folders or tuning keys, etc.) to give to music teachers as gifts or for distribution to their students.

Extend a special offer to the employees of local music stores, instructors, school music faculty, performing arts groups, orchestra and band members, etc. Create an offer to extend to the customers of local music stores.

Host a used musical instrument swap or sale event. Add starter instruments or toy instruments to your retail or purchase branded toy instruments for gift, gift-with-purchase or retail sale.

June 23 – Pink Day

Add pink items designed for women, girls, babies or even pets to impulse buy or regular retail. Hold a pink trivia contest or post interesting facts about the color pink or things that are pink on your Facebook page, blog and e-mail newsletter. Hold a contest to see who can compose the best acronym using the letters P.I.N.K. relative to your business, one of your products, services or staff members, the community, the season, or in relation to some other topic.

Purchase branded pink items or items with pink in the design (t-shirts, tank tops, hats, scarves, jewelry, pens, memo pads, tumblers, toys, totes, cover-ups, flip-flops, etc.) to add to retail or to give away as contest prizes or a gift-with-purchase. Donate pink and/or branded pink items along with a bounce-back offer from your business to members of local girl's or women's organizations, clubs, church groups, MOPS (Mothers Of Pre-Schoolers), to businesses staffed entirely or primarily by women, to local business women, etc.

June 24 – Swim a Lap Day

Sponsor a senior or child's swim class or pool facility memberships. Purchase community pool or recreation center passes to be given as gifts, gifted-with-purchase or awarded in contests or drawings. Give passes to employees for themselves and family members as a token of appreciation, as a reward for outstanding performance or as part of an employee health and fitness program.

Partner with a local swimming pool to hold a customer or employee-appreciation event. Extend special offers to the employees and patrons of community swimming, fitness and recreation facilities. Create a special offer to extend to pool patrons.

Sponsor a swimming party at your community pool for a local day care or another youth group. Become a booster of your local high school swim team.

Purchase swimming accessories (suits, caps, nose plugs, goggles, beach balls, towels, floating aids, etc.) or purchase branded swimming accessories and for retail, contest prizes or gift-with-purchase.

Send a list of tips to your community pool to be posted on bulletin boards or included on websites or newsletters telling pool patrons how to care for their hair or skin during the summer in light of extra time spent outdoors, at the beach and at the pool. Provide branded samples of hair and skin moisture-restorative products or sunscreen for distribution in swimming, fitness and recreation facility locker rooms (along with a bounce-back offer for your business).

June 25 – Let It Go Day

Partner with a local motivational speaker, relationship expert, life coach or counselor and hold a workshop for customers and/or employees who need to let go of past hurts, failures or other setbacks. Post relevant quotes, links to websites, local resources and titles of recommended reading on your Facebook page, blog and e-mail newsletter.

Think about the processes, procedures and systems in place within your business which directly impact the customer experience. Are any outmoded or non-customer-friendly? Are you making customers jump through hoops or keeping them waiting longer than they need to because of one of your systems or procedures? Clunky, onerous and disagreeable processes could lead to the loss of sales and clients. Let go of old ways of doing things and ensure that all of processes in your business are designed in as customer-centric a way as possible.

It's been almost 6 months since you made your New Year Resolutions, why not make one in reverse? Instead of promising to start doing something, promise to "let it go" and stop doing something that is holding you back, is a bad habit, or otherwise needs to go!

June 26 – Coin a Phrase Day

This one doesn't exist; I just made it up today! I'm writing this entry on the 2nd of May, 2011 after what was the coldest April on record since they started keeping records in the greater Seattle area. Yesterday was the first truly nice, warm day we've had in months, but this morning we are right back to drizzle and cold, so I am coining the phrase, "As shy as the sunshine in Seattle this spring"

On *Coin a Phrase Day*, hold a contest to see who can come up with the best new phrase about your business or a specific service, product, staff member or another aspect of your business, a phrase about the city in which your business is located—be creative! Brainstorm as a staff to coin a new phrase to use as a tagline for your business or in an upcoming marketing campaign.

Choose a phrase of the day for employees to use in the course of business (which may or may not even be relevant to the course of business, or which may be inspirational, mysterious, humorous, etc.) in order to start conversations, entertain or educate customers about some aspect of your business. Write a list of abbreviations, anagrams, slang or jargon commonly used in your industry or within your business and provide their definitions to educate customers and/or employees.

Include a coined phrase in e-mail or other marketing collateral and reward customers who return to your business and use the phrase at the point of purchase. Hold a trivia contest or post entries about the origin of common-but-wacky phrases used in society currently or in the past on your Facebook page, blog, e-mail newsletter and bag stuffers.

June 27 – Ugly Dog Day

Have an Ugly Dog Walk for charity or an Ugly Dog Contest. Solicit Ugly Dog photos online or post them on a bulletin board. Find a picture of a truly ugly mutt and have a contest to see who can come up with the best fictitious name or story about it.

Add pet items with bling or unique style to retail or an impulse buy display—collars, leashes, costumes, bowls, brushes, shampoos etc.—items that could make an ugly dog look a little bit better. Purchase branded ugly dog toys or stuffed animals for gift-with-purchase or retail sale.

Create your own branded line of ugly dog clothing, hats, mugs, tumblers, water bottles, t-shirts or tanks, pens, memo cubes, notebooks, totes, etc. featuring a unique design or humorous slogan.

Hold a benefit event to support a local animal shelter. Reward people for adopting ugly (or not-so-ugly) dogs and cats. Sponsor pet adoptions. Donate food or supplies. Put information on your Facebook page, blog and e-mail newsletter about pets available for adoption and shelter needs.

June 28 – Sunglasses Day

Purchase branded sunglasses for gift or gift-with-purchase. Purchase a youth or boutique-quality sunglasses display for summer impulse buy or point of purchase sales. Partner with local sunglasses stores and optometrists for cross or cooperative marketing. Work together to hold a screening or workshop for employees or customers.

June 29 – Camera Day

Hold a customer photo contest with seasonal categories like summer, vacations, the pool, beach or another theme. Partner with a local camera store for cross or cooperative marketing. Hold a contest or drawing to win a free camera. Partner with photographers for cross or cooperative marketing (and revisit May's National Photograph Month ideas). Partner with a local photographer to hold a workshop or series of photography classes for your customers. Set up a family photograph opportunity for your customers at a special rate, as a contest prize for your customers or as a gift for your employees.

Add coffee table books featuring amazing photography to your retail or impulse buys. Give away photography art, books or photography instruction books as gifts-with-purchase or contest prizes. Add photography instruction books or videos to retail.

Be diligent about taking pictures in the course of your business to record customer and employee events, accomplishments, charitable endeavors, corporate meetings, etc. Post event and other happy-people pictures on Facebook so people who didn't attend will know what they missed. Include high-resolution photos whenever you submit press releases; after all, a picture is still worth a thousand words!

June 30 – Save Your Hearing Day

Partner with a local hearing aid specialist or hearing professional for cross or cooperative marketing. Hold a screening event for seniors or children. Sponsor hearing checks for your employees and/or their family members.

Post information about local hearing-related businesses, medical professionals, resources, non-profit groups, etc. on your Facebook page, blog and e-mail newsletter. Hold an event or fundraiser to benefit a local hearing-impaired individual or to be donated to a related service organization, education or treatment center.

Post information about protecting hearing, common causes of hearing loss, early warning signs, statistics, etc. on your Facebook page or e-mail newsletter. To help raise awareness, give away free earplugs with purchase as a bag stuffer, or send branded ear plugs to local manufacturers, airports or other loud businesses for employee use.

Hold a summit in cooperation with other businesses to discuss accommodations that can be made to assist hearing-impaired shoppers or employees. Partner with a local educator to hold sign language classes. Add a book on sign language to your retail. Sponsor sign language classes for interested employees. Hire sign language interpreters to attend your events and extend special invitations to the hearing impaired to attend.

july
365 Days of Marketing

July Month-Long Observances

Air Conditioning Appreciation Month

Hot out? Provide refreshment and respite within your air conditioned interior and hold Air Conditioning Appreciation happy hours to help customers beat the summer heat featuring ice-cold drinks, snow cones and other cool indulgences. Extend a special invitation or even help coordinate transportation for seniors, children and others who are extra-vulnerable to suffering due to the heat.

Purchase branded eye gel cooling masks, reusable fabric-covered cold packs, reusable LED ice cubes, specialty ice cube molds, double-walled beverage glasses or insulated cold beverage tumblers to incentivize event attendance, for a gift-with-purchase on extra-hot days or to add to retail.

Partner with HVAC sale or repair businesses for cross or cooperative marketing. Exchange website links with reputable HVAC professionals in order to connect customers with reliable resources.

Anti-Boredom Month

No one likes to be bored! Use surveys to find out how customers like to spend their leisure time and what type of events they would be most likely to invite friends or family to attend. Construct events meant to help people stave off boredom (game nights, happy hours, free entertainment, activities or tournaments, etc.) Reward people who bring friends to events. Incentivize referrals. Target invitations toward desired target markets, such as Baby Boomers, Generation X, Y or all the way down to the teens, tweens and kids of the Internet or Wired Generation. Knowing "who" to target will also help you design marketing collateral, activities, contests and events that will be of interest *to them*.

Declare a war on boredom and hold one special activity or contest *every day* in June, or construct a contest that builds day after day with new clues, rewards or incentives. Hold a drawing every day in June (this could be a great way to help build a following on Facebook or Twitter if you ask followers to comment and share a post on their page or retweet your post on Twitter). As you make the daily posts or as prizes are awarded, tell everyone about the benefits of each item you are giving away.

Keep kids entertained while with parents at your business with branded coloring sheets, activity books, crayons, clay, silly putty, etc.

Cell Phone Courtesy Month

It's hard to know where to draw the line on cell phone use in most businesses. People are accustomed to being connected via cell phone 24 hours a day, 7 days a week. Give people a reason to unplug electronically and plug in socially during cell-phone-free appointments, happy hours or events.

Post cell phone courtesy tips for talking, texting, surfing or gaming on your Facebook page, blog and e-mail newsletter. Hold a texting contest. For advanced texters, hold a blindfolded texting contest; you'll be surprised at how good some people get at this! Set a time limit and provide a list of texts that become increasingly complex; may the best digit-er win!

Be sure employees know your policy on cell phone use at work so they are not inadvertently rude or disruptive to the customer experience.

Partner with a cell phone seller for cross or cooperative marketing. Purchase pre-paid cell phones or gift cards to use as contest prizes or add to retail.

Take the electronic pulse of your customers—find out how they would prefer to receive reminders, sale alerts and other announcements from your business (direct mail, e-mail or text, etc.) Use survey forms to double check and/or collect contact information in order to update your database. Begin sending text reminders to customers who opt-in by texting them a thank you and a special offer.

Family Reunion Month

Host, facilitate or cater family reunions and other events. Create a menu of party activities, kits, entertainment, food and beverages, accommodations, facilities, equipment, services or other items that you provide. Partner with party planners, caterers, photographers, bakeries, bars and restaurants, hotels/motels, group meeting facilities and related organizations for cross or cooperative marketing. Post a directory of local resources on your website, Facebook page, blog and e-mail newsletter. Make a branded print version available online for download and send it out once a year to your customers.

Partner with a local salon, makeup esthetician, independent retailer, etc. to create reunion and event makeover packages for customers who want to look their best before seeing old acquaintances. Expand your directory to include other professionals, such as fitness and weight loss experts, cosmetic medical and dental professionals, etc. Create a directory of local attractions (museums, historical sites, recreation areas or facilities, sports, etc.) which people could enjoy while in your city attending a family reunion or event. Be sure it includes reasons to visit your business!

Make a Difference to Children Month

Get involved in your city's civic organizations (Rotary, Kiwanis or Optimists/Soroptimists, etc.) These organizations regularly participate in fundraising and events that directly benefit children right in your own community.

Get involved in local Big Brother/Big Sister, mentoring or tutoring programs. Hold a fundraiser to provide scholarships for needy children to obtain professional tutoring or private education, to help with college tuition, purchase books or supplies, purchase a computer for student use, etc.

Participate in auctions and fundraisers at local schools. Donate prize baskets and help raise community awareness of local school needs. Extend a special offer to the employees of local private and public schools, to members of local PTA/PTSAs, etc.

National Parks and Recreation Month

Become a supporter of city parks and recreations programs. Sponsor a team. Donate supplies, uniforms or equipment. Volunteer to coach a team or become a referee. Host parties for your sponsored team. Provide players and parents with branded wares. Attend games and distribute branded water bottles with labels featuring a bounce-back offer. Extend a special offer to all of your city's parks and recreation leagues coaches, players and their family members.

Sandwich Generation Month

The term "Sandwich Generation" refers to individuals who are caring for aging parents at the same time they are still raising and supporting their own children. 'Sandwiched' between two generations who both need their help and support on a daily basis—these people deserve some rewards! Solicit nominations of individuals who meet these criteria and hold a drawing for one or more special prizes. Invite nominees and those who nominated them to a special Sandwich Generation reception or happy hour.

Partner with a deli, restaurant, mobile food van or caterer and provide tasty sandwich samples or full size retail options to customers. Cross market with a local bakery to provide breads to sample to customers. Purchase bread loaf minis from a local baker to gift-with-purchase or resell. Create a special offer to extend to their customers.

Partner with a restaurant or deli for cross or cooperative marketing. Give restaurant or deli gift cards away in contests or drawings (using entry forms to help build your contact database). Invite local culinary professionals or customers to participate in a "best sandwich" contest. Solicit favorite or most unusual sandwich recipes of customers, employees, local chefs, etc. to share on Facebook, your blog and e-mail newsletter.

July Week 1
July Week 1 – Be Nice to New Jersey Week

In recent years, various television shows like those featuring young adults, wives and even Jersey hair itself have drawn attention to the accents, hair styles and fashions stereotypically associated with that great state. In the next best thing to a costume party, hold a New Jersey-themed happy hour, contest or event. Hold a New Jersey celebrity look-alike contest, or a Jersey hair and fashion show.

Post facts and trivia about The Garden State on your Facebook page. Hold an online trivia contest. Solicit pictures of people sporting Jersey fashions or hair. Hold a New Jersey state report contest for kids or have a New Jersey drawing or coloring page contest.

July 1 – Second Half of the Year Day

If ever there were a random day to celebrate, it must be Second Half of the Year Day! Summer is now in full swing; how many of your customers are missing out on the best summer products or services you have to offer? Create an enticing offer around some of your most popular summer items and send a special direct mail and/or e-mail marketing piece to your customers. Hold an open house to help customers beat the heat featuring sampling, consultations, demonstrations and event-only offers.

Every good football game half time has two things in common: Entertainment for the crowd, and a kick-butt pep talk from the coach to the players. In terms of the first, hold a Second Half of the Year cocktail party or happy hour for customers, vendors, marketing partners and employees featuring live music.

In terms of the kick-butt pep talk, hold an employee event to help kick off second half of the year initiatives. Clearly communicate corporate or department goals for the back-to-school, Autumn and upcoming holiday seasons. Have an all-employee meeting. Make sure that each of your employees really understands their role relative to corporate or departmental goals. Post goals, assignments and timelines on employee bulletin boards. Send out dedicated employee newsletters. Invite key employees to participate in a strategy retreat or meetings in order to review goals for the second half of the year and brainstorm on strategies and tactics to meet them. If holiday sales are particularly important to your business, setting and communicating clear goals now gives you the time you need to design and execute clear, targeted strategies and to develop a multi-channel holiday communications plan.

July 2 – Creative Ice Cream Flavors Day

Partner with an ice cream parlor or yogurt store for cross or cooperative marketing. Work together to hold a Creative Ice Cream Flavors event or happy hours or invite marketing partners to provide samples for your customers. Purchase gift cards from a local ice cream shop to resell, gift-with-purchase or use as contest prizes.

Hold a homemade ice cream making contest, tasting or happy hour. Post trivia about the history of ice cream or creative ice cream flavors on Facebook. Hold a contest to ask customers to think of the best names for creative ice cream flavors; reward the winner with a gift card redeemable for ice cream (from you or one of your marketing partners). Use entries to help add contacts to your database. Extend a special offer to all entrants after the contest or invite them to your ice cream happy hour.

July 3 – Compliment Your Mirror Day

Hold a contest to see who can come up with the best "Mirror, mirror, on the wall…" phrase ending. In the story of Snow White, every day, the evil queen asked her own mirror who was "the fairest of them all," wanting to hear that she was in response. When you look in the mirror, what is it that you want your mirror to tell you that you are the "fairest" or best at doing? What do you want to personally master? What type of superiority do you want for your business? What would it take to get there?

Help customers get the answers they want from their mirrors. Create special offers and/or highlight the products or services you provide that help improve the outward appearance, inner health, well-being or some other aspect of customer's lives. Partner with a salon, stylist, esthetician or makeup seller and hold a "Mirror, Mirror Makeover" demonstration, workshop or event. Expand the event by including fitness and nutrition experts, cosmetic medical, orthodontic and dental professionals, etc. Extend a special offer from your business to these types of professionals in your community who work hard to improve the appearances of others.

Purchase branded or boutique-quality compacts or mirrors to add to your retail or to give away as contest prizes, client gifts or a gift-with-purchase.

Create "Mirror, mirror" compliment cards to give to employees acknowledging superior customer service skills, product knowledge, sales performance, etc.

July 4 – Independence Day

Plan ahead to participate in summer community events (including those for Independence Day). If your city has a parade, hand out business cards, flyers or even samples. Hand out ice-cold branded bottled waters. Distribute branded calendars, rulers, pens, lip balms or other items people are likely to keep and use.

Design your own branded school-year marketing calendar (August through July) featuring kids artwork, photography, local scenery, product or service knowledge and recommendations, a spotlight product or service of the month, holiday or seasonal decorating, recipes and activity ideas, your customer bill of rights or guarantees, etc. Sell or give them away as a gift-with-purchase. Send a copy to your most valuable clients, marketing partners, businesses located near yours, administrative or human resources staff of large employers, school or district offices, etc.

Support local Military and Veterans organizations and clubs. Offer to host meetings, provide refreshments or participate in fundraising. Post information about local resources and charities on a community-focused page of your website or on your Facebook page, blog and e-mail newsletter.

Chances are your city will have a street fair, festival or another summer event where you can take your brand and parts of your business out on the streets—to where tomorrow's clients are! Rent a booth; if you can't afford do it on your own, partner with another independent professional or non-competing business to share costs. Bring products, tools and equipment so you can perform or demonstrate mini-versions of your most popular, trendiest and pleasurable services, provide consultations, product recommendations and samples of some of your most popular products.

Create your own branded "prescription" form to use in your business or at events to make specific recommendations of products or services that individuals should purchase to address a specific conditioner or make their lives better. Distribute coupons or business cards with bounce-back offers. Sell or give away branded products like sun screen, lip balm, glosses, sunglasses, water bottles, shirts, cover-ups, etc. Show off the unique gift center you have created in your business with examples of the boutique, beautiful, fun, custom-designed and one-of-a-kind items you offer.

July 5 – Workaholics Day

We workaholics need your help! Create service packages for us that include quick in-and-out times, pre-set, pre-sold recurring appointments and de-stressing add-on services (such as a hand or scalp massage). Set up e-mail, text or call-ahead shopping services, automatic ordering or sales for products or services purchased on a regular basis or even a delivery service for your most loyal (and busiest) customers.

We workaholics want to work. And we don't just want to work "at work;" we'll work any time, any place, for any reason! Sometimes we even fail to take care of ourselves because we just want to work. Add wi-fi to your business and let workaholics know they are welcome to bring electronic devices and stay connected during appointments—because for us, the only thing that is better than working, is getting something else done at the same time!

Start a workaholics anonymous happy hour or support group. Invite a counselor, executive or life coach, office organization or time management expert to come and speak to us (this will help us feel like we are actually 'working' during happy hours) about how to carve out a healthy work-life balance and how to make the time we need to care for ourselves and for our family and friends. Take advantage of our brief period of captivity to tell us about products or services that can make our lives better; give us demonstrations, professional consultations, prescriptive product or service advice and samples to try at home (along with a bounce-back offer for full size purchase).

July 6 – Take Your Webmaster to Lunch Day

You should already be meeting with your webmaster at least once a month to ensure that events, promotions, new products or services, contests and drawings, new employee feature articles and other news will be updated to the internet. (If you aren't, start now!)

Create website-exclusive offers redeemable by a downloadable coupon or special code word. Using coupons, codes and other ways to track offers will help you to know which offers are working, where, when and for whom in terms of your promotional offers.

Once each month, hold a contest on Facebook, your blog or other social media sites and reward winner/s with a gift certificate or free product. Extend a special offer to members of your social networks redeemable by a special code. Build a following on Facebook, Twitter and other social media sites through giveaways and contests that require people to "like" your page, post or repost your updates, retweet your tweet, etc. Hold a (real) event for local Facebook, Twitter, blog or website followers. Collect contact information to add to your e-mail database.

Work with marketing partners and hold an online happy hour for social media followers by extending Facebook, blog or other social network site-exclusive offers. Hold online drawings and distribute product knowledge in "Did you know...?" style posts.

July 7 – Tell the Truth Day

No marketing collateral has as much impact as the individual interactions between your customers and your employees. Have you ever heard the saying, "One bad apple can spoil the whole basket?" This is because an apple with a bad spot molds, and the mold spores spread to everything around it.

It's true within your business as well; one employee with a "bad spot" such as a negative attitude, a tendency to gossip, an unwillingness to perform the tasks for which they are responsible, lack of concern for the customer or who demonstrates pessimism, cynicism, defiance or subtly mocks your corporate mission, culture or goals will be contagious and damaging to *everyone* around them if tolerated or left unaddressed. It's not just the customer who is negatively impacted, it spreads to your vendors, marketing partners and other employees as well.

Sometimes it's difficult to confront an employee, especially if you are personal friends or they have been with your company for a long time. Have you been holding back on delivering an unpleasant truth from someone on your staff? Today's the day to tell them the truth about their behavior, ask for the truth in response, and work together to craft a plan to move forward.

Maybe it's not one just employee, but *all* employees who need to hear from you. Hold an all-employee meeting to tell the truth about the health of your business in contrast to the level of health it needs to achieve. By involving employees to help craft solutions, you give them an opportunity to become more personally and emotionally invested in achieving specific goals and in the overall success of your business. Your employees may even be willing to make sacrifices in times of need and might have creative solutions for growing sales, bringing in new clients or lowering expenses which have not yet occurred to you.

Conduct customer, employee or vendor surveys designed to reveal the truth about your organization. Conduct them anonymously in order to garner raw, unvarnished responses but with the option to provide contact information to enable you to follow up on customer dissatisfaction. Afterward, tell your employees, customers, vendors, etc. what the surveys revealed and what actions you are taking as a result. Appoint a customer-experience czar or committee. Provide rewards or incentives to employees who suggest changes which positively impact the customer experience, the level of customer satisfaction or sales.

In anonymous employee surveys, ask employees what they believe to be true about the employee culture, which values they feel are (or should be) most important to your business, whether they share your values as they understand them, whether they understand their role in the organization, what support or improvements you could provide that would help them to fulfill their role, etc. Afterward, report results and tell employees how the information will be used to help shape future planning and training or what other changes you will be making as a result of their feedback. Invite employees to submit ideas or participate in helping to address concerns raised in the surveys. Create a formal process to solicit and address employee concerns and suggestions.

July Week 2

July 8 – Unplug the Drama Day

Partner with a counselor to hold a workshop about how to diffuse stressful and potentially drama-filled situations, how to avoid getting caught up in the dramas of others, how to remove oneself from drama or how to take things less personally. Solicit ideas on your Facebook page and blog for dealing with difficult situations and diffusing drama in the workplace, at home, with family members, etc. Post a list of recommended reading. Post facts about drama, stress and their effects on your Facebook page, blog and e-mail newsletter. Post local resources for professional assistance when it comes to common drama that occurs in our lives due to loss of a loved one, marital problems, divorce, family friction, etc.

Hold a staff workshop to improve interpersonal relationships and communication, increase trust and decrease drama in the workplace. Survey employees to find out where they feel the most stress occurs in the course of their work; the answers may lead you to make changes that improve things for customers as well as employees.

Partner with a counselor or family relations expert to hold a teen parenting workshop. Or hold a teen life workshop to help teens deal with drama that commonly occurs in junior and senior high school settings. Or go big! Work with marketing partners to hold a community forum on teen/tween bullying.

Hold a customer or employee-appreciation movie night event and unplug the drama by viewing a comedy or plug into a dramatic movie by choice. Solicit and share recommendations of favorite dramatic movies and books on Facebook. Poll readers to determine their all time favorite movies, books, celebrity breakups, fights or other dramas.

July 9 – Video Games Day

A video game event or tournament could be a great way to celebrate with employees or to reach out to male, tween or teenage clientele. Partner with a local game shop and/or local bar to hold a video game event or tournament.

Partner with an equipment rental or games shop and hold a Wii bowling tournament. Even senior citizens have been getting into the act, participating in Wii bowling and other game tournaments. Partner with a bowling alley or expert to provide an introductory bowling lesson for kids (or seniors) prior to a Wii bowling event or as part of a real bowling event. Use registration forms or hold a drawing in order to add contacts to your database. Afterward, thank participants for attending, invite them to a future event, extend a special bounce-back offer, hold a second-chance drawing, etc.

Add video games or game store gift cards to retail or give them away as contest prizes or a gift-with-purchase. Partner with video game stores and game rental stores for cross or cooperative marketing.

July 10 – Joke Day

Hold a joke contest at an event or take written entries on your Facebook page, blog, web-based electronic entry form or in your business. Solicit jokes and compile them into a collection to have printed into a book or to post on your Facebook page, blog, e-mail newsletter and bag stuffers. Post links to online jokes, humorous websites or comics. Purchase joke books to add to retail, gift-with-purchase or for use as prizes.

Hold a standup comedy contest and reward winner/s with tickets to a local comedy club as well as a gift card redeemable in your business. Hold a customer or employee-appreciation event at a local comedy club. Partner with a local bar and play standup comedy videos during a customer event featuring sampling, consultations and demonstrations. Hold one or more door prize drawings and use entry forms to help build your contact database. After the event, extend a special offer written in a humorous style to everyone who attended.

July 11 – Cheer Up the Lonely Day

As an employee team or on your own, volunteer at a local senior living center, for shut-ins or other individuals in need of assistance. Wash windows, weed flower beds, run errands, play games, provide companionship—whatever you can do to help cheer up these sometimes-lonely individuals.

My husband has gone to a senior living center almost every Wednesday for the last several years to visit a senior citizen he barely knows—a now-retired, founding member of the Rotary Club in the city where his business is located. He talks with this individual, reads to him, listens to him; although they aren't related, my husband feels a responsibility to do this because of the work this man did in the community. There are probably individuals just like this in your city who spent years working in and contributing to your community who would love to have a visitor like you. Contact a local senior living facility, nursing home or church to connect with individuals whose loneliness you can help relieve!

Partner with a counselor to hold a workshop on loneliness. Compile a list of suggested reading and local resources, clubs or social groups to post on your Facebook page, blog and e-mail newsletter. Hold a singles mixer or happy hour.

July 12 – Different Colored Eyes Day

Create electronic and/or print collateral promoting "different colored summer eyes" including eye makeup application steps, specific color combinations, color palettes and product recommendations. Partner with a salon, esthetician or independent cosmetics seller to hold a makeup workshop.

Invite an esthetician or makeup seller to provide mini-touchups, demonstrations and consultations for your customers; extend an offer or invitation to their customers. Add services to your menu for attending women's events, providing makeup touch-ups and demonstrating application techniques. Create a party services menu for teen and tween birthdays or sleepovers to demonstrate skin care and makeup.

July 13 – Barbershop Music Appreciation Day

Invite local barbershop quartets or ensembles to perform live in your business. Working with local musicians, organize a barbershop "flash mob" to surprise your customers or purchase branded shirts and take your barbershop flash mob to a local mall, senior center, park or another public venue. Host or sponsor a local senior event featuring Barbershop music and nostalgic activities, games and refreshments.

Post barbershop music trivia, facts and history on your Facebook page, blog and e-mail newsletter. Hold a trivia contest. Purchase albums and create music-themed gift baskets for retail sale, gifts-with-purchase or contest prizes.

July 14 – Gruntled Workers Day

Although not technically a word, the meaning of "gruntled" is clear: Disgruntled is defined as angry or dissatisfied; so, gruntled workers would be happy and content. How gruntled are your employees? The level to which they are gruntled will be apparent to and will deeply affect customers, vendors and co-workers.

Hold an employee-appreciation event or take actions designed to gruntle your workers more completely. Write thank-you notes or letters of appreciation, surprise employees with unexpected rewards, post customer raves and compliments on your Facebook page, blog, e-mail newsletter, in signage on employee bulletin boards or on tent cards in break rooms. Give one or more of your employees an extended (paid) lunch hour or afternoon off to reward them for extraordinary loyalty, customer service, sales or another achievement.

Do something to cosmetically or functionally improve an employee work, break or lunch area. Make sure employees see you working as hard as they do. Perform personal services at work like cleaning out the microwave, doing dishes, emptying the trash, sweeping the floor, cleaning up spills, etc. Treat employees to pizza, doughnuts or bagels, a veggie and fruit tray, gourmet coffee or ice cream.

Purchase branded t-shirts or tank tops for employees with a team-oriented message or a message about how much you love your team. Solicit samples or gift cards from marketing partners and create goodie bags for your employees. Hold an all-employee picnic or another family event.

July Week 3
July 15 – Gummi Worm Day

Fill a large glass container with Gummi Worms for a quantity-guessing contest (count first!) Take entries in-store and post a picture on your website, blog or Facebook page in order to solicit online entries and collect contact information. Reward the winner with the worms, a gift card and bounce-back offer. Use entries to build your contact database. Afterward, send an e-mail to all entrants (or your entire contact database) announcing the winner and extending a bounce-back offer.

Purchase branded or gourmet gummi treats to gift-with-purchase, use as bag stuffers or add to retail. Post trivia about gummis on your Facebook page. Post a variety of gummi pictures or illustrations and hold a contest asking customers to assign creative names, captions or life stories to each.

July 16 – Father-Daughter Take a Walk Day

Set up father-daughter activities, games or contests in your parking lot or hold a father-daughter event. Create service experiences suitable for father and daughter to enjoy at the same time or sell buy one, get one father-daughter gift cards where one of the two will be a customer new to your business.

Hold a father-daughter do-it-yourself building or repair class. Partner with a sports or recreation facility (golf, batting cages, etc.) to hold workshops, introductory lessons or host activities on dedicated Father-Daughter days.

July 17 – Get Out of the Doghouse Day

Hold an event at a local dog park. Distribute branded tchotchkes and/or flyers with special bounce-back offers. Take entries for a drawing to be held at the event or to be held in your business on the following or a later date; use entries to help build your contact database. Send an e-mail to announce the winner and extend a special offer to all entrants, or assemble a prize package compelling enough to hold a "must be present to win" drawing.

Add pet-themed products that have unique style, flair or "bling" to your retail such as leashes and collars, pet bowls, brushes, shampoo or treats. Partner with a construction or renovation professional to hold a do-it-yourself doghouse building workshop. Solicit pet photographs and stories on Facebook. Hold a contest for the best, most unique or strangest-looking doghouse.

Getting out of the doghouse is about making amends. Partner with a counselor to hold a workshop on making amends and repairing relationships. Compile a list of recommending reading, inspirational quotes and local and online resources to post on your Facebook page, blog and e-mail newsletter.

July 18 – Toss the Could Have/Should Haves Day

When was the last time you thought about your own dreams? What are your biggest regrets? What is your biggest fear in terms of something you may regret in the future? Keeping your dreams in focus and in the forefront of your mind will help to focus your activities.

Think about the last year. What could you have done differently—what *should* you have done differently? What will you do to ensure that you will not repeat the same mistakes, or that you will do what you should do in the future? Most people have regrets—things we could have or should have done, but didn't. Partner with a professional counselor, motivational speaker or life coach to hold a workshop on moving past regret as well as life strategies that will help us avoid them.

Take a look back at the Resolutions made in January; have you, your employees and/or your customers been faithful in pursuing your goals? Renew your commitments. Create a support group, means of accountability and rewards to incentivize employees and customers to set and pursue 2nd half of the year resolutions.

July 19 – Ice Cream Day

Partner with an ice cream parlor, yogurt, custard or coffee shop to provide samples of scrumptious frozen treats for customers or for employees. Host an ice cream social for your employees and those of your marketing partners. Hold an ice cream social or ice cream sundae happy hour at your business. Invite team members and their families of local parks and recreation sports teams to attend. Host or sponsor an ice cream social for a local senior center or youth group.

July 20 – Lollipop Day

Extend an offer to the employees of local candy and gourmet foods stores. Work with a local candy maker to create your own custom lollipop for client gift, gift-with-purchase or retail sale. Invite them to provide lollipops for your customers or purchase lollipops to gift-with-purchase, give away to kids or resell.

Place lollipops in a large glass container and hold a contest to see who can guess how many are inside (count first!) Post a picture of the container on your website so people can enter online as well as in-store. Add contact information from entry forms to your database. After the contest, send an e-mail to announce the name of the winner and a bounce-back offer to all entrants.

Post trivia or history about lollipops on your Facebook page or hold a trivia contest. To help you get started, check out the information available at http://en.wikipedia.org/wiki/Lollipop.

Gift branded lollipops to local day cares along with a bounce-back offer for parents and staff. Place branded lollipops on the tables, waiting rooms, lobbies or at the point of purchase in businesses you partner with for marketing and events. Give branded lollipops to the members of the parks and recreation team you sponsor—or enough for all the teams. Send a lollipop bouquet to the receptionists of businesses near yours, offices of local schools, senior living centers, etc.

July 21 – Junk Food Day

Partner with local independent fast food restaurants and diners for cross or cooperative marketing. Extend a special offer to the employees of local restaurants. Invite one or more of your marketing partners to provide junk food (or junk food alternative) samples for your customers.

Post trivia about junk food on your Facebook page or hold a trivia contest. Items you might include: average number of calories in certain foods, history of pricing, who established or where restaurant chains were started, etc. Hold a junk food (or junk food-alternative) happy hour. Treat employees to lunch or give them gift cards for family use.

If you are, in fact, a junk food provider, extend a special offer or send gift cards to local executives, receptionists, care givers, clergy, city officials, civil servants, etc.

July Week 4

July 22 – Ugly Truck Day

Partner with local auto sales, auto parts and repair businesses for cross or cooperative marketing. Extend special offers to their patrons and employees. Post ugly truck trivia on your Facebook page. Solicit pictures of people's ugly-but-beloved trucks. Ask customers to post pictures or descriptions of their favorite truck make, model and year or hold a poll to determine their favorite vintage truck.

Hold an ugly truck contest or car show in your parking lot. Give away branded tchotchkes, a flyer with special offers, a menu or your catalog and do product sampling, demonstrations and consultations at the event. Invite a local car maintenance expert to provide a workshop about do-it-yourself projects for Ugly Trucks (and pretty ones, too). Hold a contest or drawing for an ugly truck auto care supplies gift set (such as for car maintenance, car washing, auto detailing, etc.)

July 23 – Gorgeous Grandma Day

Hold an open house and/or set aside appointment blocks just for Gorgeous Grandmas. Extend invitations or special offers to residents of local retirement communities, senior centers and senior service agencies, clubs and organizations. Create Gorgeous Grandma gift baskets, bags or totes that include a gift card, moisturizing lotion, smoothing hair products, beautiful nail lacquers and coordinating moisturizing lipstick, scarves, gloves, beautiful books, etc.

July 24 – National Drive Thru' Day

Set up a booth in your own parking lot for people to drive through. Distribute refreshments, samples, branded items, etc. as well as a special bounce-back offer. Purchase branded items reminiscent of 1950-60's drive in restaurants to gift-with-purchase. Purchase branded glassware or create a series of designs so that you can release them for collectors as a premium or gift-with-purchase. Partner with local drive-through restaurants for cross or cooperative marketing.

Premium collectibles or gift-with-purchase products can be an inexpensive way to build profits and increase customer loyalty and engagement. Items with almost no real value in and of themselves can become collectibles important enough to be purchased on their own, and at premium prices. In efforts to attract kids in recent decades, fast food restaurants created rock star-style demand (like with Beanie Babies) for items that would otherwise be in bins to be traded for skeeball tickets. The idea isn't now, but it's proven. Is there a premium-with-purchase type of item you can envision creating for your business? Giving away specially-priced or free add-ons and gifts-with-purchase beats discounting. Discounting can leave a customer feeling like they were overpaying at the regular price, or like what you have to sell wasn't worth as much as they thought. In contrast, when you are give something away, you are add value to the customer for money spent and—let's face it—it makes you the good guy!

Can you think of a low-cost collectible type of item to release for a limited time or which you can release in a series to bring clients back and stimulate repeat purchases? An item that could be used to get your clients back more frequently than they usually visit your business? An item that could be used to expand and increase your retail sales?

July 25 – Culinarians Day

Partner with a chef or caterer to hold cooking classes for gourmet appetizers, dinners, desserts and wine pairings. Hold a cook-off for local professionals or skilled amateurs. Partner with a restaurant or bar to hold a wine tasting featuring samples of gourmet appetizers, cheeses or desserts. Add cookbooks to your retail or as a gift-with-purchase or contest prize. Create a gourmet foods or kitchenware gift basket as a drawing or contest prize or for retail sale.

Hold an event at your business set up similar to a "progressive dinner" with food, prizes, contests, consultations, demonstrations and/or other activities at each stop. Partner with a kitchenware store or independent seller to hold a workshop to introduce customers to the latest and greatest in kitchen gadgets and beautiful dinnerware. Add dinnerware, glassware, silverware, baking or cooking pans, napkins, napkin rings or other tableware to your retail or to be sold as premium items with purchases. Create your own line of food, cooking or dining-related designs or slogans to be printed on t-shirts, aprons, tumblers, key rings, license plate surrounds, etc. for retail sale, contest prizes or a gift-with-purchase.

July 26 – All or Nothing Day

Partner with a motivational speaker or life coach to host an All or Nothing workshop to talk about risks and rewards relative to the most important dreams, visions and goals to which people aspire.

Create "all or nothing" scratch cards or hold a drawing and reward one shopper with a shopping spree or the refund of a total purchase. Spin a wheel, roll dice, draw numbers out of a hat—there are a lot of ways to do it. Give customers a chance to win a variety of free add-ons with purchase using one of these methods. Hold a happy hour featuring an "all or nothing" grand prize drawing or contest.

July 27 – Take Your Pants for a Walk Day

Hold a walk to raise funds for a local charity. Join or establish a fitness group of walkers. Tell people about the health benefits of walking and encourage walking during lunches, breaks, after work, after dinner, etc. in posts on your Facebook page, blog, bag stuffers and e-mail newsletter.

'Take your own pants for a walk' and get out into your community. Meet with community leaders who have influence over rules and regulations. Introduce yourself to local newspaper and radio staff. Find out where needs exist within your community and help to raise awareness and provide solutions. Meet with the owners of businesses you want to partner with for marketing and events.

July 28 – Hacky Sack Day

Purchase branded hacky sacks for retail sale, gifts-with-purchase, as gifts for your sponsored summer league or your own children's sports teams, as a street fair toy to give away, to send to local day cares, etc. Hold a hacky sack tournament in your parking lot or a local city park.

July 29 – Lasagna Day

Partner with local Italian restaurants for cross or cooperative marketing. Hold a dinner to raise funds for a local charity featuring great food, wine and a motivational speaker. Create a take home piece for attendees noting the needs of your chosen charity and what your business is doing to make a difference.

Ask customers to share lasagna recipes and cooking tips online. Hold a lasagna cooking contest, tasting or happy hour. Sell gourmet ingredients and bakeware at your event and/or add to retail.

Lasagna is about layers, and so is customer loyalty and engagement. Neither happens by accident, nor do they suddenly appear all at once. Customer engagement is built over time, over shared values, over delicious experiences and over interest in what is coming next. Think about how you make lasagna; ingredients aren't dumped in all at once, they are intentionally chosen and built up layer by layer. If you are not thoughtfully and intentionally designing (layering) each customer experience from beginning-to-end, you are leaving some of the details up to chance! You are missing opportunities to stimulate engagement and loyalty. Some of the details that you are missing or leaving to chance may even be working against the experiences you want to create—which may be why some of the customer reactions and responses you are provoking are not what you expected or desired.

July 30 – Cheesecake Day

Partner with local restaurants for cross or cooperative marketing. Work with them to create a special offer entitling customers to a free piece of cheesecake (or even a whole cheesecake) in exchange for participation in a benefit event or as a gift-with-purchase. Invite marketing partners to provide cheesecake samples to your customers or make cheesecake available for order or retail sale.

Partner with local restaurants or stores and sell cheesecakes with a portion (or all) proceeds of sales going to charity. Donate cheesecakes to local charities. Send cheesecakes to senior centers, youth organizations, to employees of local schools, hospitals, churches, etc. Purchase cheesecakes for your employees to enjoy with lunch or to take home to their families.

Ask customers to share their cheesecake recipes. Hold a cheesecake contest, tasting or happy hour. Hold a contest for the most original or unusually-flavored cheesecake recipe or entry.

July 31 – Mutts Day

Hold an event to benefit a local animal shelter or reward people for adopting pets. Hold a mutts-only community dog show. Put together a pet owner's gift basket for contest prize, gift-with-purchase or retail sale. Add pet supplies and equipment to your retail. Create your own custom-designed mutt-worthy pet or people wear like t-shirts, tank tops and hats, or other items like mugs, tumblers, water bottles, pet bowls, leashes, collars, etc. Compose your own custom-designed mutt-worthy slogans for wall or desk plaques. Purchase pet-inspired greeting cards and gift wrap.

Give away flyers or branded, pet-themed tchotchkes at your local dog park or in cross marketing with local veterinarians, animal shelters, animal hospitals, pet groomers, pet boarders or pet stores. Extend offers to the employees of these businesses.

august

365 Days of Marketing

August Month-Long Observances

Family Fun Month

Do you offer products or services which clients purchase for themselves but who purchase similar products or services elsewhere for their spouse or children? Set family rates or create multi-unit purchasing incentives and blocks of appointments to help clients with families save money and time. Especially at this time of year, a BOGO-style offer (buy 1-get 1 / buy 1-get 1 at half off / buy 3-get 1, etc.) can make a big difference to the budget of working families with school-age children—and that can mean new clients and more loyal customers for you.

Hold an event or day-long open house full of family activities, contests and prizes. Set up a family fair with carnival games, big bouncy toys, rides, etc. Rent a cotton candy machine or popcorn popper. Purchase branded school supplies to give away as prizes or as a gift-with-purchase in August.

'Adopt' a local family in need or by way of public nomination for a day, month or even a year's worth of free services or products. Invite customers to help underwrite the cost of additional products, services or other needed items. Preserving privacy, you can still keep customers aware of the needs and progress of your 'adopted' family throughout the year in general updates. As an alternative, 'adopt' a local family services organization and donate products or services that will be distributed to families in need. Use your Facebook page, blog, bag stuffers and e-mail newsletter to raise awareness of needs and publicize your results and community service.

Partner with a local gym or a sports or family recreation business for cross or cooperative marketing. Purchase gift certificates or passes from family-friendly sports, fitness or recreation centers to give as gifts to your most valuable customers or a gifts-with-purchase to customers who purchase specific items or spend over a certain dollar amount with your business. Partner with a local family fun center to hold a customer or employee-appreciation event with free or reduced-price entrance, food or drink vouchers and door prizes. Give away branded tchotchkes and extend a bounce-back offer.

Back-to-School Month and the Education Market

Hold a back-to-school open house with prizes, special offers, fall fashion show, school supplies, makeup and hair demonstrations, a celebrity look alike makeover competition, refreshments, etc. Attract attendees by holding a drawing for a complete set of free school supplies (or a school-year's worth of a product or service). Afterward, send all attendees special offers for school-year products or services.

Create signage to draw attention to products you carry that address conditions, needs or problems common to school-age children. Include a FAQ (Frequently Asked Questions) list of common childhood needs, conditions or problems and the corresponding solutions you provide on your website, e-mail newsletter, blog, Facebook page, etc.

There are thousands of teachers in your community! Give teachers a school-year marketing calendar that includes monthly offers or coupons, a school year book of offers or a set of coupons redeemable by month. Establish a standing discount for teachers and teacher-referral incentives. Design a school year homework or assignment planner for teachers or students which also features monthly offers, product knowledge, a spotlight service or product of the month, etc.

Teachers appreciate value and convenience. They respond to special offers created for them. Their time and money is at a premium. Most of their days start early and end late, so set aside certain time blocks for teacher's appointments or hold weekly teacher's happy hours. Teachers represent large networks (teachers, students, parents, etc.) so each has the potential to refer hundreds of other community members to your business.

Contact local public or private schools, school district offices or PTAs for permission to place flyers, catalogs, samples, menus or postcards in break rooms or to be distributed at meetings, in parent mailings, etc. Ask whether you can place ads or extend offers in school newsletters. Send treats or refreshments to school secretarial staff and teachers. Support local school athletic, music, art, theater and other programs. Attend school events. Donate to auctions and fundraisers.

Public schools may have regulations or policies which prohibit you from extending offers to their employees or students, but private schools are also an option. While private schools may represent smaller student bodies; their parents may be more likely to be part of your prime client demographic targets in terms of home ownership, income, professional work status, etc.

Eye Health and Safety Month

Partner with a local optometrist, glasses or sunglasses store for cross or cooperative marketing. Invite eye health professionals to your business to conduct screenings for customers, employees, children or to hold a workshop for your customers.

Post facts about eye health and safety on your Facebook page. Promote sales of safety glasses, reading glasses, sunglasses and related cleaning or repair items. Hold a drawing for a free pair of safety, reading and/or sunglasses, a repair kit and cleaning wipes. Use drawing entries to help build your contact database.

Purchase a display of sunglasses, reading glasses or safety glasses to add to your retail or impulse buy offerings. Purchase branded sunglasses to give to children who shop with their parents, to give as a gift-with-purchase or for retail sale.

What Will Be Your Legacy Month

Partner with a financial or retirement planner to hold a workshop on preparing for retirement. Meet with a professional yourself in order to create plan for the succession of your business, retirement, sending your kids to college, expanding your business or for some other goal.

Create a mentoring and leadership development program for your employees. Incentivize employee continuing education and training. Partner with local professionals who can provide your employees with guidance or resources to help them reach personal or professional goals.

National Picnic Month

Hold a customer-appreciation picnic in your parking lot, at a local park or outdoor recreation area. Add picnic baskets or take-out lunches to your retail. Hold an all-employee picnic.

Purchase branded or boutique-quality picnic-related items such as a basket or tote, tableware, wine, wine glasses, plastic storage containers and serving pieces, napkins, a blanket, etc. to add to retail or give away as contest prizes or a gift-with-purchase. Create picnic basket/kits for retail sale or to be awarded in contests or drawings.

August Week 1

August Week 1 – Simplify Your Life Week

Partner with a professional organizer to hold a workshop on de-cluttering, organizing and other ways people can simplify their lives. Invite a financial expert to participate and speak about how people can simplify their lives by improving their financial condition, credit score, preparing for the future, etc.

Bring attention to the products or services you sell that can help customers simplify or better order their homes, offices or lives. Add related products to retail. Create a back-to-school or organization products gift basket for contest prize or retail sale.

Post simplifying and organizing tips, recommended reading, product recommendations, links to websites or local professional organizers on your Facebook page, blog and e-mail newsletter. Add recommended reading to your retail or give titles away as contest prizes or a gift-with-purchase.

Narrow your own focus to pursuit of those goals which are the most vital and important. Recommit yourself to your goals. Prioritize the way you spend your time and disregard or dispose of things that distract you from what is most important.

August 1 – Girlfriends Day / Friendship Day

Hold a girlfriend-themed event. Extend a BOGO (buy-one, get one) promotion to girlfriends or friends where one would be a customer new to your business which offers appointments or services in pairs or groups, or for a girl's night out. Offer to book appointments in pairs or groups at a special rate.

Solicit "best girlfriend" nominations or stories. Hold a famous girlfriend's in history trivia contest. Suggest specific products or services which would be great gifts for girlfriends or best friends and create promotional offers around them.

Design your own girlfriend or friendship-themed greeting cards. Purchase friendship-themed greeting cards for a point of purchase display or inclusion in girlfriend gift baskets. Design your own girlfriend-themed shirts, tumblers or mugs, notebooks, note pads, pens, totes and other items for retail sale, gifts-with-purchase or contest prizes.

August 2 – National Night Out

Officially, "National Night Out" is America's Night Out against Crime (www.nationaltownwatch.org). It was started almost 3 decades ago to heighten crime and drug prevention awareness, generate support and involvement in anti-crime programs, strengthen neighborhood spirit and police-community relations and send a message to would-be criminals that they are not welcome, and that the community is committed to working together in order to prevent crime, catch criminals and bring them to justice.

Get involved in local crime awareness, neighborhood watch and crime prevention initiatives. Support legislation intended to help reduce neighborhood crime, drug activity, vagrancy and panhandling. Have a block party or cookout and invite police to make a presentation. Work with the businesses located near yours to hire security or street patrol professionals. Examine the outside of your business for potential vulnerabilities. Improve parking lot and outdoor lighting; add motion lights and alarms.

Many neighborhoods have "Night Out" parties and cookouts in August to build community spirit and get to know one another. Hold a neighborhood event with businesses located near yours and invite people from the community to attend. Incorporate food, games, contests, drawings and give away branded tchotchkes, flyers and other marketing collateral.

Hold a fashion and makeover event for women; if male customers are more your thing, partner with a local sports facility or sports bar and hold a night out for those who want to relive the latest local championship on a big screen TV or view an upcoming game. Feature samples, goodie bags, demonstrations and consultations at events. Hold door prize drawings. Use entry forms to help build your database and extend a special offer after the event.

Compile a list of suggested activities for a night out for families, girlfriends, couples, clubs or other groups. Partner with local restaurants, bars, clubs or other night out destinations to create a bundled activity night out package. Put together date or night out gift card packages to sell via retail at a special price at all participating businesses. Add pre-event activities such as salon makeover, champagne reception or transportation options to create care-free experiences for guests.

Hold a contest and solicit nominations for a local "perfect couple" that deserves a night out on the town. Reward them with items such as a trip to a retail boutique and/or formal wear rental, salon makeover, spa services, limo or town car transportation, dinner and a destination event like a play, concert, movie or game. Use entries to help build your contact database and extend special offers from you and your marketing partners after the event.

August 3 – Watermelon Day

Partner with a local farmers market or grocer in order to gift or gift-with-purchase a watermelon to the first 10 (or 25, 50, 100 etc.) customers of the day, week or month, to those who purchase specific items or whose purchase exceeds a certain dollar amount. Sample watermelon to customers.

Solicit fruit salad recipes or have a contest, tasting or happy hour. Post trivia and historical facts on your Facebook page. Have a watermelon and wine tasting or create a watermelon-flavored drink or cocktail. Have a watermelon toss, watermelon eating contest or a watermelon seed spitting contest at a local city park or your parking lot.

August 4 – National Chocolate Chip Day

Partner with a chocolatier or gourmet foods store to provide customers with samples of chocolate chips in various flavor varieties. Take entries and hold a drawing to win gourmet chocolate chips or a chocolate chip themed gift basket.

Hold a wine and chocolate chip tasting or happy hour. Purchase branded or gourmet chocolate chips for retail sale, a gift-with-purchase or contest prizes. Post chocolate chip trivia and history on your Facebook page, blog, bag stuffers and e-mail newsletter along with irresistible recipes or product recommendations. Share recipes from local chefs or post links to online recipes. Solicit recipes to add to the collection you will have printed at the end of the year.

Solicit customers favorite chocolate chip inclusive recipes, or have a baking or cooking contest with chocolate chips. Hold a full-blown cookie fair featuring the work of local culinary professionals or that of the general public. Add baking pans, cookie mixes, pot holders, spatulas and related items to your retail or create a chocolate chip-themed gift basket for retail or contest prize.

August 5 – National Underwear Day

Partner with a lingerie store or independent seller to hold a lingerie show or charity benefit event. Ask customers to bring in new underwear in lieu of an event cover charge, in exchange for a free product or for special pricing. Donate the underwear to a local charity, treatment center or shelter.

Post trivia about underwear or lingerie on your Facebook page, or hold a trivia contest.

Create your own branded design to have printed on sleepwear tank tops, shorts or boxers for retail sale, client gift, gift-with-purchase and contest prizes. This could be another opportunity to create a premium series to be released one at a time. Create new designs for the upcoming holiday season. You might create designs or slogans to appeal to teens/tweens, pet owners, nurses, etc. which are targeted toward hobbies or occupations or which feature the name of your city.

August 6 – Fresh Breath (Halitosis) Day

Purchase branded gum or mints or create a custom design for your own line of gum or mints to add to retail or impulse buys, to gift-with-purchase or to give away at events or the point of sale. Create your own design for a tin of mints or gum to use as your business card during August (or all year). Create a design to raise awareness of a local charity and donate proceeds from sales to the charity.

Partner with a local dentist for cross or cooperative marketing. Hold a drawing or contest to win an electronic toothbrush, other professional cleaning tools or teeth whitening services.

Post information about the causes of halitosis and how to prevent and treat it on your Facebook page, blog, bag stuffers and e-mail newsletter. Post tips from a dentist or a nutritionist on the impact to breath of certain food or drinks, natural remedies, oral cleaning and care, recommended schedule of services, etc.

August 7 – National Kids Day

Purchase branded toys, activity or coloring books, crayons, clay, etc. to add to retail or gift with purchase to customers with kids. Send branded toys to local day cares, schools, churches and youth services organizations. Hold a Kid's Day featuring a magic show, clowns, fairies or mascots, bouncy toys, play sets, small rides, carnival-style games and/or refreshments.

Sponsor a Kid's Day at a local theme park for children of employees, local underprivileged kids, a church youth group, day care, etc. Partner with the theme park for free or reduced-price tickets to give to your most valuable customers, to give away as a gift-with-purchase or resell. Hold an employee or customer-appreciation day at a local family fun center.

Raise funds or hold a benefit event for a local children's charity. Establish college, private school or tutoring scholarships with applications open to the children of customers, employees and/or the general public.

Partner with pediatricians, children's dental specialists, salons and kid's clothing stores for cross or cooperative marketing. Hold a children's health services or safety fair. Post local resources on your Facebook page, website, blog and e-mail newsletter. Post recommendations on topics like children's nutrition, health care needs, when they should first see a dentist or orthodontist, common scalp or skin care problems, etc.

With school about to start again, partner with local clothing and shoe retailers to hold a children's, tween and/or teen fashion show. Invite local stylists to participate to demonstrate kid's hair and makeup styles or give kids school year makeovers. Include refreshments, live music and kids entertainment or activities. Feature door and grand prize drawings; use entries to help build your contact database. Send a special back-to-school offer to attendees after the event.

August Week 2

August Week 2 – National Smile Week

Create offers and make specific suggestions to customers for products or services that contribute to a healthy, beautiful smile or those which make people smile. Purchase branded toothbrushes to give away to local day cares or schools, use as bag stuffers, etc.

Partner with a dentist, orthodontist, cosmetic surgeon, dermatologist or skin care/makeup professional for cooperative or cross marketing. Display one another's business cards, promotional offers, gift certificates and service menus.

Create a cooperative offer with a local dentist, orthodontist, dermatologist or cosmetic surgeon and hold a contest via your website, Facebook page, blog, etc. for the "best smile." Create an online gallery with before-and-after photographs that demonstrate the power of a great smile.

Hold a "Best Smile" contest at a local bar or restaurant. Reward winner/s with a gift card and smile-enhancing products. Demonstrate and sample smile-related products during your event. Give branded lip balms to those in attendance. Sell lipstick, lip gloss or other smile-enhancing products at the event. Use registration or door prize drawing entry forms to collect contact information; afterward, extend a special offer to all attendees.

Create a kit for retail sale or for drawing or contest prize with products to help create a perfect smile including lipstick, lip gloss or branded lip balm, wrinkle reducing serum (to minimize wrinkles and fine lines around the mouth), toothpaste, toothbrush, teeth whitening products, branded floss, etc.

August 8 – Dollar Day

August 8th is the day in history that the U.S. Dollar was created. Do you still have the first dollar you made in your business? Tell the story of your first dollar or how your business started on your Facebook page, blog, website and e-mail newsletter. Extend special Dollar Day offers or designate items customers can add on to a purchase with a $1.

Post trivia about the dollar on your Facebook page or hold a trivia contest. Create a special code word exclusive to your website, e-mail newsletter, blog or Facebook page entitling customers to a $1 add-on, branded tchotchke or another special $1 offer. Differentiating promotions with a code word or trackable coupon can help you determine which offers and which means of communication are most effective at stimulating response and sales.

Purchase branded banks, money clips, wallets or coin purses for gift, gift-with-purchase or retail sale. Hold a contest or drawing to win an automatic coin sorter, branded piggy bank or money clip. Partner with a local bank to hold an event to help children start savings accounts. Partner with a financial expert to hold a financial well-being or investment workshop.

Partner with a local bar or club and hold a dollar dance for charity, or hold a dollar dance as a singles mixer, for local seniors, teenagers, etc.

August 9 – Book Lovers Day

Compile a list of your favorite books and ask employees and customers to suggest more titles for recommended reading. Take some of the best titles from this list and/or past recommended reading lists and create the ultimate Book Lover's Collection for contest prize or retail sale as a set. Include other reading "must-haves" like reading glasses, branded bookmarks, branded reading lights, etc. Hold a contest or drawing to win a digital book reading device.

Launch a book club and host meetings at your business. Create a program to reward children for reading done over the summer or during the coming school year. Contact local educators to invite their classes to participate in your reading program. Ask them for titles and create a list of recommended children's literature divided into age categories for your contest or to post on your Facebook page, blog and e-mail newsletter.

Hold a "Name that Book" trivia contest using quotes from well-known (or not so well-known) books. Hold a book swap or set aside an area for reading at your business. Hold a fundraiser in support of your local school library, a public library or a children's literacy program. Sell recommended titles with proceeds donated to a local school library, English as a Second Language or literacy program.

August 10 – Lazy Day

Purchase branded or boutique-quality travel pillows, throws, stadium seats or blankets for retail sale, contest prizes or a gift-with-purchase. Put together a Lazy Day gift basket containing things like pillows, throws, personal massagers, novels, soothing music albums, pampering lotions and oils, etc.

Do you have lazy customers? I hope so—because it's the perfect excuse to launch a telephone, text message and/or e-mail reminder system. Reminders aren't just about appointments; send alerts prior to sales, contests, drawings or to announce special events. Survey customers in order to keep your database up to date and adhere to their preferred method/s of contact.

Do you take appointments? Launch a rebooking initiative or revitalize your existing program. Make it your goal to have 100% of customers rebooked for the next appointment before they leave.

Launch delivery services, personal shopping services, call-text-or-e-mail ahead ordering for pick up, or automatically re-ship customers frequently purchased items. Start a club whose members will receive automatic shipments of select new (or regularly-purchased) items every season, in the same way that wine club members receive shipments with newly-released wines 3-4 times a year.

August 11 – Playin' in the Sand Day

Partner with a builder or outdoor play set business for cross or cooperative marketing. Set up a giant sandbox in your parking lot for kids to play in while you treat parents to samples, demonstrations and consultations. Have games or a sand castle sculpting contest and serve refreshments. Purchase branded beach balls, sand pails and shovels for kids to take home. Add sand play toys to your retail or create a prize basket for a contest or drawing. Add full size or miniature sandboxes, sand-filed zen garden kits or supplies to retail.

Partner with a party planner for a workshop on decorating with sand (in glass containers, with candles, as table décor, to create art, etc.) Purchase colored sands or sand art kits to add to retail or gift-with-purchase.

August 12 – Middle Child's Day

Those poor middle children—they've waited their whole lives for a little bit of attention! Always in the shadow of older siblings or out-cuted by younger ones; it's time to give the middle child their due!

Identify the 'middle children' among your products or services; those items that rarely enjoy time in the spotlight all their own. Create special offers and tell customers about the benefits and services they provide. Create promotions and highlight items such as the second title in a trio of books or movies, the conditioner in a shampoo-conditioner-styler set, the second of three music albums of an artist or band—every trio of products or services you offer has it's own 'middle child.'

Solicit customers humorous or sentimental middle child stories. Post information about birth order theories and related reading on your Facebook page. Feature articles about middle children who are members of your staff in your e-mail newsletter. Solicit stores about the accomplishments of notable middle children.

Create your own slogans or designs for middle child-themed greeting cards or products (t-shirts, tank tops, tumblers or mugs, notebooks, pens, etc.) Put together a gift basket with items chosen specifically for the middle child.

August 13 – Left Handers Day

Put the spotlight on products you sell that are designed specifically for left handers. Create your own left handers slogans or designs for t-shirts, tank tops, hats, mugs, tumblers, notebooks, etc. to add to retail or give away as contest prizes or a gift-with-purchase.

Post information on Facebook or hold a trivia contest about famous left handed people. Hold a contest for left handers, making them use their right hand to complete a complex project or for right handers to have to use their left. Or have right and left handers compete with one another to see who can perform complex tasks most quickly or accurately using their non-dominant hand. Create special offers or give a free add-on or branded tchotchke to left handed people who come to your store and prove their left-handedness.

August 14 – Garage Sale Day

Hold a parking lot garage sale of discontinued or aging inventory. Hold a sale from your garage door bays with cover charges collected or a portion of proceeds donated to charity.

Coordinate with other businesses near you to hold a multi-business garage or parking lot sale. Extend special day-of-sale only offers. Purchase branded water bottles, visors and/or lip balms to give away as a gift or gift-with-purchase or to sell at the event. Allow people to reserve or rent space and hold a community garage and/or craft sale in your parking lot.

Hold a special promotion for any products or services you sell related to commercial or residential garages, cars, etc. Highlight the Top 10 tools, garden supplies and/or cleaning equipment—or other items that you sell—which customers should have in their own garage.

August Week 3 – Resurrect Romance Week

Partner with a counselor, relationship expert or columnist to hold a workshop on ways to resurrect romance. Write a Top 10, 50 or 100 Ways to resurrect romance to post on your website, e-mail newsletter, blog or Facebook page, weaving some of your own romance-resurrecting products or services into the list.

Post lists or links to recommended romantic books or videos. Post the most romantic fragrances, quotes, ways to propose, ways to ask someone to prom, etc. Hold a contest for the most romantic stories about how people met, first dates, engagements, weddings or anniversaries.

Create a flyer or brochure featuring your romance-resurrecting products or services. Working with other businesses, put together the ultimate romance-resurrecting date night package including flowers, formal rentals, makeovers, dinner, activity or destination event, transportation, etc. as a contest prize or to sell at a special bundled price.

August Week 3 – Weird Contest Week

Brainstorm with employees to create a weird contest, tournament or game, or hold different weird contests all week. Solicit weird contest ideas from customers and implement one or more of the winning suggestions. Partner with a local hobby or games store to compile a list of weird games. Hold a drawing or contest to win a gift basket filled with weird games to play at home. Come up with your own weird game for employees to play as a team-building or training exercise. And don't forget, weird contests call for weird prizes!

August 15 – National Relaxation Day

Educate customers about the symptoms and common causes of stress as well as natural or unusual ways people can relax. Partner with a nutritionist and fitness expert and pass on information about foods, beverages, vitamins or exercise that contribute to relaxation or stress-relief. Partner with a local yoga instructor for an introductory yoga workshop or host a series of classes for your customers. Create a flyer listing relaxation techniques customers can do at home. Post lists of local resources and recommended videos or books.

Put the spotlight on the products or services you provide that reduce stress or help with relaxation. Offer promotions to help take strain off customers monetary or time constraints. Post information about aromatherapy on your Facebook page and e-mail newsletter and highlight products you carry that offer aromatherapy benefits.

Purchase branded stress balls or personal massagers for retail sale, client gifts, contest prizes or gifts-with-purchase. Create a gift basket filled with pampering products for retail sale, gift-with-purchase or contest prize.

August 16 – Roller Coaster Day

Purchase tickets to a local theme park to award in a contest or drawing, give to your most valuable customers or exceptional employees, to gift-with-purchase or even to resell. Partner with a counselor or life coach to hold a "life can be a roller coaster" seminar or workshop on parenting, teen life, relationships, etc. Create a list of local resources and recommended reading to post on your Facebook page, blog and e-mail newsletter, add to retail or give away as contest prizes or a gift-with-purchase.

Add theme park video games, board games or toys to retail. Partner with a photographer to take pictures of customers when entering or while dining, shopping, ordering, etc. (just like they do at the theme park when you ride the roller coaster) to create a collage, use in marketing collateral, populate a bulletin board, feature on Facebook, etc. Offer to provide customers with pictures for use on their social media profiles—this gives you another opportunity to ask for an e-mail address and add contacts to your database and connect with them on Facebook and other social media.

August 17 – Mail Order Catalog Day

When did you last re-think your catalog? Add value to your catalog or menu to give readers good reasons to keep them longer and to share them with friends:

- Articles about things that would interest readers on fitness, nutrition, hobbies, recipes, etc.
- Referral rewards program description, incentives, etc.
- Special code words to track response relative to items in the catalog or specific offers
- Calendars, weights and measures conversion charts, horoscope or personal interest items
- Inspirational or humorous quotes, comics and stories
- Book reviews, product reviews, movie reviews
- Announce contests and results
- Top 10 lists
- Local trivia, business directories, attractions directories, best places to eat, drink or go out, etc.
- News about the local business climate, economy, city government, shopping locally, etc.

No catalog? Design a brochure featuring upcoming promotions as well as some of the types of information above. Encourage customers to share your catalog with friends or to give you the e-mail addresses of friends to add to your catalog mailing list. Add value so that it's more likely to be kept for future reference. Create directories which also feature your services or products. Work with your marketing partners to create combined catalogs (and share production and print costs).

Update your mailing list. Ensure that you are collecting contact data at every customer and prospect touchpoint. Conduct a mailing that includes the cost of return/undeliverable addresses so you can clean your list of inaccurate addresses and reduce mailing costs going forward. Use Facebook, your blog, e-mail newsletter, website and forms/conversations at the point of sale to collect new subscriptions for your catalog, direct mail and electronic communications.

Hold a contest asking customers to submit the craziest, funniest, oddest or cheesiest old mail order catalog pictures or product descriptions they can find. Post strange product photos and ask customers to write a fictitious caption, product description and price for it or post pictures from old catalogs of obsolete items or dated fashions and ask customers to guess what pricing was 'then' and 'now.'

August 18 – Cupcake Day

Partner with a local bakery or caterer to provide samples for clients or purchase cupcakes to add to retail or give away as a gift-with-purchase. Purchase gourmet cupcakes for your next customer or employee-appreciation event. Create a party kit which includes party decorations, table ware, gourmet cupcakes and/or a party menu of services. Sell cupcakes at a reduced price to non-profit organizations so they can be resold with profits going to the group project or a local charity.

Working with a local baker, create a custom-decorated or flavored cupcake to sell exclusively at your business or to serve at a special event.

Provide un-decorated cupcakes for kids to frost and decorate. Create a gift basket for retail sale or contest prize with cake mix, pan, frosting, toppings, spatula and other items needed to make and decorate cupcakes. Give gourmet cupcakes to your most valuable customers, vendors or employees.

Ask customers to share a favorite recipe or pictures of their own cupcake creations. Partner with a caterer or baker to hold a baking and/or decorating class, or a series of classes. Hold a cupcake making and/or decorating contest.

August 19 – Men's Grooming Day

Partner with a local esthetician, skin care expert or cosmetics seller to demonstrate men's grooming techniques, tools and products. Work together to create a flyer or brochure to use as a bag stuffer or post online as an at-home men's grooming guide featuring grooming tips and product recommendations.

Add boutique-quality men's skin care and grooming products and tools to your retail. Create men's grooming-themed gift sets for retail sale or gift-with-purchase.

Partner with a local bar to hold a best-shaved contest. Hold a shave-off event for charity. Demonstrate men's grooming products and tools at the event. Hold a door prize drawing and collect entries at the event. Afterward, extend a special male-oriented offer to all attendees.

Partner with men's barbershops or unisex salons, cigar shops, hunting or sportsmen's clubs, golf clubs and other men's organizations for cross or cooperative marketing.

August 20 – Sand Castle Sculpture Day

Partner with a rock and sand supplier and create the world's largest beach in your parking lot (or at a local park) to hold an all-community sand castle sculpture contest or festival. Separate 8-foot square sections of sand; take reservations and hold a contest or simply let people create sand art for art's sake alone. Set up a sandbox where kids can play stocked with branded beach balls, sand pails and shovels which kids can take home. Sell or give away branded water bottles, hats, t-shirts, tank tops and other items at the event. Donate a portion of proceeds from sales or a cover charge to a local charity. Invite representatives of the charity to attend and share information with the public.

Post images of sand castle sculptures on your Facebook page or list tips and tricks for making great sand castles. Purchase a coffee table-quality book with photos of sand sculptures, beaches or related photography to add to retail, incentivize sales as a gift-with-purchase or give away as a contest prize.

August 21 – Homeless Animals Day

Hold an event, fundraiser, donate a portion of sales or donate proceeds from the sale of specific products or services to a local animal shelter. Contact shelters for information and statistics about local issues and the needs of local shelters to share on Facebook, bag stuffers, your blog and e-mail newsletter to stimulate awareness and generate campaign momentum. Design your own line of pet-themed branded shirts, mugs or other wares and donate a portion of proceeds from their sales to a local shelter on an on-going basis.

Post pictures of pets available for adoption, hold an adoption event or provide the shelter with branded items or gift cards to incentivize/reward adoptions. Ask customers to post pictures of their pets on your blog, Facebook page or an in-store bulletin board. Accept pet food to be donated to a local animal shelter in lieu of cover charge at an event or in exchange for a free add-on or branded tchotchke.

August Week 4

August Week 4 – Safe at Home Week

Partner with local law enforcement, residential or personal security experts to hold a Safe at Home workshop. Provide customers with professional tips and recommendations and post them on your Facebook page, blog, bag stuffers and e-mail newsletter. Add personal security items to retail. Partner with local alarm sellers and locksmiths for cross or cooperative marketing.

When was the last time you spoke with employees about safety and security on the job? Hold regular emergency drills and provide annual re-training for employees in crime prevention, fraud awareness, personal security, facility security, disaster and accident preparedness. Be sure every work station is equipped with an emergency kit. Update emergency exit maps. Tell customers about your commitment to their safety and how you have trained and equipped employees to help them.

Add emergency and disaster preparedness kits to your retail. Posts lists of recommended supplies, instructions for family emergency drills, personal safety, etc. on your Facebook page, blog and e-mail newsletter.

Hold a "safe at home base" gift-with-purchase promotion or hold contests or drawings for customers or employees to win tickets to local minor or major league baseball games. Purchase tickets as a gift for the coach of the parks and recreation team you sponsored or another deserving member of your community. Hold "safe at home base" happy hours to watch baseball at your business, at a local sports bar or at a recreation facility.

August 22 – Be an Angel Day

Become a team of angels! As an employee group, perform maintenance, repair, cleaning, yard work, etc. for local seniors or shut-ins. Volunteer to do yard work on the grounds of a local charity, or adopt a local section of road. Get involved in Big Brother/Big Sister, mentoring or tutoring programs. Establish a scholarship fund to be awarded to underprivileged children or for vocational job training. Establish a scholarship to be awarded annually to a student who demonstrated extraordinary community service during their high school years. Write a press release to raise additional public awareness and highlight the contributions of your business.

Take nominations of individuals who people feel are "angels" because of how they serve others. Reward one or more with a day of pampering, makeover services, boutique clothing, lunch or dinner, a night-out destination, etc. Or go big! Partner with other businesses for additional publicity, larger or multiple prize packages and to hold a joint awards reception to honor the winners. Write press releases to help publicize the contest and honor the finalists and the winner.

Purchase children's angel-themed items (costumes, halos, wings, etc.) to add to retail for kids dress-up play. Purchase or create your own line of angel-themed t-shirts, tank tops, tumblers or mugs, notebooks, greeting or note cards, stationery, pens, totes, etc. for retail sale or to give away as contest prizes or a gift-with-purchase. This could be a great collection to add before the holidays.

August 23 – Second Hand Wardrobe Day

Hold a closet sale or clothing swap event and donate proceeds, cover charge or a portion of sales to charity. Organize a swap event for clothing and shoes for school-aged children. Encourage or incentivize the donation of new or gently used items to a local shelter or mission. Contact a local charity and 'adopt' a family; raise funds or solicit donations of new clothing in the sizes they need.

Partner with a local thrift store and have a contest, giving participants $15 and 15 minutes to put together the most fashionable outfit possible. Or hold a contests for self-proclaimed fashionistas to return with the most valuable or fashionable item they can find. Contact local high schools, colleges or trade schools and invite design students to participate. Award the winner with retail clothing and shoes gift cards, a bookstore gift card, tuition scholarship, etc. Write a press release to publicize the contest and report results.

August 24 – Strange Music Day

Solicit nominations for the strangest music, albums or artists. Hold a contest for the most original or unique use of non-music items as musical instruments. Challenge contestants to form ensembles and perform at a strange music recital. Provide prizes for the most original music, use of non-music items as instruments, etc.

Hold a strange music happy hour. Purchase strange music albums for retail sale, contest prizes or gifts-with-purchase. Hold a strange music trivia contest or have a Name that (Strange) Tune contest. Feature strange live music in-store or at an event. Post links to strange music videos or make recommendations of unique music albums, musicians or groups on your Facebook page, blog and e-mail newsletter. Post links to local musicians, bands, music stores, etc.

August 25 – Kiss and Make Up Day

Partner with a local salon, esthetician, makeup artist or makeup seller to hold a makeup application demonstration or workshop. Add lipstick, plumpers or lip gloss displays or a full blown boutique makeup collection to retail. Create gift or goodie bags with lip balm, lipstick, plumper and/or other makeup as a gift-with-purchase, to incentivize event attendance or for retail sale.

Hold a kiss and makeup happy hour featuring demonstrations and a "best pucker" contest. Partner with a local counselor, clergy or other relationship expert to hold a workshop on forgiveness.

August 26 – Work Like a Dog Day

Working hard in the summer can make you pout—so many other people are enjoying vacations and taking long weekends! Hold a happy hour at your business (or at a local bar or restaurant) for hard-working clients or hold an employee-appreciation night out. If you hold a Work Like a Dog Day happy hour, consider donating a portion of proceeds or cover charge to your local animal shelter.

Partner for cross marketing with a mobile groomer so that customers can come to their appointment or shop at your store while their furry friends are being groomed outside. Partner with other pet-oriented businesses for cross or cooperative marketing.

Partner with an executive coach or counselor to hold a seminar on work-life balance. Compile a list of recommended reading and post links to management and leadership articles and resources on your Facebook page, blog and e-mail newsletter. Create a peer networking and problem-solving group to make work easier for everyone. Create an employee problem-solving committee. Add work-oriented branded items to retail or create slogans or designs for your own 'work like a dog' line of branded wares for retail sale, contest prizes or gifts-with-purchase.

August 27 – Just Because Day

Hold a special "Just Because" event and invite customers to a fall fashion style, hair and makeup show complete with step-by-step demonstrations, event-only offers, appointment prices or promotions. Design take-home tip sheets, catalogs or brochures featuring the products and step-by-steps featured at the event.

On August 27 (or any random day of the year) stock a fishbowl with a number of random, exceptional "just because" offers and let attendees "fish" an offer out of the bowl. You might include coupons for free products, services, buy one-get one offers, motivational quotes, product knowledge, tips and tricks, weird and fun facts about your business or your city, etc. Have fun—just because! If customers enjoy this, consider repeating it once a month or once a quarter.

August 28 – Radio Commercials Day (and August 20th – Radio Day)

Introduce yourself to local radio personalities and news staff. Find out where to submit press releases and contest announcements. Submit press releases to local radio stations throughout the year; they may be willing to help to publicize your contests, especially those where you are asking for public nominations or benefitting local charities.

Provide radio stations with tickets to your events, workshops and happy hours for themselves and to give away in on-air contests. Provide them with scripting for announcements.

Find out which charities your favorite radio personalities support and raise awareness, hold benefit events or conduct fundraising campaigns for these causes. Create events to which you can invite local celebrities (including radio personalities) and ask for on-air announcements and endorsements. Participate in radio station fundraisers and pledge drives.

Extend a special offer to local radio station employees. Partner with a local radio station to hold an event in September to benefit one of their favorite charities or a local animal shelter.

August 29 – Race Your Mouse around the Icons Day

Partner with computer sales and repair businesses for cross or cooperative marketing. Hold a joint event to demonstrate the latest in computer technology or hold computer software classes. Partner with a graphic design instructor or local art school to hold an introductory computer design workshop.

Hold a computer navigation, e-mail or texting contest. Create a scavenger hunt which customers complete by visiting the websites of your business, your Facebook and blog sites and/or the sites of your marketing partners in order to find codes or answer specific questions (your goal is to get people onto your website—and reading it!)

Set up a large scale version of a computer screen on the floor or in the parking lot and equip kids with cardboard "mice" cars to race around the icons, collecting prizes or stamps at each stop and receiving a special prize at the end.

Purchase branded mice and/or mouse pads (or create your own custom design) for retail sale or to give away as contest prizes or a gift-with-purchase.

August 30 – S'mores Day, Toasted Marshmallow Day

This is the perfect time to hold an end-of-summer customer or employee-appreciation event at your local park, in your store or in your parking lot. Serve S'mores or create S'mores kits for retail complete with graham crackers, chocolate bars, marshmallows and marshmallow toasting skewers.

Solicit customers S'mores recipe variations. Create S'mores cocktails or challenge local bartenders to create S'mores cocktails or mocktails for a contest, tasting or happy hour.

S'mores are so named because you eat one, then you want "S'more" (some more). Create promotions for your most irresistible products or services—the ones that customers want s'more of right away—featuring free add-ons, BOGOs (buy one-get one variations), packaged series of repeat services, bundled best-selling products, extra rewards, etc.

August 31 – Trail Mix Day

Partner with a local gourmet or organic food store and create interesting, unique and irresistible trail mix combinations to sample, gift or retail to customers. Create your own custom trail mix combination and package design and add branded trail mix to your retail.

Post information about local parks, hikes and trails on your website, blog, Facebook page and e-mail newsletter. Create a flyer or brochure with hiking and trail information that also features related "must haves" like your custom trail mix, branded or custom designed water bottles, bandanas, hats, back packs, picnic wares, etc.

Solicit customer suggestions for great local trails to hike or bike on Facebook, or post links to local outdoor recreation, wilderness, camping and hiking resources and information.

september

365 Days of Marketing

September Month-Long Observances

Classical Music Month and National Piano Month

Extend a special offer to independent vocal, piano and instrumental music teachers. Extend special offers to employees of music and instrument stores. Partner with local music teachers and stores for cross or cooperative marketing. Hold a demonstration introductory lesson or workshop to introduce your customers to local music instruction options and connect them with instrument sellers.

If you offer fashion, styling or makeup services or products, create a menu of services and/or offers for local students and professional musicians to utilize prior to recitals, performances or competitions.

Support local performing arts organizations like choirs, orchestras and ensembles. Attend concerts. Give concert tickets away in contests. Place ads in programs. Host or sponsor after-parties or post-performance get-togethers.

Courtesy Month

Customer service professionals are often the first point of contact (and some times the only point of contact) for customer interaction, taking orders, assigning consultants, completing sales, fielding complaints, etc. It's vital that they receive a thorough orientation and on-going support, scripting and retraining. Sales, growth, customer loyalty and retention—there's a lot riding on their performance! Review your orientation and training programs. Revise scripts that have become stale or obsolete. Determine whether courtesy or knowledge gaps exist among employees which indicate the need for re-training. Beyond corporate training, show employees you care by establishing a mentoring and leadership development path, demonstrating support for continuing education and bringing in guest speakers to enhance training.

Tell customers about all of the courtesy services you provide. Add a new courtesy service such as delivery, automatic repeat shipments, call, e-mail, text or fax-ahead orders, transportation for seniors, shuttles from hotel or motel, etc. Create a list of courtesy expectations—things customers can expect to experience, that you promise will be true every time they interact with anyone in your company for any reason. Ask all employees to agree to uphold these promises made to the customer as part of your employee orientation, annual employee meeting or performance review.

Self-Improvement Month

Partner with a counselor, motivational speaker or life coach to hold a workshop (or series of workshops) on self-improvement topics. Compile a list of recommended reading and post links to website or local self-help or self-improvement resources on your Facebook page, blog and e-mail newsletter.

Invite local colleges, universities, trade or specialty schools to provide your customers with information about local course offerings and adult education programs. Hold an adult learning or advanced degree continuing education fair.

Partner with individuals who are committed to self-improvement (nutritionists, trainers, fitness and weight loss experts, cosmetic medical and dental professionals, dentists, orthodontists, salon professionals, etc.) to hold the ultimate exterior-improvement workshop. Connect customers with local resources, professional tips, advice and recommended reading.

September Week 1
September Week 1 – Build a Better Image Week

In contrast to self-improvement, which often involves changes we make on the inside, building a better image is about how we appear to others—and "branding" is how your build your image. Your image, or brand, is—essentially—a promise that exists *in the customer's mind* about who you are and the benefits you provide that gets reinforced *every single time* they come in contact with *any facet* of your business.

Building a better image is about putting the stamp of the personality, values, culture, beliefs—the very essence of what you really want your business to be—on every possible customer touchpoint. Why is this important? Without a strong brand image in the customer's mind, you have to build a case for why you DESERVE their business, every single time you get ready to make a sale. Businesses with strong brands are closing deals while others are still introducing themselves.

Putting your stamp on *each and every* possible touchpoint? That's a long, long list! For a free branding workshop checklist and other resources, visit the 'Resources' page at www.12monthsofmarketing. com. Sometimes you need to put your brand into words to build a better image. Review the list below and create, tweak, evolve or simply recommit yourself to the fulfillment of your:

- **Vision Statement**
  IS NOT: what you are going to do or how you are going to do it
  IS: what your organization *ultimately* aspires to become, will resonate with customers
  and employees, will make everyone connected to your business feel proud, excited and
  that they are part of something bigger than themselves. Your vision is the good that your
  company will ultimately provide *to the world*. It explains *why* you are doing what you are
  doing and the good that success will enable your business to accomplish.

- **Mission Statement**
  IS NOT: about you, is not fluffy, ethereal or esoteric
  IS: a definition of why you (deserve to) exist; a precise description of what you do; should
  describe the business you are in. Your mission statement should give your employees a
  clear idea of how *their role* helps fulfill the vision. Your mission statement is *the practical
  route or means* you will employ to achieve your vision.

- **Tagline, Motto or Slogan**
  IS: your promise. The promise that guides the development of your business strategies and
  all the elements of your brand. It's a word, short phrase or single sentence that explains
  how you benefit your customer in a meaningful, impactful way.

September 1 – Generating Back-to-School Buzz

On average, "Moms" have more than 100 product-based conversations every week. Teachers represent thousands of other people—students, parents, co-workers, administration staff, family, friends, etc.—and they talk to one another in the parking lot, the classroom, at meetings, in the bleachers at sporting events, at the coffee shop and even in grocery store aisles. They share referrals. They ask one another where they purchased things or for the names of those who perform services for them, for their kids, their pets, etc.

Plan a Back-to-School Reception. Partner with local massage therapists or a salon or spa and invite teachers to your business to enjoy relaxing mini manicures, massages or makeovers. Partner with a local caterer and provide light snacks and beverages such as sangria or champagne to celebrate the arrival of a new school year, and set a date to celebrate with them again at the end of the year! Collect contact information and be sure that each attendee leaves with a bounce-back offer and collateral featuring your teacher's offers, referral and loyalty rewards.

September 2 – Truancy Prevention Day

One last school-and-student-related theme: Support parent and teachers efforts to prevent truancy. Design a pledge form for students to sign at the beginning of the school year with a goal of perfect attendance. Make print copies available for signature in-store and create a web version of the pledge form which can be signed electronically. Use forms to collect contact information.

Invite everyone to attend mid- and end-of-year parties with goodie bags for all, door prizes and a grand prize drawing (such as a college scholarship or summer vacation trip) to honor and reward those who did not miss a day of school all year. Invite parents to attend. Feature student fashions, hair and makeup. Do product demonstrations and provide professional consultations. Give away samples of new or best-selling products.

Establish a student rewards program where students accrue points for attendance, good grades, scholastic and other accomplishments throughout the year that can be redeemed for branded tchotchkes, products, services or other prizes. Create online student galleries featuring the art, writing, scholastic achievements and awards, etc. of local elementary, junior and senior high school students.

September 3 – The 1st Monday in September is Labor Day

Hold a Labor Day promotion, sale, event or happy hour. Have a cookout in the parking lot and give away hot dogs and sodas in exchange for a donation for a local charity. Post Labor Day trivia on your Facebook page. Purchase branded school supplies like #2 pencils, pens or notebooks for contest prizes or to give away as a gift-with-purchase. Labor Day marks the end of summer, so it's a great time to have a customer or employee-appreciation open house or party.

September 4 – Read a Book Day

Share a recommended reading list including favorites of your staff and customers. Poll customers and reward the one who has already read the most titles on your recommended reading list.

Hold a 'read-in' event featuring storytelling, alphabet or reading flash card contests and games for younger children. Hold a 'read in' to benefit a local library, literacy program or another charity. Compile a reading list for elementary, junior and senior high school levels and reward local students for reading books on the list. Launch a book club for adults.

Support local literacy and English-as-a-Second-Language (ESL) programs. Extend special offers to tutors, teachers and para-educators. Establish a $500 scholarship to be awarded to one student annually who is entering or already attending college as an English or Literature major.

Purchase multiple copies of your favorite children's books (mine is "The Fire Cat" by Esther Averill) and keep them on hand to give away along with a branded or personalized baby blanket, picture frame or another keepsake to employees, vendors or customers upon the arrival of a new baby.

September 5 – Be Late for Something Day

For which of your personal, professional or business goals are you running late? Now is the perfect time to get back on track, or to set up a new timeline and list the incremental steps you will take in order to meet them. My dad likes to say, "You're not late, unless you don't show up." So show up again—don't give up on your dreams!

Purchase branded watches or travel clocks for retail, client gift or gift-with-purchase. Begin designing your own marketing wall or desk calendar for next year to give (or sell) to customers, vendors and employees. Design a beautiful, funny or otherwise-customized branded calendar to sell via retail. Ask customers or children to submit designs to be used as artwork for each month. Set up an employee committee to choose among submissions—you'll need 14; one for each month of the year and one each for the front and back covers. Note holidays and observances you plan to incorporate into your marketing plan and intersperse reminders, special offers, product knowledge and other recommendations into the publication.

Implement a reminder program to reduce late arrivals and no shows. Use your rewards program to incentivize 100% on time appointments and no-cancellations or rescheduling. Collect customer contact information and preferences so that you can utilize telephone, text or e-mail reminders for appointments, sales, weekly promotions, events, changes in store hours, etc.

Hold a promotional event with door prizes and special pricing for those that are there when your doors open, or for those who are there during your last hour of the day.

Reward employees for 100% on-time arrivals and/or for working all of their scheduled hours in a month, quarter or year.

September 6 – Fight Procrastination Day

Partner with a motivational speaker or counselor to hold a workshop on procrastination. Post tips and tricks for fighting procrastination on your Facebook page, blog and e-mail newsletter.

There are many reasons we procrastinate that have nothing to do with our desire to do something or how badly it needs to be done. Determine the most common reasons that you procrastinate— you may be afraid of failing, you may not know where to begin, you may dread doing certain tasks, you may be overcommitted or may simply be too overwhelmed to begin something new. Identifying the reason/s you procrastinate can help you to overcome them; you'll know whether you need additional help or knowledge to begin, or whether you need to incentivize yourself to do something unpleasant.

One of the best ways to avoid procrastinating is to have some means of external accountability. Identify a friend, mentor, trusted peer (or even your spouse) with whom you can discuss things honestly and share your timeline of incremental steps and long-term goals.

The same holds true for your employees. Some individuals are self-motivated and need little direction, some need a lot! Establish the means to hold employees accountable, remembering that one of the roles of a manager is to hold employees to promises they make to the customer, the company and to one another. Ask employees to make public commitments to goals and standards. If an employee is not living up to a promise, don't just let it go because it may by unpleasant to deal with. Remember that saying, "one bad apple spoils the whole barrel?" One employee who is allowed to disregard commitments made to the company, the customer or co-workers can quickly become more than one. It can impact the morale of everyone in the company. Co-workers may come to believe their own behavior does not matter either, and others will be resentful that co-workers are not held to the same standards they are.

September 7 – Grandparents Day is the 1st Sunday after Labor Day

Hold an open house with activities, contests and games for grandparents and their grandchildren. In a variation of "The Newlywed Game," ask grandparents cultural questions about their children's interests, and find out how much kids know about what happened in the world when their grandparents were young.

Solicit stories about grandparents on your blog or Facebook page. Ask people to share the best advice or funniest one-liners their grandparents used to say. Solicit nominations of great local grandparents and create two prize baskets, one for the grandparent, one for the grandchild who nominated them.

Purchase or design your own greeting cards with sentiments suitable for grandparents or grandchildren. Make specific suggestions to customers relative to products and services you offer that would make great gifts for grandparents or seniors.

Hold a senior open house or social event. Organize or sponsor a local senior group bus tour, visit to a tourist attraction, wine tasting, trip to the zoo with grand kids, or another fun field trip. Work with local senior living communities to coordinate transportation to your business for shopping, events, appointments, etc. Set aside senior shopping hours or extend a senior citizen discount.

September Week 2

September Week 2 – Clean Hands Week

Purchase branded hand sanitizer for gift, gift-with-purchase or retail sale. Post recommendations about hand washing products or techniques and statistics about germs and hand washing on your Facebook page, blog, bag stuffers and e-mail newsletter. Add latex gloves in fun colors to your retail.

Remind employees about regulations or policies relative to hand washing and/or their responsibility to help keep your facility clean—even if it is not one of their formal job responsibilities. Make sure employees understand how the appearance and cleanliness of your business directly impacts the customer experience. Double check that the signage you are required to post in public bathrooms or other public areas relative to employee hand washing or any other standards of behavior looks new, is clean and readable. Replace old signage.

Purchase hand sanitizing stations or wipes to place near your entrance for customers who want to wipe down the handle of a shopping cart, their own hands or the door handle on their way in or out of your business.

Partner with a nail salon to extend a special offer to your customers. Purchase nail salon gift cards for gift-with-purchase or contest prizes. Purchase branded manicure kits to add to retail or give away as a gift-with-purchase.

September 8 – Wonderful Weirdos Day

Acknowledge and reward Wonderful Weirdos like teenagers who own their own businesses and super-smart 4.0 over-achieving students with extra rewards points, samples or freebies. Additional achievements to acknowledge might include scholastic and other school awards, honor roll, perfect attendance, recitals or performances, sports championships, etc.

Ask customers to tell you what their definition of a Wonderful Weirdo is and to nominate someone who qualifies. Honor some of these Wonderful Weirdos in press releases and in posts on Facebook, your blog and e-mail newsletter. Or go big! Solicit nominations and work with marketing partners to hold a Wonderful Weirdos reception or awards show.

Hold a Wonderful Weird Stuff sale. Purchase wonderful things in wild, weird colors. Partner with clothing and shoes retailers, a salon or stylist, cosmetic medical or dental professionals, piercing or tattoo artists, etc. in order to offer Wonderful Weirdo makeovers to your most unusual and individualistic customers.

September 9 – Teddy Bear Day

Purchase branded teddy bears to donate to a local children's treatment center, children's hospital, shelter, children's services organization, pediatrician or dentist's office or another of your marketing partners. Use branded teddy bears as gifts, as a gift-with-purchase or for retail sale.

Purchase a giant teddy bear to award in a contest or drawing. Hold a teddy bear story or drawing contest. Ask customers to post pictures of their own teddy bears on your Facebook page. Post teddy bear history and trivia online. Hold a kids teddy bear activities event or happy hour.

September 10 – Swap Ideas Day

Create a support network among peers in your industry and/or other small business owners. Have monthly meetings to share challenges, solutions and inspiration and for cross or cooperative marketing

Hold a charity-benefit swap event with cover charge where clients can bring-one, take-one of items like jeans, jewelry, books, shoes, home accessories or some other category.

Why should Starbucks have all the fun? Set up a reading area within your business (or in cooperation with another nearby business) with a book swap library.

Add a "Swap Ideas" question and answer blog or an online bulletin board to your website or Facebook page where clients can ask questions and get information about local resources, service providers, tourist attractions, dining or entertainment, shopping, etc.

September 11 – No News is Good News Day

Declare September 11th a bad-news-free zone and post only happy stories and thoughts on your Facebook page, blog, bag stuffers and e-mail newsletter. Solicit customers' good news, stories about great kids, accomplishments, promotions, anniversaries, birthdays, good deeds and happy thoughts.

Add inspirational thoughts, over-the-top thank-yous and other happy slogans, quotes or notes to customer receipts, invoices and statements. Surprise customers by putting branded tchotchkes, free add-ons or samples in with shipments.

September 12 – Popcorn day

Rent a commercial popcorn cart for the day and greet or send customers home with a bag of hot, fresh popcorn. Purchase branded bags for popcorn or add a hangtag to each with a bounce-back offer, coupon or preview of an upcoming promotion. Purchase branded packaged microwave popcorn to give away as a client gift, gift-with-purchase or for retail sale.

Create popcorn-themed gift baskets and promote them as a great gift for teachers, coaches or co-workers throughout the year and during the upcoming holiday season. Hold a contest to see who can submit the best recipe incorporating popcorn, photos featuring the most original use in decorating or another popcorn-related theme. Hold a popcorn eating contest. Have a popcorn tasting or happy hour featuring flavor and topping variations.

Post popcorn trivia, history and nutritional facts on your Facebook page. Hold a contest and reward the first 1, 5, or 10 people who respond with a popcorn fact. Reward customers who use the code word "popcorn" with a free sample, add-on, extra awards points or another special offer with purchase.

Partner with a local theater to hold a customer and/or employee and family appreciation event with hot-buttered popcorn and a private movie screening. Send branded bags or balls of popcorn to local schools, day cares or church youth groups or to the office staff of local schools, large employers, businesses located near yours, members of your Chamber of Commerce, Rotary or other civic organizations, etc.

September 13 – Positive Thinking Day

Partner with a counselor, life coach or motivational speaker to talk about the power positive thinking can have in our lives, helping us transform fear, worry and negativity into energy we can spend focusing on dreams and goals instead. Compile a list of recommended reading and add one or two of the best titles to your retail or give them away as a gift-with-purchase.

Create your own slogans or designs for positive-messaged t-shirts, tank tops, tumblers and mugs, totes, wall plaques, notebooks and other items to add to retail or give away as contest prizes or a gift-with-purchase. Post inspirational quotes on your Facebook page, blog, bag stuffers and e-mail newsletter.

Living in a spirit of gratitude benefits you as well as the recipient of your appreciation. Extend compliments, kudos and gratitude to customers, vendors and employees—liberally. Write thank-you notes every day. Reward and recognize behavior you want more of!

September 14 – Boss-Employee Exchange Day

Swap places with one or more of your subordinates for 30 minutes or even longer. Let other employees and customers see you doing things that are "not your job" on a regular basis. Lead by example if you want employees to go beyond the call of duty.

When it comes to exchanging information with your employees, how well is it working? Do employees readily buy in to new initiatives and ideas, or do you feel like a one-man band who is beating the drum for more customers and more sales with no one else helping to carry the tune? The following strategies can help you introduce change, marketing programs, customer initiatives and other improvements to your staff.

Communicate thoroughly, effectively, and often. Don't assume employees understand your motives or know what lies behind your desire to make changes, even if the reasons to do so seem painfully obvious to you. Explain precisely why each change is necessary. Periodically restate and discuss changes made and those you are pursuing over the long term to ensure that everyone stays on the same page. Don't be surprised if you have to talk about things more than once or that you have to remind some employees about their role and responsibilities in the process.

Explain to staff not only why planned changes are good for your business, but also what the negative consequences will be to the organization overall and to individual employees of not implementing them.

Most importantly, tell employees clearly and specifically how the changes will benefit them. Beyond improvements to the bottom line of the business (which will ultimately affect payroll, benefits, equipment, etc.), this may mean that initiatives need to be accompanied with employee incentives for incremental as well as long-term or final results. Salaries and performance reviews should be tied to corporate initiatives and goals, both to incentivize participation and to give you the means to hold employees accountable.

Reward behavior you want more of; rewards occur in many forms. They may include monetary inducements but can also be expressed through acknowledgement, recognition, paid time off, empowerment and thank-you notes and letters.

Introduce ideas to influential employees ahead of time in order to garner support or head-off opposition before it occurs. Having one or more of your staff already 'on board' before introducing an idea to the rest of your staff can help ensure a warmer reception.

Don't introduce new programs in the form of general, vague suggestions. If you are serious about an initiative it should be accompanied by a system and schedule for implementation, scripts, training, incentives, a method for tracking results, and the measures by which you will hold staff accountable — and consequences, if needed. Initiatives should be presented with your resolve for their implementation, a firm schedule, a commitment to tracking results and the means to staff accountable.

If this will be the first time in a long time that you have made accountability part of a new initiative, a change in employee standards, a change in customer relations, etc., and if you have employees who regularly subvert or even openly oppose or ridicule change, then this is your moment. This is your chance to show that you are putting the business first, because that is what is best for the customers, best for all employees, and best for your business.

Finally, when you make hiring decisions, do so not only with creative talent and technical skills in mind, but be sure that you also allow your desired employee culture to play a major (or even deciding) role in the process.

September Week 3

September 15 – Hat Day

Purchase branded hats or visors for client gifts, employee wear, gift-with-purchase, contest prizes, incentives, rewards or retail. Purchase branded beanie hats for winter/holiday season retail, gift-with-purchase, to incentivize purchase of men's products or services, or as employee or client gifts.

Partner with a local salon or stylist and boutique clothing and shoes retailers to hold a "no hat needed" hair and clothing fall fashion show. Hold a wine tasting featuring celebrity-inspired, stylish, easy-to-manage fall hair and makeup styles (and the products needed to create them).

How many 'hats' are you wearing? My guess is it's more than one! Many times small business owners have to fulfill roles far outside of their own areas of interest, experience and expertise. You might not have realized that when you signed on to own your own business you were also signing on to do your own accounting, taxes, human resources, marketing, cleaning, property management and so much more. As a small business owner and entrepreneur, I completely understand.

It would be easy to believe that I must become an expert in every area of my business in order to succeed; however, I learned a valuable truth prior to launching my own business as a result of watching Marcus Buckingham's short video series (6 videos that are each 10-15 minutes long) called *Trombone Players Wanted*. (I highly recommend that you purchase the series to watch yourself, and to watch with co-workers as a staff development and team building exercise, regardless of your business type. There is a link to this video series on the bottom of my blog at www.savvystylist.net and on my website at www.12monthsfomarketing.net.)

The main theme of this short but profound, transformative series suggests that you will be the most successful, happy and fulfilled when you work in your strengths and within areas of personal passion most of the time. You may have the intellectual ability to do your own marketing, but no passion for it. Or like me, you might have the ability to do your own bookkeeping and taxes, but you might also dread and dislike those tasks.

Buckingham makes the point that you will thrive, be most productive and most profitable working in areas that you love. And that while for a time you may be forced to work in areas that are not your strengths and perform tasks you personally dislike, your goal should be to work yourself out of those tasks, either by becoming profitable enough to outsource them or by delegating or 'trading' tasks with other individuals who do enjoy those areas of responsibility.

By hiring strategically to your weak areas, and giving staff a chance to grow and take on new responsibilities, you are working to create an environment where you can spend most of your time working to your strengths, where staff have a path for personal growth and for developing their own careers by taking on new responsibilities. You will be creating the best atmosphere for employee satisfaction, development, morale, continuous learning, maximum productivity and profitability—not to mention, you will get to spend more of your time doing those things you most love!

September 16 – Working Parents Day

Work with your marketing partners to create a combined business directory designed to help working parents save time; identify great restaurants, clothing, shoes and school supply retailers, tutors, babysitters or day cares, dry cleaners, family physicians, dentists, stylists, entertainment, recreation— businesses and organizations that would be important to a busy family. Add a family-oriented community directory to your website. Feature resources for working parents in posts on Facebook, your blog and e-mail newsletters. Create a print version to be used as a bag stuffer or mailer, handed out at parades or street fairs, distributed by your marketing partners, featured in rack card displays at local tourist points of interest, etc.

Take nominations or hold a drawing and reward local working parents with prizes like free catered or delivered meals, dry cleaning, housekeeping, etc. Post quotes or trivia about famous working parents on your Facebook page. Make specific suggestions of products or services you sell that make great gifts for working parents, or which are pre-packaged for purchase by working parents to help them save time. Post time-saving tips and tricks on Facebook, your blog, e-mail newsletter and bag stuffers and promote specific products and services that help working parents save time and resources.

September 17 – Citizenship Day, Constitution Day

Post a link on your Facebook page to the official page of the Constitution, Declaration of Independence and Bill of Rights. (http://www.archives.gov/exhibits/charters/constitution.html) Post trivia about the constitution, founding fathers and history of the country on your Facebook page, blog, bag stuffers and e-mail newsletter. Hold a history contest for customers or their kids.

Create your own customer bill of rights. Tell customers about guarantees you provide or promises you make relative to the performance of products, quality of services, the customer experience or level of customer service, etc.

Purchase branded miniature flags to sell or gift-with-purchase or to distribute in November at a Veteran's Day parade or event. Add full size flags to your retail (or plan to add them prior to Veteran's Day, Memorial Day and/or Independence Day).

Post links to local, state and national government and city resources on your website, such as links to city hall or the mayor's office, state and federal representatives, voter's registration or polling places, department of licensing, small business resources and to utilities such as water, power, trash pickup, recycling and landfill sites.

September 18 – Cheeseburger Day

Partner with a local independent fast food restaurant or diner for cross or cooperative marketing. Invite them to sample sliders or cheeseburgers to your customers. Create your own custom cheeseburger or cheeseburger-ish substitute (wrap, pizza, appetizer, salad, etc.)

Hold a cheeseburger recipe or cooking contest, tasting or happy hour. Poll customers for favorite local cheeseburger recommendations. Ask customers to describe their own perfect cheeseburger combination. Post ideas for cheeseburger variations (wraps, pizzas, appetizers, salads, etc.) on your Facebook page, blog, bag stuffers and e-mail newsletter. Post trivia about cheeseburgers on Facebook. Hold a contest and ask customers to make up a fictional story about the origin or benefits of cheeseburgers.

September 19 – Talk Like a Pirate Day

Included because it's my daughter Sarah's favorite! On Talk Like a Pirate Day, encourage staff to dress in pirate garb and tell "mateys" (customers) to "walk the plank" (instead of saying goodbye). Concoct your own custom pirate punch, appetizers, snacks or treats. Place a treasure chest at your entrance (or on tables, workstations, desks, point of purchase, etc.) displaying seasonal retail available for purchase, free add-on or branded tchotchkes or which are full of gold-wrapped branded chocolate coins for customers to take.

Hold a happy hour for the pirates among your customers, or hold an event in partnership with a caterer, local bar or restaurant featuring "fishy" food and games for families, couples, singles, etc.

September 20 – Fortune Cookie Day

Purchase branded fortune cookies or create your own custom fortune cookie line filled with inspirational quotes and messages. Gift fortune cookies with purchases, serve them at an event or make them available in the waiting area, on tables, etc.

Randomly intersperse special offers or give away free add-ons, branded tchotchkes or samples in fortune cookie messages. Give away samples of new products or services that you want your clients to get excited about. Branded, customized fortune cookies could be a great product to distribute in cross-marketing efforts with other businesses, to utilize at events or to create some excitement at the cash register.

September 21 – Play Dough Day

Purchase branded play dough, clay or silly putty from a promotional products vendor and make it available for retail sale, gift-with-purchase or as an incentive for clients to book their children's appointments when they book their own. Purchase play dough or silly putty for children to play with when customers are accompanied by children at your business.

September Week 4

September Week 4 – Keep Kids Creative Week

Hold contests or exhibits in children's art, writing, photography, music composition, music or dance performance, or even hold your own 'idol' contest. Solicit photographs or videos of children's work or performances on your Facebook page, to add to an online gallery or to post on a (real) bulletin board. Write a press release about extraordinary children in the community or who are represented among your client and/or employee base.

Partner with local artists or art teachers to hold a workshop, introductory lesson or a series of art classes for children or adults. Invite a local graphic design expert or teacher to hold an introductory demonstration or series of classes. Establish a scholarship to award to a child annually to subsidize tuition for art school, graphic design, dance, art or other creative classes taken at a community or vocational college, summer art camp, etc.

Hold a fundraiser or donate a portion of sales to support a local school art program or youth art center. Add art kits and supplies to retail. Put together a gift basket with art supplies for contest award, gift-with-purchase or retail sale.

Invite children in your community or from among your client base to submit original photographs, writing or art done by hand or on the computer. Create a marketing calendar for the next calendar year featuring one piece of original art on each month, plus art for the front and back covers. Be sure entrants (and their parents, if they are minors) sign a release allowing you to re-use the artwork for business purposes. Sell calendars via retail or utilize them as client gifts, gifts-with-purchase or contest prizes. Give a copy to your most valued customers, your employees, vendors, marketing partners, area businesses, large local employers—customers and prospects you want to attract in the coming year. Resources to help you create your own customized marketing calendar is available on the 'Resources' page of my website at www.12monthsofmarketing.com.

September 22 – Dear Diary Day

Begin to document the life of your business by making a short entry every day in a journal (by hand or on the computer). Photo-document the life of your business; take pictures at all customer and employee events, take an annual all-employee photograph and take pictures when major changes or renovations are made, when your menu of products and/or services changes, of seasonal displays, to record employee awards, to document contests and drawings, to send with press releases, etc.

Purchase branded notebooks or journals or create a unique, custom design or slogan to have printed on journals, notebooks, bookmarks, pens, pencils, reading lights, etc. for retail sale, gifts-with-purchase or contest prizes.

Partner with a local author or literature expert to hold a workshop on journaling or writing an autobiography. Post trivia or passages from famous diaries. Ask customers to write a funny or clever fictional "journal entry of the day" for your Facebook page. Have a contest asking customers to write a diary entry representative of your business or your products or services; reward the winner/s with a gift card or corresponding free product or service.

September 23 – World Gratitude Day

World Gratitude Day was started by a group within the United Nations for the purpose of expressing gratitude to those who make a positive impact on the world around them. Write notes of thanks to acknowledge individuals who contribute to the good of other s. These could be people who have made notable singular contributions, or individuals who work every day for the good of others such as police, fire and emergency responders, clergy, doctors and nurses, volunteers or leaders of charitable organizations, parents who volunteer time at their child's school or help lead school fundraisers, etc.

Design and purchase one-of-a-kind blank note cards, thank-you note cards or boxed sets of greeting cards to add to retail. Be sure blank notes are near your gift card display and sized appropriately so they can be easily paired by customers for gift giving.

Purchase branded thank-you cards, gift certificates and award certificates for use in your business. If you are not in the habit of writing thank-you notes to *at least* your most loyal or valuable clients, start today. Commit to writing at least one thank-you note every day; write one to each client, if possible.

Thank employees for their work and acknowledge outstanding performance, extraordinary customer service or even positive personal traits with a personal note sometime this month. A spirit of gratitude tends to be contagious, spreading not only to recipients, but putting the sender in a more positive state of mind as well. Plus, acknowledging behavior you want more of, tends to bring you more of the same!

September 24 – Punctuation Day

Post trivia about punctuation and grammar on your Facebook page, blog and e-mail newsletter. Compile a list of grammar and punctuation guidelines, recommended reading, guide books and online resources for aspiring writers to post on your Facebook page, blog and e-mail newsletter.

Write a story flooded with grammar and punctuation errors and hold a contest for local school kids to see who can find the most errors and/or successfully correct the copy. Or hold a contest pitting school-aged children against adults (my daughter Sarah gleefully stumped her language arts teacher in the 6th grade several times!) Put together a writing or reading-related gift basket to award as a contest prize or sell.

September 25 - Comic Book Day

Just saying the words "comic books" probably brings you back to your youth and memories of hot, lazy summer days gone by when you raced to the corner store, eager to read *Mad Magazine* or find out what Betty, Veronica, Archie and Jughead were planning to do next. Hold an open house and invite customers and/or local comic book sellers to show off collections, swap or purchase comic books.

Add comic books to your retail and help a new generation get hooked; do some research and try to find a local comic book writer or a good comic book series that is not already being sold everywhere else to add to your retail, then work to build a loyal following among your comic-loving customers.

Hold a comic writing and/or illustrating contest for adults or children. As part of a contest or for fun, solicit (or commission) an illustration from a local artist and ask customers to write captions for it, or write a caption and hold a contest for people to draw corresponding illustrations. Post comic book trivia on your Facebook page, blog and e-mail newsletter. Post links to entertaining comics. You can purchase a comic for business use from sites like andertoons.com, cartoonistsgroup.com, etc.

September 26 – One Hit Wonders Day

Do you remember that great song in the 1980's from that awesome band you never heard from again? How about the car that was going to revolutionize the industry that ended up in junk yards across the country? There have been many inventions over the years that seemed like a sure thing, only to be made obsolete or reveal too many inherent weaknesses for sustainability. On One Hit Wonders Day, use your Facebook page to remind customers about some of these great stories.

Ask customers to share their favorite 'one hit wonder' product or service, or to share ideas for the greatest products that were never created at all (products that don't exist, but should). Give away One Hit Wonder albums or iTunes cards as gifts, gifts-with-purchase or contests prizes.

September 27 – Love Note Day

Distribute 'love notes' (to your customers) on bag stuffers all month. Print them as part of receipts and invoices, include them in your e-mail newsletter or mail postcards or letters to customers. Encourage customers to write a love note about their favorite employee, product or service. Tell your employees them what you love most about them in notes.

Partner with a local author or literary expert to hold a love note writing workshop for customers. Hold a singles event where communication or flirting is carried out via 'love note.' Hold a contest for customers to write the best, worst, funniest, etc. love note. Solicit stories about the first love notes people wrote or received. Share famous love notes in history on Facebook, your blog and e-mail newsletter.

Create your own custom-designed note cards or wares with love-themed sentiments. Suggest scripts for love notes, thank-you, apology or sympathy notes, birthday, anniversary, engagement, shower and other greeting cards.

September 28 – Ask a Stupid Question Day

Asking questions can be a great way to stimulate retail product sales—and that's never stupid! Create or update the 'Frequently Asked Questions' (FAQ) on your website with answers to commonly-asked questions, suggesting services and products which address common problems or conditions. Create signage and post some of the most compelling questions/answers in-store on shelving near products, on end cap displays, on public bulletin areas, at the point of purchase, as station talkers, etc. Post frequently asked questions and answers on Facebook, your blog, e-mail newsletter and bag stuffers.

Hold a contest to see which of your customers can ask the most creative, thought provoking, funny, profound—or even stupid—question. Post question entries online and in-store for public vote. Make asking questions part of your daily customer routine in the form of exit surveys and polls. Post results online as well as actions or improvements you made to address concerns and answers to customer's questions.

September 29 – Miniature Golf Day

Kick off the fall season with a customer-appreciation miniature golf event or partner with a local miniature golf course to extend a special offer to your customers. Purchase gift cards or passes to gift to your most valuable customers, vendors or employees, to gift-with-purchase, to award in a drawing or as a contest prize, or even for resale to customers.

September 30 – Birthdays Day

This isn't an official observance; however, it could be an effective way to build rapport and strengthen relationships and loyalty with customers (and employees, vendors, etc.)—because almost nothing is more personal to someone than their birthday! Implement a birthday greeting and/or birthday rewards program for customers. Update your data collection forms to include birthday and wedding anniversary dates. Ask customers for birthday and/or anniversary dates in order to receive free gifts via e-mail, postcard or text message. Send an e-greeting or a signed corporate or personal greeting card to your most valuable customers (or all customers) and to all of your employees on their birthdays and/or anniversaries.

Hold a monthly birthday party open to anyone born in that month featuring demonstrations, consultations and free birthday goodies to take home. Incentivize bookings or sales with event-only offers and sampling. Make it feel like a real party with decorations and refreshments and encourage birthday boys and girls to bring friends along.

Hold a monthly birthday party or luncheon for all-employees or give each employee a personal gift on their special day. Can't afford a gift? Ask your marketing partners for free products or reduced-price gift cards you can give to employees on birthdays. Give employees paid time off in the form of a chance to leave a couple hours early or come in late, an afternoon or an extra whole day off. If your employee benefit package is short on paid holidays, this could be a very nice gift!

Partner with a party planner or caterer to hold party planning, cooking and/or decorating workshops for birthday parties, anniversaries, bridal showers, receptions and other themes—this could easily become a series of classes! Post tips and ideas on your Facebook page, blog and e-mail newsletter.

Create birthday party kits with the decorations, tableware, invitations, thank-you notes and other items needed to throw parties for kids, tweens, teens or grownups and for parties that can be held in or out of doors. Create party kits. Compile and post lists of suggested supplies for other types of parties as well (anniversaries, bridal or baby showers, receptions, corporate events, etc.) on your Facebook page, blog and e-mail newsletter.

Establish a plan for the coming 5 years of your business anniversary—this will give you the time you need to build to those big "5" and "10" year anniversary parties which need to be more special than the others. Establish an employee hire-date anniversary recognition program. Utilize all of your channels of communication and write press releases to highlight and celebrate the accomplishments and contributions of your business and its employees.

october

365 Days of Marketing

October Month-Long Observances
Breast Cancer Awareness Month

Donate proceeds from one day of sales or from October sales of specific products or services to a national or local breast cancer charity or treatment center. Partner with a local salon or spa or invite stylists from throughout your community to come together to hold a haircutting event to benefit Locks of Love (www.locksoflove.org), a local cancer treatment facility, the City of Hope (www.cityofhope.org) or a Susan G. Komen (www.the3day.org) 3-Day Walk for the Cure team. Organized charities can often provide you with marketing collateral, support materials, guidelines and ideas for conducting fundraising campaigns and holding benefit events. Check with your tax professional to be sure you structure fundraising events appropriately so that donors contributions (and yours) will be legally tax-deductible.

Charitable-giving guidelines prohibit dictating the amount that a participant must donate, but you can set a "suggested donation;" most people will probably meet or exceed this. And you can let all customers know their donations are welcome (whether they are participating in event activities or not). Invite corporate and individual sponsors to match donations. Write a press release beforehand to publicize the event, and afterward to report results and talk about how the funds raised will benefit the local community. Use Facebook, your e-mail newsletter, blog and website to help raise awareness, build momentum, display photographs and links and report results.

There may be a cancer treatment facility in your community which would welcome the donation of products and/or services for patients or family members use. Many treatment centers have adjoining housing or apartments where family members can stay during treatment. 'Adopt' a local cancer patient for a year's worth of free products or services. Invite other businesses to contribute funds or products as gifts for holidays, birthdays, anniversaries or other special occasions in the patient's life during the year.

Color a World Without Cancer

Hold an art and/or coloring contest titled, "Color a World Without Cancer." Award prizes to the winners and extend a special offer to all who enter. Write a press release and send copies of finalists' work to local media, city hall, treatment facilities or cancer charities, etc.

Purchase special pink and/or pink ribbon products and tools to add to retail in October. Design your own unique awareness-messaged t-shirt, tank top, mug, water bottle or other branded tchotchke for retail sale with proceeds or a portion of each sale going to a national or local cancer charity.

Clergy Appreciation Month

In addition to ministering to their own congregations, many churches also take part in performing community service and giving assistance to the needy. Find out what churches in your community are doing. Extend gratitude to those who are making your city a better place to live or helping meet the needs of others. Solicit stories from customers about projects the churches they attend are doing in your community. Compile a list of local church service organizations to add to the community resources page of your website or to feature on Facebook, your blog and e-mail newsletter.

Make a donation or hold a fundraiser to benefit a church-run charity. Extend a special offer to members of local church youth, singles, women's, men's, seniors or couples groups. Extend a special offer to clergy in your community, or to all church and parochial school employees. Plan to hold a Halloween alternative event at the end of the month and extend invitations to members of local churches.

Customer Service Month

According to a 2011 American Express Global Customer Service Barometer (a survey done in the USA and 9 other countries relative to attitudes and preferences toward customer service), 70% of Americans said they would be willing to spend almost 15% more with businesses they believed (really) provided excellent customer service. With such an indicator, you would think that businesses would make customer service a top priority; but in the same survey, 60% of respondents said they don't believe businesses are making customer service a high priority. In fact, 26% said they think businesses are actually paying *less attention* to service.

When was the last time you asked customers how their experience with your business stacks up against their expectations? When was the last time you asked what they expected, or what constitutes exceptional service to them? When was the last time you received a complaint, a compliment—or any feedback at all related to customer service?

Maybe many business owners simply don't understand what customer service 'is,' or maybe they misinterpret or fail to deliver what it is their customers *really want*.

When you say the words "customer service," what comes to mind? A telephone service agent, headset in place, waiting to take your call or working on a long queue of calls; or maybe it's the smocked sales associate standing behind the counter at the far end of the building, just under a specially titled "Customer Service/Returns" sign. If any of these images constitutes what customer service is to you, or is representative of the people responsible to provide it, your definition needs some work.

According to Wikipedia.org, "*Customer Service is the provision of services to customers before, during and after a purchase*," so far, so good, there's not much there to change the basic understanding held by most people. But the description goes on to reference Efraim Turban's 2002 book, "Electronic Commerce: A Managerial Perspective" where he says that customer service is "*a series of activities designed to enhance the level of customer satisfaction—that is, the feeling that a product or service has met the customer expectation*."

Whoa—that's a whole different take! According to this line of thinking, the definition of customer service is not contained in the actions of a person taking a phone order, fulfilling a web order, receiving a return or complaint, performing a service or selling a product. Customer service isn't an action, it's a *process*—an *intentionally designed system*—meant to enhance the customer's experience and which influences whether a customer *feels* satisfied or dissatisfied by a product or service.

A sales transaction, product or service on its own is not enough to produce customer satisfaction. You must systematically examine and strategically improve each and every aspect of the customer experience, at every possible touchpoint. You must create a system *designed* to *enhance* the customer experience. Do you know what *that* really means? According to thefreedictionary.com,

> **en-hance** (*verb*) means:
> 1) to make greater, as in value, beauty, or effectiveness; to augment
> 2) to provide with improved, advanced or sophisticated features

It's not just about making the customer experience "better." It's about making it greater in value, bigger (augmented) and/or more sophisticated—more than that of the competition and more than the customer expects—so that it stands out *to the customer*. To do that, you must thoroughly know and understand your customers, and you must train, educate and empower employees to respond to requests, complaints, unique situations and individual customer's needs and desires.

If you wonder why people don't always agree with the claim you make that your business provides "exceptional customer service" or why the customer experience at your business is not helping you gain and retain clients, it's because what you have in place is not actually enough to influence the customer to *feel exceptionally satisfied*. It may technically be "good enough" but if t's not more than expected and doesn't set you apart from the competition, it's not good enough!

October Week 1
October 1 – World Vegetarian Day

Partner with a local vegan nutrition expert to hold a workshop or to provide information and resources to your customers about Vegetarian diet and lifestyle choices. Partner with a vegetarian restaurant for cross or cooperative marketing, or to provide gift cards or a special offer to your customers. Provide samples of related products or menu items. Give customers information about food or ingredient substitutes which can help them adhere to special diet restrictions.

Put the spotlight on products or menu items you offer which adhere to some of the dietary restrictions people have: Vegetarian, gluten-free, free of eggs, wheat, nuts or other common allergens, etc. Hold a reception, open house, happy hour or wine tasting event which adheres to the needs of individuals with dietary restrictions.

Partner with specialty restaurants, organic or gourmet grocers, caterers or other professionals for cross or cooperative marketing. Partner with a local chef to hold a workshop or series of vegetarian, gluten-free, allergen-free or other specialty cooking classes. Hold a cooking exhibition or contest, have a tasting or solicit customers specialty recipes to share or to add to the recipes you are collecting for a printed cook book. Create a brochure featuring specialty recipes as well as the relevant products, ingredients or menu items that you offer.

October 2 – Name Your Car Day

Americans are known for having a long-standing love affair with the automobile. Whether it's the freedom or the feeling, the love some people have for their cars rivals their affections for others. Get someone talking about their favorite or first car, and you are likely to hear stories about drive in restaurants and theaters, road trips, cruising the main drag and listening to the Beach Boys.

Tell customers about products or services you offer to help clean, care for, maintain or repair their beloved cars and trucks. Create gift baskets for contest prizes or retail sale that contain the perfect products for keeping automobiles bright, shiny, new looking and smelling great. Partner with auto sales, service, repair and parts stores for cross or cooperative marketing.

Ask customers to tell you which are their favorite cars or tell you their favorite car-related story on your Facebook page or blog. Ask what they would (or have) named their car and why. Hold a contest and post a picture of an interesting-looking, luxury or run down car or truck and challenge customers to come up with the best name and/or fictional story about it. Post history about famous cars or hold an automobile trivia contest.

October 3 – Frugal Fun Day

Create Frugal Fun offers around family-oriented products or services. Hold a Frugal Fun event with activities or offers specially-priced for families, students, singles or another of your target markets.

Partner with local recreation and family fun centers, sports facilities, theme parks, etc. for cross or cooperative marketing. Hold a customer or employee-appreciation event, or buy passes for resale to customers, contest prizes, client or employee gifts or to give away as a gift-with-purchase.

Hold a Frugal Fun event with free activities like cards, board games, quizzes and contests. Hold a customer-appreciation cookout at a local park or wilderness area where guests can enjoy the scenery, skate, play ball or hike. Remind customers about the free fun we had as kids by holding a Hide and Seek, Mother May I, Red Rover or Kick the Can tournament. Post a list of these types of backyard games and instructions for play on your Facebook page, blog and e-mail newsletter.

Create a Top 10 Frugal Fun list of things to do you in your community for dates, family outings, places to eat or drink, entertainment, live music, etc. Hold a contest or solicit customer suggestions for the best-and-most-frugal date or family outing ideas.

October 4 – Child Health Month

Create a directory of local children's health and dental specialists, nutritionists, health food stores and other resources to post on your website, Facebook page, blog and e-mail newsletter. Suggest books for recommended reading and post links to websites with information and guidelines about children's health and well-being topics. Solicit customer recommendations of local service providers.

Or go big! Invite local professionals to take part in a community-wide children's health fair featuring refreshments, entertainment and children's activities. Create a take-away piece for attendees listing online resources and local children's health and dental practitioners, immunization clinics, allergists, optometrists, hearing specialists—you can even expand your directory to include tutoring and reading teachers, music teachers, etc.—businesses that provide children's products or services.

Put the marketing spotlight on the products or services you provide that contribute to children's health and well-being.

Partner with a photographer to hold a children's I.D. card event. Take family photographs (this would be a great time for families to get a professional photo for their holiday greeting card). Demonstrate and/or sample the products or services you provide which contribute to children's health and wellness.

October 5 – Improve Your Office Day

Think about ways you can make your office run better, more smoothly, less expensively or more efficiently. Review all of the processes you have in place that keep your business up, running and reported on every day—especially those that directly impact customers.

More specifically (since this *is* a book about marketing) improve your office by reviewing all of your communications with fresh eyes. Are receipts, statements or invoices worded in such a way that they convey gratitude to your customers or do they sound like they come straight from a collection agency? Are your postcards, flyers and other advertising pieces loaded with restrictions and disclaimers? Would your signage be likely to make people with kids feel unwelcome? Do customers spend time on hold listening to dead air, to tired, expired scripting or a radio station that might actually be feeding them competitor's ads? Are all of your communications well-branded, and is your contact information easy to find on each and every piece of print and electronic collateral?

Think about the vendors, suppliers and manufacturers with whom you do business. Even if *you* have the best intentions and your staff are well trained to help customers, indifference or incompetence on the part of one of your suppliers may impact the customer experience. In this case, *you* are the customer; work with vendors and manufacturers who share your values when it comes to your dedication to the customer and who you know truly understand how to create customer satisfaction—because they do it for you!

Think about the atmosphere in your office and your employee culture. Your employee culture is impacted by a number of factors; not only by the experiences and personalities of the employees themselves, but also by your corporate mission, vision, goals, values, client and employee policies, etc. To improve your employee culture, focus on identifying and defining the components that most directly impact your marketing:

- What is your official corporate mission and vision? Is it communicated to employees? Is it demonstrated in day-to-day operations or just words in a pretty frame on the wall? Would customers be able to guess what values and promises are represented in your mission and vision statements *based on their experiences* with your business?

- What policies do you have in place regarding employee standards of behavior, conversation, attitude, conduct, dress and appearance? How are they communicated to employees? Do employees follow them? Do you? Are there consequences for those who choose to violate policies or fail to deliver on your promises to the customer — especially when these standards are clearly communicated or when it damages customer relationships?

- Are you afraid to impose standards on others out of a reluctance to appear authoritative, a fear of losing friendships or a desire to maintain a "cool," laid-back working environment?

- How are decisions made and communicated? Do employees have a say in the process? Are there certain employees who dominate decision-making? How is negative feedback from employees expressed, and how do you handle it in response? How are disputes between employees resolved?

- Do you have written standards relative to staff communication with one another in front of clients or inappropriate types of conversation in public areas? Do you have a policy to protect customer, vendor and employee privacy? Does it cover employee gossip inside and outside the walls of your business?

- What do you want the atmosphere in your business to feel like? What do your customers want it to feel like? It's more important that the atmosphere in your business reflect their desires than it is for the atmosphere to reflect your desires (or those of your employees) where those two things do not align from décor to music to policies, etc.

Whether you are building a business from scratch or reshaping your business culture through education, accountability and normal employee turnover, determining which characteristics you want to define your employee culture will help you make better training and hiring decisions as you move forward.

No matter how idealistic your intentions and no matter how obvious you feel it is that your business needs to grow, ultimately, to create the kind of culture needed to serve your clients and grow your business necessitates that you obtain employee buy-in, support, and engagement. In other words, your employees must consciously choose to support the environment you want to create and demonstrate agreement in their attitudes, behaviors and actions.

Multiple surveys taken over the last decade reported that the number of employees who feel they are truly engaged at their place of work hovers around 30% on average. That means that at any given company, *7 out of every 10 people* do not feel especially connected to, or invested in, the good of the organization they work for. It's just a paycheck to these individuals; they save their passion, talent and energy for investment elsewhere.

As a small business, you might enjoy a greater degree of employee engagement for the simple reason that it's more difficult for disillusioned, disgruntled or disengaged employees to fall off your radar. Imagine how your business could grow and thrive if _all_ your employees were positively charged, fully engaged and shared your ideals when it comes to customer service, growing your customer base, increasing retail sales, introducing new services, expanding and increasing profits?

Imagine the good your business could do if all of your employees supported your community involvement and charity initiatives. Imagine not just the revenue that would come your way but also the enhanced reputation of your business, your reputation as a leader and the positive impacts your business would make in the lives of your employees, clients and the community.

Your employee culture is a reflection of the sum total of the values, beliefs, attitudes, ideas, experiences, assumptions and behaviors shared by your staff. And for better or for worse, this culture is reflected back to your clients in every area of your business. If your employee culture is characterized by negativity, laziness, carelessness, cynicism or indifference, it is because that trait is present in one or more of your staff, and because it's been left unaddressed or is tolerated *by you*.

Does this mean that you should only hire people who think exactly like you? Not at all. It is the very variety of experiences, talents, skills and interests—the differences within us as people, when shared—that leads to higher levels of creativity, imagination, resourcefulness, abilities and strengths. But your business will grow and thrive only to the extent that these strengths, passions and creativity can be harnessed to pull toward the same goals in a spirit of positive energy and optimism (rather than cynicism and negativity).

Have you ever seen a marching band in action on the field during halftime at a football game? You might see a fifty to a hundred or even more people, all working together to play the same song. By mutual agreement, combining their individual strengths, abilities and different instruments to deliver a performance for the audience. Every step they take is intentionally choreographed to engage and entertain the audience visually—even beyond the music. Band members work together to create a visual, dynamic design that (like the music) is made up of unique routes and roles, purposefully designed and choreographed to create a visual whole made up of the sum of all its parts.

Each band member has different skills and strengths; many are skilled soloists in their own right as musicians and/or dancers. But as band members they come together with an understanding that the good of the whole is greater than the glory of any one individual. They agree to pool their strengths, skills and abilities in order to achieve a group goal—to perform the same song, to the same beat, as directed by the band leader—in order to please *their customers* (the audience).

School band members know they will only be playing together for a short time, maybe only a few months; yet they still come to this agreement and shared goal. In the case of your business, where some of you may work together for decades, isn't it even more important for you to agree to work together toward the shared goals of attracting and pleasing clients? Of meeting customer needs and making them feel that they are vitally important to everyone who works for your business?

I have worked in companies that harbored employees who were well-known to regularly thwart ideas, offend customers or co-workers, undermine initiatives or even overtly defy orders. Leaders within these companies knew they had these problem individuals, but they often chose to retain them for years, and in some cases, even to promote them. They may have believed these employees had irreplaceable skills, knowledge or power, or may have thought they could 'win them over.'

Apparently, they discounted the negative impact these employees had on co-workers and even customers. Some were retained out of compassion and some out of a sense of absolute loyalty to the employee. The employer failed to recognize that this often led to the loss of other individuals who could potentially have become their best and most productive, loyal employees. Some even lost customers out of this misplaced sense of employer loyalty.

Whatever the reason a leader retains individuals who negatively impact the workplace, they are also choosing (whether they know it or not) to reward behavior they do not want more of, negatively influencing the overall employee culture. These individuals will continue to demonstrate cynicism, lack of motivation, rude or bullying behavior, resistance to change and even outright defiance—and all the more so when they are rewarded with tolerance, continued power, and the knowledge that they have the ability to control the corporate environment and initiatives through negative behavior. Furthermore, they are teaching their co-workers that this behavior is effective. These people damage the morale and stifle the creativity of their more positively inclined, enthusiastic co-workers.

Employer loyalty is a highly-laudable quality, especially now, when so many companies have been forced to downsize and there is a larger supply of qualified, talented individuals who are in the job-seeking market (so employers have the ability to pick and choose from among the cream of the crop to fill any open position or even to replace low-performers). But employer loyalty is misplaced when it is the cause for retention of an individual that is damaging your company from the inside-out, or even actively damaging your customer relationships and impeding initiatives.

Am I advocating a no-tolerance, slash and burn policy where your employees are concerned? No; but I am suggesting that you have an obligation to think about the extent to which the behavior and actions of each employee contributes to or works against your team as a whole and enhances or detracts from the good of your customers and the goals of the entire organization.

Only you can determine the point at which the damage being done to employee morale, initiatives or client relations outweighs the value you believe an individual contributes to your company. Only you can determine at what point you believe an individual is not open to change or is un-teachable when it comes to modifying their behavior for the good of the organization.

But with those "only you" statements comes a great deal of responsibility, because *only you* have the power to protect your business, employees and customers from a destructive employee or an initiative-killing staff member.

October 6 – Beer Day

Not officially held on this date but worth a mention both for the nature of the topic and its origin. "Beer Day" is a US Naval term, so named because it's the one day that the crew at sea are issued and allowed to consume beer (usually just one or two). Way back in 1794, the US congress set a daily ration for alcohol for sailors and in 1914 a general order was issued which ended all alcohol consumption. The only exception that is made occurs when a ship has been out to see for at least 45 continuous days without a port call, at which time the Commanding Officer can call for a Beer Day. Once had, another 45 day interval must pass before another Beer Day can be authorized.

With that bit of history in mind, here is my suggestion by way of marketing. Create some of your own 45 day rules. If you have not heard from a client in 45 days, make contact, send a postcard, extend a special offer, e-mail or text them—let them know that you miss them.

Even if you normally don't see your clients more than twice or even once a year (such as in dental or medial practices), make *some kind* of contact with your clients at least once every 45 days. An e-mail newsletter, a postcard announcing new services or products, a letter introducing a new associate or caregiver, connecting customers with other community resources or city events, an invitation to "like" your Facebook page or follow you on Twitter—send them something!

Don't go more than 45 days without having a one on one conversation with each of your employees, or at least with each of your direct reports. Don't go more than 45 days without meeting one on one with your immediate supervisor, the director of your board, without making contact with your investors, etc.

Don't go more than 45 days without learning something new about and/or getting feedback directly from customers and employees through the use of surveys or polls. Don't go more than 45 days without touching base with your marketing partners to discuss ways to generate more referrals, to refresh your joint marketing collateral or to extend a special offer to their customers or employees.

The second point relative to this story I would make is this: If you are having a customer event that features alcohol, refrain from drinking (you and your staff). *Not drinking* draws an important distinction— it tells your customers that you have good judgment and it reinforces the level of professionalism you want your customers to assign to you. It reminds staff that they are, in fact, working, and will help to preserve decorum. On a practical level, it will prevent unnecessary problems and criticism. Just like the good men and women of our armed forces do, wait until you are off duty and away from the workplace to consume alcoholic beverages.

October 7 – Techies Day and Computer Learning Month

Partner with experts proficient in the use of social media, e-mail and common computer software programs to hold workshops with/for your marketing partners, employees and customers. Invite local business owners and managers to attend a social media marketing workshop led by a local marketing professional.

Improve your knowledge relative to technology, programs and applications available to you. Don't be overwhelmed by believing you have to master them all; determine which would be of most use to your business right now, and which you will add later. Find out who among your employees has an aptitude for communications and technology and enlist their help.

Learn what each is primarily or most effectively used to achieve (in other words, is it used for direct sales, customer relations, brand awareness building, etc.) and learn about how to measure these forms of marketing for return on investment, hits, comments, "likes," forwards, etc.

October Week 2

October Week 2 – Pet Peeve Week

One year in early February I was reading through a few e-mails for inspiration, a kick in the pants—whatever would connect with me the most. I clicked on a link to a marketing article titled "28 Days for the Heart," to discover that the article was filled with great marketing ideas—ideas that I would have needed to start on at least 6 weeks before in order to utilize. I thought to myself:

> *"Dear Author: Thank you so much for these great ideas which I will now file away to use next year, provided I still remember they exist ten months from now."*

So, still needing some practical inspiration, I opened up a fresh trade magazine and read about Valentine's Day marketing ideas. I thought, "Valentine's day is Saturday, let's see, um, today is Tuesday—so if I *hurry,* I can frame out this idea, lay out a campaign, send 2 postcards and 2 e-mail newsletters to my customers, order in the retail I need, get custom-designed gift certificates, partner with a restaurant to set up a cooperative gift package and sell through about 50 of these. In 4 days. *Rrrrrright."*

Opportunities missed make me crazy! This is one of my pet peeves, when someone teases me instead of giving me something of practical value. This is one of the reasons I give so many ideas away on my blog. I want ideas I can use to build business now. I want ideas I can use to revitalize my creative energies now. I want ideas to breathe some life and fun back into this slow economy NOW!

So here's what I propose: Schedule a *designated* time every month to plan ahead for at least the next three months. Plan this time. Carve it out. Protect it. It's easy to become so consumed by the demands of daily business operations that creating an actual plan seems impossible. But it may well be the time you spend creating a plan that will mean that you won't be as overwhelmed with 'busy' moments in the months to come.

October Week 2 – Home-Based Business Week

Reach out to entrepreneurs, independent sellers and other home-based business professionals by letting them know you understand their unique needs. Stretched in several directions at any one given time, running every aspect of their business by themselves and usually also meeting the needs of a spouse and children at home—these busy working professionals might appreciate it if you carved out some time just for them each month. Hold a breakfast, lunch or happy hour during times convenient for them. Demonstrate relevant useful products and services, provide professional consultations, give away samples and extend special offers.

Connect them with other small business owners online. Create a directory of independent and home-based businesses to share with customers on Facebook, your blog and e-mail newsletter. Share these contacts with your marketing and event partners in order to further help support other local, independent businesses and professionals and in order to boost the local economy.

October 8 – American Touch Tag Day

Hold a customer or employee touch tag tournament or join with other businesses to hold a city-wide inter-business competition. Form business or public teams and have a Touch Tag tournament or field day at a local park or field.

Create an in-store version of Touch Tag for employees where they must tell a customer about a product or service before 'tagging' the next employee who must then do the same. Or use this as a training exercise to test product and/or service knowledge among employees.

Play Touch Tag with customers. 'Tag' a customer and ask them what their favorite product or service is and why. Ask customers to answer a set of 3-4 questions designed to let you know how they found your business, what they came to purchase or research, and what they feel will be the most important or deciding aspect relative to their purchasing decision. Ask what would turn them into more frequently-returning or more exclusively-loyal patrons.

Create a Touch Tag promotion where offers move around the store. Change the special of the day. Move a surprise add-on, reward or offer from check stand to check stand or station to station whenever someone takes advantage of an offer.

Send a Touch Tag coupon or code word offer out by e-mail or text (the customer gets the offer, add-on, free item or special price when they 'tag' you with the word at the point of sale, online, etc.) Extend a Touch Tag offer, add-on or reward on Facebook (the next 1, 5, 10, etc. people to 'tag' your Facebook page with a post, a "like," a shared status update, etc.)

Review your shelf tags. Do they provide the customer with any useful knowledge? Are they legible? Do they help educate the customer? How do they help support or detract from the brand image you want to reinforce in the customer's mind?

October 9 – Curious Events Day

Post curious events on your Facebook page, blog, bag stuffers and e-mail newsletter. Re-write your business story as a sequence of curious events and release the story post by post on Facebook, put it on your blog, send it out in an e-mail newsletter or overwrite your current "about us" website content.

Put "Did you know...?" style posts about your business, employees, products, services, city, local leaders, celebrities—anything your customers would be especially curious about—in posts on your Facebook page, blog, bag stuffers and e-mail newsletter.

Despite my rant on the last page for Pet Peeve Day, there is a time and place for a good tease! Learn to write marketing copy and social media posts in such a way that your audience is teased – intrigued – enough so that they simply have to know more, try a product, experience a service or come to your business to see what is new.

October 10 – Universal Music Day

Partner with local music studios, instructors and dance studios for cross or cooperative marketing. Create menu options for music students, teachers, band members and directors with the products or services you sell that would help them or their students prepare for performances, competitions or recitals. Hold receptions or celebrations following performances or recitals. Extend special offers to local musicians, music instructors, music store employees and school music teachers.

Hold a special music-centric happy hour featuring music from around the world. Purchase albums by local artists for retail sale, client thank-you gifts or for contest prize basket inclusion. Add items like music players, iTunes gift cards or accessories to your retail. Feature live music at your business.

Purchase concert tickets or tickets for local performing arts, art shows, orchestra, choirs, dance studios, etc. for contest prizes, to give away as a gift-with-purchase or for retail sale. Follow local musicians and cover bands and let customers know where and when they will be performing. Hold employee or customer-appreciation events at these venues, offering to pay the cover charge for your guests, provide them with gift cards, albums, drink or food vouchers, etc.

Post information on Facebook about local performing arts including those at local schools. Become a booster of local performing arts, school theater and music programs. Place ads in their programs, donate to auctions and fundraisers, display event posters up in-store and publicize events online.

October 11 – Cake Decorating Day

Partner with local bakeries and wedding caterers for cross and cooperative marketing. Work together to hold a cake decorating class or a series of on-going baking, decorating and party planning classes. Hold a drawing for a professionally baked and decorated cake. Feature pictures of the work of local bakers and caterers on your Facebook page and connect customers with catering and party planning resources. Add decorating tools and instructional books to your retail. Post step-by-step decorating instructions, ideas and photographs on your Facebook page, blog and e-mail newsletter. Post links to other decorating sites, patterns, recipes and pictures.

Ask customers to share pictures of their own decorated cakes, cupcakes and cookies. Solicit customers favorite recipes or tips and tricks for frosting and decorating. Have an amateur cake decorating contest split into age or theme categories.

October 12 – Moment of Frustration Day

Examine and redesign the customer experience in order to eliminate anything which might cause frustration for a customer. While we all know life isn't perfect and things don't always run smoothly, a moment of frustration for a customer can result in a lost sale, a lost opportunity or even a lost customer, because one of the things your customer is paying for is for their experience to run "right."

Here are a few potential pitfalls that could result in customer frustration to review and address today:

A customer cannot find your phone number, address or hours of operation without:

- an extensive hunt on your website
- walking up to your store windows and peering in to see if the lights are on
- a lengthy wait on your automated phone answering system
  or worse, having to punch in numbers trying to get to the right automated answer
  or even worse, not having business hours displayed or available at all

Scour your first points of contact. Make it *as easy as possible* for customers to find you. Put your phone number, address and hours of operation "above the fold" on your website landing page (or every page), *and* on your blog *and* on your e-mail newsletter *and* on your Facebook page (and *all* social media sites). Place your phone number and website address and hours of operation on the outside of your door or business location and make it easy to find and easy to read (simple, plain, readable fonts in sizes large enough to see from the street or sidewalk). Provide customers with an e-mail address or phone number to call after hours. If you make a change to contact information or hours of operation, *immediately* update all of your signage, website and automated phone messages to reflect these changes.

A customer found your website and you caught their interest; they want to know more about you, your products or the solutions you provide and so click on a link only to find that it's broken, and the information they wanted isn't available.

Schedule a time or assign responsibility to an employee to revisit your website every month (at least) and check *all* web links to ensure that links to content and to other sites have not changed or been removed. You can boost website traffic by putting current, relevant information that would be interesting to the customer on your website and updating your content often.

A customer purchases a product, tool or equipment from you and upon arriving home

- it doesn't work
- they can't remember what you told them to do to make it work

Don't just tell, show. Where use of a product or tool is not obvious, tell the customer how to use it, ask them to tell you what you told them and/or ask them to use it in front of you before they leave. Provide the customer with written instructions on branded collateral that gives them step-by-step information needed to use a product where it is not necessarily obvious or intuitive.

Collateral should include "who" to call or e-mail for help or instructions. Requests for help should be acknowledged immediately and answered as quickly as possible. Enhance collateral by featuring specific options for upgrades, add-ons and accessory items to stimulate future sales. Make add-on or accessory promotional offers time-sensitive at a special price.

A customer is in your store but can't get the nearest associate to break off from a personal phone call or a conversation with a co-worker in order to ask a question about your products or services.

A customer can't even find an associate to help them, or who can help them.

A customer is placed on hold but when their call is finally taken by a "real person," they are routed to a series of extensions, none of which are apparently staffed by people who are knowledgeable enough to help them.

A culture of dedication to the customer starts at the top. Hiring, orientation and training must all be used to reinforce these values. Employees must be held accountable for poor customer service whenever it occurs. Employee expectations must be clearly defined and clearly communicated, repeatedly. Reward, acknowledge, incentivize and/or thank employees who display behavior you want more of.

Employees should be adequately cross-trained to be of assistance in areas outside of their expertise and/or in the absence of co-workers. Cross training will also help make jobs more interesting and can clear the path for advancement to individuals who display initiative and aptitude.

Don't rely only on verbal training; provide employees with written lists of frequently asked questions on a variety of common topics and with an employee directory that lists the organizational chart not only by job title, but which also describes the types of solutions an individual or department provides for customers. Make training and re-training part of the culture of your business for every employee, in every department. Incorporate quizzes and tests to gauge employee knowledge of other roles/departments as well as their own.

A customer walks in, sees a room full of other people waiting and walks out.

Configure your point of entry, lobby or waiting area so that no matter how many people are assembled there, customers are greeted by an associate who can help them 'check in' or register, told how long the wait (if any) will be and/or explain why there are so many people gathered in the entry area. Ensure that people who are waiting have an inviting, hospitable and comfortable place to do so, are provided with periodic updates or asked if they need anything, or are routed directly to where they want to be or to an individual who can provide them with immediate assistance.

One of your associates makes a disparaging remark about a co-worker, the customer in the next aisle, your chief competitor or another local business... who happens to be your customer's cousin... etc.

The climate, personality and spirit of your business, as displayed by any employee, starts *at the top*. Make it clear that gossip or slander about other employees, customers, vendors and even competitors is unacceptable in policy and as demonstrated by your own behavior. Saying nothing is preferable to making a disparaging or negative remark, even when it comes to the competition. You want customers and employees to trust you. You want people to leave with the best possible impression of your business *and* the employees you have chosen to deliver the customer experience. The *only* way to have a positive climate and culture is to focus (*only*) on the positive.

A customer finds out that the product or service they want today was just on sale last week.

You are out of the product the customer wanted, or you no longer carry it.

Send weekly (or at least monthly) e-mail / text / direct mail communications that tell customers about dwindling stock and current promotions including expiration dates. Send a personal e-mail or note to customers who regularly purchase specific items that will be part of a special time-limited promotion ahead of time. Tell customers about products or services that will be discontinued, are in short supply or are limited to supplies on hand. Tell customers about new and improved or substitute product or service options. Extend special ordering options to your most valuable customers.

October 13 – Kick Butt Day

Partner with a motivational speaker, counselor, life or executive coach, fitness trainer/gym, kickboxing instructor, nutritionist/weight loss expert, stop smoking resources, etc. for cross or cooperative marketing. With marketing partners or on your own, hold a workshop, seminar, class or series of classes on how to "kick butt" at life in general or relative to a specific topic, such as job search, interpersonal relationships, success in the workplace, how to kick butt reaching diet, exercise, fitness or weight loss goals, how to kick butt (literally) in a kickboxing class, and/or how to kick butts (stop smoking), etc.

Posts for Facebook/social media, Blog, E-mail, Bag Stuffers and/or Website:

- Inspirational "kick butt" quotes
- Solicit customer stories about an area of life where they have or do "kick butt"
- Ask customers what things they would like to have the ability or knowledge to "kick butt" doing (this can help you develop solutions for them, and it can give you an opportunity to provide them with expert advice or connect them with resources)
- Feature employees, manufacturers or local community members who "kick butt" in some area of life, performance or community service
- Recommended reading and/or online resources
- Local resources and options to support goals for smoking cessation, fitness or weight loss, workplace success, personal success, growth and development

Ask the public to help you "kick the butt" of a cancer, disability or disease by attending an event, making pledges, by making purchases and/or raising awareness.

Add to retail, gift, gift-with-purchase or contest prizes:

- Branded or custom-designed t-shirts, tank tops, mugs and tumblers, totes, wall plaques and other items featuring inspirational "kick butt" messages or quotes
- Brandware or custom-designed clothing and accessories for attendees or participants of "kick butt" classes, charity events or support groups
- Recommended reading, videos or other resources related to workshops such as exercise wear, water bottles, yoga mats, workout towels, etc.

October 14 – Dessert Day

Partner with local bakeries, caterers, restaurants, dessert shops, gourmet food or candy stores, party planners and/or nutritionists for cross or cooperative marketing. With marketing partners or on your own, hold a workshop, seminar, class or series of classes on dessert preparation, party planning, hosting and/or decorating for parties, dessert alternatives or substitute ingredients for those with dietary restrictions.

Hold a dessert competition or exhibition for local chefs and caterers, or the general public. Hold a dessert tasting event or happy hour featuring desserts you offer (or that are offered by some of your marketing partners).

Provide free or reduced-priced desserts that can be sold for non-profit fundraising. Send branded, packaged cookies or other desserts to the offices of a local charity or community service organization.

Posts for Facebook/social media, Blog, E-mail, Bag Stuffers and/or Website:

- Ask customers to share favorite dessert recipes; compile into an online collection or add to the recipes you are collecting for a cook book to be printed for client gift, class participants, retail sale, etc.
- Solicit customer recommendations of great local restaurant/shop desserts
- Trivia about the history of desserts, about specific types of desserts you feature or for which you will hold competitions/happy hours
- Dessert or ingredient substitutions for healthier options or individuals with dietary restrictions
- Recommended reading, cookbooks, celebrity recipes or recipe websites
- A code word that can be redeemed for a special dessert-related offer in your business or that of one of your marketing partners

Add to retail or give away as a gift-with-purchase or contest prize:

- Brandware or unique/boutique-quality specialty items like aprons, pot holders, bakeware, utensils, recipe collections or cookbooks
- Branded packaged desserts, cookies, candies or chocolates
- Wares with a dessert, chocolate, sweet or related slogan or custom design such as mugs, glasses, tumblers, totes, notebooks, t-shirts or tank tops, nightshirts, pens, wall plaques, greeting cards, etc.

October Week 3

October Week 3 – National Food Bank Week

Designate your business as a point of collection for money, food or other donated items for a local food bank or shelter. Enlist the participation of businesses near yours, members of your Chamber of Commerce or civic organizations, your marketing partners, etc.

Create a poster, flyers, point-of-purchase display, web page or web graphic, etc. soliciting donations and noting your business as a designated drop-off for a local food bank. Put signage on your windows or doors. Ask businesses located near yours and those of your marketing partners to place signage in their businesses, links on their websites and e-mail newsletters and displays at their point of purchase during the campaign period. Hold a friendly competition with your marketing partners, between departments or among individual employees to see who can bring in the most donations or raise the highest dollar amount.

Give customers a branded tchotchke, free add-on, entry in lieu of cover charge or another special offer when they donate a new item or cash in support of your initiative. By yourself or with employees, volunteer your time at a local food bank or shelter for a one-time event or on an on-going basis.

Write a press release to publicize efforts, raise awareness and let the public know how they can help. Enlist the support of local news or radio personalities to help raise money and solicit donations.

Posts for Facebook/social media, Blog, E-mail, Bag Stuffers and/or Website:

- Website links and/or a directory of local food banks and shelters
- Highlight services provided and the needs of local food banks and shelters—especially in light of the upcoming holiday season
- "Did you know...?" style facts/statistics about hunger, homelessness and poverty in your community
- Suggested shopping list of items for donation to food bank or shelter

Purchase brandwear or create a custom design that your employees and/or those of your marketing partners can wear during a campaign or while performing community service work as a team.

October Week 3 – Massage Therapy Week

Partner with massage therapists and with salons and spas which offers massage therapy for cross or cooperative marketing. Extend a special offer to massage therapists (and/or all salon or spa employees) in your community, hold a happy hour or another event exclusively for customer-pampering professionals. Invite local massage therapist/s to come to your place of business and provide free mini-services, a workshop or demonstration for your customers.

Hold a customer drawing or contest to win a free massage. Take nominations for the best local massage therapist and reward the winner (and the individual who nominated them) with a gift card or pampering product gift basket. Use entries to build your contact database and extend a special offer to all entrants.

Posts for Facebook/social media, Blog, E-mail, Bag Stuffers and/or Website:

- Information about pampering, stress relieving or therapeutic products or services you sell
- Recommended reading about massage or stress relief, links to online guides and resources
- Solicit customer recommendation or nominations for best local massage therapist
- Tips and tricks for self-relaxation and stress relief
- Recommendations / listing of local massage therapy services

Purchase branded personal massagers and branded or boutique-quality pampering, stress-relieving, aroma-therapeutic items like lotions, massage oils, candles, incense, room sprays, air fresheners, etc. to add to retail or to give away as contest prizes or a gift-with-purchase.

October 15 – Get to Know Your Customers Day

Yes, I know we observed a *Get to Know Your Customers Day* in January, but nothing is more important to the health and growth of your business than truly knowing your customers—what they really want and need, and more importantly, what they really want or need that you have the ability to provide. Giving customers the means to provide you with honest, no-holds-barred feedback gives you the ability to measure the performance of your business and employees against what you claim to be your corporate vision, mission and values.

One way to get more information about your customers is to simply ask for it. So that you don't overwhelm (or frighten) your customers, set up a series of short surveys to ask over the course of the coming year. Ask a new, short set of questions each month (or at the same frequency at which customers generally return; for instance, a dental practice might only see clients once every six months).

Create a written form or an online survey linked to your e-mail newsletter, website, blog, Facebook page and other social media profiles. Reward participation by extending a special offer, holding drawings or giving away branded items or samples to thank them for taking their feedback. Intersperse questions from several different sets of questions in order to build robust profiles of your customers over time without seeming intrusive or pressing hard in any one given area in a single survey.

Some of the things you might want to know about your customers:

Demographics and identifiers:

- name
- e-mail address
- gender
- age range; such as, 10-18, 19-24, 25-34, 35-44, etc. This can help as you analyze trends in different age groups and as you try to target specific offers to clients.
- zip code (to see if customers or prospects are clustered in certain neighborhoods; this can help you design targeted marketing for those neighborhoods in the future, identify neighborhoods to canvass or in which conduct a door-hanger campaign, etc.)
- address, phone number, mobile phone number

Preferences:

- whether they prefer contact by e-mail, text, direct mail or phone for information such as;
- newsletters, sales, promotions, events, classes, new products or services. charity drives, community news and events, volunteer opportunities

Other:

- how they heard about you
- whether they generally come to your business alone or with a friend, family member, child, co-worker, etc.
- how much time they spend on average each time they visit your business
- how many products or services they regularly (or occasionally) purchase from you
- what types of products or services they regularly purchase from you
- what they like most about doing business with you
- whether (and how) any of your employees exceeded their expectations
- whether (and how) any *other* business regularly exceeds their expectations
- how they would rate your facility in general or about specific areas such as cleanliness, décor and furnishings, rest rooms, food, music, seating, lighting, check in, check out, etc.
- which products or services your provide that most excite or intrigue them (whether or not they have purchased them)
- whether they have ever been disappointed with any aspect of your business (and in what/ why)
- what products or services they wish you offered
- what types of promotions most entice them to make unplanned purchases (free upgrade or add-on, gift-with-purchase, coupon, discount, BOGO)
- what type of special offer they last participated in (at your business or any business)
- what characterizes their ideal experience as a customer
- what words they would use to describe your business, your staff or your products or services

October 16 – Boss's Day

Celebrated on October 16th annually, or observed on the work day falling nearest if the 16th falls on a weekend, Boss's Day is a great opportunity for you to reflect on your performance as a leader, solicit feedback from your employees and take steps to improve in areas where you may need to develop skills or gain knowledge.

Beginning 4-6 weeks ahead of time, use your e-mail newsletter, bag stuffers, signage, Facebook and other social media sites to tell people that Boss's Day is coming. Make specific gift suggestions, add boss-appropriate greeting cards to your retail and provide sample scripts for notes-to-bosses to take the pressure off of subordinates. People who want to give a card or gift to their boss will probably want it to impress; add boutique-quality, one-of-a-kind items to your retail guaranteed to help subordinates make a good impression or express sincere appreciation for a great boss.

Partner with a business or communications expert to hold a workshop on relationships in the workplace, business communications, customer relations or dealing with a difficult boss (or co-workers).

Participate in local "Best Places to Work" competitions (generally held by city magazines or network newspapers). Hold your own contest and take nominations for the best local boss or best place to work. Support, encourage, provide or sponsor professional development and education for your staff. Subsidize continuing education and/or flexible schedules for employees who are taking classes or attending college. Establish a scholarship fund open to employees or their children.

Just as you communicate employee expectations to your staff, create a list of values and behaviors they can expect from you. Create an employee bill of rights and responsibilities. Establish a safe, formal system to garner feedback from employees. Meet with an executive coach, peer or trusted friend to determine areas where you may have blind spots or need to improve in order to be a better boss.

Posts for Facebook/social media, Blog, E-mail, Bag Stuffers and/or Website:

- Tips and tricks for impressing the boss or getting noticed by those responsible for corporate advancement
- Ideas for dealing with difficult people in the workplace, recommended reading, links to serious or light-hearted websites
- Recommended reading, online resources or local support groups for individuals who are their own 'boss' or for individuals want to get on the path to self-employment or business ownership
- Top 10 bad or good leadership traits, Top 10 Worst Bosses in History (or best), etc.
- Solicit customers humorous worst boss stories, boss or workplace jokes or cartoons

Add work-related humorous or inspirational wares such as notebooks, memo cubes, pens, wall plaques, clothing, folios, computer bags or totes, mouse pads, etc. to your retail or to give away as a gift-with-purchase or contest prize.

October 17 – Wear Something Bold and Gaudy Day

Partner with costume shops, clothing, shoe and accessory retailers, salons and spas or independent beauty professionals for cross or cooperative marketing. On your own or with marketing partners, hold a fall fashion show or go all out and hold a bold and gaudy holiday fashion show between now and the holidays. Create a directory of local, independent clothing, shoe and/or accessory boutiques and highlight the benefits to the community of shopping at locally-owned, independent stores.

Clip celebrity and fashion magazine photos and promote similar clothing, shoes, accessories, makeup, hair services, etc. you offer that can be used to re-create the same styles or fashions. Use celebrity photos to help promote sales of seasonal items by pointing out fashion and style trends and making specific product or service suggestions.

As a publicity stunt, set aside a day for employees to wear a costume, brightly colored pajamas or special bright, bold and gaudy branded shirts in support of a charitable cause, promotion or event. Hold an adult costume party (or plan to hold one for Halloween). Tell customers where they can get bold, gaudy costumes for themselves or their children in the weeks leading up to Halloween on your Facebook page, blog and e-mail newsletter. Have employees wear bright, branded shirts or costumes and invite kids to trick-or-treat, enjoy refreshments games and activities at your business for Halloween or as part of a Halloween-alternative event.

October 18 – No Beard Day

Partner with barbershops, salons, men's grooming professionals, waxing estheticians and independent sellers of men's grooming, skin care products or tools for cross or cooperative marketing. Create promotions around men's grooming products and services you provide. Put the marketing spotlight on the benefits that your related products, tools or services provide for male customers. Promote women's facial waxing services and products. Purchase gift cards for waxing or barbering services to give away as contest prizes or a gift-with-purchase in October.

Hold a "shave off" event to promote sales or to benefit a charity at your business, or partner with a local sports bar to hold a happy hour or evening event. Ask stylists to donate time and ask participants and attendees to make donations to a local mean's health or cancer-related charity. Partner with a photographer to photo-document the event and take before and after pictures of contest participants. Sample or demonstrate products or services that you sell. Hold door prize drawings and use entry forms to collect contact information; extend a special offer to everyone after the event.

Raise awareness for men's health issues or diseases by promoting "Noshavember." While Noshavember was created simply to give men an excuse not to shave in November, there's no reason you can't co-opt this theme into some ways to build business:

- Hold a 'shave off' at the end of November to demonstrate and sample products and services, as a contest for local barbers, to benefit a local charity or to raise awareness for men's health issues or diseases
- Register participants at the end of October with a clean-shaven face and award winners at the end of the Noshavember for best beard, best mustache, best goatee, etc. then hold a shave off and reward winners for the smoothest shave, biggest transformation, etc.

October 19 – Evaluate Your Life Day

Partner with a motivational speaker, counselor, life or executive coach, fitness trainer/gym, nutritionist/weight loss expert or another specific area-of-life expert to hold workshops to help attendees evaluate a specific aspect of their life and lay out a plan for the future and for cross and cooperative marketing.

Identifying specific goals is crucial to crafting effective, strategic solutions. Evaluate the life of your business: Where is it in the cycle of maturity and what should be your top priority?

- Just starting out with the overriding need to attract new customers
- Established but just getting by, with a need to:
  1. attract more customers or sell more products or services to existing customers
  2. add more products or services in order to attract customers or sell more
  3. improve customer retention, close a 'revolving back door'
  4. increase frequency of customer visits
  5. hire more employees
  6. hire better qualified/trained employees
  7. improve employee retention rate and decrease turnover
- A mature business with a strong following of loyal customers that needs to:
  1. evaluate and identify new products or services in order to grow
  2. reach out to a new generation of consumers
  3. reach out to attract and motivate a new generation of employees
  4. retrain or re-educate employees to remain competitive due to advances in technology or radical changes in the industry

"Customer life cycle" is a term used to describe a measure of customer relationship management (CRM). While there are variations, and customers may not fall cleanly into one category or another, the life cycle generally includes these phases:

- customer acquisition – in this phase you are introducing yourself to a customer and educating them about what you have to offer and "who you are" (vision, mission and values)
- customer retention – a customer has made at least one initial purchase, your focus is on generating repeat visits and stimulating purchases of more products or services
- cross-selling / up-selling – a customer has made multiple purchases from you, is relatively loyal and your focus is to sell them additional/different products or services or upgraded versions of those they regularly purchase
- lapsed customer – a formerly loyal customer has stopped purchasing from you, has reduced the amount they purchase from you or is not coming in as often (or at all); your main focus should be to find out why, address any dissatisfaction, re-introduce yourself and persuade them to be restored to their previous level of engagement with your business

Understanding the customer life cycle should help you identify where you are in relationship to most of your customers and, based on that, what type of marketing and outreach should be your focus with each. Trying to up-sell or cross-sell to a customer who is pulling back from their relationship with your business would likely only hasten its dissolution. Continuing to introduce yourself to loyal customers may be consuming valuable time better spent in up-selling. Tailor and personalize your marketing, especially with your most valuable clients, to maximize your opportunities and give yourself a chance to make amends if something has gone wrong.

October 20 – The 3rd Saturday in October is Sweetest Day

Partner with local restaurants, bars, clubs, theaters, salons, formal rental or clothing boutiques, limousine or town car services, etc. for cross or cooperative marketing. Partner with these (or other) types of businesses to create Sweetest Day couples packages with bundled or ala carte selections at a special price which will be offered and sold through all participating businesses. Partner with a counselor or relationship expert to hold a workshop on dating. Partner with a local bar or restaurant to hold a singles mixer or happy hour.

Create BOGO offers or service packages which couples could attend or enjoy together. Create his/hers product/service duos or gift baskets. Create graduated "sweet, sweeter and sweetest" offers that incentivize the purchase of multiple products or a series of services that will be used over time (such a series of massage services for 1, 3 or 6 months or graduated pricing based on length of appointment time).

Provide branded chocolates or another sweet treat as a VIP client gift, as a gift-with-purchase or for retail sale for Sweetest Day along with custom-designed greeting cards. Add love-themed items to retail or create a your own love (or even humorous anti-love) sentiments, quotes or designs to have printed on wares like wall plaques, notebooks, journals, t-shirts, tank tops, memo cubes, etc.

October 21 – Support Your Local Chamber of Commerce Day

If you haven't already, join your local Chamber of Commerce and find out how to become involved in decision-making that impacts the local business climate and economy. Recruit other members to join. Volunteer for a committee and help with street fairs and events. Be supportive of your Chamber at city council and other community meetings. Attend Chamber meetings, raise concerns and make specific suggestions. Run for a board or leadership position or chair a committee. Write a press release or send a letter to the editor noting recent work done by the Chamber, promoting future initiatives and speaking about the business climate of the city.

Volunteer time in support of community initiatives. Help promote fundraisers through donations, raising public awareness, donating products or services for beneficiaries or for use in auctions or as drawing prizes, answering calls on a phone bank, etc.

Attend Chamber meetings and events. Get to know the owners of member businesses. Patronize the businesses of other members. Participate in 'Buy Local' campaigns or launch a local 'Buy Local' merchant cooperative. Place a link to the Chamber on your website. Host or help sponsor a networking, educational or social event. Give branded tchotchkes to other members.

Create a special offer which can be extended to the customers of businesses that are members of the Chamber or special offers for their employees.

Posts for Facebook/social media, Blog, E-mail, Bag Stuffers and/or Website:

- The work your local Chamber is doing or post community service accomplishments

- Proposed/new taxes, ordinances or rules that will impact the local business climate and economy, and how the public can make their voice heard

- Benefits to the community of shopping locally-owned, independent businesses

- Trivia/history about your city

- Tell the public how they can become involved in the Chamber or support community initiatives, influence legislation or help improve the local economy

Create your own line of wares featuring your city's name and/or a custom slogan or design for retail sale, gifts-with-purchase or contest prizes (t-shirts, tank tops, hats, towels, glasses, mugs and tumblers, nightshirts, totes, notebooks, memo cubes, lunch bags, pens, pencils, snow globes, paperweights, etc.) Or purchase some of these types of items to be sold on behalf of your local Chamber of Commerce and/or member businesses with funds going to benefit the Chamber, a community service project or a charity.

October Week 4

October Week 4 – Freedom from Bullies Week

Throughout modern and ancient history, and even from the Biblical story of the first 4 people ever created (Adam and Eve, Cain and Able), bullies have existed, wielding destructive power with often tragic consequences. In recent years, our society has been saddened and challenged by the stories of children who were bullied to the point that they were willing to take their own lives. Whether there *is* actually increased bullying in the world today or we are just more aware of it because of the media, the seriousness of the problem mandates the need for awareness and for the eradication of bullying from any setting—including from the workplace.

Partner with local school officials, counselors, law enforcement and other experts to hold a workshop or even a community-wide forum on bullying. Meet with your marketing partners to hold a round table on bullying in the workplace. Post information and links to online and local resources on your Facebook page, blog and e-mail newsletter. Give parents information about how to protect their kids online, at school, how to identify early warning signs, how to discuss bullying with their children, etc.

Hold a workshop for employees on bullying in the workplace. Announce or reaffirm your commitment to maintaining a bully-free workplace. Talk about the values you hold which underlie employee-to-employee standards of behavior, boss-to-subordinate and vice versa, inter-departmental, etc. Enforce your policies and hold employees accountable for any and all inappropriate bullying behavior—starting at the top (that's you!)

Posts for Facebook/social media, Blog, E-mail, Bag Stuffers and/or Website:

- Links to local resources for parents or for kids, recommended reading and related websites
- Tips and techniques for dealing with bullies at school, in the workplace, at home or in the neighborhood, in other organizations or social settings, etc.
- Ideas and techniques for working out differences between people
- Quotes about bullying or positive interpersonal behaviors
- Information about your corporate anti-bullying policy and values

Add wares with anti-bullying slogans or designs to retail or give them away as gifts-with-purchase or contest prizes. Purchase branded anti-bullying-themed shirts for employees to wear on a given day to raise awareness, to be sold or given away at an event, to be sold with proceeds going to a related charity, etc.

October 22 – National Nut Day

Partner with gourmet food, organic foods and candy stores for cross or cooperative marketing. Invite marketing partners to provide nut or nut-treat samples to customers. With marketing partners or on your own, hold a cooking contest, happy hour or tasting featuring nuts or foods with nuts (such as breads, chocolate covered, salads, candy bars or balls, cheese balls, etc.) Hold a contest and blindfold contestants to see whether they can guess what kind of nut they are eating.

Posts for Facebook/social media, Blog, E-mail, Bag Stuffers and/or Website:

- Nut-related facts, history or trivia
- Humorous sayings or quotes about people who are 'nuts'
- Solicit customer stories about the 'nutty' people in their lives or hold a nuttiest-story contest
- "Celebrities gone nuts" or the favorite nuts of various celebrities
- Nut-related health and nutrition benefits
- Uses of nuts
- Solicit customers recipes containing nuts in general or for specific kinds of nuts

Create "we've gone nuts" or similarly titled promotions or offers. Add nut crackers, branded or gourmet nuts, nut-containing goodies, breads, etc. or holiday nut and candy gift boxes to retail or to be given away as a gift-with-purchase or contest prize.

October 23 – iPod Day

From boom boxes to modern day personal music devices, music devices got bigger and bigger, then the trend reversed and now thousands and thousands of hours of music fit on devices half the size of a business card, and nearly as thin. In recent years businesses have used the lure of winning or receiving a free iPod to incentivize purchases, bolster contest entries and contact databases, attract customers to events and keep them there ("must be present to win!") We load them up with music, books, movies and other media and take them with us on vacation, to appointments, on long car rides, for walks, runs and hikes. Few products have rivaled the iPod for popularity, and for popularity across generational and gender lines—you know you want one!

Hold your own contest or drawing for a free iPod. Use the lure of winning an iPod to incentivize competitions among customers and employees alike—the most referrals, purchases, sales—whatever consumer or employee behavior you want the most of! Add iTunes cards or iPod accessories to your retail, use them as contest prizes or incentive sales by giving an iPod, iTunes card or accessories away as a gift-with-purchase.

Provide iPods for customer use during appointments or long waits loaded with music from a variety of genres, movies, audio books or even your own podcasts. Create your own videos and podcasts for employee training, customer education, sales presentations, etc.

Post trivia about local music artists or book authors (whose work is available on iTunes) on your Facebook page, blog and e-mail newsletter. Ask customers for the names of their favorite songs, artists or albums. Post links to iPod apps (applications), accessories or resources, iPod facts, trivia or history.

October 24 – Make a Difference Day

Your company's point of difference (also known as your "unique selling proposition") is a marketing term that refers to what sets your business apart, how it is differentiated—or unique—from that of your direct and indirect competitors. Your unique selling proposition should be reflected within (or may be a product of) your vision, mission, tagline and corporate values.

Your unique selling proposition (USP) should be something that differentiates you in such a way that people would _prefer_ to do business with you specifically _because of your USP_. In other words, it's not just something about your business that is unique, it is something unique about your business that is meaningful and relevant to your customers and the individuals that comprise your prime target markets.

Posts for Facebook/social media, Blog, E-mail, Bag Stuffers and/or Website:
- What differentiates your business from your direct and indirect competitors
- What is special about the products and/or services you provide; how they benefit your customers or members of your prime target markets
- The benefits to the customer of doing business with you (how your business makes a difference in their lives)
- How your business makes a difference in your community or the local economy
- How your business makes a difference to your employees

Volunteer, donate products or services or raise funds for organizations whose mission is to make a personal difference in the lives of others, like Big Brothers/Big Sisters, YMCA, tutoring and mentoring services, after school programs, etc.

Invite a local high school or college student to intern with your business to help fulfill graduation requirements or to gain practical experience in an area related to their field of study. Establish an apprenticeship program within your business (and/or in partnership with other businesses) to provide opportunities for cross training and advancement for students, interns or employees.

October 25 - World Pasta Day

Partner with local caterers, restaurants, gourmet or specialty foods stores for cross or cooperative marketing. With marketing partners or on your own:
- Hold a pasta cooking, sauce or a homemade pasta making contest
- Hold a competition for local professional chefs, caterers or restaurants
- Hold a pasta tasting or happy hour event
- Hold a pasta and wine pairing hands-on cooking class or workshop
- Hold a cooking class or pasta making workshop
- Hold a customer-appreciation dinner with pasta on the menu
- Hold a 'spaghetti feed' to benefit a local charity
- Partner with an Italian restaurant to provide lunch for your employees or to hold an employee-appreciation family event

Posts for Facebook/social media, Blog, E-mail, Bag Stuffers and/or Website:
- Trivia, history or pasta-related facts
- Resources for people who make homemade pasta
- Cookbooks, recipes and pasta-making tips
- Nutrition information
- Local pasta dining recommendations
- Solicit customers favorite recipes to post online and/or to add to the collection you will have printed at the end of the year for gift, gift-with-purchase or retail sale
- Solicit customer recommendations for best local pasta

Add to retail or give away as a gift-with-purchase or contest prize:
- Cookbooks and recipe collections
- Pasta making kit, supplies or equipment
- Gourmet pasta sauces or sauce mixes
- Branded or pasta-themed aprons, pot holders
- Cookware, serving bowls and utensils
- Restaurant gift certificates

October 26 – Internet Day

Once the stuff of science fiction, today's Internet finds its roots in a 1967 contract worth a whopping $19,800 issued by the US Defense Department for the purpose of studying the "design and specification of a computer network." From those seeds sprung studies, science and technological advances in the US and throughout the world, eventually growing to the gargantuan proportions it boasts today—both in its seemingly limitless size and sphere of influence. To brush up on your Internet history, visit www.fcc.fob/omd/history/internet/.

While there are still some holdouts (yes, dad, I'm talking about you) in terms of use, very few people on the planet can claim that the internet has not improved their life in some way. Having instant access to a virtually limitless amount of information and resources and the ability to communicate and share information with nearly anyone, anywhere, at any time has revolutionized modern society and changed the way business "does business" forever.

Formerly, large companies or those with vast financial resources had all the advantages in advertising and marketing. Now, with the internet, for little-to-no money at all, the internet bridges the gap between the smallest 'single shingle' and its largest, richest competitor.

The simple fact is, if *you* are not taking advantage of the Internet to grow your business, learn, advertise, communicate with customers, prospects, vendors and others—if you are not leveraging internet opportunities to your advantage, you are missing out on potential growth and profit.

In observance of Internet Day, create a checklist for internet marketing, including:

- A company website with your own domain name (a real website, not hosted by a blog, directory, or another 3rd party directory). Visit www.12monthsofmarketing.com and click on any of the 1and1.com logos to set up your own website or check for domain name availability, or contact me for a quote or referral for website services.

- A company e-mail address that ends in your domain name (not .aol, .gmail, .hotmail, etc.) such as "elizabeth@12monthsofmarketing.com." Most website hosting packages include dozens (or up to many thousands) of unique e-mail addresses available ending in that domain name, and give you the ability to create your own names for the first part of the address (the "elizabeth" in the e-mail address example above).

- A blog for you as the leader of your company (you may want to have both an internal blog or intranet for your employees and a public, corporate blog for the general public).

- Facebook, Twitter, LinkedIn and other social media pages; you may choose to utilize several different social media sites. But don't just tweet to for tweeting's sake—learn which social media applications are best relative to your business goals. Adding all of them may be a significant waste of your most precious resource—your time.

- An e-mail marketing host (this could be a service provided by your web hosting company or an e-mail marketing application like the one I use, Constant Contact). Visit the Resources page of www.12monthsofmarketing.com for a link to Constant Contact and instructions for establishing an account.

- Listings in online yellow pages, community resource directories, industry directories, etc. Some of these will be for-pay and some will be free. Monitor your listings in directories that feature public ratings, complaints and raves. Ask customers to visit location-based directories and provide you with positive reviews, vote for you in "best of" polls, etc.

Make it your goal to collect 100% of your customers e-mail addresses. Request e-mail addresses from prospects on registration or check-in forms, subscription forms, contest or drawing entries, blog or Facebook submissions, etc. Update your database with new contacts and send an initial e-mail to welcome readers as soon as possible. Set up a regular schedule for e-mail marketing that you can maintain and/or solicit help from co-workers so that your social media sites, blog, website updates and e-mail marketing tasks can be accomplished as often as is desired to support your business goals.

Use online contests to help build numbers among the ranks of your social media site followers and e-mail marketing database; but remember, if the main or only reason someone "liked" your page, "retweeted" your post or subscribed to e-mails was for the chance to get something for nothing, there's a good chance they may fall outside of your target markets and ideal client base. But it's still a numbers game, and in order to reach more people via social media, you have to reach more people.

Content is still king; bore your readers and they will quickly lose interest. Entertain, educate, stir passions and reward people with some type of pay off, and they will keep visiting your sites, read your e-mails, and they will recommend and share your e-mails and sites with friends, family, co-workers and even the strangers they are linked to only by way of online social media webs.

October 27 – Cranky Co-Workers Day

Partner with an expert on interpersonal relationships or relationships in the workplace to hold a workshop on cranky co-workers, communication or interpersonal relationships or to hold a team building communication exercise for your employees.

Promote the virtues and health benefits of having a positive attitude. Make positive interpersonal communication one of the standards of employment in your company (and as with all standards, accountability starts at the top!)

Conduct an employee survey to gauge morale and identify perceptions relative to the tone and effectiveness of your corporate communications. Use anonymous surveys to solicit information about areas of potential problems among co-workers or where corporate communication may need to change in tone.

If potential problems are identified, deal with people privately and discreetly, giving them the benefit of the doubt. Address problems with the primary goal of providing support and re-training needed to modify behavior and thought patterns, or by providing people with a dignified way to choose to exit the company, request a transfer, etc. Set a standard of positive communications for all managers; lead by example.

Posts for Facebook/social media, Blog, E-mail, Bag Stuffers and/or Website:
- What customers should expect in communication interactions with your employees
- Quotes about bad attitudes, good attitudes, positive thinking and happiness
- Solicit cranky co-workers stories

Add branded humorous or inspirational cranky co-worker-themed t-shirts, tank tops, notebooks, memo cubes, pens, pencils, totes, lunch bags or other wares to your retail or give them away as contest prizes or a gift-with-purchase Create your own line of humorous or inspirational designs for items to be sold to customers as well as marketed to the employees of other local businesses, members of your Chamber of Commerce, 'Buy Local' merchant cooperatives or civic organizations, etc.

October 28 – Knock, Knock Jokes Day

Partner with a novelty, toy or hobby store for cross or cooperative marketing. With marketing partners or on your own, hold a kids standup comedy or joke writing contest. Add joke books to your retail or give them away as contest prizes or a gift-with-purchase.

Select neighborhoods in your community to target and conduct a door hanger campaign to introduce residents to your business. Talk about your products or services; tell them about other people 'in the neighborhood' who patronize your business and what the benefits are of doing business with you. Give recipients one more reason to keep your door hanger by incorporating a removable fridge magnet, year at a glance calendar, weights and measures conversion chart, local professional or college sports team schedules or some other useful feature into the design. Since this is something you want people to keep; rather than designing collateral that is 'all business,' you might make more of an impression if you incorporate humor, a cartoon or beautiful graphic that will draw the eye every time the homeowner walks past.

Feature the phrase "Knock, knock!" in big block lettering at the top of a posters, displays, door hangers, e-mails, newsletters or the front of postcards; it is sure to grab attention. Write your own marketing messages that begin with "Knock, knock! Who's there?" and go on to answer the question in a punny way, drawing attention to products or services that provide solutions to common customer needs.

Grabbing and keeping the attention of customers and prospects is no joking matter! According to *Shopper Marketing, Providing a 360° View of Your Shoppers and Consumers* on www.deloitte.com, experts estimate that the average US Consumer is exposed to upwards of 3,000 separate marketing messages *every day* in one form or another; a consumer could view up to a whopping 20,000 plus SKUs or more in just one trip to the local grocery store!

You not only need to get the attention of a reader; you need to get their attention long enough for them to absorb and connect with a message about how your products or services can bring them specific benefits and/or how doing business can make a positive difference in their lives. Here are a few guidelines for creating attention-grabbing subject lines and content to keep in mind:

To *get* the buyer's attention with subject lines:

- Keep it short, 5-8 words at most
- Use punchy, short, commonly-understood words
- Use statistics, percentages, dollars and numbers
- Use "you know you want…" phrasing to imply that they already know it's a good thing or a phrase that implies they are "too smart not to…" take a desired action
- Ask a question that points to a specific problem in their lives (such as, "Dry, flaky scalp?" or "Tired of high gas prices?")
- Imply that you are giving out brand new, little known or secret information
- Use a play on words, pun or humorous title
- Stimulate shock or surprise, like headlines a Hollywood gossip magazine would use
- Use a "join the group" or "who else wants" type of headline implying membership in an elite, smart, rich, successful, intellectual, philanthropic or otherwise desirable trait exclusive group of people
- Use an "if you liked such-and-such, you'll LOVE this" type of statements
- Avoid clichés (in the last few years this would have included phrases like "recession-proof" and "stimulus package")

Once you've got someone's attention, here are some guidelines for *keeping* it:

- Keep paragraphs short; no more than 2-3 sentences each
- Limit copy to the main 2-3 main points likely to be most important *to the customer*
- Use bullet and number lists to break up copy and to create concise, memorable lists
- Mention the most compelling, important, engaging, surprising, etc. buyer benefits first
- Break up long passages by interspersing bold, larger-lettered sub-headlines into the text
- Use color and imagery that illustrates the theme or reinforces product or brand awareness
- Write conversationally, as if you were talking to someone (contractions might be ok, grammatical and spelling errors are not and profanity is never ok!)
- Include a call to the specific action you want them to take next (buy something, visit your business, register, subscribe, read an article, contact someone at your company, etc.)

October 29 – Caramel Apple Day

Provide caramel apples for clients during appointments or as a gift-with-purchase when leaving. Provide caramel apple kits or flavored candies, coffee drinks, etc. for sampling.

Solicit customers caramel apple making recipes and tips, as well as recipes for other caramel apple-flavored items like cocktails, coffee drinks or candies. Post tips and recipes online as well as caramel apple-related trivia or history.

Working with the businesses near yours (or on your own) hold a caramel apple day as part of a kid's safe trick-or-treating or Halloween-alternative event with activities, games, candy and entertainment.

October 30 – Candy Corn Day

Partner with candy stores and grocery stores for cross or cooperative marketing. Purchase branded packages of candy corn for retail or to give away as a gift-with-purchase or bag stuffer; or, sample candy corn to customers while shopping or during appointments.

Purchase branded packages of candy corn in a color and flavor mix unique to your business—perhaps matching your logo colors? Send branded packages of your custom candy corn mix:

- home with customers as bag stuffers
- to large local businesses to be placed in lunch or break rooms
- to local schools and/or district offices, teachers or to be enjoyed by a high school sports team, band, choir, day care, youth services organization or church youth group
- for employees of local hospitals and nursing homes, city hall, police and fire stations
- to be placed on tables of local restaurants or bars
- to businesses located near yours or with which you partner for marketing and events, to members of your Chamber of Commerce, Rotary, local merchant association, etc.

Fill a large glass container with candy corn (count first!) and let customers guess the quantity; reward one or more winner/s with a prize, gift basket, gift card, branded item, etc. Post candy corn trivia or solicit customer recipes for cooking or decorating with candy corn on your Facebook page, blog and e-mail newsletter.

Hold a candy corn throwing contest by setting up a group of plastic cups and letting customers throw candy corn into them (like a carnival game). Either reward customers for any candy corns that land in cups, include special colored cups or color code the bottom of cups so that candy corn landing in specific cups would receive a special prize, add-on, branded item, gift card toward next purchase, etc.

October 31 – Halloween

In partnership with businesses near yours, hold a Trick or Treating or Halloween-alternative event for children. Hire a magician, clowns or other costumed entertainers. Invite local stylists, makeup artists or independent makeup sellers to provide face painting for kids (and grown ups!) in exchange for the opportunity cross market their services as a stylist or promote their salon or spa. Set up carnival-style games and/or a big bouncy toy. Rent a commercial popcorn cart. Go 'old school' and bob for apples. Provide parents with samples, short demonstrations and professional consultations. Include a bounce-back offer and branded tchotchkes as well as treats in goodie bags for kids.

Purchase branded scented candles, lotions or other Autumn or Halloween-themed items for contest prizes, retail sale or to be given away as a gift-with-purchase during October or during the week (or just the day) of Halloween. Extend a Halloween day, week or month-long offer.

Working with businesses near yours or those with which you partner with for cross or cooperative marketing, hold a Halloween costume party for clients or employees at a local bar or restaurant. Extend special offers to the employees of these businesses.

november

365 Days of Marketing

November Month-Long Observances

Drum Month

Renew or establish cross or cooperative marketing partnerships with local music stores and music teachers. Invite a local percussion instructor or performer to hold a demonstration or introductory lesson at your business for customers. Post links to local musicians, bands or party disc jockeys on your Facebook page, blog and e-mail newsletter or create an online directory of live music options for businesses, parties, weddings, etc. Invite local bands and musicians who perform at weddings, anniversaries, birthdays, bar mitzvahs, corporate events, etc. to provide live background music at your business or host a showcase event where they can perform and take bookings.

Many street and barter fairs feature the work of folk drum and musical instrument makers; solicit customers to show off drums, folk or handcrafted instruments they have invented at your business in an exhibition, in a photo gallery on your website, blog or your Facebook page. Post links to folk drum building instructions, artist or crafting supplies on your Facebook page, blog and e-mail newsletter.

Customers might be looking for affordable instruments to purchase as holiday gifts for their children, so hold a music instrument swap or 'garage sale' event. Partner with a local music instrument store for special holiday offers to extend your customers. Post links to local instrument sellers and instructors on your Facebook page, blog and e-mail newsletter or add these resources to your online music/musicians directory.

Add custom-designed or branded drumsticks, guitar picks and other music accessories to retail or give them away as contest prizes or a gift-with-purchase. Add toy drum or percussion sets to retail as children's gifts. Add handcrafted drums or other percussion items to your retail for holiday sale.

Post trivia about the history of drums, use of drums across different cultures, drum photos or videos, etc. on your Facebook page, blog and e-mail newsletter.

Real Jewelry Month

Partner with local jewelry stores, artists who make handcrafted fashion jewelry, fashion jewelry party sellers and craft stores for cross or cooperative marketing. With marketing partners or on your own, hold a workshop or series of classes for making handmade jewelry. Hold kids, tweens or teens jewelry-making classes. Create a jewelry-making birthday party service to add to your menu. Hold a jewelry swap event.

Posts for Facebook/social media, Blog, E-mail, Bag Stuffers and/or Website:
- Jewelry crafting or repair products and services
- Solicit customer photos of handmade jewelry (such as the work of local independent artists)
- Solicit pictures of homemade jewelry made by kids (such as those made as gifts for parents)
- Solicit customer recommendations or favorite jewelry stores
- Links to or a directory of local jewelry stores, repair professionals, appraisers, jewelry-making equipment and supplies, etc.
- Links to websites or Facebook pages of local fashion jewelry artists
- Links to local jewelry or crafting fairs or bazaars (there will probably be many held at local churches/schools in the weeks leading up to the holidays)
- Jewelry-related trivia or history

Purchase a holiday jewelry display specific to a current trend/fashion, with holiday-themed jewelry or jewelry designed to appeal to specific age groups (kids, tweens and teens, etc.) to add to retail during the holiday season. Restock the display in the new year with seasonal items for Valentine's Day and continue restocking with new themed merchandise throughout the year (Mother's Day, prom, graduation, bridal jewelry, summer, etc.)

Add jewelry kits or children's jewelry crafting kits to your retail or to give away as contest prizes or a gift-with-purchase. Display handmade jewelry of local artists or partner with local artists for cooperative handcrafted jewelry sales. Add jewelry making tools, equipment and supplies to retail. Purchase branded jewelry repair kits to add to retail or give as a gift-with-purchase. Hold a jewelry repair clinic. Add a watch battery placement and basic jewelry repair service to your menu.

Military Family Appreciation Month

Use your website, Facebook page, blog and e-mail to extend a special offer to local military members and their families or invite them to a military family-appreciation open house. Send a copy of your offer to the newspapers of local military bases for distribution to military families. Send copies of promotional brochures, business cards and/or menu to the offices of military/family service organizations.

Take nominations from clients or contact your local military base and 'adopt' a military family or service member for free products or services for a year, for a holiday shopping spree, date package, etc.

Even if you don't live near a military base, you can still extend an offer to the Veterans in your community. Deliver copies of your brochure, business card, menu, manufacturers samples, etc. to the office of your local V.A. (Veteran's Administration) or other Veteran's organization or club.

Invite people in your community to sign or submit thank-you notes or holiday greeting cards to be sent to troops overseas. Solicit handmade cards and drawings from children. Solicit donations and gifts suitable for sending to troops overseas during the holidays. Hold a benefit event. Donate funds/ products for care packages for military personnel on deployment over the holidays. Put posts on your Facebook page, blog and e-mail newsletter conveying gratitude to local military members and to family members who have loved ones on deployment.

Sleep Comfort Month

Partner with local mattress and furniture stores for cross or cooperative marketing. Tell customers about products or services you offer that contribute to better sleep. Partner with a medical professional or sleep expert to hold a workshop about improving sleep quality. Partner with a dream specialist to hold a seminar on the interpretations of dreams.

Posts for Facebook/social media, Blog, E-mail, Bag Stuffers and/or Website:

- Tips, recommendations for ways to improve sleep quality or duration
- Tips for getting kids or new babies to sleep better
- How much sleep people need, the benefits of sleep
- Products or services you sell which contribute to better sleep, relaxation, improved energy, etc.
- Dream-related trivia
- Recommended reading, links to local specialists or other resources

Add branded travel pillows, throws, kids pillows or convertible pillows (like those that transform into tote bags or stuffed animals), baby blankets, pet beds, etc. to retail or give them away as contest prizes or a gift-with-purchase.

November Week 1

November Week 1 – Chemistry Week

Invite a local chemistry professor, high school teacher, members of a science club or other experts to hold a chemistry exhibition or workshop in your store. Invite college and high school students and science junkies among your customers to attend. Feature fun, cool or interactive science demonstrations and retail science kits and supplies. Or go big! Work with marketing partners and local schools to hold a community-wide science fair featuring the work of students. Extend a special offer to participants and their families, teachers and/or all school employees. Distribute branded tchotchkes and copies of your catalog or service menu.

Posts for Facebook/social media, Blog, E-mail, Bag Stuffers and/or Website:

- Links or news about local science clubs, current projects or accomplishments of local college or high school science programs, student achievements, or follow the work of a science club all year
- Links to interesting at-home experiment sites for kids, students or adults
- Resources for science tutoring

Take this theme in a less scientific direction and partner with a relationship expert to hold a workshop on interpersonal chemical attraction or how chemistry between people affects relationships from friendship to romance and even between co-workers.

Partner with a personal fragrance expert to hold a workshop on creating personal fragrances. Add essential oils, fragrance sprays, scented candles, incense, room sprays or air fresheners to your retail, to give away as a gift-with-purchase or award as contest prizes. These could be great items to add year round, to feature as holiday gift ideas or to give as holiday gifts to your clients.

November 1 – Zero Tasking Day

Zero Tasking Day is observed on the day after most US households turn their clocks back an hour (at the end of Daylight Savings Time). It's meant to be an hour you give back as a gift to yourself to do nothing—one of the very few hours in your life that remains unclaimed. As a business owner or working professional, you probably don't have many unclaimed hours—in fact, there's probably a tug-of-war for between responsibilities at home, at work, from family, friends, co-workers, pets—the list goes on. Some time during this busy month, block out an actual hour of waking time when you can "just be" somewhere quiet, free of electronics, communications, pens, paper or staplers. Zero Tasking Day was created to give you the gift of an hour; take it!

Whenever I take on a new job, I pull it apart, analyze tasks and responsibilities, find out what can be done better or more efficiently and re-engineer it so that tasks can be easily handed off to other individuals or to whomever will succeed me in that position. It's my belief that it is healthier to evolve, cross-train others and document the responsibilities of a job—to the point that you could be replaced at any time—than it is to hold on to power, knowledge and tasks out of a false sense of power or job security. Stop thinking that you are (or even that you should be) irreplaceable as an employee, manager or even as the owner of your business. As a *person*, you are irreplaceable and unique, as an *employee*, your job is to share information, cross-train and mentor others so that you can put yourself in a position to own "zero tasks"so that you can be ready to take the next step in your career, accept a promotion, expand your business, retire, etc.

November 2 – Look for Circles Day

Look for no deeper meaning; Look for Circles Day is a day to look for circles. Having no beginning or end point, the circle is symbolic of unity and infinity. It is represented in nature by the "royalty" of our universe; our sun and moon and our own planet.

Fill a large glass container with marbles, rubber balls, gum balls—any circular item will do—and have customers guess the quantity. Post a picture online so people can enter on Facebook or a web entry form. Use entries to build your contact database and extend a special offer to all entrants (how is that for a circular process!)

Have a ring toss tournament or set up an activity area for kids. Place circles on the floor for a door prize-type of game with music (like a cake walk or a game of musical chairs); each time the music stops, an individual left without a circle to stand on is "out" and one more circle is removed, until there is only one circle, and one winner, left.

365 days of marketing

Place a circle in an envelope and seal it; put it on a board with a number of empty envelopes. Set a price and sell all the envelopes with proceeds going to charity at an event, or allow customers to choose an envelope when they make a purchase. Reward the individual who picks the winning envelope (the one with the circle) with a gift basket or another prize, gift card, shopping spree, etc.

Ask customers to see how many circle shapes they can find in a picture or a puzzle. Challenge people to create art using circles. Place circles throughout your store that indicate special hour-long (day-long, etc.) special offers.

Add "circles" to your retail, contest prizes or to give away as a gift-with-purchase, such as:

- Toy balls for kids, ring toss, croquet, volleyball, bocce or other backyard games with balls
- Branded or custom-designed circular computer mouse pads, memo cubes or notebooks
- Round-shaped coin purses, bags, purses or evening bags for holiday wear or gifts

November 3 – Sandwich Day

Create promotions that 'sandwich' a product or service between two others bundled at a special price or as a free add-on. Sandwich a series of services together (such as a series of 3 hair cuts, 3 oil changes, etc.) at a special price, to be redeemed within a specified period of time.

Partner with caterers, party planners, delis and restaurants for cross or cooperative marketing. With marketing partners or on your own:

- Sample sandwiches to your customers
- Provide wrapped sandwiches or box lunches for retail sale or as a gift-with-purchase
- Provide delivered sandwiches to local businesses or as a party menu option
- Hold a class on entertaining with sandwiches, specialty sandwiches, sandwich alternatives (like wraps, pita pockets, salads, etc.)
- Hold a sandwich recipe contest for customers
- Hold a sandwich competition between local chefs or restaurants
- Hold a happy hour or tasting event featuring sandwiches
- Compile recipes to create your own sandwich recipe book

Provide sandwiches for employees at lunch or give them gift cards redeemable for sandwiches at the businesses of one of your marketing partners.

Posts for Facebook/social media, Blog, E-mail, Bag Stuffers and/or Website:

- History/trivia of sandwiches
- Solicit customer recipes
- Solicit customer's local favorite sandwiches/shops
- Hold polls to determine the most popular sandwich of customers, kids, etc.
- Links to delicious seasonal, shower and party sandwich recipes

November 4 – Cliché Day

At www.thefreedictionary.com a *cliché* is defined as: A trite or overused expression or idea; or, a person or character whose behavior is predictable or superficial.

You don't want to use the first, and you definitely don't want to *be* the second! Avoid the use of cliché phrases. While it may seem fun to jump on the band wagon—like in 2010 when companies were all out advertising "stimulus package" promotions—it gets old, fast. And *using* cliché words and phrases in your marketing makes you *look* like a person whose behavior is predictable or superficial!

Hold a tagline writing contest for customers (or employees) relative to their favorite products or services. Hold a contest to see how many famous business taglines or campaign phrases your customers can recall. Write a list of taglines and see whether customers can match them up to the company or product they were used to promote. Write a list of cliché statements and see whether customers can match the list to the origin or meaning of the phrase.

Posts famous clichés, taglines or slogans or trivia about the origin of common cliché phrases (the rule of thumb, the pot calling the kettle black, etc.) on your Facebook page, blog and e-mail newsletter.

November 5 – Men Make Dinner Day

Work with a dinner preparation business or caterer to hold a cooking class (or series of classes) for men who want to improve their day-to-day cooking skills or to help them prepare to cook for dates, entertaining or the holidays. Hold a men's cooking contest.

Create "take and fake" substitute options that include last-minute at-home eating, serving or other preparation instructions. Create kits for retail sale that include all ingredients needed to make specific recipes. Create an offer which includes dinners prepared for pick-up or which can be delivered, catered, etc.

Add other options to your men's dinner package, such as floral bouquet, wine glasses, tableware, napkin rings or glass charms, background music, candles and candlesticks, etc. Post links to local florists, gift shops, kitchenware retailers, etc. on your Facebook page, blog and e-mail newsletter.

Post links to celebrity recipes. Post links to local culinary schools or cooking classes. Create a directory of restaurants that provide take-out options to share on Facebook, your blog and e-mail newsletter or as part of a community directory on your website.

Post links to celebrity recipes or recipes that are easy to make for holidays, entertaining or families on your Facebook page, blog and e-mail newsletter. Post tips for setting a beautiful table, decorating for the holidays or throwing birthday parties.

November 6 – Marooned without a Compass Day

Partner with a local counselor, life coach or motivational speaker to hold a workshop on what to do when feeling "marooned" or lost. Compile a list of recommended reading, audiobooks and videos. Add some of the best titles to your retail or impulse buy offerings, or post them online.

Post links to local resources on your Facebook page, e-mail newsletter or blog. Work with marketing partners and local education institutions to hold a career or job fair for adults, college or high school students. Work together to establish job shadow and intern programs. Create a community support group for job seekers or employers, or set up a specialty job listing resource online. Invite marketing partners to participate in regular meetings to discuss ways to "map out" pathways to improve local economic health in order to benefit independent businesses and the community.

Create a formal mentoring or apprenticeship program within your business for your own employees, local students, adults in need of vocational training, etc. Help subsidize or provide resources for continuing education for your employees.

The last thing you want is for someone to be "marooned without a compass" at your business, unable to find what they need. Be sure in-store signage is up to date. Create directory signs to be placed at eye level at the ends of aisles. Create a floor map directory noting the route to the offices, departments, rest rooms, reception or other areas that visitors to your building most commonly visit. Post it in your entry, reception desk or waiting room, give copies to first-time guests, post it on your website or include it in an annual e-mail newsletter.

It's only natural that from time to time you will need to reorganize or renovate parts of your building. Draw up a new floor map following any remodel, renovation or re-organization project to e-mail and/or direct mail to customers and prospects, or one that can be handed to customers at the door or utilized at an open house event. Use this opportunity to draw attention to new products or services and hold an open house with door prize drawings, contests, entertainment and refreshments as well as product demonstrations, professional consultations and product sampling.

Educate customers as to products or services—solutions—you provide that they may not have been previously aware of, or which they may not have needed previously (but do now). Throughout the year, use your communications channels and events to put the spotlight on various products, services, departments, specialists, etc. Use your e-mail newsletter, blog, Facebook and other social media and your website to introduce new employees, products or services to your customers as soon as possible. Create time-limited promotions to help fill appointments books for new employees or to support the launch of new products. Pair new items in promotions with best-sellers and clearly define their benefits in messaging across all of your communications channels.

Create brochures listing local attractions, the best dining, entertainment and family recreation centers, activities for rainy days, options for hiking, swimming, golf, etc. and which also features relevant products or services. Solicit ideas and recommendations from customers and post links on Facebook. Send copies to local hotels, motels, car rental agencies, travel agencies, etc.

November 7 – Tongue Twister Day, Aid and Abet Punsters Day

Hold a contest for the best (or most groan-worthy) puns, tongue twisters or jokes submitted in-store or online. Post entries on your Facebook page, blog, e-mail newsletter and/or website as well as in-store and all people to vote. Post famous or fun puns, tongue twisters, riddles or jokes on your Facebook page, blog and e-mail newsletter.

Challenge customers to compose a tongue twister about your business or one of your products or services. Hold a tongue twister recitation contest. Challenge customers to tackle a tongue twister at the point of sale or as part of a contest in exchange for a special offer, gift card or branded tchotchke.

Compose a tongue twister to use in a marketing campaign. Add books with jokes, tongue twisters and puns to your retail or give them away as contest prizes. Add pun, play on words, or humorous wall plaques, t-shirts, tank tops, notebooks, tumblers or mugs and books to your retail or to give away as contest prizes or a gift-with-purchase.

November Week 2

November Week 2 - National Hunger and Homeless Week

During the holiday season, raise awareness of the needs of local shelters, food banks, missions and similar charitable food and housing providers. Extend a special offer or give branded tchotchkes as thank-you gifts to clients who donate money, food, or clothing to these charities. Donate a portion of sales from product or service sales in November to a local charitable meal provider. Publicize efforts and raise awareness within your community in press releases submitted to local radio and news stations/reporters, local newspapers and city magazines.

Posts statistics about the local hungry/homeless population on your Facebook page, blog and e-mail newsletter. Post trivia such as the average cost per day needed to make a difference at local charities or ways that people can volunteer or provide personal assistance.

November Week 2 – Pursuit of Happiness Week

Partner with a motivational speaker, life coach or counselor to hold a pursuit of happiness seminar. Compile a list of recommended reading to post on Facebook, your blog and e-mail newsletter; add some of the best titles to retail, to gift or gift-with-purchase, or to be awarded as contest prizes.

Posts for Facebook/social media, Blog, E-mail, Bag Stuffers and/or Website:
- Highlight the services or products you provide that make customers most happy, or poll customers for their favorites
- Links or directories of local fun activities and recreation centers
- Happy inspirational quotes
- Ask customers what simple things make them happy
- Solicit pictures of happy kids, funny pets, etc.
- Poll people for favorites that make them happy such as entertainers, movies, music, restaurants, books, etc.

Create "pursuit of happiness" add-ons or special offers. Create your own design or slogan to have printed on happy or smiley-themed items such as mugs, tumblers, t-shirts, tank tops, hats, notebooks, memo cubes, journals, pens, greeting cards, etc. to add to retail or give away as a gift-with-purchase or contest prize.

November 8 – Cook Something Bold Day

Cook up a bold challenge for your customers, employees, marketing partners and/or local businesses. Set an ambitious goal in support of a local food bank, homeless shelter or another charity and work together to conduct fundraising campaigns, hold benefit events and raise awareness throughout the community. Buy campaign-branded items to sell with proceeds going to charity and make them available for purchase at all participating businesses.

Add bold gourmet sauces or mixes to retail or to give away as contest prizes or a gift-with-purchase. Partner with local restaurants and caterers for cross or cooperative marketing. With marketing partners or on your own, hold a bold cooking class featuring bold holiday or entertaining recipes. Hold a bold cooking contest for customers, or hold a bold cooking contest for local professional chefs or restaurants. Hold a bold wine and appetizer happy hour. Create a bold palette cook book or recipe collection to be printed for retail sale.

Using Facebook/social media, Blog, E-mail, Bag Stuffers and/or Website, put the marketing spotlight on any bold menu items, ingredients or foods you sell. Create bold promotions for some of your most popular products or services, or create bold holiday promotional offers (e.g., a "bold look," "bold fashion," "bold attitude," etc.) Solicit customers favorite bold cooking recipes on your Facebook page, blog and e-mail newsletter.

November 9 – Young Readers Day

Support local reading programs through donations, holding benefit events or helping to raise public awareness. Hold a "read-in" for kids, an all-nighter publicity stunt or another reading event. Give away award-winning children's books as contest prizes or a gift-with-purchase. Add great children's literature to your retail.

Design your own (branded) alphabet and/or number flash cards to have printed for retail sale or available for free download from your website. Design your own alphabet and/or number, color, etc. game pieces for matching game play. Create your own custom design to have printed on wooden alphabet blocks for retail sale.

Compile a young readers recommended reading list or solicit customer recommendations on your Facebook page, blog and e-mail newsletter. Solicit teacher's recommendations of books for various age ranges. Post links to websites that feature educational games and activities for preschool and early elementary-aged children.

Make recommendations of support or learning materials for parents, child care providers or babysitters or post links to related websites. Post links to local literacy programs, tutors or reading specialists.

November 10 – Parents as Teachers Day

Home-schooling consortiums and support groups exist in most communities; extend special offers to home-schooling families in your community. There are several websites dedicated to the home schooling segment of education. One such site that has listings for home school cooperatives in all 50 states, and also features listings for international cooperatives, is Homeschool World; their directory listings are located at www.home-school.com/groups/.

November 11 – Veterans Day

Extend a special offer to Veterans, military servicemen and women and their families. Hold an open house, happy hours or another event for Veterans in your community. Hold a benefit event or donate a portion of today's (or November's) sales to your local Veteran's Administration or a military support agency. Take part in your city's Veteran's Day parade or other community activities.

Don't know where to start when it comes to honoring and supporting past and present members of the military? Veteran's support and social organizations exist in all 50 states, and other countries have their own Veteran's organizations as well. I found a list containing both on *wikipedia* at http://en.wikipedia.org/wiki/List_of_veterans'_organizations.

Say "thank you" to Veterans in posts on your Facebook page, blog, e-mail newsletter and bag stuffers. Solicit 'shout outs' to Veterans and military members from the public on your Facebook page.

November 12 – Area Code Day

Use the numbers of your area code to create a special offer for services and/or products. For instance, let's say you own a salon in an area like Seattle, which is in the vicinity of 4 area codes—206, 253, 360 and 425. Use all four of the local area codes to create special offers. A "206" might include a pre-sold package of two hair color highlights at $6 off each, a "253" might be a pre-sold package of 3 haircutting appointments sold at $25 each, a "360" could be $3.60 off any 1 or 2 retail products and a "425" could be a "must be present" in-store, must be listening radio station or must be 'live' on Facebook drawing held daily at 4:25 P.M.

Hold employee or customer contests for the most creative area code promotions. Poll customers to determine their most common area codes as part of a drive to collect mobile phone numbers for special event or sale text message marketing.

November 13 – Set a Record, Do a Stunt Day

November 13th is Guinness Book of World Records Day. Set a new world record or hold a publicity stunt on your own or with marketing partners. Solicit ideas and participation from customers, your marketing partners, employees and/or the general public. Add copies of the latest edition of the *Guinness Book of World Records* to your retail for the holidays. Post links to interesting world records or the official Guinness Book site on your Facebook page, blog, bag stuffers and e-mail newsletter.

Working with the music or arts department of a local school or music/dance studio, organize your own dance or choral "flash mob" to take place in your business or in another public venue. Provide participants with branded t-shirts or tank tops. Afterward, ask participants to hand out copy of a special offer, a branded tchotchke, business cards, etc.

Invite local choral, dance and other performing group to provide live entertainment in your business during the holiday season. Ask local school and church choirs to provide holiday caroling outside (or inside) of your business, to visit businesses located near yours or those of your marketing partners, to 'carol' with your employees at a local senior or assisted living facility, etc.

November 14 – Loosen Up, Lighten Up Day

Partner with beauty professionals, fitness experts and cosmetic medical or dental professionals for cross or cooperative marketing. With marketing partners or on your own, begin to construct New Year Resolution cooperative offers and solutions for customers.

Partner with local fitness and beauty experts to hold a cooperative "loosen up, lighten up" weight loss and makeover promotion. Help customers prepare to look their best for the upcoming holiday season by providing them with a workshop, demonstration or boot camp that might include fitness, weight loss, dietary and skin/makeup consultations. Sell bundled sets of pre-selected makeup palettes or give participants the option to purchase bundled services to help them meet their holiday goals.

Partner with local beauty professionals to hold a skin bar happy hour focused on helping clients "lighten up" complexions by freeing skin from buildup and reducing the effects of stress and environmental damage, and to "loosen up" wrinkles with skin firming and wrinkle reducing products or services; and with a

- Cosmetic surgeon who can help remove wrinkles permanently; and with a
- Dentist who can "lighten up" teeth through whitening services; invite a dentist to provide whitening services in your business at an event or on an on-going basis; and
- Partner with a caterer or restaurant to provide light refreshments at your workshop. Give clients copies of recipes for this light party fare and suggestions for making healthier dietary decisions, ingredient substitutes, etc.

Post eating-light recipes and recommended resources, cookbooks or recipe sites, links to local restaurants or caterers with low fat/low calorie options, etc. Post recommendations from your marketing partners for ways to achieve a healthy weight, reach fitness goals, improve the appearance of skin and teeth, makeup application tips, etc. on your Facebook page, blog, bag stuffers and e-mail newsletter.

November Week 3

November Week 3 – Family Week, Game and Puzzle Week

Add games and puzzles to your retail for the holidays or put the spotlight on those you sell. Create a special offer for bundled sets of games/puzzles or multiple purchases. Hold a family game night at a local restaurant. Sponsor a teen game night and invite local church youth groups or other youth organizations to attend. Hold a game or puzzle tournament at your business. Have a poker or card game tournament at a local bar for charity. Have a photograph of your business, your logo, your employees, etc. made into a puzzle or have your logo printed onto a simple puzzle for young children.

Posts for Facebook/social media, Blog, E-mail, Bag Stuffers and/or Website:
- Links to kids learning games, puzzle and activities sites
- Suggest games that can be played with common household items
- Links to rules for common games or instructions for card games
- Create a list of activities families can do together for little or no money; include things that can be done both in and out of doors
- Solicit customer family game night suggestions, photos and stories

During November, let clients have fun by solving puzzles or participating in shower-style quizzes and games in the waiting area or while shopping, dining, etc. Hold a contest for speed and/or accuracy or create your own game with client rewards. For a shower-style game that can be played by clients or can be utilized by employees as a training exercise, write down a list of your top 20 products or services, and a list of the specific benefit each provides, additional or secondary benefits like vitamins, SPF protection, aromatherapy, the product's intended use, the problem it solves, the solution it provides, etc. Reorder the list of products randomly and see whether clients (or employees) can match up the product or service with its characteristics.

Create a special word of the month like 'turkey,' 'pumpkin' or another seasonal word. If a customer says or guesses the word, give them a chance to drop an entry form in a fishbowl for a drawing to be held at the end of the month. Create a prize basket with pumpkin, cloves, spice or another aromatherapy lotion, candle, etc. plus a gift card redeemable at their next visit to your business. Help spur referrals by including a second gift certificate for your customer to give a friend, co-worker or family member who would be a new customer to your business.

November Week 3 – Don't Text and Drive Week

Post trivia or statistics about the risks and consequences of texting and driving on your Facebook page, blog and e-mail newsletter. Hold a benefit event for a local family that has been impacted by a texting and driving accident. Raise awareness by posting information about what constitutes "distracted driving" on your Facebook page, blog and e-mail newsletter.

Post an electronic petition or pledge form online; ask customers to sign it as a pledge that they will not text and drive. Make copies available for download for use by other businesses in your community. Link the form to your Facebook page, blog and e-mail newsletter. Or go big! Enlist the help of other businesses and work together to hold a community-wide petition drive for signatures with a culminating event.

November 15 – I Love to Write Day
(and November is Novel Writing Month)

Work with a local author or literature expert to hold a workshop for aspiring authors. Discuss the writing process, connect participants to resources for artwork, editing and publishing, provide them with information about self publishing or promoting books to publishers or directly to the public. Establish a writer's club or hold a series of classes to walk participants through a novel writing process. Visit the Resources page of www.12monthsofmarketing.com for self-publishing artwork, editing and publishing resources.

Posts for Facebook/social media, Blog, E-mail, Bag Stuffers and/or Website:
- Compile a list of recommended reading and resources for aspiring authors
- Compile list of favorite novels with input solicited from employees, customers and the public
- Post literary and writing tips, tricks and advice
- Post quotes from famous novels (or hold a "name that quote" contest)

Add writing supplies and branded, boutique quality or your own custom designed notebooks, pens and journals to your retail or to give away as contest prizes or a gift-with-purchase.

November 16 – Button Day

Create humorous, inspirational or branded designs to customize your own buttons to add to retail, gift or gift-with-purchase, or as 'flair' for employees to wear. Hold a button design contest for customers in support of an upcoming charity event, a community happening, a product or service campaign, the holidays, or some other theme.

Create "Ask me about…" buttons for employees to wear (and signage for shelving, entryway, the point of purchase, etc.) to encourage customers to ask about new products or services, upgrades, add-ons or time-limited promotions. Write "Did you know...?" and "Ask me about..." posts for Facebook, your blog and e-mail newsletter to get the attention of readers and stimulate interaction.

Make sure your website has buttons with links for Facebook, Twitter and other social media and in order to subscribe to your e-mail newsletter. Set aside time each month to make sure all of your website buttons work or assign this responsibility to a staff member. Add "like" and "retweet" buttons to your blog posts to stimulate more cross traffic and article sharing. Encourage readers to forward your e-mails and share your blog, Facebook and Twitter posts.

Post button trivia or images of famous or amusing buttons (like those used for political campaigns, in marketing, for causes, etc.) on your Facebook page, blog and e-mail newsletter.

Post links to local craft and sewing supply stores or to online stores that sell buttons. Partner with a local craft artisan to create sets of beautiful clothing buttons to add to your retail.

November 17 – Electronic Greeting Card Day

Send an electronic greeting card your customers thanking them for their patronage and wishing them a Happy Thanksgiving. This might also be the perfect time to send a corporate greeting by mail (vs. one that might get lost in the pile during December holidays). Add an offer to your electronic greeting card by way of a code word redeemable for a specific discount, free add-on, branded tchotchke, etc. Send personalized, individual electronic greeting cards to your most valuable customers, vendors or marketing partners. Post links to electronic greeting card sites on your Facebook page.

Add unique, custom-designed greeting cards to your point of purchase or regular retail for the holidays, or in support of holidays and seasons that occur throughout the year. Stimulate greeting card sales by pointing out upcoming holidays and observances and pre-packaging your gift certificates with seasonal cards. Hold a greeting card design and/or sentiment composition contest. Solicit pictures of handmade cards (such as those made by kids) on your Facebook page.

November 18 – Preaching to the Choir Day

The term "preaching to the choir" is used to describe a situation where one is speaking to a group of already-converted 'believers.' You could liken it to a situation where you have gathered a group of your most loyal customers together—people already engaged with your business on a regular basis who really 'believe in' what you have to offer. They don't need to be persuaded to buy in, they just need to be led to the next level—and they are willing to be led there.

I've personally sung in many choirs, so as I started thinking about the phrase, I thought of more ways to apply it to marketing, especially how the phrase would relate if you replace the word "choir" with the word "employees." Because in the case of your employees, it is more than reasonable to expect that they are all 'believers'—or at least pretend to be! But however much that *should be* true, it is not always so.

Every employee's unique ideas, prejudices, experiences, likes and dislikes impact your employee culture. Just because someone joins your team, it doesn't necessarily mean they have the same level of commitment and enthusiasm you desire or even demonstrate. Even if someone does join your team with a high level of enthusiasm for your business, it still doesn't ensure that they will agree with *your* ideas on how to build your customer base, or even "who" your 'ideal clients' should be! And joining your employee team does not mean they a person will agree with what it is you promise that all your customers will experience in every interaction with your business.

Just as with a choir, differences aren't necessarily a bad thing. After all, not everyone sings tenor or bass or soprano. Nor do choirs all sing the same notes at the same time, or even the same words at the same time. But they do all sing from the same measure of the same page of the same movement of the same score at the same time. Each sings their unique note and word at the right time, so that the whole of the song is produced for the audience.

In the same way, not all of your employees perform the same task at the same time in the same way; but all employee roles are—or should be—designed so that in performing their unique task at the right time to the best of their ability, they are part of the overall production that gives the customer the experience you want them to enjoy each and every time they interact with your business.

Fill your employee 'choir' with people who have diverse abilities so that all the roles necessary to create the desired customer experience can be fulfilled. It's not necessary that everyone think or feel exactly the same; it is, however, vital that everyone sing from the same page. Choir members who fall behind, jump ahead, can't actually sing at all or are singing a whole different tune need to be addressed if they don't realize the problem on their own and self-correct. They may need to be directed to find their place again, might need re-training or reassignment, or might even need to be encouraged to join a different choir.

It's not unreasonable to ask an employee who is not fulfilling the role you need them to play either to choose to 'sing their part' in concert with other employees and according to the 'song' of your vision, mission, tagline, performance expectations and the promises you have made to customers— or to choose to join the 'choir' of a different business where they might be a better fit. If the situation cannot be remedied they may choose to leave, but you may have to fire them because of their choice not to 'sing their part' in your business' choir. Singing out of harmony with your business mission and objectives, being out of rhythm with other employees and their responsibilities and damaging your customer's experience is not acceptable for a choir member, or an employee!

November 19 – Great American Smokeout

Participate in, sponsor and/or promote Great American Smokeout activities held in your community. With just about a month still remaining before New Year Resolutions will be made, this is a great time to connect customers with smoking and habit cessation counselors and resources.

Post links and tips for smoking cessation on your Facebook page, blog and e-mail newsletter. Post statistics about smoking and the harm that it causes; www.quitsmoking.com provides free, reproducible articles and statistics as well as links to resources and support for people who want to quit smoking.

Launch a drive to get as many people as possible to stop smoking beginning now or with the New Year. Host an on-going support group; set incentives and rewards for participants who make it 3, 6, 9, and/or 12 months without smoking. Solicit customer suggestions or stories about how they kicked the habit to share on your Facebook page, blog and e-mail newsletter.

November 20 – Beautiful Day

Hold a Beautiful Holidays open house or holiday fair in conjunction with independent beauty and fashion industry professionals (stylists, makeup artists, boutique clothing retailers) and/or independent sellers of jewelry, party supplies, clothing, accessories, kitchenware, giftware, etc. Invite the customers of all participating businesses (as well as the general public) to attend.

Create holiday party tablescapes and pre-package the items used to create them for bundled sale. Show off holiday fashions, accessories and party hairstyles. Pre-package holiday makeup kits to sell in addition to regular makeup products, nail products, etc. Invite local stylists to provide hair and makeup demonstrations, makeup touch-ups, mini-manicures and pedicures. Provide attendees with step-by-step instruction sheets telling them which products they should purchase and how to recreate the looks at home.

Combine resources with your marketing partners for marketing, communications and the event itself. Put together goodie bags for attendees with branded tchotchkes and samples from all participating businesses. Take videos of demonstrations at the event to be used as podcasts on YouTube and your website. Collect contact information at the event on registration and/or drawing entry forms. After the event, extend a bounce-back offer. Include lists of suggested items for purchase and instructions for recreating decor or looks featured at the event. Create web pages that show videos, examples and provide lists of products needed and step-by-step instructions for recreating at home.

If you want to have a beautiful holiday this year, jump start holiday sales by holding a Holiday Shop in-store or cooperatively in a marketing partner's space. If you can't hold a Holiday Shop, contact local churches and schools to find out about participating in local holiday bazaars. If you participate in an off-site event, be sure that your kiosk features more than just gift card and gift certificate sales. Distribute branded tchotchkes, business cards, menus, contest entry forms for data collection and ads for coming events and promotions. Bring a travel kit and do free demonstrations, consultations and give away samples.

Extend a new-client incentive to entice people to give your services and products a try before the end of December. Make sure all take-away materials and downloadable electronic collateral include your contact information. Merchandise your own business for the holidays from the outside, in. Lure shoppers in through displays and posters visible from windows or doorways. Set up a sandwich board on the sidewalk or in the common area or lobby of your building. Partner and cross-market with other businesses near yours to cooperatively promote holiday offers and events.

Purchase non-traditional items to add to your retail which clients would be likely to buy by themselves or in conjunction with gift cards for holiday or hostess gift-giving like branded, boutique-quality, bling-ed out, holiday-themed or custom-designed t-shirts and tanks, chocolates, candies, wine, candles, interior decor items, holiday dishes, pampering products or services, etc.

Cater to holiday party-goers by partnering with a local transportation business, restaurant and event destinations to create bundled packages. Partner with a local salon or spa so that customers can enjoy a salon makeover or spa service prior to the event. Host a champagne or cocktail hour to get the evening started.

November 21 – World Hello Day

Craft a Thanksgiving message to send to your contacts by e-mail. Reach out personally to clients whom you have not seen in a while, or have not rebooked or returned at their regular frequency.

Man your own doors as a greeter or hire a greeter for the day or even the entire holiday season. If it's getting cold and wintry out, shoppers will appreciate a warm, welcoming greeting, someone to hold the door, walk them to their car with an umbrella, etc. Provide valet parking services on wintry days (or every day). If you already provide valet parking, make this service fee for the day or give away free parking validations with purchase.

Post "hello" in different languages on your Facebook page, blog and e-mail newsletter. Share trivia about various cultural greeting traditions and taboos on your Facebook page, blog and e-mail newsletter.

Say "hello" to new residents in your community by partnering with realtors for cooperative or cross marketing, subscribing to new move in mailing lists from the post office and conducting door hanger campaigns in targeted neighborhoods.

November Week 4
November Week 4 – Long Range Planning Week

Set aside at least one full day this month to create, review, measure or report results relative to the formal long range plan of your business. Set aside time with employees to talk about the mission and goals of your business, get employee buy in and create a blueprint for the coming year. Invite employees to contribute ideas. Put your plan on paper and give copies to a mentor or trusted friend; review progress at least quarterly in the coming year. Invite employees, vendors and/or a marketing professional to review your plan in order to obtain additional resources and expertise. Visit the 'Resources page of www.12monthsofmarketing.com for long range planning resources.

November 22 – Better Conversation Day

Sometimes we use the phrase "a better conversation would be..." to reference the fact that while we are talking about one thing, there is a more important point to be made. In your case, "better conversations" would be those most important and relevant to your customers; because unless what you have to offer is relevant, needed, wanted and understood *by the customer,* the length of your business' life could be short.

Focus conversations with employees on their impact to the customer experience. Keep conversations with suppliers and vendors focused on the needs and desires of your customers. Be sure the conversation you are having with each customer is a two-way conversation (i.e., it's not just you, shouting marketing messages at them). In reality, your marketing messages should be responsive; meaning, you understood, heard, and took to heart precisely what your customers told you they needed or wanted. Your customers spoke, you listened.

If it's been a while since you listened, get a new fix on the needs of your customers with a comprehensive or targeted customer survey. Ask them not only about what they want, but ask customers what they want to know or learn more about. Ask employees about the types of conversations customers are having with them, what they request or ask for that you don't sell, etc.

Perhaps at no time in human history has conversation changed as quickly or drastically as in the recent past; globalization and the advent of entirely new means of communication (instant messaging, texting, etc.) has made some of our conversations nearly incomprehensible as compared to those of previous generations. To help ensure that the art of rich conversation does not become a lost one, partner with a language and conversation expert to hold a workshop on communication and "better conversation" skills. Add books about conversation or books featuring literary, humorous or inspirational quotes to your retail or to give away as contest prizes or a gift-with-purchase.

Put posts with quotes about conversations or rules for conversational etiquette on your Facebook page, blog, bag stuffers and e-mail newsletter. Use social media, e-mail and in-store polls and surveys to solicit customer and employee feedback and opinion on a regular basis. Report results as well as any changes made as a result of their feedback.

November 23 – National Cashew Day

Partner with a local candy and nut store, gourmet grocer or another vendor to provide cashew or cashew-containing samples to customers. Add branded or gourmet cashews to your retail or to give away as contest prizes or a gift-with-purchase. Hold a customer recipe contest (requiring use of cashews) or solicit cooking, snack and dessert recipes. Compile recipes into an online cookbook or create a print version for retail sale, contest prizes or a gift-with-purchase. Hold a tasting or happy hour featuring cashews. Post information about nutrition benefits, uses for and trivia/history of cashews on Facebook.

November 24 – Celebrate Your Unique Talent Day

We touched on the idea of the Unique Selling Proposition in the entry for October 24 – Make a Difference Day, but this is one of those "better conversations" you should be engaging in with all customers and prospects, at all customer touchpoints. Why? Because for nearly everything they want or need to purchase, your customers and prospects have choices—sometimes they have dozens or even hundreds of other choices when it comes to purchasing the same products or services you provide.

Take coffee, for example.

As an unrepentant addict (I blame it on my Scandinavian heritage) requiring at least one and usually two venti mochas (with a splash of hazelnut) daily, I have my local favorites when it comes to purchasing coffee drinks, but when I travel, I always go to Starbucks. Why? Because I know exactly what the mocha will taste like every time and how to order it (non-fat no-whip two-pump venti mocha) to my own preference.

Let's say that you sell coffee, but you are (unfortunately) located within a block or two of a Starbucks or another business that is better known than yours and which has a loyal customer following and good reputation. How will you compete?

Something about your business has to be different and better than the competition in such a way that it provides a compelling decision-maker to the customer. And (here comes the marketing part) you have to find a way to communicate that compelling point of difference to your customers (to turn them into more loyal followers) and to prospects (to get them to try your products).

Chances are you already have an idea about what sets your business apart from competitors. (Please don't say, "it's our people"—every company says their people "set them apart"—it's cliché. What's more, it's an irrelevant truth; every company has it's own unique blend of people who possess unique experience, education and talents. Every company is therefore 'different' due to their employees. Plus, let's say you have a 'bad egg' among your employees or one of your usually-stellar employees is having a really bad day. By telling customers it's your employees that set you apart, you have just told them that the bad experience they had with your business today is characteristic of the experience they can expect to have with all your employees and in every interaction with your business.

While it's not your employees who set you apart, it may very well be the level of customer service or types of services they have the ability to provide. For instance, do you provide delivery service? Call, e-mail, web or text-ahead ordering? Do you provide employees with specialized customer service training or do they sign off on and adhere to a customer bill-of-rights? Having employees doesn't set you apart; the services those employees provide, and the way in which they provide them, had better!

Or maybe it's the coffee you use; is it fair trade, sustainable crop management, refined in a unique way, processed by your barista in a unique way or a different kind of brewing process? What benefits does the coffee you use or your process provide? Lower acidity? More flavor? Environmental benefits? These are all very different types of benefits that would appeal to different types of customers; so, knowing your unique selling proposition (USP) can also help you to identify the ideal types of customers that should be on the receiving end of most of your marketing efforts and resources.

For instance, my mom has acid reflux; nevertheless, coffee is one of her indulgences and something that she does not want to have to completely eliminate from her diet. Several other people among my family and friends have conditions which cause digestive problems due to acid; knowing that a certain kind of coffee or a certain brewing process offers them the ability to continue to enjoy something they love, while also reducing the chance that their body will hate them for drinking it, is a point of difference worth talking about. On the other hand, other people I know would be far more interested in knowing that you only buy coffee from growers who practice fair employment and pay practices and as-green-as-possible growing and sustainability.

Two very different target markets, two very different messages. You need to know what sets you apart so that you can leverage your USP to competitive advantage and so that you can more efficiently pursue those individuals who truly represent your ideal customer types and/or target markets.

Not sure what really sets your business apart? your Unique Selling Proposition (USP) should answer this question: How does my business benefit *my* customers better than anyone else can? The exercises below can help you answer that question (or at least get you closer!)

1. What problem/s does my business solve? What do you (literally) provide to customers/ clients; and, what all do you offer?

2. What types of people do you believe make up your target market?

3. What types of characteristics would you use to describe your ideal client? (And does this correlate, or where does it cross over, with your answer to question #2 above?) What would they care about? What kind of lifestyles, professions, interests, hobbies, etc. would they be most likely to enjoy?

4. What promise/s do you make to your customers? What is your tagline or slogan?

By analyzing and combining the answers to these questions into one or two summary statements, you should have some idea of what your true corporate points of difference are.

More? Now that you have a good idea of your real unique selling proposition, answer this question: If you could do anything at all to change, expand or improve your business, what would you *want* your USP to be? What would it take to get there?

To help people observe *November 24 – Celebrate your Unique Talent Day*, work with businesses near yours, members of your Chamber of Commerce and/or your marketing partners to hold a community-wide unique talent show. Solicit photos, videos or stories about your customers unique talents on Facebook. Post links to videos, articles about people with unique or weird talents, a list of your and your employees weirdest talents, etc. on your Facebook page, blog and e-mail newsletter.

Partner with local dance, music, gymnastics, golf or other sport instructors and studios for cross or cooperative marketing, to hold a workshop or to provide free introductory lessons for customers.

November 25 – Shopping Reminder Day

Although technically officially observed annually on November 26th, I suggest that you make the Wednesday or Monday before Thanksgiving 'Shopping Reminder Day' for your business. Put your business back into the spotlight in the customer's mind when it comes to holiday shopping.

If your business is not the type of business traditionally viewed as a resource for holiday gifts, you should be continually working to create awareness about the great gift options you offer for holidays and throughout the year. And hopefully you, yourself, are developing a mindset beyond the products or services you typically sell in order to expand and add variety to your retail. Becoming a true gift resource for clients will mean more frequent client visits, more gift card sales and more referrals. Build a bigger role for your business in the lives of your clients!

Create promotional collateral featuring shopping lists that make specific gift suggestions for parents, grandparents, children, teachers, coaches, friends, co-workers, hostess gifts, etc. Mail them as direct mail pieces, distribute them at your entry and post them in a downloadable format online so that customers can print them from e-mail, your website, blog or Facebook page and return to your business to pick up the items suggested and/or to redeem an associated offer, gift-with-purchase, add-on (such as a free $20 gift card with purchase of a $100 gift card for someone else) identified by coupon or code word on these lists.

Set up customer e-mail reminders for Black Friday (the day after Thanksgiving) and Cyber Monday (the Monday after Thanksgiving) promotions. In the weeks before Thanksgiving, put sneak previews for Black Friday, Cyber Monday and holiday promotions on your Facebook page, blog, website and e-mail newsletter.

November 26 – The 4th Thursday in November is Thanksgiving

Take time to reflect on all of the good people and blessings in your life. I have come to the conclusion that achieving 'happiness' in life may be as simple as choosing to live in a spirit of gratitude. You can choose to spend most of your time and energy worried and focused on past, present or potential problems, or you can spend most if not all of your time and energy enthusiastically envisioning the future you desire, focused on taking the next step of the plan in pursuit of your dreams.

Partner with a party planner, caterer or restaurant to provide customers with catering, take out or dining options for Thanksgiving in order to leave people free to simply enjoy their time with family and friends. Or hold an employee Thanksgiving Dinner party now, in lieu of a holiday party in December when people are likely to be extra-busy with activities, concerts, and school and family events.

Partner with a caterer and party planner to hold a class on throwing perfect football parties or other sports-related social gatherings including recipes/food planning, table setting, décor, etc. Sell Thanksgiving or football party supply kits. Hold an event at a local sports bar for customers and/or employees to enjoy Thanksgiving Day football games. Hold a post-game happy hour for those who want to extend the day's social celebrating.

November 27 – Black Friday is the Friday after Thanksgiving

Create compelling, one-day-only offers for Black Friday if you hope to attract deal-hungry shoppers. Give customers get a preview of your deals during the 1-2 weeks prior to Thanksgiving in signage, direct mail flyers, e-mail newsletters, and on your blog and Facebook page.

Create options to help speed customers in and out more quickly on Black Friday, such as take-out, pre-shopped items for pickup, text, e-mail or fax ordering options or even delivery or shipping options. Or position your business for afternoon or evening patronage by marketing your business as the last stop for weary shoppers—a place where they can slow down, relax, enjoy refreshments and experience either a soothing place to unwind and put their feet up or enjoy some kind of entertainment for the evening with friends or family.

November 28 – Toy Drive Day

Become a corporate sponsor or designated point of donation for the US Marine Corp's "Toys for Tots" campaign (www.toysfortots.org). Use Facebook, your blog, bag stuffers and e-mail newsletter to help raise awareness, tell customers about needs in your community, invite donations of toys or cash and report results. Write a press release to tell the public and local media about the difference your campaign made to the local community, to help raise additional awareness and to generate enthusiasm for next year's campaign or your next charity initiative.

November 29 – Inspirational Role Model Day

Take nominations of local "Inspirational Role Models" and select or draw a winner to receive a free gift card, prize package, etc. Put posts about nominees, finalists and the winner on your Facebook page, blog and e-mail newsletter. Write a press release and set up an in-store display to honor the winner as well as some of the most notable nominees.

Establish an intern or apprenticeship program for employees. Invite students from local high schools or colleges to participate in a day in the life of your business. Make a video or PowerPoint presentation about your industry, your business or your life story which can be shared online, featured on your website or used in seminars or workshops.

November 30 – Cyber Monday is the Monday after Thanksgiving

Make every Monday a Cyber Monday—use your website, Facebook, Twitter, text messaging and/or e-mail marketing every Monday during the holiday season (if not all year) to let clients know about holiday specials, gift giving ideas, open appointments, charitable drives, etc. Populate electronic communications with holiday party ideas, quick and easy recipes, holiday tablescapes, fashion, style and makeup looks, tips and tricks, photos showing holiday indoor and outdoor decorating, etc.

Make Cyber Monday part of your marketing habit and utilize technology on Mondays throughout the year to extend cyber offers and information to your readers. Update your blog with a new post every Monday and share the article link on Facebook, Twitter, LinkedIn and other social media sites. Set aside 30 minutes every Monday to read marketing, management and leadership blogs or articles to further your own development and get inspiration and ideas. Create personal cyber habits that will help maximize your marketing outreach and more deeply engage your customers and prospects.

december

365 Days of Marketing

December Month-Long Observances
Bingo Month

Hold a bingo-style contest based on purchase of specific items or create a bingo-styled rewards card. Bundle a set of 5 products at a special price or reward clients for every 5 products, services, combination of products or services, etc. they purchase in December.

Conduct a "Bingo" campaign in conjunction with partnering businesses where customers receive a free gift or entry in a bundled prize package drawing if they visit each of the businesses featured on a card or flyer. (Credit for this idea goes to my friend Celia Bender, a self-employed marketing and design genius, who employed this contest as part of a regional 'Buy Local' campaign in Enumclaw, Washington.) Make sure the information from all drawing entries is entered into your contact database and that each receives a special offer in the New Year.

Many bingo-loving seniors may feel lonely or left out this time of year. Partner with a local senior center to sponsor a Bingo Tournament. Enlist the help of your marketing partners to create prizes designed to bring seniors into your business and those of your marketing partners for redemption. Or hold a bingo tournament at your business (or at that of one of your marketing partners) for youth or senior groups.

Write a Business Plan Month

There are many good reasons to develop a business plan and engage in formal long range planning, annually—regardless of what type of business you own. You will need a business plan to attract investors or get funding, grants or bank loans. You may even need a business plan in order to work with manufacturers or vendors that limit themselves to partnering with select organizations. Your business plan may help you entice influential industry leaders or key executives to become part of your team. Following are some of the components common to traditional business plans, and which you should review annually as part of your long range planning process:

1. **Executive Summary:** Although listed first, you will probably write this last. The executive summary is just that—a summary of everything in the business plan itself. It should be optimistic and bold, but also realistic. You want potential investors, banks, vendors and your team members to be confident, but you don't want to set people up with false expectations or appear as though you are not grounded in reality.

2. **Vision Statement:** What your organization ultimately aspires to become. Your vision should resonate with customers and employees and make those connected to your business feel proud, excited and that they are part of something bigger than themselves. It is the good that your company will ultimately provide to the world. It explains why you are doing what you are doing and the good you want to achieve through your success.

3. **Mission Statement:** A definition of why you (deserve to) exist. Your mission statement should provide a precise description of what you do and describe the business you are in. Your mission statement tells your employees how their roles help to fulfill the vision. Your mission statement is the route you will follow and/or the means by which you expect to achieve your vision.

4. **Company Description**
   a. The history, present state and future of the company
   b. Description of products and services
   c. Description of current customer demographics

5. **Marketing Plan**
   a. Overview of your Industry as a whole
   b. Identification of target market/s
   c. Analysis of direct and indirect competitors
   d. Your Unique Selling Proposition (USP) or point of difference

6. **Operations and Management:** How your business operates; the departments, your organizational chart including both positions and main responsibilities, description of key team members, annual/seasonal schedules, reporting cycles, etc.

7. **Financial Statements, Financial Plan and Projections**

8. **Appendix of Supporting Documents**

Write a Friend Month

Purchase blank greeting cards, holiday cards or boxed sets of stationery and note cards for retail sale. Add a holiday greeting card display to your point of purchase or retail with one-of-a-kind cards that clients cannot find anywhere else.

Purchase or design a corporate holiday card to send to customers. Express appreciation for their patronage and extend best wishes for the new year. Sign each personally. Include a business card and a special holiday or New Year offer. Capture this moment in the life of your business with an all-employee photo and create beautiful, zany, or otherwise one-of-a-kind holiday greeting cards for use in e-mail or electronic greetings, on your website, as a printed greeting card and/or in advertising during the holiday season.

If your client gift budget is $0, you can still give a meaningful gift to everyone on your list, including clients and staff. In 2009, inspired by a popular religious book, my friend Dawn Taylor (owner of Salon Bella Dea in Auburn, WA) wrote a personal letter and sent it to all of her clients telling them how they have impacted her life over the years. She thanked them not only for their business, but also thanked those clients who knew her parents and had prayed for her mom while she was battling cancer, for all she feels her clients teach her and how much she appreciates their trust.

Dawn said that the idea was to tell people what she would tell them if she knew she had only a short time left to do so—without being morbid, the result was a letter written to people telling them they have impacted her life in ways they might not even know and to inspire them to continue to make a personal difference in the lives of others when they can. The gift she gave away nearly free, but priceless!

December Week 1

December 1 – Day With(out) Art

Remind customers how important the arts are to our society and civilization. Partner with a local art instructor or studio to hold an introductory class or workshop for your customers. Hold on-going specialty art classes at your business or in partnership with a local studio. Feature the work of local artists in displays at your business or by links on Facebook, your website, blog and e-mail newsletter.

Posts for Facebook/social media, Blog, E-mail, Bag Stuffers and/or Website:
- The history of the arts
- Links to the work of local artists
- Highlight local school arts programs, achievements and instructors
- Connect customers with local music, dance and art studios, instructors and performing groups
- Create a directory or community resources page on your website where local music, dance and art teachers can promote their services, events and specialties

Partner with a party planner to provide gift-wrapping instructions, tips or ideas on a flyer/brochure, in posts on Facebook, your blog and e-mail newsletter, or to hold a gift-wrapping class. Solicit gift wrapping photos on Facebook or post links to beautifully-wrapped gifts. Hold gift wrapping contests based on appearance and/or speed.

December 2 – Dice Month

Hold a happy hour featuring Bunco or other dice games; I found a long list of dice games and playing instructions at http://en.wikipedia.org/wiki/Dice_games.

One simple game you can play with 6 dice is called "6 x 6" (Six by Six). The object is to roll as many sixes as possible with the six dice in consecutive rolls. A player rolls all six dice at once and you keep track of how many sixes came up on that roll, then they roll all six dice again, and you add those sixes to the first roll. The player keeps rolling and keeps accumulating sixes until they roll all six dice and no sixes come up. The winner is the player with the most total sixes rolled in consecutive tries. If you have a tie, have roll-off rounds to determine the winner.

Design a dice game unique to your business to hold at the point of purchase to determine whether a customer will receive extra reward points, a chance at a special prize drawing, a free add-on, a gift card, a branded tchotchke, a set of branded dice, playing cards or a board game, etc.

Add branded dice to your point of purchase, games or other retail display. Purchase large "fuzzy dice" to add to gift wares or give away as contest prizes or a gift-with-purchase.

December 3 – Roof over Your Head Day

We often think that we need to go outside of our own resources or come up with a genius new idea in order to stimulate sales. Often we overlook simple and obvious ways to grow that are (literally) right over our heads. Here are 8 ways to use the roof over your head to build business:

- Does your business share a roof (in a mall, business park, etc.) with other businesses? Partner with these businesses to hold a special holiday open house or sale event.
- Exchange and display the website links of the businesses with which you share a roof on your website, blog, Facebook page, in your e-mail newsletters, etc.
- Extend special offers to the employees who work in businesses near yours
- Extend your own employee discount to the employees of local businesses for a limited time.
- Create offers to extend to the customers of businesses that share a roof with you and ask them to display your offers, hand out your bag stuffers, or include your offers in their mailings, newsletters, on their websites, etc.
- Extend offers to the landlord and/or all employees of the management company that owns your building, parking lot, business park, neighboring businesses, etc.
- Partner with local roofing, construction, and home renovation businesses for cooperative or cross marketing.
- Partner with local home repair or renovation professionals to hold a special 'how to' class or workshop for your clients on a particular do-it-yourself project (or hold a series of classes).

December 4 – Santa's List Day

Feature your business as a location where children can drop off letters to Santa in November and December on Facebook, your blog, website and e-mail newsletter as well as signage in your business. Provide a decorated mail box and when children drop off a letter for Santa, give each a candy cane or branded yo-yo, hacky sack, watch or another toy (along with a bounce-back offer for mom and dad).

Create "Santa's List" marketing messages keying in on themes like naughty or nice or that begin with a phrase such as "Santa called, and this is what he said…" Or create personalized shopping checklists for naughty and for nice people.

Purchase branded Santa or Elf hats for employees to wear and/or to sell or give away as a gift-with-purchase. Hire a Santa for the month or hold a special event featuring kids activities, games, toys and an appearance from Santa.

'Adopt' a local needy family (preserving their privacy) and as staff, donate a day of proceeds or have staff or clients donate items needed to help this family have a "Merry Christmas." Be "Santa" to a local needy individual or family by giving them the gift of a year's worth of a product or service in the New Year, a shopping spree, gift cards from your business and those of your marketing partners, etc.

Say thank you and extend holiday greetings to your most valuable clients in some way. Extend your brand beyond your walls by gifting branded travel mugs, t-shirts or tank tops, unique nail files or other fun, buzz-worthy, low-cost items. Sell some, too!

December 5 – Bathtub Party Day

Create a Bathtub Party gift set or purchase boutique-quality or branded bath and personal items (towels, robes, bubble bath, room sprays, personal fragrances, scented candles, etc.) for retail sale, to give away as contest prizes or a gift-with-purchase, as gifts for staff, vendors, your landlord, etc.

Purchase boutique, guest-quality hand towels to be given as client gifts, gift-with-purchase or for retail sale along with branded hand sanitizers, hand soap, boutique soap dispensers or soap dishes, scented candles or incense burners, etc. Use branded towels, hand towels and napkins in the course of services provided at your business, for cleaning, in rest rooms, at hospitality stations, etc.

Partner with a hot tub/spa seller for cross or cooperative marketing. Recommend hot tub-related products to their clients (and yours) and create an offer to extend to their customers.

December 6 – Mitten Tree Day

Set up a "Mitten Tree" and decorate it with customer-donated mittens, hats, coats and other cold weather gear to be given to a local charity, social services organization or a needy family. Partner with a charity or social service organization to host a "Giving Tree" where clients can choose to purchase specific items to donate to local needy children or a family. Write a press release to publicize efforts and help solicit donations. Thank those who donate with gift cards, products, samples, free add-ons, branded tchotchkes and/or bounce-back offers.

Purchase unique, boutique-quality cold weather gear like scarves, hats, gloves, umbrellas or other accessories to add to holiday/impulse-buy retail offerings. Purchase branded cold weather accessories like scarves, beanie hats or headbands for retail sale or to give away as a gift-with-purchase, contest prize or employee gift.

December 7 – Pearl Harbor Day

The term "the greatest generation" was coined by Tom Brokaw to describe the generation of people that grew up during the great depression and whose members fought in World War II. This generation grew up in a time of incredible and sometimes even painful want, yet had the backbone and determination to face and overcome some of the most difficult challenges imaginable. Pearl Harbor Day is the perfect day to honor "the greatest generation" for the sacrifices they made, for their wisdom and for the much of the prosperity we have enjoyed in generations since.

Famous members of this generation include people like John F. Kennedy, Robert Kennedy, George H.W. Bush, Walter Cronkite, Joe DiMaggio, Billy Graham, Charles Schultz, Ronald Reagan, Jackie Robinson, and many more who went on to make major contributions in shaping the world and our society as we know it.

Honor members of "the greatest generation" by soliciting stories and nominations of local individuals who are members of this generation, holding an open house, extending dedicated happy hours or shopping hours, giving special awards or honors or by extending a special offer or free gift to them.

In recent years many reports and articles have been written as to the characteristics of different generations, how to market to them, how to manage them as employees, etc. At a minimum, you should be familiar with the general breakdown:

- **The Greatest Generation:** Born between about 1909 and 1942, they've seen it all when it comes to advertising. They are savvy consumers who are careful about who they do business with. They want to know more about your business *and about you*, before doing business with you. Keen on value, they don't shop just for fun. Having spent their early years in the Great Depression, they try not to waste anything if they can help it.

- **Baby Boomers:** Born from about 1943 and 1965, on average this generation outspends other generations by $400 billion per year. They have exceptional drive and the ability to evaluate (and see through) advertising to find out whether something has real value. This group is projected to grow to represent as much as 20% of the total population by 2030.

- **Generation X:** Born between about 1965 and 1980, a somewhat overlooked generation whose members are now entering/in their peak earning and buying years. Generally very tech savvy, they love to shop. They put a high value on education and knowledge. Prestige is a draw for this generation, but value trumps labels.

- **Generation Y:** Born from about 1981 and 1990, the children of Baby Boomers, many members of this generation lived longer at home than did previous generations. Tech savvy, Gen Y members process information quickly and tend to be brand loyal.

- **Gen Z or the Internet Generation:** Born between 2000 – present, the children of the youngest Baby Boomers. The only generation to be born fully in the internet era and the only generation whose parents are also (generally) more accepting of technology.

For more information about national and regional demographics, visit www.census.gov.

December Week 2

December 8 – National Brownie Day

Partner with local candy stores, restaurants, caterers and bakeries for cross or cooperative marketing. Invite a marketing partner to provide free samples or brownies to customers while shopping, at appointments or for dessert. With marketing partners or on your own, hold a brownie making contest for customers, hold a brownie eating contest or hold a tasting or happy hour featuring brownies.

Posts for Facebook/social media, Blog, E-mail, Bag Stuffers and/or Website:
- Solicit customers best recipe or cooking tips
- Post links to celebrity or celebrity chef recipes
- Post history or brownie-related trivia

Add wrapped single brownies to impulse buy offerings or add brownie pans, pot holders, mixing bowls, aprons, spatulas, etc. to retail. Develop your own unique brownie recipe to share with customers or create a brownie mix for retail sale or to be part of a gift basket for contest prize, a holiday client gift or given away as a gift-with-purchase.

December 9 – Christmas Card Day

Send a Christmas greeting card to your customers. Have a group photo taken of your employees during the holidays each year for holiday card use, to be displayed at your business and to help photo-document the life of your company. Post a holiday greeting or New Year wish, quote or sentiment on your Facebook page and blog every day between now and the New Year. Post holiday entertaining and party ideas and trivia about holiday traditions on your Facebook page, blog and e-mail newsletter. Solicit and share customer and employee holiday stories, family traditions and customs.

Add custom-designed or boutique-quality holiday greeting cards, gift tags and wrapping paper to your retail during the holidays. Create your own line of cards for holiday gift-giving which coordinate with your business' gift cards or gift certificates. Partner with a local stationer or handmade card artist to create displays featuring one-of-a-kind seasonal greeting cards, gift tags, gift bags or wrapping paper and supplies to sell throughout the year.

December 10 – Cookie Cutter Day

Partner with an independent kitchenware seller for cross or cooperative marketing. Purchase unique cookie cutters to sell during the holiday season. Purchase boutique-quality or branded cookie cutters to use as ornaments for your holiday tree and/or to give away as a client thank-you gift or a gift-with-purchase in December. Post links to local resources for kitchen wares including cookie cutters and/or to custom-made cookies on your Facebook page, blog and e-mail newsletter. Hold a cookie baking or decorating contest.

Collect and share the favorite holiday cookie recipes of employees and customers on your Facebook page, blog, bag stuffers and e-mail newsletter. Post cookie cutter trivia, history, or ideas for alternate uses for cookie cutters. Compile cookie recipes to share with customers during the holidays or add them to the marketing cookbook or calendar you will have printed for gift or sale in the new year.

Tell your customers why yours is not just another "cookie cutter" company by identifying and highlighting your Unique Selling Proposition (USP) in your marketing. Tell customers about how your products and services are different and better than those of competitors. Talk about the strong points of your customer service, business processes, facility and the strengths of your employees. Talk about your mission, vision and values and the benefits your business provides in terms of jobs, benefiting others in the community, boosting the local economy, etc.

December 11 – Cotton Candy Day

Partner with a party and equipment rental company for cross and cooperative marketing. Rent a cotton candy machine to give customers cotton candy at your business or a branded bag to take home. Post cotton candy trivia, history or recipes on your Facebook page or e-mail newsletter.

December 12 – Poinsettia Day

Send a poinsettia or another holiday floral arrangement to a local senior center, school, charity or church. Send poinsettias to thank your most valuable clients, employees, vendors, marketing and event partners, etc. Partner with local florists and nurseries for cross marketing, and/or sell miniature poinsettias in your store during the holidays.

December 13 – The 2nd Sunday in December is International Children's Day

Host a holiday party for children or provide kids with activity pages to color, games to play, branded toys or treats on December 13th (or during the entire month of December). Sponsor a party at your business for a local youth services organization, club, day care or church youth group.

Hold a benefit event or donate a portion of sales to a local children's charity, local children's hospital or another youth organization. Use your Facebook page, blog and e-mail newsletter to raise awareness of local children's charities and holiday needs.

December 14 – Recipe Greetings for the Holidays

Design (print or e-mail) corporate greeting cards that feature a favorite holiday recipe, a complete perfect holiday party or dinner menu, recipes of local chefs or recommendations of great local holiday party catering or restaurant fare. Weave in gift, tableware, catering, décor, beauty, fashion and style or other suggestions from among the products or services you sell.

Posts for Facebook/social media, Blog, E-mail, Bag Stuffers and/or Website:
- Solicit customers favorite holiday recipes for parties, Christmas Dinner, New Year's Eve, etc.
- Share your and/or employee recipes for holiday appetizers, dinners, eggnog, cocktails, etc.
- Share and/or solicit sugar cookie recipes and/or photos of decorated cookies
- Share and/or solicit party table setting and décor ideas and photographs
- Solicit pictures of customers' events, décor and table settings/food
- Suggest wine, appetizers, desserts or other pairings
- Post links to pictures of professional or celebrity holiday décor, table setting, food presentation, etc.

December Week 3
December 15 – Cat Herders Day

Cat Herder's Day was created by a couple in California (who have established several other whimsical observances) in order to draw attention and honor to individuals whose responsibility it is to manage almost impossible tasks—like herding cats. While I did not speak to any actual cat herders for the writing of this entry, one might surmise that two aspects of their job which could be very frustrating is that they don't always see the results of their work and that 'herdees' won't always be herd-ed.

What about you? Do you give up on new initiatives, policies or changes that you want to make In your business due to lack of immediate gratification or when you encounter employee opposition or lack of enthusiasm?

I don't know about "cat drives" but if you've ever watched any old Westerns, you know that cattle drives were undertaken by a small handful of 'cowhands' usually supported by no more than a cook driving a supplies wagon. They covered long distances and endured hardships, deprivation, threat of theft, risk of loss and even risk to life and limb. In the movies, opposition almost always came from 'the competition' (people trying to steal cattle or people trying to stop the drive in order to put the rancher out of business) but sometimes even came from within in the form of disgruntled, dishonest and sometimes even traitorous staff.

Sound familiar? If you have been in business for very long, you can probably tell some stories that correlate to these scenarios.

The point is, don't give up. Don't give up on changes that need to happen within your business. Don't stop trying to get employee buy in; but by the same measure, be alert so that you won't be caught unawares if an employee is doing damage to your customer relationships, to employee morale or is demonstrating opposition to your policies or campaigns. Reward behavior you want more of. Let employees who demonstrate a lack of understanding or lack of commitment to your business know that they must make a choice, either to become an effective, enthusiastic and productive part of the team or to leave, with your blessing.

Hire strategically and put as much weight on character, integrity, enthusiasm and personality as you do on relevant experience, or at least let those traits tip the scales between candidates when all else is more or less equal. And once hired, invest in training for your employees. Be sure your employee orientation and annual training provides for the review of your corporate vision, mission and goals and how each employee role contributes to them.

December 16 – Chocolate-Covered Anything Day

Partner with candy stores, chocolatiers, grocers, caterers, etc. for cross or cooperative marketing. With marketing partners or on your own, hold a contest for blind-folded contestants to guess the content of various fruits and/or nuts covered with chocolate. Hold a chocolate-covered anything happy hour complete with themed treats and beverages.

Solicit customers best chocolate covered anything recipes on Facebook. Share recipes and presentation ideas (such as for pretzel bouquets) on your Facebook page, blog and e-mail newsletter. Connect customers with local chocolatiers or chocolate covered gift ideas for the holidays in a directory or posts on Facebook, your blog and e-mail newsletter.

December 17 – Cut Out Snowflakes Day

Partner with craft, hobby and stationery stores and specialty paper providers for cross or cooperative marketing. Partner with a local stationer, craft or hobby store and add specialty gift, craft and letter-writing paper to retail during the holidays or on an on-going basis.

Hold a snowflake cutting or full-blown origami exhibition or workshop. Have a contest for children; following the contest, ask children to sign their snowflakes to be sent as greeting cards to a local nursing home, senior center, to a local children's hospital or cancer treatment center, overseas to soldiers, etc.

Posts links to snowflake cut-out patterns or decorating idea sites on your Facebook page, blog and e-mail newsletter. Solicit customer pictures of homemade snowflakes. Hold a cut-out snowflake contest for kids or adults; post contest results and pictures online.

Use large, cut-out snowflakes to decorate your windows, walls, shelving or to hang from the ceiling to create an indoor winter wonderland in your business.

December 18 – Bake Cookies Day

Partner with bakeries, caterers, restaurants and specialty cupcake and cookie stores for cross or cooperative marketing. Partner with a local caterer or bakery to provide cookie samples for customers. Give gourmet cookie gift packs to your staff, VIP clientele, vendors, marketing partners, local charities, employees at city hall, the staff and teachers of local schools, etc.

Purchase pre-wrapped snack cookies or specialty cookies from a local store to sell during the holidays or to offer to clients during appointments. Use cookie-fragranced candles, incense or room sprays to create the illusion of fresh-baked cookies in your business. Add cookie-fragranced candles, room sprays or air fresheners to your seasonal or regular retail. Purchase cookie-scented items to give as a client gift or gift-with-purchase in December.

Work with a nutritionist to compile a collection of healthy cookie recipes and ingredient substitutes so that clients don't have to choose between indulgence and their health or waistline during the holidays. Hold a healthy baking workshop. Include cookie nutrition tips on bag stuffers, blog and Facebook posts and in your e-mail newsletter.

Hold a cookie-making contest, tasting or happy hour. Share recipes with customers and solicit their favorite holiday cookie recipes, decorating tips and photographs on Facebook.

December 19 – (Look for an) Evergreen Day

Partner with local Christmas tree sellers for cross or cooperative marketing. Provide them with samples or a gift certificate redeemable in your business to give tree buyers as a gift-with-purchase. Purchase branded ornaments as customer or employee gifts. Add unusual or unique ornaments to retail to enhance holiday/impulse sales, to promote as hostess gifts or to give away as a gift-with-purchase. Create your own design featuring your business name, logo or the current year (such as "2011") for retail sale as the first in a series; each year, release a new ornament as a collector's item.

Purchase live tree starts from a local nursery to give away at an event or as a gift-with-purchase.

December 20 – Go Caroling Day

If you or your employees love to sing, go caroling together! Take your holiday entourage on the road to brighten the season for businesses located near yours, the businesses of your marketing partners, area nursing homes or sing as a "flash mob" caroling performance in a mall or another public venue.

Invite choirs from local schools, private schools or churches to sing at your business as part of a community-wide choral holiday fair or on weekend or evening times during the holiday season.

December 21 – Winter Solstice

Just the opposite of its June 21st Summer Solstice counterpart, by definition, this is the day with the shortest amount of daylight in the northern hemisphere—which makes it a great day to hold events characterized by cheer and sunshine! Replace outdated fluorescent fixtures with more efficient, modern or natural lighting, skylights, more windows, etc. Set up a natural light display or add natural light lamps or bulbs to your retail.

Partner with a local bar or restaurant and hold a well-lit winter solstice happy hour. Have a natural sunlight party featuring products or services that provide natural lighting, contain vitamin D or have characteristics representative of other sunshine-related benefits. Purchase branded LED flashlights for retail or to give away as contest prizes or a gift-with-purchase. Add specialty flashlights or light up toys to retail as stocking stuffer gift items.

December Week 4

December 22 – Holiday Makeover Day

Partner with a local salon, stylist, makeup esthetician and/or independent makeup seller to hold a drawing for holiday makeover services. Partner with a personal organizer, housecleaning professional and/or home decorator for a home holiday makeover drawing. Partner with a party planner or home decorator to hold a workshop on making over the home for the holidays, how to make over the table for holiday dinners or parties, etc.

Plan activities to hold during the week between Christmas and New Year's Day like kids activities and/or games or family, seniors, couples, singles, etc. game nights. Hold a happy hour or a New Year's Eve party. Hold a New Year's Eve or post-Christmas party with your employees or hold a larger party including the employees of your marketing partners, businesses located near yours, fellow members of your Chamber of Commerce, etc.

December 23 – Eggnog Day

Sample or sell eggnog. Hold an eggnog recipe contest or solicit recipes to share on Facebook, your blog, e-mail newsletter and bag stuffers. Post links to eggnog recipes of local chefs or celebrities. Hold an eggnog happy hour to celebrate the eve of Christmas Eve (December 23).

December 24 – Christmas Eve and December 25 – Christmas Day

Send a corporate electronic greeting card or dedicated e-mail to your customers, vendors, etc., wishing them and their families a happy holiday. Write your own Christmas wish or sentiment. Tell people—employees, vendors, customers, etc.—how important they are to you and to your business. Express gratitude for their patronage, loyalty and referrals.

December 26 – Thank-You Note Day

Don't procrastinate, get right on it! Write thank-you notes to vendors, employees, marketing partners, landlord, businesses located near yours and customers who gave you a gift, or to whom you wish to extend a special, personal thank you before the end of the year.

Add custom-designed, clever, funny, beautiful or otherwise one-of-a-kind thank-you notes and blank note cards to your retail. Create a special design for the holiday season to promote as coordinated greeting, gift and thank-you note card sets. Post a display sheet with ideas for thank-you note scripts near your greeting card display and on your Facebook page, blog and e-mail newsletter (along with the suggestion that they purchase your custom-designed cards for thank-you note writing!)

December 27 – Re-Gifting Day

Purchase branded items like hats, t-shirts, tank tops, notebooks, totes and other wares and offer to let customers exchange unwanted gifts for them.

Solicit and share stories about bad gifts (or great ones) on your Facebook page, blog and e-mail newsletter. Ask customers to tell you about the most meaningful gifts they have given or received. Post trivia about bad gifts in history. Talk about your return policy and post etiquette or guidelines for making returns. Post creative ideas for re-gifting of unwanted items.

Tell customers about what types of gift items, New Year Resolution helpers or other products or services will be coming to your business in the New Year on your Facebook page, blog, website, bag stuffers and e-mail newsletter. Take pre-orders or reservations for items that will be available for sale in January.

December 28 – Card Playing Day

On your own or with marketing partners, hold a card game tournament or happy hour. Add branded decks of cards to your retail or to give away as contest prizes, client gifts or a gift-with-purchase. Add custom-designed playing cards featuring the year of the New Year (such as "2012") for seasonal retail sale. Post links to instructions for card games that families or friends can play at home on your Facebook page, blog and e-mail newsletter.

Hold a contest for customers to see who can bring in the largest quantity of holiday cards received that year, for the most unique card received, for the ugliest card received, etc.

December 29 – Tick Tock Day

The New Year is coming! Make up your mind as a business owner to analyze your business from a client-experience point of view. Obtain resources and support for renewal and re-energizing, both for yourself personally and for your business. Create a plan to help support staff development in technical as well as personal areas.

Map out a plan for next year's marketing, promotional, charitable and other initiatives. Create a list of businesses with which you want to partner, and a list of businesses/organizations to which you want to extend special employee or patron offers in the New Year.

Partner with fitness, nutrition and weight loss experts, motivational speakers, counselors, coaches, organizers and other professionals for cross and cooperative marketing in order to connect your clients with more resources in their community. Compile an online directory to share on your website, Facebook page, blog and e-mail newsletter. Establish support groups to help people meet New Year Resolutions and goals.

December 30 – Out with the Old, In with the New

Take some time to evaluate the past year and make professional as well as personal New Year Resolutions for the coming year. You may be planning to start or expand your business, become an educator, provide consulting services, enter a competition, publish your work, expand your product or service lines, or it might be time to update your pricing.

No matter what your goals, putting them on paper and noting the incremental steps you need to take in order to reach them will help you avoid procrastinating. Take the first (or next) step toward each of your goals. Share your goals and goal timeline with a trusted friend or mentor—this can be another way to help hold yourself accountable.

Measure and analyze the initiatives, marketing efforts, events, and cross-marketing partnerships you undertook during the last 12 months against the goals set for each. As you do so, think about more than just your bottom line goals—sometimes you learn valuable lessons beyond direct outcomes. Take note of unexpected or indirect benefits or downsides: what worked well, what you enjoyed the most, which customers enjoyed the most, which drew the most participation, which seemed to stimulate customer engagement, which your employees enjoyed most (or least) or which garnered the most employee buy in (or resistance), those that had problems you had not anticipated or where you fell short in efforts to market, promote or create buzz around your promotions.

Speak to a few key customers about what kinds of programs or packages would induce them to take action. Asking loyal clients and employees to participate in focus groups and garnering feedback on a regular basis can help you construct more effective promotions and events, avoid unforeseen pitfalls and give clients what they really want as you try to build a bigger role for your business in their lives. Use all of this information to make adjustments to your marketing plan for the coming year as you prepare it for launch.

December 31 – New Years Eve

Prepare for the New Year, including putting the finishing touches on your marketing plan. During the last week of December when you may be closed for the holidays or things are on the slow side, set aside time to take stock of where you are, how far you have come during the past year, and make New Year's (business) Resolutions. Set aside time to appreciate and celebrate with mentors, co-workers, customers, vendors, family and friends; celebrate the end of a great year—and the beginning of a promising new one!

Take a step back to examine the experience provided to clients in your business. When was the last time you truly viewed the experience from the customer's point of view? It's not always easy to see things from their perspective. When you are there, performing your role day in and day out, it can be easy to overlook details that might escape your notice simply because you have become accustomed to seeing them. One way to overcome this tendency is to actually analyze the client experience in a systematic way or to think about it from a non-traditional point of view.

With that in mind, think of your business as a theater, of your employees as main cast members and your customers as hopefully-recurring characters. View each client experience as a "scene" in your so that you can give direction to cast members, create scripting and set the stage for success.

The customer experience occurs "on stage" which includes "sets" that lie both outside and inside of your business. Scenes play out not only within your walls, but on the phone, your website, by e-mail, at events and at any other touchpoint where a customer or prospect interacts with you or with any member of your business. The first step in improving the customer experience is to set the stage—where ever scenes might play out. As this year winds down, take your analysis of the client experience and see what improvements or changes you want to make to each of the sets where interaction occurs between individuals and your business.

Find ways to enhance the client experience. Do something unexpected. Create intrigue. Look for ways to enhance the customer experience in ways that will set your business apart from others and keep customers coming back for more. Product samples, demonstrations, consultations, engagement with employees that go beyond simply directing customers to an item, the gift of a genuine compliment and a sincere thank you to every client—there are so many options.

Draw other actors to your stage. Make a list of businesses in your physical proximity or who are connected to you through family, friends, or clients. Set out to contact these businesses for cooperative and cross marketing opportunities that will support your marketing goals during the coming year. Just one good idea can be the catalyst to launching a series of events, drawing your clients into closer relationship with your business and resulting in new clients.

As you plan to write your marketing "script" next year, create events and promotions for each month that are purposefully designed to create moments of customer-centered pleasure: wine and chocolate, a fashion show, mini-massages, a bridal fair, a demo on applying makeup, a workshop on personal development or empowerment, a charitable campaign, food or clothing drive to bring some of the simple pleasures of life to those less fortunate in your community—the possibilities are endless. View the value of promotions and services from the customer's point of view—not the manufacturers, distributors, or even your own—and create messages that highlight client pleasure and benefits.

The end of a year is the beginning of the new one: Commit yourself to continual learning and improvement and to the continual analysis and improvement of every aspect of the client experience. Then: Lather, rinse, repeat!

afterward

I've read a lot of books about marketing—you probably have too.

There are a lot of great books and online resources available for those who want to gain in-depth knowledge of traditional marketing, branding, communications, social media marketing, viral and word-of-mouth marketing, holding customer events and the like; but there aren't many resources that marry creative, practical ideas and content to the 'how-to' of what to do, when it comes to marketing.

That's where 365 Days of Marketing comes in.

365 Days of Marketing is a book that can be used by anyone to grow their organization, get followers, stimulate referrals and build business. Beyond that, it is a resource that will put marketing and branding into a new light for non-marketing business professionals. 365 Days of Marketing will give you every-day, practical, nutritious "helpings" when it comes to marketing concepts in such a way that you will see how they fuel nearly every aspect of your business.

Marketing doesn't have to be your passion. If you are passionate about your customers, your employees and your business, utilizing 365 Days of Marketing will help you build a bigger role for your business in the lives of your clients, develop customer loyalty and employee engagement, stimulate referrals, increase brand awareness and the influence you have in your community using traditional, social media, community and event-based marketing.

Elizabeth Kraus

www.12monthsofmarketing.com

Elizabeth Kraus is the owner of Be InPulse Branding, Marketing and Design and the author of other marketing publications including Make Over Your Marketing and 12 Months of Marketing for Salon and Spa.

Marketing and business education combined with professional, hands-on work experience with manufacturers, distributors and small and mid-sized businesses resulted in a unique, 360 degree perspective for the author. Elizabeth Kraus understands the unique needs of smaller businesses and knows how to maximize resources when it comes to the challenge of building clientele, loyalty and sales in a tight economy, for both profit and not-for-profit organizations. Find more ideas and inspiration, subscribe to e-mails and connect with the author at www.12monthsofmarketing.com.

www.ingramcontent.com/pod-product-compliance
Lightning Source LLC
Chambersburg PA
CBHW080353060326
40689CB00019B/3996